Black Resistance White Law

Black
Resistance
White
Law

A History of Constitutional Racism in America

Mary
Frances
Berry

ALLEN LANE
THE PENGUIN PRESS

ALLEN LANE THE PENGUIN PRESS
Published by the Penguin Group
Penguin Books USA Inc., 375 Hudson Street, New York, New York 10014, U.S.A.
Penguin Books Ltd, 27 Wrights Lane, London W8 5TZ, England
Penguin Books Australia Ltd, Ringwood, Victoria, Australia
Penguin Books Canada Ltd, 10 Alcorn Avenue, Toronto, Ontario, Canada M4V 3B2
Penguin Books (N.Z.) Ltd, 182–90 Wairau Road, Auckland 10, New Zealand

Penguin Books Ltd, Registered Offices: Harmondsworth, Middlesex, England

This edition first published in 1994 by Allen Lane The Penguin Press,
an imprint of Viking Penguin, a division of Penguin Books USA Inc.

1 3 5 7 9 10 8 6 4 2

Copyright © Mary Frances Berry, 1971, 1994
All rights reserved

An earlier edition of this work was first published in 1971 by Prentice-Hall, Inc.

LIBRARY OF CONGRESS CATALOGING IN PUBLICATION DATA
Berry, Mary Frances.
Black resistance/white law : a history of constitutional racism in
America / Mary Frances Berry.—Rev. ed.
p. cm.
Includes bibliographical references.
ISBN 0-7139-9102-X
1. Afro-Americans—Civil rights. 2. Afro-Americans—History.
3. Afro-Americans—Legal status, laws, etc. I. Title.
E185.61.B45 1994
323.1' 196073—dc20 93-9089

Printed in the United States of America
Set in Janson
DESIGNED BY BRIAN MULLIGAN

For my mother,
Frances Berry Wiggins,
and Minerva Hawkins,
teacher and friend

Contents

Preface   xi

1   Foundations of Repression   1

2   The Law of Black Suppression   5

3   Defiant Slaves and Defiant States   14

4   The Seminole War as a Black Freedom Movement:
Phase One   27

5   The Seminole War as a Black Freedom Movement:
Phase Two   41

6   Abolition and the Abrogation of Civil Liberties   53

7   Controlling Blacks During the Civil War   61

8   The Bottom Remains on the Bottom   69

9   Changing Modes of Oppression: 1877–1900   81

10   Riots, Lynchings, and Federal Quiescence   97

11   Moving Off Dead Center   108

12   The Illusion of a New Era   122

13   Toward Federal Protection   135

CONTENTS

14 The States Act Despite Themselves   146

15 Riots, Rebellion, and Repression   166

16 Protests and Renewed Violence   193

17 More Rebellion and Repression   216

18 Still the "Disquieting" Presence   240

      Notes   245

      Bibliographical Note   289

      Appendix: Excerpts from the *United States Code*   295

      Index   305

"Law and order must prevail" has become the cliché of the 1960's and the biggest lie, because the American black man has never known law and order except as an instrument of oppression; and it has prevailed upside his head at every available opportunity. It exists for that purpose. The law has been written by white men, for the protection of white men and their property, to be enforced by white men against blacks in particular and poor folks in general.

—Julius Lester
Look Out, Whitey! Black Power's Gon' Get Your Mama!

Preface

This book is an attempt to describe and analyze constitutionally sanctioned violence against blacks and violent suppression of black resistance—the outgrowth of a government policy based on essentially racist, not legal, concerns—throughout the American experience.

Black people have been a disquieting presence in America since the arrival of the first twenty Africans at Jamestown in 1619. To most blacks, their status, usually as slaves until 1865 and as second-class citizens thereafter, has been unacceptable; to some, it has been intolerable. Before 1865, in addition to aiding in the suppression of slave revolts, the national government ignored or approved—on constitutional grounds—white mob violence directed at blacks and their few white supporters even when local officials participated in the violence. Those blacks who did not become involved in conspiracy and rebellion before the Civil War were not necessarily "docile"; they lived in the grip of a system of violent control institutionalized under the Constitution. The years since Reconstruction, when blacks became nominally free, are littered with incidences of white riots against blacks, burnings of black homes and churches, and lynchings, while federal and local law enforcement agencies stood idly by. And while federal law enforcement disregarded white violence, pleading lack of jurisdiction under the Constitution, it endorsed and contributed to rigorous campaigns of surveillance and control of rebellious blacks, using "constitutional" military force against them with impunity.

Whether its policy was action or inaction, the national government has used the Constitution in such a way as to make law the instrument for maintaining a racist status quo. Some legal theorists might describe the American political system as one in which law represents the will of the majority while providing room for the protection of minority rights, but this is not an accurate description of the system in operation. Though the Bill of Rights, the Civil Rights Act of 1866, and the Fourteenth Amendment purport to protect individuals in their lives, liberties, and property, these ringing phrases have in fact afforded little protection to black people as a group. Law and the Contitution in the United States have been a reflection of the will of the white majority that white people have, and shall keep, superior economic, political, social, and military power, while black people shall be the permanent mudsills of American society.

The upsurge in racial intimidation and violence in recent years led me to believe that a new edition of this book would be timely and useful. My general conclusion—that the implementation of the law by federal executive branch officials perpetuated racial subordination—remains valid today. Millions of African-Americans, whose lives have improved enormously due to the social and economic changes of the last several years, nonetheless are at disproportionate risk of police abuse. They also remain largely unprotected by their government from racially motivated violence perpetrated by groups and individuals. New victims of racial violence have added their names to the rolls of those injured or killed because they were black. In most instances today's assailants, as yesterday's, have escaped with little or no punishment for their deeds. The Rodney King incident in Los Angeles in 1991, the Michael Griffith murder in Howard Beach in 1986, the murder of Yusef Hawkins in Bensonhurst in 1989, and the shooting of National Urban League President Vernon Jordan in 1980 are only the most widely publicized examples of a familiar story.

Throughout the country increases in bigotry, racial intimidation, and violence have been documented by the United States Department of Justice, Community Relations Service, and the Federal Bureau of Investigation as well as by private groups such as Klanwatch. Experts agree that the crimes are probably underreported. Many victims do not report their abuse to police, and police prefer not to identify incidents as racially motivated.

In the African-American community the increases in racially motivated violence only add to the social problems needing resolution. High suicide rates, particularly among African-American males, murder rates from black-on-black violence accompanying the drug menace, and persistent poverty require major remedial efforts by individuals, black community organizations, and black institutions. Racism and interracial tensions may increase community solidarity as they become a common burden to bear. They also, however, increase community frustration and reinforce black nationalist tendencies among those who are alienated.

Asian-Americans, Latinos, and Native American Indians are also the target of white violence. There are tensions between African-Americans and other racial, religious, and ethnic minorities as well, and among and between nonblack minority groups, all of which sometimes lead to violence. In our increasingly multicultural society, however, nonblack racial minorities enjoy greater acceptance by whites and experience less discrimination in housing than African-Americans and are less segregated and ghettoized as a result. Most racial violence is still initiated by whites and directed at blacks. According to the most recent FBI Report of Hate Crimes in 1991, offenses by whites against African-Americans constituted the largest number of reported incidents. Black-white tension remains the most likely precipitant of racial conflict.

The president and executive branch agencies have advanced the idea of federalism as a rationale for customarily leaving the punishment of black attackers and the control of white violence to local officials. When the violence is perpetrated by African-Americans or other racial minority groups, however, the federal government intervenes with the help of the FBI and federal troops; Justice department indictments quickly follow.

In preparing this new edition of *Black Resistance/White Law*, I have carefully considered reviews of the first edition and the comments of colleagues, teachers, and students. I have corrected errors in the text and taken advantage of new work in the field to reassess explanations and evidence and to revise where necessary. I have also added new material covering the period since 1971.

I must thank V. P. Franklin, Genna Rae McNeil, and Melinda Chateauvert for their careful reading of the text. I also thank my graduate research assistants James Johnson and Anne Bailey for their help. My editor, Mindy Werner, and her assistant, Michael Hardart, shepherded this project to its conclusion. Krishna Toolsie, my executive assistant, helped in so many ways to make sure I could complete this work.

—M.F.B.
Washington, D.C.
September 1993

Black Resistance White Law

1

Foundations
of
Repression

HE FEDERAL PATTERN of constitutional interpretation, which
has been successfully utilized to maintain the continued social, economic, and political subordination of black people,
evolved from policies and theories developed during the British colonial period. The British theory of federalism, the division of
power and responsibility between the central and local governments, which arrived in America with the first colonists, has become
a handy philosophical tool for maintaining white superiority. Federalism as a policy has been advanced to explain national noninterference when state agencies refused to protect nonconforming blacks
from white violence intended to keep them in their place; and then,
it has been cited to explain the compulsory use of national force
when state agencies found themselves unable to successfully ward
off black attacks on white persons or their property.

Black suppression in America began with the introduction of the
system of slavery in the late 1600s. Slavery was permitted and even
encouraged by the British government, even though slavery made
blacks a potential enemy in the midst of the colonists. Very early,
the rapid increase of the slave population and the rebellions that followed brought the need for an adequate instrument of defense. The
British federalist policy placed the responsibility for the use of force
on local colonial officials because the British government was unwilling to use military force unless all civilian and local police measures were exhausted.[1]

1

The colonists' principal instrument of slave control was the local militia. By the time the American colonies were established, the militia in England was largely a debilitated institution; however, the establishment of the colonies demanded it be revived as the primary military organization in America. Although the king technically had full authority over the militia, these groups were largely supported and controlled by the individual colonies, with the governor of each colony acting as commander. In times of crisis, such as slave revolts, British regulars supplemented colonial militia forces.[2]

As the number of blacks increased alarmingly in the colonies, some southern colonists made efforts to control the slave trade. However, slavery had become such an economic boon to British merchants that every attempt to interfere was vetoed by the British government. A body of custom, judicial sanction, and statutory law evolved to institutionalize the system. Slavery was officially recognized as an institution in colonial laws by the 1660s. In 1697, Parliament expressed the view that blacks were property of great value to the kingdom, and ten members of the Court of King's Bench agreed that slaves were merchandise that could be regulated under the Navigation Acts.[3]

When the Treaty of Utrecht ended the war of Spanish Succession in 1713, the British government expanded its interest in slavery by obtaining a British monopoly on the colonial slave trade. Having no control over the increasing number of slaves arriving in the colonies, the colonists began to strengthen the militia. The most critical areas for slave control were those in which the slave population was large, the white population small, and the distance between the settlements great. Bands of hostile Indians greatly aggravated conditions in several colonies. In 1710, the population of the colony of Virginia was at least twelve thousand blacks as compared to eighteen thousand whites. At this time, the governor confided to the legislature that the militia was in such a disreputable state that he feared trouble should word reach the slaves and Indians. In an effort to obtain revenue to arm the militia more adequately, the Virginia legislature enacted a duty in 1723 on the importation of liquor and slaves, to be paid by the importer.[4]

The colony of Carolina, with its extremely small white population, the presence of hostile Indians, and the large number of slaves, was particularly concerned with slave control. There were 10,500 blacks and 6,250 whites in Carolina in 1715; in 1724, there were three times as many blacks as whites; after the split of the colony into North and South Carolina in 1729, the situation was not significantly changed. By 1765, there were an estimated 90,000 blacks and 40,000 whites in South Carolina. Selected slaves were used to augment the militia against the Yamassee Indians in 1715, but a slave uprising in 1739 shattered confidence in the employment of blacks for defense and led to renewed efforts to strengthen the militia. Numerous programs for increasing the white population were debated in the colonial assembly, but no resolution was adopted. After 1743, the British government responded to requests for aid by stationing three regular infantry companies under the control of the governor of South Carolina to protect that colony and Georgia from possible slave revolt.[5]

Despite the presence of regular British troops, the fear of insurrection persisted in South Carolina. In 1757, at a meeting of the governors of North Carolina, Pennsylvania, Virginia, and Maryland convened to plan colonial defense for the duration of the French and Indian War (the Seven Years' War, 1754–1763), South Carolina's predicament elicited great concern. In a letter to Lord Lyttleton, governor of South Carolina, the governors stated that British regulars would remain stationed at Charleston so that the local militia could be moved to defend the frontier. The British soldiers were intended to keep the blacks "in awe."[6]

Numerous other instances of actual or feared slave rebellions occurred during the colonial period, and the statute books were peppered with legislation designed to control the slave population. Blacks could not gather in groups, carry weapons, or travel without the permission of their masters; white males periodically searched black quarters for weapons and kept the blacks under surveillance. Militia laws were primarily designed for slave control. Internal control of blacks by militia and adjunct patrols, assisted in times of stress by British troops, was a well-established system by the time of the American Revolution.[7]

During the American Revolution, colonists in the South continued to express fear of black revolt. The defection of large numbers of slaves to the British compounded these fears. Southern delegates to the Continental Congress expressed unwillingness to use their militias outside their own borders. In 1779, a committee of the Continental Congress reported that South Carolina could provide very little manpower for the war effort because the militia was needed as a home guard to suppress rebellious movements among the blacks.[8]

As a result of the American Revolution, state governments were free to make whatever regulations they desired on slavery and the control of blacks. Article II of the Articles of Confederation recognized the retention of state control over domestic institutions—which included slavery. The national government under the Articles had neither the authority nor the force to suppress domestic disturbances. It followed, therefore, that in cases of black revolt, states would be forced to rely on their own resources. The end of the British government in the colonies marked the end of British protection.[9] Since the northern states soon either abolished slavery or put it on the way to ultimate extinction, constitutional and legislative provisions for slave control were of minor importance above the Potomac. The southern state governments recognized the continued existence of slavery as an institution by reenacting and expanding the body of colonial laws on the subject. The militia and citizen patrols remained primarily responsible for control of the black population.

As the confederation moved toward constitutional government, issues of internal security were found to require careful consideration. The maintenance of the system of slavery through the use of force was a primary problem of colonial defense. The fear of black insurrection, the absence of regular troops to augment local militia, and the obvious inability of the central government to suppress internal disorder hastened the development of an adequate military system patterned on the federalist model. Black oppression through the system of slavery had survived the Declaration of Independence and American Revolution and would now become an integral part of American constitutional law.

2

The
Law of Black
Suppression

HERE WAS LITTLE DOUBT of the need for a stronger central government as the delegates to the Constitutional Convention met in Philadelphia in May 1787. Debtor disturbances, among them Shays's Rebellion, a revolt of impoverished farmers against taxation and the judiciary, which had threatened a federal arsenal at Springfield, Massachusetts, had stressed emphatically the weakness of the central government under the Articles of Confederation. The government had been helpless; it lacked an effective national military organization and the authority to interfere in the domestic affairs of the states. Convention delegates insisted that the new government provide a means for suppressing disorders which were designed to subvert the execution of laws and the judicial process. State militia organizations could not be depended upon to end rebellions, particularly if the militiamen sympathized with the aims of the rebels, as they did in Shays's Rebellion. The delegates wanted both a stable militia and a stable national standing army, providing the states could prevent uninvited national interference. Without too much difficulty, they agreed that the national government should guarantee each state a republican (representative) form of government and should protect the states from domestic violence upon a request from the state legislature, or the governor when the legislature was not in session.

In the debate on the military clauses of the Constitution which would empower Congress to provide the militia to quell internal disorders, no one explicitly stated that the national military power might be used to suppress slave revolts. The precedents for slave control as a local responsibility were well established. However, while debating the proposal to prohibit the slave trade, Rufus King of Massachusetts introduced the relationship between slavery and the use of national military forces. King felt that importing additional slaves would make national defense more difficult and costly. He believed it unjust not only that the North was obligated to defend the South in the event of slave revolts while the South was free to import more slaves, but that southerners were bitterly opposed to the levying of export taxes which would compensate the federal treasury for this additional defensive burden. Since theirs was an agricultural exporting economy, southerners were generally opposed to export taxes. John Rutledge of South Carolina did not believe the South would encourage the slave trade or, in an unconscious contradiction, that slave insurrections would occur as a result of further importations. Rutledge suggested that if the North's disapproval of the slave trade was based on military considerations, the South should be willing to exempt northern states from an obligation to protect the South from slave rebellion. No other southerner agreed with him, and there is no evidence that northerners endorsed his proposal or tried to convince others to accept it. The Constitution as finally drafted, in conformity to southern wishes, forbade Congress from prohibiting the slave trade before 1808 or levying a tariff on exports from any states.[1]

In the debate over apportionment of representation, Gouverneur Morris of New York opposed counting slaves as only three-fifths of a person both for taxation and representation. The southern states, he commented, ". . . are not to be restrained from importing fresh supplies of wretched Africans, at once to increase the danger of attack, and the difficulty of defense." While gaining nothing from the Three-Fifths Compromise, northern states bound "themselves to march their militia for the defense of the Southern States; for their defense against those very slaves of whom they [Northern opponents of slavery] complain."[2] The convention ignored Morris and accepted the compromise formula.

The Fugitive Slave Clause of the Constitution was also adopted with little debate. Some opposition arose over the proposal to make the governor of the state responsible for insuring the return of fugitive slaves. James Wilson of Pennsylvania felt that the responsibility would be too burdensome for the governor, and possibly too costly, if military force became necessary. The proposal finally adopted does not specifically give the responsibility to any governmental official, but ultimately, the rendition of fugitive slaves fell on the president under his duty to enforce the Constitution and laws.[3]

When the military clauses of the Constitution were considered by the state ratifying conventions, the same issues, the need to protect states' rights and to insure state control over the movement and disposition of state militias, received earnest debate. The slavery issue was brought into the debate in the Virginia convention by George Nicholas, who pointed out the additional security for slavery provided in the Constitution. Along with the power of the state to use its militia to control the slaves, "it will be the duty of the general government to aid when the strength of the union is called for."[4] The Fugitive Slave Clause was scarcely noticed by northern delegates to the ratifying conventions, but in the South, it was used as a definite selling point. James Madison particularly emphasized its usefulness in Virginia, as did some of the Federalists in the North Carolina convention. These debates lend credence to the view that the southern states would not have ratified the Constitution without the proslavery compromises. The Fugitive Slave Clause and the commitment of the national government to protect slavery, but not interfere with it, were indispensable parts of the Constitution.[5]

The military system provided by the Constitutional Convention and ratified by the states was entirely consonant with the principles of federalism developed during the American colonial and revolutionary experience. The language in the Constitution was vague enough so that Congress, in drafting enabling legislation, could use its own discretion to fill in the substance. The military clauses, as stated in the Constitution, provided that the states would keep order within their own borders, but if invasion occurred, the national government was responsible for defense. If overpowering rebellion occurred, the state government could request federal aid, but the national government could not intervene at will. However, Congress had the power to utilize the militia or regular forces to enforce federal laws. The maintenance of internal security and slave control primarily remained a local responsibility but the national government was explicitly bound to insure the return of fugitive slaves and to support state governments in suppressing domestic violence which could include slave insurrections.[6]

In the First Congress on September 29, 1789, a bill was passed to implement the military clauses of the Constitution; the act recognized the small military contingents established under the Articles of Confederation and authorized the president to call militiamen into service to protect the frontier from Indian raids. In the Second Congress, a bill was passed on May 2, 1792, which provided that the state militias could be called out to execute the laws of the Union, suppress insurrections, and repel invasions. This additional legislation, which gave the president the power to federalize the state militias when the United States was endangered or upon a state request for aid in time of domestic violence, was based on the recognition that regular forces were too small to be used for anything except manning seacoast fortifications and protecting the frontier. By 1807, when the regular military forces were increased to ten thousand men, the statute was changed to authorize the president to call out the land and naval forces of the United States or the militia. The House debates on the Militia Act of 1792 consisted largely of controversy over what conditions constitute an insurrection and the possibility of the national government utilizing the military in a tyrannical fashion. Significantly, the act does not say that the president *must* call out the militia but only that "it shall be lawful" for him to do so. This principle was clearly expressed in the act of 1795 which repealed the Militia Act of 1792: the president was given sole discretion, without further consultation or congressional action, to determine when an exigency requiring the use of the military existed.[7]

Congressional interpretation of national responsibility for the suppression of slave disturbances was clearly expressed in debates concerning the abolition issue. Quakers and other reformers initiated an abolition movement in the early days of the Revolution, and their activities persisted throughout the antebellum period. On March 8, 1790, when Congress received a petition against slavery and the slave trade from the Quaker Pennsylvania Society for Promoting the Abolition of Slavery, Representative James Jackson of Georgia insisted that discussion of the slavery issue would cause insurrection in the South.

When the discussion continued unabated, Representative William Smith of South Carolina made a lengthy speech in defense of slavery. One argument northerners frequently used was that slavery made the South weaker in case of invasion, and Smith felt this view was erroneous; he believed that blacks might, in fact, make good soldiers and could be used to defend the South. After considerable debate, the House decided to adopt a general statement of its power over slavery under the Constitution without acting on the Quaker petition. As the situation appeared to the House members, the Constitution forbade prohibition of the slave trade until 1808, and Congress had no authority to interfere with slavery in the states.[8]

The proslavery supporters in the First Congress became increasingly sensitive to any discussion of the slavery issue, constantly asserting states' rights and pointing out the danger of fomenting slave revolts as a defense against anything remotely resembling antislavery argument. Even the alleged "kidnapping" of free blacks from Pennsylvania by North Carolinians who insisted they were runaway slaves was to many southerners not a matter of congressional concern, since states' rights might be infringed upon if the national government became involved in the issue. A representative from Pennsylvania brought the subject before the Fourth Congress, after being informed that some free blacks from his state had recently been kidnapped. Smith of South Carolina, who had been willing to make long arguments in defense of slavery, now adamantly opposed any discussion of the kidnapping question because agitation might promote insurrectionary conditions in the South. The House, evidently impressed by his argument, agreed and resolved that "it is not expedient for this House to interfere with any existing law of the states on the subject."[9]

The Pennsylvania kidnapping issue remained unsettled. Representative John Swanwick of Pennsylvania succeeded in presenting a petition from some blacks in his state who complained that slaves who had been manumitted by Quakers in North Carolina were being forced back into slavery. Smith of South Carolina once again objected, explaining that the plight of the blacks resulted from a North Carolina statute which forbade manumissions and gave any claimant the right to reduce persons, freed in contravention of the statute, to slavery. Some of these freed blacks had escaped to Pennsylvania; persons claiming ownership to the runaways, as provided in the Fugitive Slave

Act of 1793, took them back to North Carolina. James Madison of Virginia asserted that this petition did not deserve the time or attention of the House; he believed that if these petitioners were free, they could settle their grievances in the North Carolina courts, but if they were slaves, the Constitution gave them no hope of being heard in Congress. The petition was rejected by a vote of 33–50.[10]

In June 1796, when the crisis brought on by French attacks on American shipping demanded increased military preparation, the possibility of slave uprisings again drew the attention of Congress. A bill was passed authorizing the president to require state governors to hold a total of eighty thousand militiamen in readiness, apportioned according to the number of white inhabitants in each state. In the House, Smith of South Carolina suggested that the bill ought to provide for apportionment in each state based on the total number of whites and three-fifths of the blacks. The southern states would therefore call out more men but, Smith asserted, if war came, the additional men would be needed. Abraham Venable of Virginia found Smith's thinking unclear. He stated that if the South needed more troops for its protection, the Constitution provided that they must be supplied from other states as well; there was no need for the three-fifths formula. Joseph McDowell of North Carolina reminded Smith that if his plan were adopted, with the large number of whites assigned to military duty, those at home would be left defenseless against the blacks. Smith hastily withdrew his proposal. George Thacher of Massachusetts, who consistently attacked the proslavery forces while he was in Congress from 1789 to 1801, could not resist needling Smith by asking him whether he meant that three-fifths of the blacks should be armed and used as soldiers. Smith stammered that he had no such intention. The bill was passed without the three-fifths proposal.[11]

The proslavery tactic of pleading the danger of insurrection as a technique to squelch antislavery arguments had not yet completely served its purpose. In November 1797, when the Quakers presented their annual petition begging for the end of slavery and the slave trade, fear of revolt was again successfully invoked by proslavery congressmen. Nathanial Macon of North Carolina denounced the petition and the petitioners, who were, in his opinion, warmongers "bent on bloodshed" rather than peacemakers.[12] In January 1800, Representative Robert Waln of Pennsylvania presented another petition of free blacks asking for an end to the slave trade, which met the same harsh reception given the Quakers' petition. While debating whether to submit the petition to a committee, Harrison Gray Otis of Massachusetts endeared himself to the proslavery elements by drawing attention to the crude lettering of the petition. He suggested that the petitioners were illiterate and had no notion of what they were signing. The discussion was interrupted by John Rutledge of South Carolina who introduced the issue of the successful slave revolution against the French in Haiti in August 1791. He claimed that emissaries from Haiti had been sent to America to stir up unrest and that, once again, the discussion of abolition and the slavery problem might encourage insurrection. Another representative from South Carolina, Robert Goodloe Harper, added that the petition was just another Quaker petition; apparently, since the previous petitions were rejected, the Quakers had induced unknowing blacks to sign the present one. The House resolved that the petition created disquiet and should therefore not be entertained by the House. George Thacher cast the lone dissenting vote. The proslavery position decrying antislavery agitation was overwhelmingly accepted.[13]

When, in December 1803, the manpower needs of South Carolina's expanding cotton and rice production required her to reopen the foreign slave trade, the possibility of insurrection again became a national issue. Representative David Bard of Pennsylvania proposed that the national government levy a tax on each slave imported. The congressmen from South Carolina defended the state's actions on the basis of state sovereignty. They claimed that the action of South Carolina was an expression of the Tenth Amendment in which powers reserved by the states could not be usurped by the national government; what South Carolina did about the slave trade was of no concern to the national government or any other state. Bard and John Smilie of Pennsylvania then subjected the South Carolinian's argument to a devastating attack. As importation of slaves meant the importation of enemies into the country, Bard asserted that the concern of the other states and the national government was understandable. Smilie was even more explicit. The reopening of the trade, he insisted, would weaken the defense of the entire nation and it was common knowledge that the military power of the nation was constitutionally bound to suppress slave insurrection. The House, unimpressed by Bard and

Smilie, postponed consideration of the tax. South Carolina continued the foreign slave trade until Congress exercised its power to prohibit it by the act of March 1807 which went into effect on January 1, 1808. The concern of Bard and Smilie was well founded, for in the four years before importations were made illegal, some 39,075 additional Africans were brought into the already large slaveholding state of South Carolina.[14]

As seen from the Congressional debates, the southern viewpoint in 1804 was that Quakers and other outside agitators were inciting insurrection, and any discussion of opposition to slavery in Congress would create incendiary conditions. Further, slavery was a local practice which the national government had no authority or right to regulate. And yet, if the southern states requested aid for slave insurrections or the return of fugitive slaves, the military force of the nation was constitutionally obliged to comply.

The proof of whether the proslavery theories elaborated in the first congresses could be successfully implemented came when two rebellions involving opposition to federal tax laws compelled the use of national power. In the Whiskey Rebellion of 1794, the governor of Pennsylvania refused to call out the state militia. The federal courts appealed to the president since the laws of the United States were "obstructed by combinations too powerful to be suppressed by the ordinary course of judicial proceedings. . . ."[15] President Washington called fifteen thousand militiamen from Pennsylvania and surrounding states into federal service and issued two proclamations calling for an end to the rebellion. The insurrection petered out with little opposition. Similar action was taken in response to the other instance of local obstruction to a federal law, Fries Rebellion, which erupted in Pennsylvania in 1799: President Adams issued a proclamation of rebellion, asked the governor of Pennsylvania to call out one thousand militiamen, and the affair was promptly suppressed.[16]

The action taken in these rebellions demonstrated that the national government could discharge its responsibilities under the sections of the military act designed to end obstruction to federal law. In view of the concern that Shays's Rebellion and other debtor disturbances had created at the Constitutional Convention, the response of the government was of a kind anticipated by the framers. Still to be tested, however, was the section of the military act designed to end insurrection within a state upon a state request for federal aid. Statements made regarding the use of national power to suppress slave revolts in the convention and the first congresses indicate a clear awareness of the national responsibility in such cases: national military power would be invoked to quell black insurrection and to remand fugitive slaves when, and if, it became necessary.

3

Defiant Slaves
and Defiant
States

IN THE LATE SUMMER of 1800, Gabriel Prosser, a young slave of Henrico County, Virginia, was executed, along with forty other slaves, for daring to attempt revolt against the slaveholders. Prosser's projected insurrection ushered in a turbulent period of some thirty-five years when, in the crucible of slave rebellion, the congressional interpretation of national military responsibility in a republic was tested. The machinery that had successfully quelled opposition to federal taxing power in the Whiskey and Fries rebellions was now confronted with racial disturbances *within* a state.

In a period of quiescence after the adoption of the Constitution, southern slaveholders continued to rely upon their own resources to control the black population, just as they had done during the colonial period. The systems of patrol and militia duty, already in existence, were legislatively reestablished in the new nation. After the enactment of the national militia law of 1792, patrol remained an integral part of the military, both forces drawing from the same class of males. However, when no warfare or revolt threatened, it was difficult to keep patrol performance at a high degree of efficiency; militiamen performed drill and muster inadequately, if at all. Many instances of drunkenness, improper conduct, failure to report for duty, and brutality toward innocent slaves and free blacks were reported. But when necessity dictated, the patrol was adept in suppressing rebellion without outside help.[1]

The example of black revolt in Haiti, which began in August 1791, and the influx of terrified French refugees into the seaboard cities of the United States created sufficient fear of insurrection to keep the local patrols and militia in a state of readiness. Congressmen and local officials in the South continued to make persistent references to the Haitian revolution and its incendiary effects. As reported plots were an everyday occurrence, residents in areas with large slave populations feared the necessity of sending militiamen to defend the western frontiers. Local patrols had sufficient reason to be assiduous in their duties.[2]

Gabriel Prosser attempted to execute his plot in this atmosphere of crisis. The planned revolt appeared to be a well-organized project involving about one thousand blacks in the vicinity of Richmond. The slaves gathered on August 30, 1800, but disbanded because a violent storm and flood made military operations impossible. During the next month, many blacks, including Prosser, were arrested. Although the plot failed, the reaction it engendered is significant. Governor James Monroe and other public officials in Virginia had heard rumors of the revolt, and on the day of the disturbance, two faithful slaves reported the plan to their masters. Local and state government officials were sufficiently aroused by the propsect to ask for aid. Monroe requested and received the use of the federal armory at Manchester. Although federal intervention was unnecessary, the plot being aborted and the leaders captured before any slaveholders were killed, the immediate federal response to Monroe's request established a precedent.[3]

A heightened uneasiness persisted after Prosser's plot, and the continuous rumors of slave conspiracies in the next few years led many states to enact more stringent measures to control both slaves and free blacks. Although free blacks had no discernible connection with Prosser's plot, southerners believed that the social events at which they were present furnished the occasion for planning the rebellion. Southern legislatures passed laws strengthening local militia and patrol units; they also restricted the internal slave trade, fearing that slaveholders might attempt to sell insurrectionary blacks to their unsuspecting neighbors in other states. Virginia's House of Delegates, directing its enmity toward free blacks, authorized Governor Monroe to discuss with President Thomas Jefferson the possibility of purchasing lands where such "unsettling" persons could be sent. Jefferson was sympathetic to their proposal yet refused to spend federal money for the purpose. Although he did suggest that Virginia buy land in the Northwest Territory, he indicated that this area would someday be joined to the Union. Jefferson thought the difficulty would lie in finding an area in which free blacks would not only be welcomed but slaveholders also assured that the blacks would not instigate and support slave revolt anywhere in the United States. The colonization effort was abandoned. However, in 1806, the Virginia legislature passed an act which required free blacks who were manumitted to leave the state. Many free blacks left the Lower South to resettle in the Upper South and Midwest. States in these areas began enacting legislation to prevent the entry of free blacks within their borders. As the number of free blacks in the United States increased from 59,000 in 1790 to 319,000 in 1830, many blacks faced the problem of finding a place to live. Even Massachusetts felt compelled to expel many free blacks.[4]

Although the ever-present rumors abounded, the next large-scale insurrection did not occur until January 1811 in Louisiana. The fear generated by the Haitian revolution and the large population of free Negroes in the area coupled to accentuate the tension. Further aggravation was caused by a dispute between a group of free Negroes and the territorial governor over efforts to disband a Negro militia organization which had been in existence since about 1736. When news reached the city that 400 to 500 slaves had revolted in the parishes at the Andry plantation outside New Orleans, it caused an uproar. Since the territorial militia was inefficient due to lack of training and interest, General Wade Hampton, who had control of military forces in the territory, hastily assembled two companies of the most efficient volunteers he could find, along with a company of regular army troops, and put down the disturbance. About 660 soldiers reportedly took part in the engagement. The free Negro militia ingratiated themselves with the white community by offering to assist in military operations against the slaves. Eighty-two of the Andry rebels were killed or executed soon after capture. The governor's letter books indicate continued reliance on federal forces; troop movements in the area were planned to maintain the mobility required to suppress possible uprisings.[5]

Following the Andry revolt, southern state governments continued to tighten restrictions governing the activities of free blacks, refusing passage to some, expelling others, and emancipating loyal slaves who informed on alleged insurrectionaries. Renewed interest in colonization led to the organization of the American Colonization Society in 1817 with some prominent southerners as members. Opposition developed rapidly. Some abolitionists criticized the society on the grounds that no native American should be expelled from his country; others argued that if the colonizers were sincere, they would only colonize slaves and not free blacks; some proslavery interests regarded it as an emancipationist tool. In addition to restrictive legislation directed at blacks and southern interest in colonization, southern state legislatures enacted measures to suppress abolitionist literature and discussion which might incite the slaves to rebel. Nevertheless, the southern states found little real comfort in their legislative programs; the slave problem required their sustained activity in order to maintain the will of the national government to insure slave control.[6]

The debates over the admission of Missouri to the Union beginning in 1819 provided the southerners with reassuring evidence of the will of Congress to defend the slave system. James Tallmadge of New York explained that he had not suggested free soil in Alabama because free blacks would then be too near slaves in adjoining states, thereby increasing the likelihood of rebellion, but he thought a boundary for slavery expansion should be set at Missouri. State legislatures responded to Tallmadge's proposal with a spate of resolutions. The northern legislative position essentially hinged on the unfairness of increasing proslavery representation in Congress under the terms of the Three-fifths Compromise. Considerable discussion also emphasized the position that extended enslavement of blacks would increase the possibility of internal disorder. Proslavery legislatures stood firmly on the Louisiana Purchase treaty which insured the right to property of persons in the area; they also believed that continued opposition to slavery in Missouri would create bitterness and distrust in the South as well as slave discontent.[7]

In the congressional debates, the battle lines closely conformed to the resolutions passed in the states. Representative William Plumer of New Hampshire most clearly expressed the concern of northerners in a lengthy speech in February 1820. He succinctly noted that the Constitution was established to provide for the common defense and to insure domestic tranquillity; constitutionally, slavery was a domestic institution which the national government could not touch unless an insurrection compelled state officials to request federal aid. It seemed altogether reasonable to Plumer that since this burden of protection was placed upon the entire Union, Congress should act to reduce the likelihood of insurrection which necessitated the use of federal troops and money by preventing the expansion of slavery. Plumer further noted that the slave states had always been a great burden to the rest of the nation; in times of war, southern militiamen were needed at home to "awe" the slaves. Representative Charles Rich of Vermont and other northern congressmen advanced much the same argument. Representative Harrison Gray Otis of Massachusetts, although opposing the further extension of the system, expressed a view which was gaining great favor with proslavery spokesmen: slavery was a beneficial institution, not only to the South, but to the entire country; there were strong economic ties between the two sections and a slave revolt would be economically disastrous to the nation, in addition to placing the lives of northerners in jeopardy. Said Otis, "All considerate persons in every section of the Union should unite with one accord with their masters in putting down every species of revolt and insurrection, as pregnant with dreadful consequences to the whole section."[8]

During the Missouri Compromise debates, the ideas and proposals presented may have encouraged rebellion against the institution of slavery. There is evidence that Denmark Vesey, who planned an insurrection in Charleston, South Carolina, in the summer of 1822, seized on such antislavery discussion to convince his associates that attempted revolt might bring outside help. Vesey, a literate free black, plotted the only large-scale city revolt during the history of slavery in the United States. His plot is a landmark in black American history in that it was led by a free black who was willing to risk his life to free others; all too often slaves were emancipated for informing on alleged insurrectionaries, and free blacks seemed more concerned about maintaining what semblance of privilege they had than in improving the circumstances of the enslaved blacks. The nine thousand men under Vesey were prepared to enter Charleston and begin a general massacre of not only whites but also those blacks who did not join the revolt. Success would enable the rebels to move to Haiti where further plans would be made. However, the plot was discovered before fruition, again through the disloyalty of slaves who informed their masters. Vesey and five of his lieutenants were captured, tried by a jury of two judges and three white citizens, and hanged on July 2, 1822. The investigation continued and eventually thirty-five blacks were hanged and forty-two sent into exile. Another four white men were convicted of collusion with the insurrectionaries; it was alleged they had hoped to acquire loot if Vesey's plot succeeded. They were sentenced to short prison terms and assessed fines. The controversy which developed between the governor of South Carolina and the city court over the handling of the trials led to the publication of detailed histories by both sides which remain the chief source of information concerning these events and the continuing debate over the magnitude and nature of the plot.[9]

In regard to the military response to Vesey's plot, there remains considerable evidence of willingness on the part of the national government to supply military aid. Extensive military preparations had been made by state authorities when they were informed of the existence of a plot, although they did not deem their resources adequate. During July, after many of the supposed insurgents were captured and when trials and continued investigations were at their height, Governor Thomas Bennett wrote to Secretary of War John C. Calhoun, later to become the chief theoretician of the proslavery forces, describing the insurrectionary situation and requesting additional federal troops. Bennett pointed out that the nearest fort held a large quantity of powder which the insurgents might seize and that only five men manned this garrison. Immediately, Calhoun ordered a company of artillery from St. Augustine, Florida, to Charleston and instructed the commander to cooperate with the governor in suppressing the disturbance. The troops arrived in Charleston on August 15. Governor Bennett later asked for additional forces to frighten blacks in the area. Since the South Carolina legislature was not in session, the governor was acting within the Constitution and statutes by asking for aid on his own authority. However, his request should have been directed not to the secretary of war, but to the president, who under the statute had nondelegable authority to decide whether the disturbance warranted federal intervention. The apparent concern for strict conformity to the statutes was obviously lacking in the military response to both the Vesey and Prosser plots.[10]

The South Carolina legislature reacted frantically in the aftermath of the Vesey plot. Measures were passed to prevent the return of free blacks who had left the state, to imprison black seamen whose vessels entered harbors of the state until time of departure, and to execute persons who aided projected or actual insurrections. The enforcement of the Black Seaman's Act, which overstepped the bounds of state police power, brought immediate protest from the masters of vessels whose sailors were imprisoned. In the test case of *Elkison v. Deliesilline*, which was decided in 1823, federal judge William Johnson, a citizen of South Carolina, held the law invalid. Johnson felt that the act conflicted with both an 1815 convention with England which provided for mutual free ingress and egress of naval personnel and with the exclusive power of Congress to regulate foreign commerce. Nonetheless, South Carolina, joined by other southern states that had passed similar legislation, continued to enforce the law despite the court decision, asserting that state sovereignty and powers reserved under the Tenth Amendment to the Constitution supported her position. Protests from the British government and resolutions of condemnation from northern states brought no response from the southerners. President Monroe used no federal troops to enforce this decision of the district court or to uphold the supremacy of national authority and its treaty-making power under the Constitution. Secretary of State John Quincy Adams requested that the legislature repeal the act in question, while suggesting to the British government that under the federal system, indirect measures were sometimes effective and reassured the British that if violations continued, the national government would intervene. The violations continued; the president and Congress did nothing.[11]

Little additional legislation was passed in other areas of the South in response to the Vesey conspiracy. The southern states now relied on tightening enforcement measures already on the statute books and increasing the alertness of the patrols. When Secretary of War James Barbour sent a circular letter to state governors requesting information on military preparedness in July 1826, considerable concern about slave insurrection was reported. The lieutenant governor of Mississippi felt that volunteers who could respond quickly would be much more effective than the militia should a slave revolt occur, adding that his state was especially sensitive to this problem because of a large population of slaves. The adjutant general of Virginia believed that some means of insuring a speedy response from the militia might alleviate the problem. In summarizing the reports for Congress, Barbour stated that since the presence of large numbers of slaves kept the South perpetually on guard, great reliance for military defense would continue to be placed on the regular army. Nevertheless, he believed that the planters of the Lower South should be required to raise sufficient militia, including artillery and cavalry, to aid the regulars in manning the forts in the area and "to keep the black population in check."[12]

In 1831, "unusual uneasiness" again prevailed in the South. Rumors of revolts and insurrections were rampant. Military units were increasingly wary and kept the black population under careful surveillance. In Louisiana, officials informed the War Department that a major revolt threatened and requested that additional troops be sent to the area; troops in the vicinity were put on alert. Along the eastern seaboard, army units were moved from northern states into the South to prevent suspected insurrection.[13] The rumors were partly fulfilled in Southampton, Virginia in August 1831, when Nat Turner instigated a revolt with approximately seventy slaves. State military volunteers, with the aid of federal troops, moved in to suppress the rebellion. The mayor of Norfolk sent notes requesting aid to the commander of Fortress Monroe and to the naval vessels *Warren* and *Natchez*, of the West Indian Squadron, stationed off Norfolk. Three companies of artillery with a field piece, a marine guard, and a detachment of seamen from each ship left for Southampton on the steamer *Hampton*. Disembarking at Suffolk and marching twenty-five miles, they stopped overnight and arrived the next day at Jerusalem where they joined the commander of the state militia, General Richard Eppes. According to the military report, the presence of the troops reassured a small group of white women and children gathered there. Although the regular troops had no opportunity to engage in actual conflict with any insurrectionaries, their commander thought that the "celerity" with which they acted and the "demonstration made by them during the march across country will undoubtedly have a lasting and salutary effect on the future conduct of that deluded people [blacks] against whom they were intended to act." The commander of the naval yard at Norfolk issued seven hundred stands of arms and twelve thousand rounds of ammunition to local white citizens. Approximately sixty-five white persons were killed. The rebels, with the exception of their leader, were all killed or captured within ten days after the outbreak of the disturbance. Nat Turner, who was not captured until October 30, was executed after confessing on November 11; eventually, eighteen of his companions were executed.[14]

On the heels of the revolt, fear mounted in other communities and local officials requested aid from army officers. Arms and ammunition were issued from the federal arsenal at Fortress Monroe to the citizens of Hampton, Virginia. The authorities at New Bern, North Carolina, requested and received a detachment of army troops from the same fort to quell rumors and fear of disorder. These requests for aid were handled in an informal manner without regard to constitutional statutes. When Colonel James House at Fortress Monroe, Commodore J. D. Elliott, who commanded the West India Squadron, and Commander Lewis Warrington at the Norfolk navy yard reported their actions during the Turner disturbances to the Navy and War departments, they received assurance that the president gave his "entire approbation" to the "promptitude" with which they had acted.[15]

A comparison of the manner in which the federal government exercised its military responsibility in several instances reveals some striking differences. When federal law was violated and federal courts defied in the Whiskey and Fries rebellions, the president acted scrupulously and carefully within the limitation of the statute before invoking the use of troops. The federal government deferred action when South Carolina defied the federal courts in the Black Seaman's Controversy. In rumored or actual slave revolts, however, troops were utilized without the least thought of statutory requirements for invoking aid, yet the president gave his stamp of approval to prompt quasi-legal military action. This legal variation might be explained on the grounds that federal revenue was a sufficiently important motive for military enforcement, but apparently the legal status of black seamen was not. In the cases of black insurrection, the president and War Department may not have believed that protocol should interfere with the national enforcement of the proslavery compromises of the Constitution. In any event, the Constitution proved to be a firm protector of the institution of slavery. Federal troops were sent even when they were not needed; in New Bern, North Carolina, after the Turner revolt, the captain commanding the regular troops reported that some of the "principal citizens" admitted that federal aid was unnecessary, that troops had been requested precipitously, and that their continued presence would only make the citizens less vigilant when they finally left. The captain asserted, however, that if the local citizens were asked, many of them would demand a permanent federal garrison of troops as additional protection.[16]

The 1832 crisis in South Carolina offers another convenient vantage point from which to consider the uneven application of federal military power. In the Black Seaman's Controversy in 1823, South Carolina had demonstrated that a federal court decision and treaty could be successfully ignored; they now proposed to nullify a federal tariff law. South Carolina's increasing sensitivity on the antislavery issue, coupled with an economic decline in the 1820s, stimulated efforts to find a convincing formulation of the state sovereignty position which had been used to defend slavery since the first congresses. The philosophy found its fullest expression in the works of John C. Calhoun. Calhoun insisted that slaveholders were the real defenders of the Constitution, while those who challenged their interpretations were its enemies. Thus, in opposing the unwanted high tariffs, the public officials of South Carolina draped themselves in a constitutional theory of strict constructionalism and state sovereignty to evade a distasteful federal law, while they invoked broad constructionalism and national responsibility in order to demand federal aid to suppress black revolts. Ironically, Calhoun, who as secretary of war had dispatched federal troops to aid white South Carolinians after Vesey's Plot in 1822, worked out an elaborate theory to support insurrection by white South Carolinians against that same federal government.[17]

Although Andrew Jackson and Secretary of War Lewis Cass had congratulated the military commanders involved for their "promptitude" in dispatching unneeded federal troops at the time of the Turner Revolt, they vacillated when confronted with South Carolina's nullification of the federal law. Jackson responded to South Carolina's announced intention to defy enforcement of federal tariff collection by issuing a proclamation on December 10, 1832, which asserted that the law would be enforced. However, the president also ordered Cass to inform General Winfield Scott, who commanded the troops in South Carolina, to consult with the local district attorney and collector of customs, but to stand by for further instructions. South Carolina called out twelve thousand volunteers to resist federal law enforcement. Meanwhile, Jackson announced that he would take no positive action until he saw certified copies of the Nullification Acts, which had been passed by a special state convention. On January 6, 1833, in response to Jackson's request for further authority, Congress passed the Force Bill, which extended the jurisdiction of federal courts in revenue cases and empowered the use of any additional forces necessary to uphold the laws. At the same time, Congress passed an act reducing tariff rates. On March 15, the South Carolina convention repealed the state ordinance nullifying the tariff law, and yet three days later, in an expression of defiance, the convention nullified the Force Bill. No confrontation occurred because no attempt was made to enforce the law. In effect, South Carolina had again successfully defied the national government.[18]

Jackson's dilatory policy could be attributed to a belief that federal military law did not provide for cases of state defiance, which was the position of the governor and legislature of South Carolina. However, a careful reading of the statutes indicates no distinction between insurrections *in* a state and insurrections *of* a state. The military provisions of the Force Bill added nothing to presidential authority; the only real amendment was a provision relieving the president of the necessity of issuing a dispersal proclamation before using the army and navy. Jackson's sympathy with slaveholders, as he was one, clashed with his nationalistic and assertive tendencies, and he felt that avoiding bloodshed among white South Carolinians was more important than law enforcement. His interpretation of presidential power in such cases was evidently shared by some members of Congress. In the debates on the Force Bill, Senator Theodore Frelinghuysen of New Jersey, who was on the committee that drafted the bill, explained that the president did not have the power to intervene under existing statutes, but that he was given that power in the Force Bill.[19]

While expressing the interest of his state in the continuance of the protective tariff during the House debates on the Force Bill and the 1833 lowering of the tariff, Tristam Burges, from the manufacturing state of Rhode Island, gave his opinion of the connection between nullification, military responsibility, and slavery. He stated that South Carolina proposed to take up arms for the glorious purpose of making slaves more valuable by rendering the product of their labor more valuable. He did not see why northern states should aid them in this endeavor. Instead, southerners should support northern manufacturing by paying the tariff. If manufacturing declined, the cities would decline, the population would become more dispersed, and the militia would be scattered and not easily gathered in an emergency. Regular troops might have to be recalled from the South, where they were primarily located to provide slaveholders with protection, and distributed more equitably around the country. (At this time, the approximately seven thousand men in the regular army were stationed largely in the South and West.) Burges further asserted that he saw no specific language delineating national responsibility for the suppression of slave insurrection in the Constitution; however, the Constitution had been consistently interpreted that way and northerners had not generally objected since they were deeply concerned about the safety of southerners. Burges indicated that he did not mind providing protection for southerners so long as they paid for it, and he felt a tariff beneficial to northern industry would be sufficient payment. Nullification made it possible to support the economic power of slavery on the one hand and to avoid payment for protection of the system on the other. Burges's effort was wasted. By 1832, it was well established in opinion, law, and precedent that the entire nation was responsible for the military protection of slavery and slaveholders.[20]

In the period from 1800 to 1833, the military arm of the United States proved its reliability to the southern slavery interests in the Prosser, Andry, Vesey, and Turner revolts. Yet, in the confrontations with South Carolina in the Black Seaman's Controversy and the Nullification Crisis, the national government merely demonstrated its hesitancy to act. The contradiction in response is obvious. Although the blame for this contradiction might be placed on the desire to prevent bloodshed or the need to confine the defiance to South Carolina, the most likely explanation is the powerlessness and extralegal status of black people. Blacks were nonpersons whose condition, whether slave or free, was of no constitutional concern to the national government. On the other hand, the perpetuation of the slave system and the protection of white people against slave revolt had become a constitutional responsibility of the government. It was more politic to change the law or ignore the plight of those damaged by failure to enforce a federal court order than to antagonize white southerners. During this thirty-year period, the proslavery provisions of the Constitution were reinforced by a body of tradition and practice; federal responsibility for the defense of slavery became more deeply entrenched in national policy, perhaps even beyond the possibility of reversal.

4

The Seminole War as a
Black Freedom Movement:
Phase One

I N 1839, a pamphlet published by William Jay, son of the first Chief Justice of the United States, reviewed the federal government's legal and financial support of the institution of slavery from 1789. Among the instances chronicled by Jay were the ruthless suppression of slave insurrection and the relentless offensives against the Seminole Indians in the name of the Fugitive Slave Act even to the point of disregarding the territorial rights of foreign powers. Jay, like most abolitionists, was particularly incensed by the warfare waged against the Seminole Indians and the blacks residing among them because of southern proslavery interests and threats of secession. In words which support the repeated assertion that abolitionists were worse disunionists than southerners, Jay maintained that separation would be a good solution to the dissension; at least slavery would no longer have federal protection. For then, "should the slaves attempt to revolt the masters would be left to struggle with them unaided by the fleets and armies of the whole Republic." As an additional consequence, fugitive slaves would be free as soon as they crossed the southern boundary of the North.[1]

A review of the events cited by Jay will offer some basis for determining the validity of his position. The fugitive slave problem on the southeastern frontier dated back to the colonial period. Very early, slaves who escaped from the vicinity of South Carolina sought sanctuary in nearby Spanish Florida, hoping to avoid capture by living among the Seminole Indians. Since there were no Spanish claimants to their persons, their chances for maintaining their freedom were relatively high. They were evidently easily integrated into the Indian community. Quite naturally, this refuge for runaways was a provocation as well as a threat to southern slave interests.

When the colony of Georgia was established in 1733, South Carolina at first approved the idea of forbidding slavery in the new colony, thinking it would act as a buffer between South Carolina and Spanish Florida. But when slaves began fleeing to Georgia as well, South Carolinians changed their minds and encouraged the introduction of slavery in Georgia. The colonial anxiety was not unwarranted as records reveal that by 1736, there were sufficient numbers of runaway blacks and their descendants to establish settlements in Florida. The problem was compounded by the Spanish crown's refusal to grant British requests for extradition of the runaways, to the consternation of the British and the southern colonies.[2]

The Seminole component of the problem emerged in 1750. That year, many Creek Indians left Georgia because of tribal dissatisfactions and migrated to Florida. Their numbers were augmented from time to time by additional Creeks who disagreed with tribal decisions or who were opposed to tribal treaties made with the United States. One large group emigrated in 1814 because of opposition to the terms of the Treaty of Fort Jackson made by some Creek leaders with the American government. These emigrant Creeks became known in their language as *Seminoles*, which means *runaways*. Under Spanish colonial policy, these exiles were incorporated into the Spanish population and could acquire title to land and claim the protection of Spanish laws. Some of these Seminoles formed fast friendships with blacks in Florida and, in a few cases, acquired title to blacks under Spanish law in order to ward off attempts by slavecatchers to return the former slaves to Georgia.

The Spanish government defended Indian-black interests against Georgian claimants but not from altruistic motives. Spain, fearing territorial incursions, regarded Florida as a buffer between the British colonies and her colonies to the south. In order to avoid the possibility of Indian attack on Spanish settlers in East Florida and to enlist the aid of Indians in the colony's defense if necessary, Spain sought to appease the Indians. Although the Spanish did not encourage slaves to flee to

Florida, they feared offending the Indians by remanding the fugitives to their alleged masters. Spain enjoyed disconcerting the Americans, but avoided a confrontation.[3]

Under Spanish administration, the Indians and blacks in Florida prospered. Spanish administration of that territory, interrupted briefly by the cession of East and West Florida to Great Britain at the end of the Seven Years' War in 1763, was tolerant and unobtrusive. In the colonial period, the British stationed a few regular troops in South Carolina, largely to prevent slave rebellion; during the Seven Years' War, the number of troops was increased. The British military did not pursue or in any way molest the blacks in Florida during the colonial period or during the British control of Florida from 1763 to 1783. Their garrisons were too weak and torn by strife between military and civilian officials to suppress or capture the fugitives and Indians, even if that had been their policy. Their presence, however, did act as a deterrent by reducing the number of slaves escaping to Florida from Georgia and South Carolina until the Revolution. During the Revolution, the British encouraged the flight of slaves and welcomed their support.[4]

The movement toward American independence left the problem of the treatment and disposition of the Florida Indians and blacks in the hands of the colonists. Georgians and South Carolinians expected the Continental Congress to afford them at least as much protection against the escape of slaves as the British had; Georgia's Council of Safety informed the Continental Congress in 1775 that a large force of troops would have to be sent to prevent slaves from accepting the British invitation to join those fugitives already in Florida. The two colonies continued to be a defensive problem throughout the war. In March 1779, Congress noted that South Carolina was unable to deploy troops effectively in the national crisis because they were needed to control her slaves. Although Congress was sympathetic to southern requests for aid, it also indicated that the army could not be expected to keep slaves from running away to the British; other military matters of colonial defense were more critical at this time.[5]

When Spain reacquired Florida in the peace settlement after the Revolution, the Georgians were disturbed. They were well acquainted with the Spanish position on the extradition of claimed fugitives, and they felt this issue was too central to their existence to dismiss or allow any compromise. Believing that the situation required immediate action, the government of Georgia planned to circumvent claims by Spain and obtain support from the American government under the Articles of Confederation. They asserted that after the peace settlement in 1783, the government of Georgia had made a treaty with the Creek Indians providing for the return of all slaves resident among the Creeks to Georgia claimants and, by logical extension, the return of the blacks residing among the Seminoles, who were merely runaway Creeks. Georgia demanded national enforcement of the alleged treaty in the face of several inconsistencies: the Creek denials that such a treaty had ever been made; the difficulty of establishing the slave status of persons who had lived free in Florida for a generation or who were born in Florida; and the fact that Georgia could not even produce a copy of the treaty.

When the Georgian claim was presented to Congress for action, Congress pointed out that under the Articles of Confederation, treaties could only be made by authority of Congress. In 1785, therefore, Congress appointed commissioners to negotiate with the Creek nation. When only two of the one hundred settlements comprising the Creek nation sent representatives to the meeting, the federal commissioners would not negotiate. The representatives from Georgia, however, proceeded to treat with the Creeks despite the legal prohibition against state treatymaking.[6]

The ensuing illegal treaty bound the entire Creek nation to return all slaves resident among them, and all fugitive slaves who sought refuge in the future, to Georgia claimants. The treaty was, of course, invalid on both sides, and frontier hostilities continued between Creeks and Georgians. Georgia was unable to repossess slaves living among the Creeks, who were slaveholders themselves, or to force the Creek nation to assume the extralegal responsibility of recapturing blacks in Florida. Georgia was therefore happy to be among the first states to ratify the new Constitution with its proslavery compromises. Clearly, they believed that the Fugitive Slave Clause and the military clauses of the Constitution would insure the suppression of Indians and the return of fugitives from Florida.[7]

There can be little doubt of the influence of the Fugitive Slave Clause and the military enforcement power of the national government on Georgia's haste to ratify the Constitution. On January 4,

1789, General Anthony Wayne of Georgia wrote to a delegate, James Wilson of Pennsylvania, requesting him to support prompt congressional approval for the establishment of a military district on the southern frontier similar to that established under the control of General Arthur St. Clair in the Northwest Territory. Wayne stated that the situation in Georgia, "from the depredations of the Indians . . . [and] the insidious protection afforded by the Spanish to our runaway Negroes," was so alarming "as to threaten the state with ruin and depopulation" unless timely aid was given by Congress.[8] On December 25, 1789, Wayne also wrote to Henry Knox, the new secretary of war, urging immediate strong military occupation along the southern frontier before the Spanish gained increased influence among the Indians. He suggested that troops sent to Georgia be stationed so as to prevent fugitive slaves from "taking protection under the Spaniards. . . ."[9]

One of the first treaties made by President Washington supported the claims of the Georgia slaveholders. The August 7, 1790, treaty with the Creek Indians in Georgia reasserted the demands made in the earlier invalid treaties: the Creeks were bound to return black fugitives to their masters, even if these fugitives were living in Florida among the Seminoles. Promptly denouncing this indirect effort to interfere with their affairs, the Seminoles in Florida made it clear that Creeks from Georgia bent on enforcing the treaty could anticipate trouble. Further, Spanish authorities in Florida announced that resident blacks as well as Seminoles were under their territorial jurisdiction, and no subjects of the Spanish crown would be extradited to slavery. Impediments to enforcement also increased when even the southernmost Creek tribes rejected the idea that the treaty applied to the Seminoles. Temporarily thwarted, the Georgians sought new ways around these obstacles in their effort to maintain the system of slavery.[10]

Undaunted, President Washington appointed another commission to make a new treaty which all parties would accept as binding. The treaty, negotiated in 1796, again bound the Creeks to return fugitive slaves and implied that the Creeks were also acting for the Seminoles. The reasoning behind the continued insistence on that fiction is obvious: if the Creeks claimed that the Seminoles were really Creeks, then an argument could be made for Creek jurisdiction over the "Creeks" in Florida, Spanish sovereignty notwithstanding. A further argument could be made that failure to abide by the treaty gave the United States, as one of the high contracting parties, the right to take military action against the recalcitrants, even in Spanish territory. In a secret article, the treaty provided for payment of fifteen hundred dollars annually to the Creeks forever, of twelve hundred dollars annually to their principal chief, and one hundred dollars to six other chiefs for assiduous performance of the treaty obligation. In effect, a national bounty was promised for the capture of fugitive blacks.[11]

Despite the treaty, little progress was made in subduing the hostile Indians and blacks in Florida. Impatient with the unwillingness of the president to invade the Spanish possession openly, Georgia officials sent the state militia to Creek country to force the Creeks to comply with the treaty. They were repelled by the Creeks and blacks. Georgians, seeing their military efforts fail, thereafter urged the necessity for annexing Florida to the United States so that the vexing problem of Spanish sovereignty would be removed.[12]

In 1811, Congress, sympathetic to Georgia's viewpoint and also interested in American expansion, approved a measure providing for the annexation of Florida. Soon after its passage, an insurrection encouraged by the federal government was incited by a few malcontents in the northeastern part of Spanish territory and in Georgia. American forces took possession of Amelia Island in order to put down the "insurrection." When the Spanish government protested, President Madison, who had connived in the uprising, disavowed any federal connection in this shameful episode.[13]

Frustrated by the failure of the latest tactic, the state of Georgia again sent state troops into Florida in the fall of 1812, this time to *exterminate* the Seminoles and reenslave the refugee blacks. To Georgia's consternation, the southernmost Creeks aided the Seminoles, and together they defeated the militia. It was now obvious that repeated military efforts by a single state were doomed to failure. At that time, the Monroe administration, occupied with the War of 1812 on the northern frontier and with efforts to negotiate the acquisition of Florida from Spain, was reluctant to arouse Spanish and Indian antagonism on the southern frontier.[14]

During the War of 1812, the problem was further compounded by the British invitation to American slaves to join their naval service or to immigrate to the West Indies. A British officer whose forces had been driven out of Pensacola by Andrew Jackson furnished arms to the Indians and blacks in Florida and organized a small military unit. After the Battle of New Orleans, a strong fort was erected on the Apalachicola River by the British. When the British withdrew, the blacks were given possession of the fort with its artillery and military supplies. At that time, Spanish sovereignty was no obstacle to British territorial incursions; Spain was distracted by a revolution and civil war in her Latin American colonies.[15]

Southerners, however, were infuriated at the possession of a fort by persons whom they regarded as potentially destructive to the institution of slavery. Secretary of War William Crawford of Georgia, sympathetic to complaints from his state on this issue, carried on a lively correspondence laying the plans for the destruction of the fort with General Edmund Gaines, who commanded the southern frontier, and Andrew Jackson, who commanded the southwestern military district of the United States. On May 16, 1816, Jackson ordered Gaines to blow up the fort "regardless of the ground on which it stands." Gaines sent a regular army regiment and a contingent of upper Creek allies, together with artillery and the aid of two off-shore naval gunboats, to reduce the fort. Obviously, the fort was demolished without difficulty, and approximately 270 black women and children were killed, reportedly when an early shell hit a magazine of stored ammunition. A few survivors were turned over to Georgia slaveholders who claimed that their ancestors had owned ancestors of the prisoners. Weakly protesting this outrage, the Spanish government made avowals of friendship and blamed the British for erecting the fort in the first place. The naval gunboat commander explained to the Spanish that the United States had the legal right to punish the exiles under authority of treaties made with the Creeks, who had jurisdiction over the exiles. The weakened state of the declining Spanish empire in part explains her lack of real effort to defend her sovereignty; now at best, Spanish protection for the exiles in the face of American appeals to the "immutable laws of self-defense" would prove unreliable.[16]

In the wake of the Apalachicola Fort affair, the Indians and blacks, as well as the American forces on the southern frontier, prepared for increased hostilities. In mid-November 1817, General Gaines and a regular army force of three hundred men attacked a southern Creek settlement at Fowlton near the Georgia-Florida border in order to "punish the Indians" for their failing to adhere to the treaty of 1796. A gunfight ensured in which a number of Creeks were killed. These Creeks had persisted in their opposition to American plans for the Indians and blacks in Florida.[17]

On November 30, 1817, a group of Seminoles and blacks attacked a boat descending the Apalachicola River with supplies for the American outpost at Fort Scott in southern Georgia. Thirty-five American soldiers and the wives of six soldiers were killed in the assault; six soldiers and one woman were taken prisoner. The American public was infuriated by this "perfidious" Indian attack. In his message to Congress on March 25, 1818, President Monroe pointed to the "unprovoked" warfare of the Indians and charged that the Seminoles were bound by the 1796 treaty with the Creeks not to commit depredations against Americans. The regular army was authorized to prepare an invasion of Florida to "punish" the Seminoles.[18]

At this point, General Andrew Jackson took personal command of the expedition which was to become known as the First Seminole War. With an army composed of 3,000 volunteers from Georgia and Tennessee, his home state, as well as 1,000 regular troops from Fort Scott, Jackson set out to subdue the Indians and blacks. At the time of the Fort Scott incident, General Gaines estimated that of the 2,400 exiles in Florida, only 400 were black. As Jackson pursued them in Florida, about one-half of the exiles were reported killed, and only a few were enslaved; the others escaped. The most celebrated incident of this campaign was the summary execution of two British subjects, Alexander Arbuthnot and Robert Ambrister, who, according to Jackson, were inciting the Indians to violence.[19]

Jackson, reporting to the War Department on his expedition in May 1818, explained that the campaign was designed to "undeceive" the Seminoles, who thought they would be protected by Spanish sovereignty. In correspondence between Jackson, the governor of Pensacola, and the Spanish military commander at St. Marks, which Jackson enclosed in his report to the War Department, the Spanish insisted that they had no connection with the Seminoles and blacks and that they had not directed raids against any United States citizens. Jackson's response to the Spanish was that they had neglected their duty to prevent such outrages because of impotence and enmity toward the United States. Jackson then took over the Spanish fort at St.

Marks, ignoring the defenseless commander's protests, as well as the fort at Barrancas. In his communications with the Spanish and the War Department, Jackson kept insisting that the United States had a right to engage in warfare on Spanish territory. In his view, the United States' mission and justification dated from the Fort Scott "massacre." No mention was ever made of the 270 deaths at the Apalachicola fort or the punitive expedition against the settlement at Fowlton.[20]

Jackson's defensive position of his actions was necessitated by criticism both in Congress and by the new secretary of war, John C. Calhoun. Calhoun's criticism was not a result of legal or humanitarian concern, but was a politically motivated effort to tarnish Jackson's reputation. The congressional opposition stemmed from both political motivation and the necessity of displaying to the British some concern for the hanging of two English subjects. Senate and House committee reports on Jackson's expedition circumvented any discussion of the actual conflict over the fugitive slave issue. The house majority stuck to criticism of the summary execution of Arbuthnot and Ambrister, whom Jackson had accused of inciting this "savage and negro [sic] war." It was suggested that under the circumstances civil proceedings might have been preferable to a court martial. However, the Senate report strongly denounced Jackson's disregard of Spanish sovereignty and his circumvention of the war-making power of Congress as delegated in the Constitution.[21]

Jackson replied to their criticisms by summarizing the report he had sent the War Department earlier, with two significant additions: Congress had approved the war by making appropriations for it; additionally, the president as commander-in-chief was the only person who could decide whether he had carried out his orders faithfully, and as the president had in fact approved his conduct, Congress had no grounds for objection. The controversy fizzled on that note, and Jackson, the hero of New Orleans, was now also the savior of Florida.[22]

Justification by the administration for military actions in Florida became less complicated in 1819. The difficulty Spain was experiencing with her rebellious Latin American colonies and the impossibility of gaining English support in any military action against the United States finally led her to cede Florida to the United States in the Adams-Onis Treaty. Florida was now American territory and military power could be legally used to enforce the Fugitive Slave Act of 1793 without further explanation. Since any black person was presumed to be a slave, free blacks found in Florida could be adjudged as slaves who had fled some rightful owner. In order to remain true to the proslavery compromises of the Constitution, the national government was forced to make war upon the Indians and blacks in Florida; there was no solution short of armed confrontation, unless the blacks would surrender. The southern states quickly demanded that blacks be remanded under authority of the Fugitive Slave Act, as well as under the treaties made with the Creek nation which was still regarded as semi-sovereign. Any treaty-making would, of course, have to be done with the Creeks so long as the Seminoles refused to make any agreement affecting the rights of blacks living in Florida.[23]

In 1821, Secretary of War Calhoun appointed commissioners to make an additional treaty with the Creeks containing the same clause which provided for the rendition of blacks. The commissioners were ordered to negotiate for the benefit of Georgia, whose officials had traditionally insisted on this clause and had sent observers to insure and protect her interests. When one of the federal commissioners remonstrated against the Georgians dictating the terms of the treaty, Calhoun replaced him with one of the Georgian observers. The Creeks candidly told the commissioners that, while they could return black people within their nation, they could not be responsible for the Seminoles who were not under their jurisdiction. The commissioners insisted on the opposite view, reminding the Creeks that this was the settled construction accepted by the United States government since the treaty of 1796. In the resulting Treaty of Indian Springs, the Creeks ceded about five million acres of land to the United States for which they were to receive $200,000. The United States also agreed to reimburse parties who claimed to have slaves among the Creeks, thus gaining title to the slaves. Everyone was apparently satisfied: Georgians subsequently received $109,000 for slaves and other property lost; the Creeks received payment for their land; and the United States government became a slaveholder with title to those elusive blacks.[24]

But the problem was not solved yet, nor the last blood shed. Fugitive slaves continued to seek asylum in Florida, even after the First Seminole War. In 1822, a congressional committee was appointed to explore solutions to the problem. One of the committee's first moves was to ask Andrew Jackson, as an expert on Indian matters, for advice. Jackson responded helpfully with a suggestion that the Seminoles be forced to reunite with the Creeks and return to Creek country and that runaway slaves be remanded to Georgia claimants.[25]

Meanwhile, President Monroe decided that the Creeks were right in their protestations that the Seminoles were a separate tribe. Therefore, he sent commissioners to negotiate with the Seminoles in September 1823. Even though the majority of the Seminoles distrusted the Americans, the Camp Moultrie Treaty was made with a few of their members. The provisions of the treaty provided that the United States government protect the Seminoles from all persons whatsoever and prevent white persons from intruding on their lands. In return, those Seminoles present promised to prohibit fugitive slaves from joining their ranks and to apprehend and return them to their masters upon request. No claims were made to blacks resident in Florida at the time of the treaty. In addition, the Indians were to retreat to their own district in the south of Florida, an area with the least salubrious climate and poorest soil in the territory. The Indians voluntarily removed to the lands set aside for them.[26]

The presidential election of 1825 dropped the problem into the hands of John Quincy Adams. As secretary of state, Adams had approved Jackson's conduct in Florida and had shown more interest in the acquisition of Florida from Spain than sympathy for the Seminoles and blacks. During his administration as president, the Bureau of Indian Affairs handled the problem in conformity with the interests of slaveholders. In 1825, the bureau directed its agents to take any black identified by a slaveholder as a runaway slave to St. Augustine where the dispute would be decided by a federal judge as provided in the Fugitive Slave Act. However, the agents were given the authority to judge the validity of any counterclaims made for the same black by the Seminoles. If the agent felt the Indian making the claim was truthful, the Indian was permitted to keep the black until the judge decided the issue; if the agent did not believe the Seminole, he could ignore his claim. The alleged slave had nothing to say in the matter. The only evidence that would be permitted to rebut the presumption of slave status and immediate enslavement was the possession of manumission papers. No recent runaway or any person descended from those who had fled since 1660 could possibly produce such papers.[27]

With this mandate, slaveholders claiming blacks as their property now entered Florida in large numbers. Contrary to the law, some agents surrendered blacks without a court decision, and regular army troops at Fort King in Florida were assigned to aid in the arrest of fugitives. The poorly supported and reckless claims of slavecatchers, even to blacks for whom the Seminoles could prove title, as well as the incursions of whites into Indian areas supposedly protected under the treaty of 1823, led to an increasingly tense situation.[28] Consequently, in May 1828, Colonel George Brooke, who commanded the United States Army in Florida, and the federal district judge at St. Augustine ordered Indian agents to cease giving slaves claimed by Indians to slaveholders until title was established by the court. This policy was designed to decrease friction with the Indians, not to protect blacks who were defenseless without the possession of "free papers." The national government faced an impossible dilemma: on the one hand, it had to enforce the Fugitive Slave Act which would allow slaveholders to enslave practically every black in Florida; on the other hand, it was bound to abide by the Indian treaty which insured no penetration of Indian territory. Failure to keep white persons off Indian land could precipitate war.[29]

After rejecting one solution to the Florida difficulties—leaving the Indians and blacks in peace—the national government adopted the policy of "removing" the Indians west of the Mississippi, an action which would leave the way open for settlement of Florida by slaveholders. The Indian Removal Act of May 1830 authorized the president to negotiate with the tribes east of the Mississippi, offering to pay them for their land in the east and granting them land west of the Mississippi River to which perpetual title would be attached. The act itself did not dictate coercion, but it was federal law which the president was expected to uphold even if military force became necessary.[30]

Andrew Jackson, who assumed the presidency in 1829, was ill-suited to handle the Indian problem. He had successfully "punished" the Indians during his expedition of 1818 and had shown his lack of concern for Indian interests when he refused to enforce a Supreme Court decision favorable to the Cherokees in 1832. The Indian Removal Act, however, promulgated a policy he favored, and he stood ready to enforce it. The first step in its enforcement was the 1833 Treaty of Payne's Landing made with the Seminoles, which provided that eight chiefs go west to approve the land set aside for them, accompanied by Abraham, one of the blacks among them, to act as interpreter. If the chiefs found the country suitable and believed reuniting with the Creeks feasible, they would agree to further articles of the treaty providing for removal westward. Other articles of the treaty provided for an exchange of land based on the provisions in the Indian Removal Act and the United States' liquidation of slaveholders' claims to blacks among the Seminoles, so that the blacks could join them in the move beyond the Mississippi. While in the West, the chiefs were induced to sign an additional treaty on March 28, 1833, in which they expressed satisfaction with the area set aside for them and agreed to permanently move westward on lands separate from the Creeks.[31]

When the Seminole chiefs returned, they told the Indian agents that they would report on conditions in the West to their people and decide whether to move. To this, the agents replied that when the chiefs agreed to move, they had bound the entire Seminole nation and also indicated that the Creeks had advised the War Department that the Seminoles should now be reunited with them and be placed under Creek jurisdiction in the West. The Creeks had also asserted that since the United States acquired title to any slaves among the Seminoles in 1821 by agreeing to pay Georgia claimants, these "slaves" would become the property of the Creeks when they moved west. This assertion was a crushing blow to the hopes of the Seminoles and the blacks. If they went west, all blacks would again be in danger of enslavement—now by Creeks! Further, as far as the national government was concerned, the Camp Moultrie Treaty, setting aside land for the Seminoles in Florida, was void; the Seminoles had no alternative—they must go west.[32]

The Seminoles and blacks tried to obtain a change in policy from the War Department through the intercession of their agent. The Indian agent bluntly told the commissioner on Indian affairs that the reason the Seminoles were so slow in preparing for the move west was that they knew the blacks would be reenslaved by the Creeks. They were also sure that if they remained in Florida, white people would reenslave the blacks unless the government gave them separate land and protection. Meanwhile, slaveholders petitioned Jackson to accelerate the process of Indian removal from Florida, because the slave system could not be firmly established if free blacks and Indians remained in the territory. Estimates of the number of Seminoles and blacks involved vary, but most authorities agree that there were approximately two thousand. The War Department replied to the Seminole agent and white petitioners that the removal policy would be carried out as speedily as possible. The Seminoles and blacks prepared for war.[33]

5

The Seminole War as a Black Freedom Movement: Phase Two

HE OLD LINES of battle in the Seminole War were redrawn: the government remained committed to the removal of the Seminoles and the reenslavement of the blacks; the Indians and blacks insisted upon their right to remain free and in Florida. The Second Seminole War began late in 1835, when Wiley Thompson, an Indian agent, arrested and consigned to slavery the part-Negro wife of Osceola, a Seminole chief. Apparently, when Osceola protested too vigorously in June of 1835, Thompson confined him to jail for six days. Upon his release, Osceola vowed retribution; on December 28, Thompson was slain by the Seminoles in retaliation. The incensed Indians and blacks also successfully ambushed a regiment of American reinforcements en route to Fort King, Florida. Seminoles and blacks then stormed through Florida, attacking settlements and creating great fear among the white inhabitants. Pressure for action mounted in Washington, but the prolonged failure of the Americans to change their perspective, or to accurately define the issues, allowed this protracted war to continue for almost another decade, ending not in victory for either side, but in dismal confusion.[1]

Congress, at least publicly, exhibited a singular lack of understanding of the causes and nature of the Seminole War. Jacksonian Democrats, such as Senator Thomas Hart Benton of Missouri, defended the administration and the enormous war expenditures and lent their support to Democratic generals, such as Thomas Jesup. The anti-Jacksonians, Whigs or the Federal Party, attacked the administration for expenditures in a war against a "ragtag band of naked savages," yet praised Whig generals, such as Winfield Scott and Zachary Taylor, who were "hampered" by the inefficiency of Jacksonian war departments. The United States was hopelessly mired in an endless war where regular army tactics did not work and critics made the most of it. Discussion about the war in Congress mainly concerned requests for appropriations. That the nation must expand into Florida and make it safe for slavery was not questioned. Since the nation's military power was pledged to defend and support slavery, there was no point in discussions hostile to slavery interests. Proslavery advocates were already sensitive enough after the slave revolts, the Nullification Crisis, the Missouri controversy, and the fight over abolitionist petitions in Congress. Both Democrats and Whigs wanted to gloss over sectional differences and cement party loyalties, not divide the country. Consequently, Congress approved the policy of not discussing antislavery petitions by adopting a series of "Gag Resolutions," which postponed indefinitely the entertainment of the sticky issue. Little mention was ever made of the real reason for the Seminole intransigence—the fear that the Florida blacks would be enslaved. Congress refused to acknowledge that the war would have been unnecessary if some assurances had been given the Seminoles that the blacks would be left alone.

When the war appropriation bill came up in January 1836, Daniel Webster, reflecting the general tenor of the Senate, said that he knew nothing about the war except what he read in the public gazettes. He had deduced that the cause of the conflict was the attempt to remove the Indians. Henry Clay chimed in that he knew nothing either. In reply, Benton explained that the killing of white people by the runaway blacks was a partial cause of the war. In his opinion, the loss of so many lives resulted from abolitionist agitation. When succeeding administrations were asked about the aims of the war, the standard reply was that the immutable laws of self-defense, as well as the Fugitive Slave Act and the preservation of the institution of slavery in Georgia, South Carolina, and Florida, dictated the use of American military might against the Indians and blacks. National policy was to remove or exterminate the Indians and blacks in Florida even though the current conflict centered on the failure of the Indians to uphold treaties which were fraudulently obtained by the United States.[2]

Soon after the hostilities recommenced, General Winfield Scott was given command of the army in Florida. As the war dragged on with little success, he was severely criticized. Jackson, comparing Scott's failure with his own success in 1818, removed him from command in 1837. At this time, the army had captured about 124 women and children, but not one warrior.[3] General Thomas Jesup, one of Scott's critics, replaced him. Jesup succeeded in obtaining a surrender from the Indians on March 6, 1837. The agreement provided that the Indians and blacks were to migrate together to the West under the protection of the United States Army. The army was reduced in size, and the exiles and Seminoles began peaceably moving westward.[4]

The war was almost immediately resumed, however, when Jesup failed to keep his agreement. He had met resistance when the slaveholders in Florida and Georgia, insisting that the blacks were their property, refused to permit the blacks to migrate; in addition, Osceola had been captured when he came in to parley under a flag of truce in October 1837. Jesup, although properly criticized in the press for his violation of the laws of war in capturing Osceola, regarded this violation as a necessary step in concluding the war. There was considerable legal authority, however, for the slaveholders' insistence that blacks not be taken west. Jesup could not legally permit property to be transferred unless there was some judicial determination of the rights of the parties concerned. The army, under the Constitution, was pledged to protect slaveholders in the use and enjoyment of their property. The 1832 Treaty of Payne's Landing had supposedly solved that problem for Jesup by providing payment from the federal treasury to liquidate any claims to blacks living among the Seminoles. Claimants of slaves were to file with the United States' government, both for blacks residing among the Indians at the time of the Treaty of Payne's Landing and, by extension, for any others who joined the Indians while they were in the process of moving westward. However, the slaveholders did not accept this solution. At first, they wanted to restrict any operation of the treaty to those residing among the Indians when the treaty was made. Later, they wanted to overturn the treaty provisions altogether by saying one could not tell one group of blacks from another and, in any case, all blacks should remain in slavery.

General Jesup and the War Department promptly yielded to the slaveholders' demands and delivered claimed blacks to the claimants rather than permitting all blacks to go west with the Seminoles as promised. The war was supposedly waged to enforce the Treaty of Payne's Landing and also the surrender agreement of March 1837. Officers and men were detailed to take blacks who joined the Seminoles for transportation westward to places where claimants could conveniently reenslave them.[5]

When the Seminoles and blacks responded to this perfidy by refusing to cooperate in their removal, Jesup renewed warfare. In the summer and fall of 1837, Jesup, desperate for success, made an agreement with the Creeks and the Florida militia, granting them ownership of any unclaimed black exiles they captured. This agreement had the approval of the War Department. Consequently, the Creeks gained title to some ninety captured blacks; the Florida militia claimed varying interests in other blacks. On September 6, 1837, Jesup ordered payment to the Creeks for the value of their ninety blacks, detaining the blacks at Fort Pike, Louisiana, until the government decided what to do with them. The secretary of war approved his action on October 7, 1837. Subsequently, the Creeks refused reimbursement, stating that they preferred possessing the slaves. The War Department then persuaded a Georgia slaveholder to offer the Creeks fifteen thousand dollars for the ninety blacks, which the Creeks accepted after some debate. Meanwhile, the ninety slaves had inadvertently been moved to a fort west of the Mississippi. When the Georgia slaveholder sent an agent armed with a War Department order to claim the slaves, the commanding general refused to comply because he lacked sufficient forces to control what he feared would be a violent Indian reaction. Now the Seminoles and blacks were in disarray; some blacks had been sent west and others had been reenslaved; still others remained hidden in Florida, hoping for a change in national policy.[6]

Meanwhile, in conjunction with an administration request for an additional appropriation for the war in September 1837, Secretary of War Joel Poinsett circulated a letter he had written to Silas Wright, chairman of the Senate Finance Committee, explaining the administration's position on the war. Congress was also referred to a five-volume War Department preparation which contained correspondence and reports on the topic of Indian removal. Poinsett's letter indicated that since the Seminoles had agreed to move west and then unexplainedly failed to comply, the government was solely attempting to carry out the removal policy enacted by Congress and to protect Floridians from violent outrages. Thirty-five administration critics would not permit the matter to rest there. On September 19, 1837, Representative Henry Wise of Virginia proposed that a select committee be appointed to inquire into the causes, the corruption, and the expenditures of the war. The House spent the next session trying to decide whether such a committee was necessary. Critics and defenders alike, however, assumed that the only problems were the savage fighting ability of the Indians and the insalubrious climate and swampy terrain of Florida.[7]

In an effort to capture the blacks and Seminoles remaining in Florida, the government now invoked the aid of the Cherokees, who were convinced that the best policy for the Seminoles was to go west to avoid annihilation. When several Seminole chiefs, who came under a flag of truce to parley with the Americans and Cherokees, were taken prisoner and sent west, the strategy failed. The Seminoles resolved not to submit to the United States or move without guarantees of protection for the blacks.[8]

Since Jesup did not want to fail in Florida as ignobly as General Scott had, as early as July 1837, he hinted to the War Department that it might be necessary to permit the remaining Seminoles to stay in the southern part of Florida. In 1838, his policy in shambles and his army disgruntled, Jesup was ready to give up military efforts against the Seminoles. He met with some Seminole chiefs to see if they would accept terms permitting their people to remain in the Everglades. The Seminoles found this solution acceptable. Jesup wrote to Poinsett, a South Carolina slaveholder and a good Jacksonian, asking for approval of the policy. Poinsett replied that the Treaty of Payne's Landing, made under the authority of the Removal Act of 1830, was the law of the land and its execution was the constitutional duty of the president. Poinsett's position had been reversed from his attitude during the nullification controversy in which he counseled Jackson to have patience with South Carolina in the face of her violation of federal law. He chose to ignore the terms of the surrender agreement made by General Jesup in March 1837, stating that it was not a treaty and thus not the supreme law of the land. Administratively overruled, Jesup capitulated and continued to capture as many blacks as possible for reen-slavement. Before the end of Jesup's command in Florida, some nine hundred Seminoles and three hundred blacks had been removed. To compound the military problem, the Seminoles were assigned to Creek lands in the West and, not surprisingly, they refused to live with the Creeks. The Cherokees, conscience-stricken as a result of their efforts to persuade the Seminoles to surrender, gave them temporary use of part of their territory.[9]

By 1838, the cost of the war approached twenty million dollars, and the Whigs were still making political capital out of this fact. In response, on May 31, Representative Hopkins Turney, a Democrat from Tennessee, asserted that Indian removal was a beneficial policy and that the Whigs were aligning themselves with abolitionists, who were Indian and Negro lovers, by criticizing the policy. Further, opponents of removal were the same people who under the garb of religion "strained every nerve for the nefarious purpose of exciting the slaves of the South to insurrection and bloodshed." Wise of Virginia said that he failed to see why the Indians could not remain in peace in Florida until they gradually became extinct. In addition, Indian agents had told him that the Indians had not really approved the Treaty of Payne's Landing, thus making the entire program of removal fraudulent. Charles Downing, delegate from the territory of Florida, jumped to attack Wise, maintaining that Indian agents had obtained their information from Indians and blacks. Since white men had told Congress that the treaty was valid, he declared that the word of the whites should be believed in preference to that of the blacks and Indians. Wise retreated.[10]

In the Senate on June 8, 1838, Samuel Southard of New Jersey attacked the administration's position, insisting that the war was being pursued to enforce an invalid and fraudulent treaty. Benton was well prepared for the defense on this occasion. He outlined the entire history of American-Seminole relations since 1831 from the administrative point of view. He concluded that the Seminoles had independently decided to go west because game was exhausted and white settlers were approaching their land. Further, Benton felt that the real motive for the delay in removal was the "desire for blood and pillage" on the part of the Indians but still more "on the part of the five hundred runaway Negroes mixed up among them." These Indians and blacks, he continued, believed they could raid white settlements forever and run back to hide in the swamps; consequently, the American military establishment proposed to "undeceive" them of that notion. Benton read from the Treaty of Payne's Landing, skipping over Article VI, which provided for the liquidation of slaveholder's claims to blacks so that they could peacefully go west with the Seminoles. Next, he chronicled the bloody deeds of the Seminoles and exiles, making no mention of the injustices they had suffered. Anyone who defended the Seminoles, according to Benton, was indulging in "mawkish sentimentality on behalf of yellow and black men," whose leaders ought to be summarily executed as Jackson had executed Arbuthnot and Ambrister during the First Seminole War. Benton optimistically predicted an early end to the war since the Indians and blacks were surrendering or being killed in encouraging numbers. The war, however, was to continue for another three years.[11]

When the new Congress met in December 1839, Poinsett reported that the Indians were still hostile and their number not significantly lessened, despite Benton's sanguine prediction of the year before. The administration, anxious to end the war before the next election campaign, introduced an armed settler bill for the settlement of Florida. Speaking in favor of the bill, Benton reversed his previous position and explained that the Indians could no longer be caught and removed, since there had been no real battles in Florida for two years, only massacres and assassinations. Regular army tactics were apparently doomed to failure. However, he believed that placing ten thousand armed settlers in Florida who would receive land grants for their service when the war was over might prove to be an effective strategy. These settlers were to live in stockades, receive government supplies, and have a small number of regular army personnel stationed among them. When the Indians were forced to come out of hiding, the settlers would exterminate them. The Whigs were opposed to the proposal. William C. Preston, Whig senator from South Carolina, insisted that the government clear all the Indians and blacks out of Florida before settlement proceeded. As the settlement in Florida would consist primarily of plantations with slaves, slavery could not exist in an area where Indians and blacks could entice slaves away from their masters. Senator Robert Strange of North Carolina, although asserting he was an administration supporter, agreed with Preston and proposed that

47

bloodhounds be used against the Indians and blacks. Preston suggested that the administration put General Zachary Taylor, a Whig, in charge of a riding squadron to search and destroy the enemy. Benton attempted to reply to the critics by saying that Florida should be settled by yeoman farmers who wanted to work their own land, since large slaveholdings would make the area even less defensible. He believed that the government recognized that it must change its policy since the old policy had not worked. Florida must be settled promptly, he continued, and Whigs were opposed to a policy which would facilitate this because they thought the state would vote Democratic. According to Benton, Whigs and the abolitionists who wanted Florida to remain a haven for runaways were in agreement. Despite thhe administration's efforts, the armed settler bill failed to pass, and the war continued as before.[12]

When Zachary Taylor succeeded Jesup in May 1838, he would not temporize or attempt reconciliation in Florida and again began a course of action aimed at moving every Indian and black westward. However, he would have nothing to do with efforts to reenslave blacks. Despite this change of attitude, the Indians refused to trust the Americans. American military efforts were a fiasco. Finally, President Van Buren and Secretary of War Poinsett, in desperation, decided to make a new treaty giving the Seminoles land in Florida—the same suggestion previously proposed by General Jesup and Indian agents which had been rejected. At this time, however, the Jacksonians were suffering increasing criticism for their inability to end the war. An agreement was made with the Indians on May 18, 1839, that they and the blacks could remain in southern Florida, and the war was declared at an end.[13]

Some blacks and their Indian friends were unconvinced and refused to believe that the whites would leave them in peace. They decided to ignore the government's demands for their surrender and organized resettlement. They had been deceived too often by promises from the military. Stymied, the army and militia of Florida now began hunting the Indians and blacks in order to force their surrender. Bloodhounds were brought in from Cuba to aid in the hunt, but this technique proved ineffective. In the early spring of 1840, after almost two years in Florida, Zachary Taylor was granted his request to be relieved of his station.

The remarkable Indians and blacks were not only capable of evading the army but were able to attack white settlements at will. At this point, the regular army had about five thousand troops in Florida, although many of these were incapacitated by recurring tropical fevers and the oppressive heat. The expenditures for the war became an issue in the presidential campaign of 1840, partially contributing to Van Buren's defeat. The American public, including many members of Congress, knew little of the black problem as it related to the war; however, they were aware that the war was very costly. In desperation, the War Department brought several Seminoles back from the West to tell those in Florida of the glories of removal, but this action only further infuriated the Indians and blacks, who by this time were determined to fight to the finish.[14]

When the Taylor administration took office, Colonel William Worth was assigned to take command in Florida on May 19, 1841. Worth was ordered to reduce expenditures and find some means of bringing the war to a close. The regular army had become increasingly discontented with its role in the war over the last ten years. They were assailed by slaveholders for their failure to prevent the escape of slaves and to return all blacks in Florida to slavery. Further, the people of Georgia and Florida successfully undermined any workable agreements or solutions the army made with the enemy. The army payroll was swollen with payments to Floridians as commissary workers and contractors and with the expense of rations supplied to Floridians driven from their homes.[15]

Colonel Worth adopted a policy that Jesup had dishonestly tried earlier, which involved holding a chief hostage in order to entice the Indians and blacks out of hiding. Worth told the chief to send five of his braves to explain the new removal policy to his people. The government guaranteed not to enslave the blacks; yet if the Indians and blacks did not surrender, the chief would be hanged. As a result of this ploy, about two hundred Indians and blacks came out of hiding during July 1841. They were immediately sent west. Claimants of blacks were told to seek compensation from the national government. Thereafter, convinced of the honesty of this policy, Seminoles and exiles readily came forward to emigrate.

Worth cut expenditures by sending people who were on government rations home and discharging civilians on the army payroll. He also relied on regular army troops and refused to utilize the Florida and Georgia militias. In response to this action, the governor of Georgia, as well as the congressional delegate from Florida, protested to President Tyler. Worth responded that the militia was too expensive, seemed more interested in capturing and enslaving blacks than warfare, and intimated that they were a hindrance to efforts to end the war. Secretary of War John Spencer told the protestors that Worth would be advised of their position and would take whatever action was proper.[16]

The war in Florida was finally closed in August 1843. The few hostile Indians remaining in the territory agreed to stay in southern Florida. Most of the Seminoles and blacks had willingly moved west, and at least some of the blacks had evaded the reenslavement. On January 25, 1845, the government made a treaty with the Seminoles and the Creeks that the blacks and Seminoles would live separately in a part of Creek country with partial autonomy. Any dissension over transactions occurring before the treaty date would be decided by the president of the United States.

Travesty was to compound treachery, for as soon as the blacks moved to Creek lands, attempts were made to enslave them. They fled to Fort Gibson, where the military commander accorded them temporary protection until he could get instructions from Washington. President Polk was disconcerted by the incident, and upon finding a written basis for the blacks' claim in the surrender agreement made with General Jesup in March 1837, he wrote Jesup, requesting an interpretation of this document. Jesup replied that the agreement made them free from all claims. Polk also wished to have a supporting opinion from the attorney general. However, there was some difficulty because the Attorney General was Nathan Clifford of Maine, who might take too favorable a view of the black claim for freedom. Therefore, Polk waited to secure an opinion until after Clifford left to become minister to Mexico in 1848. John Mason of Virginia, who was given an interim appointment by the president, wrote an opinion on this matter, before being replaced by Isaac Toucey of Connecticut. Mason's opinion was that the blacks were entitled to their freedom, but that the executive arm could not use the military power of the United States to protect them. The blacks saw the handwriting on the wall; after twenty years of fighting for their freedom, they fled to Mexico in September 1850.[17]

Relentlessly, slaveholders continued to pursue their claims to blacks who had been transported west, still insisting that any black found in Indian Territory was a slave. Although, in August 1838, Attorney General Benjamin Butler had prepared an opinion for the secretary of war indicating that the Constitution and laws obliged the president to use military power to remand fugitive slaves found only in a *state* and not in Indian Territory, this did not settle the issue. In February 1854, Caleb Cushing, attorney general under Franklin Pierce, decided that Butler was mistaken. Cushing's opinion had been solicited when a Mississippian requested military aid to claim a group of blacks who were allegedly living among the Choctaws. Cushing explained that when Article IV, Section 4, of the Constitution required the national government to protect the states against domestic violence, it included territories by extension; therefore, Article IV, Section 2, meant persons held to labor in a territory as well as a state. Further, the Fugitive Slave Act specifically provided for the rendition of runaways in the northwestern and southwestern territories. Since these were the only territories possessed by the United States at the time, the provision should be extended to territory acquired thereafter. Another argument he advanced was that Indian Territory was south of the Missouri compromise line, which was to be the northern boundary for slavery in the Louisiana Purchase territory; and in slave areas, all black people were presumed to be slaves unless proven to the contrary. Finally and most importantly, Cushing stated that the Act of Congress of June 30, 1834, granted the commissioner of Indian affairs the authority to remove anyone from Indian territory who was there contrary to law and gave the president the power to use military force for compliance. Fugitive slaves did not belong in Indian Territory; therefore, claimants could call upon the president to use the army to remand them if necessary.[18]

Although it is possible to discount Cushing's opinion as inapplicable to the blacks among the Seminoles since it specifically referred to the Choctaws and, on the additional basis, that the Treaty of Payne's Landing laid a legal basis for the presence of blacks among the Seminoles, the blacks who remained in Indian Territory were obviously in danger. The terms of the treaty, which had not withstood claims by the Creeks nor changed administration policy, offered them little support. The exiles who fled to Mexico in 1850 were wise to do so.[19]

The history of the United States in its relations with the Seminoles and blacks during the First and Second Seminole Wars clearly illustrates the use of military power to support the institution of slavery at any cost. The Indians and blacks could not be left in Florida even when it meant violating Spanish sovereignty. Blacks were not permitted to move peaceably westward because slaveholders were not willing to allow even one black person to obtain his freedom. There was no niche or corner of safety for the free black in a slave society. If even one little enclave of Indians and blacks remained unmolested, it posed a threat to the institution of slavery; the Indian removal policy was therefore thought necessary. The enforcement of that policy was the major concern of the federal army for twenty years, and by the end of the war, military costs alone were well over twenty million dollars. As William Jay said in 1839, it was a war which had the primary objective of saving Florida for slavery.

6

Abolition and the Abrogation of Civil Liberties

T HE NATIONAL PROSLAVERY policies demonstrated in the Seminole Wars found further reinforcement during the pre-Civil War period as federal troops were consistently used to suppress the increasingly active abolitionist movement. At the same time, constitutional military power was withheld when protection was needed for antislavery activists in the exercise of their civil liberties. Abolitionists in both the North and South were left to the mercy of local officials who usually refused protection. The national government felt no legal obligation to protect antislavery activists and, in truth, reacted indifferently to attacks upon them. In fact, the Supreme Court, in *Barron v. Baltimore* (1833), reinforced the legal position of the proslavery forces by asserting that Congress could not interfere with the exercise of the freedoms included in the Bill of Rights, since no such prohibition applied to the states; the national government could not intervene if a state chose to prohibit free speech. The consequences of this decision, combined with a federal obligation to prosecute those who interfered with the rendition of fugitive slaves, made the federal government the enemy of abolitionists, who were left legally defenseless.[1]

Had the national government been sympathetic to the antislavery cause, there was sufficient legal and constitutional authority to protect abolitionists from physical violence. When the mechanisms of law and order within a state failed to prevent or suppress disturbances, the national government was obligated to intervene. In instances of slave revolts or plots, national power was utilized, often without even consulting the president or state officials; later, civil authorities were only too happy to ratify federal action after the fact. In cases of abolitionist activity, however, local officials did not want antiabolitionist mobs suppressed; indeed, suppressionist mobs were often led by prominent judges, militia officers, lawyers, merchants, and planters. The "Doughface," or southern dominated, administrations of the period were no more interested in protecting abolitionists than were the local governments. Consistent with the current constitutional practices and interpretations, southern states passed laws prohibiting discussion of antislavery doctrines and the circulation of abolitionist literature, again using the overworn rationale that such activity "stirred-up" slave rebellions.[2] Tyranny, terror, and mob violence were used to coerce antislavery activists. Suspected abolitionists were tarred, feathered, and run out of town; antislavery literature was burned.[3]

Abolitionists and antislavery supporters were generally received no better in the North than they were in the South. Northern states did not enact legislation prohibiting discussion of slavery, but mob violence often awaited antislavery spokesmen. As in the South, mobs attacking the abolitionists were often led by the leading citizens in the community, and police officials made little effort to interfere. For example, in 1829, antiabolitionists and antiblack mobs roamed through Cincinnati's black area wreaking destruction and devastation. In July 1834, rioting against abolitionists in New York City resulted in mass destruction of the black section. The mayor of New York did call up the militia, but when the violence subsided, he blamed the disturbance on abolitionists. Ironically, the defenseless black community suffered the misdirected violence generated by abolitionism. Further, in Philadelphia in 1838, the members of the local antislavery society received threats that their meeting would be disrupted, and fearing violence, they asked the mayor for protection. No protection was given; the police stood by as fires and rioting terrorized the city. Finally, blacks and abolitionists were subjected to so much injustice and violence that a reaction formed; some northerners feared that all freedom of expression might ultimately be endangered. As a result of this change in temper, as well as a decline in abolitionist activity, blacks and abolitionists were much safer in the North after 1840.[4]

Civil liberties were also denied antislavery spokesmen attempting to exercise their freedom of the press. Indignant mobs often vandalized the presses and ran abolitionist editors out of town. Northerners who generally professed a belief in editorial freedom recanted when it came to the publication of literature attacking slavery. Mesmerized by fears of disunion, they were reluctant to impinge, judge, or interfere with the South's peculiar institution. Also, many northerners who had proslavery leanings or who were genuinely neutral saw no benefit in discussions of such an explosive issue. The publication and circulation of abolitionist literature grew in spite of public pressure. In 1835, southern legislatures asked northern states to pass legislation suppressing abolitionist publications. Most northern legislatures seemed to favor the requests but found it difficult, within the framework of existing state constitutions, to draft legislation which would suppress only the abolitionists. The contradictions in public sentiment were expressed in a violent episode involving Elijah Lovejoy, an antislavery publisher, who founded a press in Alton, Illinois, in November 1837. The attorney general of Illinois called public meetings in an effort to find a way to shut down Lovejoy's press. When the meetings became volatile, the mayor of the city attempted to pacify the aroused citizens, but he admitted that civil authority could not disperse them. As a result, Lovejoy was killed and twelve of his supporters were tried in January 1838 on the strange charge of organizing to use force in an effort to protect Lovejoy's press, an action which was described as an "unlawful defense of property." They were acquitted, but so were several mob members who had been charged with inciting to riot. The absence of military protection for the abolitionists in Alton lends credence to legal indifference that bound the country at this time. In the aftermath of the Turner Revolt, the mayor of Norfolk had called for military assistance and received it; the mayor of Alton could have asked for the dispatch of federal troops to keep order. He did not; in fact, he incorrectly claimed that Lovejoy and his associates, in asserting their civil rights, had created the disorder.[5]

The Fugitive Slave Act of 1850 generated a wave of violence inundating those who persisted in helping slaves to gain freedom. The distinctive authority of this new act made both national and state governments responsible for the capture and return of runaway slaves. The act further stipulated that those who harbored or aided runaways or interfered with the legal processes were subject to imprisonment or fines. Marshals could summon bystanders and citizens as a "posse comitatus" and even regular troops and the militia to enforce the act. Since the Fugitive Slave Act of 1793 had no such stringent provisions, the new act was obviously designed to close the legal loopholes which had allowed citizens who aided fugitives to evade punishment.

The federal government worked vigorously to enforce the new act and to suppress attempted violations. On February 15, 1851, Frederic Wilkins, alias Shadrach, a waiter in a coffee house in Boston, was arrested on a federal warrant which alleged that he was a fugitive slave. Public reaction was voluble in its opposition to the federal government. In response, President Fillmore issued a proclamation asking citizens to cease interfering with law enforcement officers. At the same time, Secretary of War Charles M. Conrad ordered the commanding officer of the troops in Boston to make troops available if the marshal needed aid. In defiance, antislavery advocates, most of whom were black, forced their way into the courtroom and liberated Shadrach from the custody of the marshal, and later arranged for his safe escape to Canada. In the aftermath, several persons were arrested; five were tried and acquitted for violating the Fugitive Slave Act.[6]

Its authority challenged, Congress held hearings on the problems associated with enforcing the Fugitive Slave Act; both houses entertained a resolution which supported the president's authority to use the military to enforce the act when civil authority proved inadequate. It was manifest that the president already had sufficient statutory authority to dispatch troops in instances of opposition to federal law, but Congress wanted to substantiate its position in an effort to pacify southerners who were leaning toward secession. However, some southerners, concerned with providing a legal basis for secession, upheld the theory that the national government could not coerce a state to comply with federal law. They were unwilling to support the resolution which gave the president the military responsibility to enforce the act. They wanted *state* authorities to enforce the Fugitive Slave Act to avoid establishing new precedents for national intervention in state affairs. Jefferson Davis of Mississippi, for example, refused to vote for the resolution, arguing that if Massachusetts did not want to enforce the Fugitive Slave Act, she could do what all states were free to do, "take the extreme medicine, secession." Despite the southern opposition, both houses passed the resolution. The effects of its passage was felt almost immediately when a second fugitive slave was captured in Massachusetts on April 3, 1851. The slave was placed on board a vessel bound for Georgia which was heavily defended by militiamen, marines, and regular army troops. A group of blacks attempted rescue, but the armed forces present were too formidable.[7]

In 1851, the enforcement of the Fugitive Slave Act precipitated violence in Christiana, Pennsylvania. Christiana's large population of free blacks and fugitive slaves formed a league of mutual protection against southern slavecatchers who were continually kidnapping blacks to return them to alleged owners. On this occasion, Edward Gorsuch and his son, along with a marshal from Philadelphia and a few other people, arrived in Christiana with a warrant to claim a fugitive slave. The alleged fugitive was sheltered at the home of William Parker, one of the black leaders of the league. When the slavecatchers' demand that the slave be brought out of the house was answered with a warning shot, some member of the Gorsuch party fired twice into the house. By this time, a crowd of blacks had gathered and a riot ensued. Gorsuch was wounded and his son killed. The alleged fugitive, along with Parker and the other black participants, managed to escape. Immediately, city authorities organized a civil posse, and with the aid of forty-five marines, they arrested thirty-five blacks and two Quakers, Castner Hanway and Elijah Lewis. They were charged with resisting the Fugitive Slave Act. At Hanway's trial, the counsel for the government, concurring with President Fillmore's position, maintained that those who resisted the Fugitive Slave Act were opposing the Fugitive Slave Clause of the Constitution and were therefore guilty of treason. However, the charge of treason is fallacious, because the Constitution defines treason as the act of levying war against the United States or giving aid and comfort to its enemies. Hanway was possibly guilty of violating federal law, but was not guilty of treason. He was acquitted, and all charges against the remaining defendants were dropped.[8]

Disturbances broke out in Boston again in May 1854, when Anthony Burns was ordered remanded to his master in Virginia as a fugitive slave. Bostonians, black and white, could no longer countenance the incarceration and reenslavement of persons who had lived among them for years. A belligerent crowd of some fifty thousand gathered around the court house. A disorganized attack was mounted and repulsed. To control the crisis, fifty federal artillerymen, along with two pieces of artillery, as well as a detachment of federal marines and the state militia called out by the governor, were sent to reinforce the marshal. The federal troop commander dispatched his troops on the authority of a letter received in February 1851, the occasion of the Shadrach incident. The United States marshal also wanted General Winfield Scott to deploy troops for support, but Scott refused to comply until he received orders from the president. Although a few prominent antislavery spokesmen were arrested, they were subsequently acquitted on a technicality. However, Burns was successfully transferred to a federal revenue cutter and returned to Virginia under the escort of several naval vessels. An indication of the continued tension in Boston in the aftermath of this incident is the fact that troops were quartered in the city until June 2.[9]

In 1854, when another alleged fugitive, Joshua Glover, was arrested in Racine, Wisconsin, and taken to Milwaukee, his plight aroused a local abolitionist group in Milwaukee who assisted in his escape from jail. Action taken by local officials was thwarted when their request for troops to aid in Glover's recapture was refused by the commanding officer at Fort Brady on the grounds that he wished to await confirming orders from Washington. The commander was not inclined to use regular army troops in pursuit of alleged fugitives, particularly at the discretion of local officials. Since the fugitive had escaped to Canada, the affair was closed before orders came from Washington.[10]

In the midst of the antiabolitionist riots and the disorders caused by the enforcement of the Fugitive Slave Act, the specter of secession hounded the halls of Congress. The congressional proslavery compromises had brought only temporary appeasement. When the great battles over whether to receive and debate abolitionists' petitions began in 1836, proslavery forces successfully introduced a series of Gag Resolutions, making it virtually impossible to discuss the slavery issue in Congress. Antislavery advocates regarded the petition strategy as a means of adding civil libertarians to their forces, and they succeeded. However, Congress was placed in the awkward position of denying the right of petition on the grounds that slavery was a domestic concern, which applied not only to slavery in the states, but also to the District of Columbia where Congress had the constitutional duty of governing. On January 7, 1836, Thomas Hart Benton, who had so vigorously supported federal action against the Seminoles and blacks in Florida, attacked abolitionists for sending petitions to Congress, contending that these petitions made slaves think that they had allies ready to come to their aid if they rebelled. Senator John Tyler of Virginia asserted that his state could put down any insurrection occurring in daylight without aid, yet feared the possibility of midnight assassinations. He concluded by stating that Virginia asked only for the disavowal from other states of any intention to interfere with slavery. Silas Wright, senator from New York, assured southerners of the North's intention to quell, not promote, insurrection. At this point, John C. Calhoun of South Carolina stated that all discussion was unnecessary since it was common knowledge that there were men in the North "who were ready to second any insurrectionary movement of the blacks."[11] In his opinion, the petition struggle only gave comfort to these agitators. This southern diversionary tactic was effectively used to maintain "the Gag" in Congress for eight years.[12]

The proslavery forces in the national government gathered momentum in the 1840s and 1850s. Texas was annexed and the Mexican War fought in part to provide territory for slavery expansion. Along with a more effective fugitive slave law, the Compromise of 1850 promised no interference with slaves in the District of Columbia. The Supreme Court, in the critical *Dred Scott v. Sandford* decision (1857), affirmed the southern claim that slave property was guaranteed in all the territories and that the federal government lacked the power to prevent its extension. Since 1790, Congress had quailed before southern rantings about slave insurrections and disunion. "Doughface" presidents and secretaries of war used the statutes to dispatch troops in defense of proslavery interests and to withhold them from providing protection to antislavery activists.[13]

The incident at Harpers Ferry was the last of a series of domestic disorders to occur before the Civil War. When John Brown and twenty-one armed followers, including five blacks, took possession of the army arsenal at Harpers Ferry, West Virginia, in October 1859, fears of revolution were aggravated among southerners and sympathetic northern allies. But the slaves did not "rise up" as Brown had dreamed, and the "invasion" was suppressed by local militia, along with a detachment of marines under Lieutenant Colonel Robert E.

Lee. A detachment of eleven officers and one hundred and forty-two men were also sent from Fortress Monroe, and President Buchanan issued a statutory proclamation declaring a state of rebellion. Although this affray was clearly of little military significance, it provided the southerners with comforting evidence of the continued governmental willingness to respond swiftly when the South was threatened. Congressional reaction was predictable; the Democrats responded to the Brown affair by blaming "Black Republicans," antislavery Republicans, who then denied complicity; the southerners blamed abolitionists and northern antislavery supporters, who praised Brown but denied any intention to incite a rebellion.[14]

The Harpers Ferry episode culminated a tradition dating from 1790 in which national military power was used to defend slavery and suppress those who would attack or subvert it. The North had stood by the proslavery compromises in the Constitution. Many abolitionists' heads had been bloodied and civil liberties abused without benefit of federal protection. The approaching Civil War revealed no federal intention to alter protocol or withdraw that protection. It was southern secession that precipitated emancipation and an end to federal support of slavery. The South left federal protection out of the fear of losing slavery; the federal government did not abandon the institution of slavery.

7

Controlling Blacks During the Civil War

ESPITE THE FEDERAL government's support of the proslavery compromises of the Constitution before 1860, the South seceded from the Union after the election of Abraham Lincoln. The southern conviction that the Republicans were bitter enemies of slavery precipitated this decision. John Brown's raid and the sympathetic reaction in the North, as well as a series of insurrection scares in 1860, blamed in part on northern agitators, accelerated the southern secessionist course. Upon leaving Congress to return to Louisiana in 1861, John Slidell of Louisiana articulated southern apprehension concerning slavery by predicting that if Lincoln were inaugurated with southern assent, a general slave revolt would occur. Slidell stated that the slaves, believing Lincoln meant to free them, would rebel against being held in bondage illegally. Jefferson Davis of Mississippi emphasized in his farewell message that slaves never revolted unless there was some outside inducement, citing the example that if the United States elected to use military force against southern planters, it would leave the slaves free to revolt. He was sure that the national government would not wish to be responsible for a bloody slave uprising. In another attempt to explain secession, South Carolina submitted a resolution which listed the following grievances: the incitement of slaves to revolt by northern agitators, the conviction that the Republicans would abolish slavery, and the belief that the federal government would become the enemy of the South rather than its protector. The Mississippi resolution of November 30, 1860, was an echo of the others. In short, the southern states believed that Republicans would refuse to enforce the proslavery compromises of the Constitution and would use federal troops to destroy, rather than protect, the system of slavery.[1]

Secession became a reality in 1860 when federal fortresses and military depots were seized by the Confederacy. When President Lincoln's attempt to provision Fort Sumter in South Carolina failed because the Confederates fired on the supply boat, Lincoln issued a call for 75,000 army troops from the states in April 1861. The army called up by Lincoln was to be used to repossess federal property confiscated by southern insurgents, but the troops were instructed not to interfere with peaceful southerners or their property. On May 31, 1861, Lincoln called for an additional 83,000 men, one-half to serve as volunteers for three years unless discharged sooner, the remainder to bolster the strength of the regular army and navy. Despite the obvious implication of this manpower increase, the army still was not intended to interfere with the property of peaceful southerners, even if the property consisted of human beings.[2]

When Congress met in July 1861, the statute of 1795, providing for enforcement of Article IV, Section 4, of the Constitution, was amended to meet the exigencies of total insurrection of a state. This amendment gave the president the power to declare a state(s) in rebellion and to prohibit commerce between citizens of the United States and the citizens of a rebellious state(s). Under the authority of this statute, Lincoln issued a proclamation on August 16, 1861, declaring the seceded states in rebellion since July 15, 1861. As the war was territorial, a civil war, between the federal government and the Confederacy, Congress had to authorize or enact necessary legislation. By amending the 1795 statute, Congress affirmed the steps Lincoln had taken before they met and enlarged his powers to deal with the continuing emergency.[3]

Having seceded because of their fear of "Black" Republican hostility toward slavery, southerners expected no aid from national troops if their slaves rebelled nor assistance in recovering fugitive blacks who sought refuge with the Union Army. However, the Lincoln administration, fearing disaffection in slave-owning border states and uncertain of the nature of its powers during a massive civil disturbance, adopted a conservative policy. Southern protestations to the contrary, the 1860 platform of the Republican party had supported state control of domestic institutions and had denounced raids, such as John Brown's, as unconscionable interference in state affairs. Southern fears were not allayed even when Lincoln, in his first inaugural address, declared that he would not interfere with slave property in the states as it was clear that the Constitution forbade such interference. Further, even though the moral sensibilities of many northerners were offended by the Fugitive Slave Act of 1850, it too would be enforced. Lincoln, and the Union, in effect, guaranteed to support the proslavery compromises of the Constitution.[4]

During the first year of the war, that promise was kept. The intention of the national government not to engage in emancipation of the slaves became apparent immediately as more and more blacks came under Union authority wherever northern troops advanced. In the spring of 1861, General Benjamin F. Butler permitted fugitive slaves and black refugees to remain in his camp at Fortress Monroe in Virginia, declaring that since they had helped erect Confederate defenses, they were contraband of war. Initially, the War Department accepted this legalistic definition of slave status. As increasing numbers of displaced blacks, most of whom had not worked on Confederate defenses, came to Butler's camp, the general permitted them to stay and used many of them as laborers. The War Department did not give explicit approval to Butler's disposition of these additional blacks. Many of the slaves who came to Fortress Monroe had, in fact, been abandoned by their masters when the Union Army advanced.[5]

After federal troops gained control of the Sea Island district of South Carolina in November 1861, numerous blacks deserted by the masters, as well as fugitive slaves, were employed and maintained by the Union Army. Legal problems created by the disposition of blacks in Virginia and South Carolina were rare, principally because no masters came to claim the slaves. If claims had been made, there is evidence to indicate that the army would have been happy to reconsign the slaves and have them off army rations and payroll. Some Union commanders even continued to uphold the antebellum policy of protecting resident slaveholders from slave revolts. In Louisiana in the fall and winter of 1862, General Butler and General Nathaniel Banks dispatched Union troops to suppress slave uprisings reported by local plantation owners. On several occasions, slaveholders expressed fears of slave rebellion to Union commanders and were assured that the army would control the slaves. The preservation of the Union, not the emancipation of the slaves, was still the primary objective of the Lincoln administration. In territory subjugated by the Union Army, slavery was protected and enforced, just as it had been before the war. A legal issue was raised, however, in areas where slaves of loyal Unionist masters fled and sought protection from federal troops. Policy was inconsistent in Missouri and Kentucky; some commanders permitted fugitive slaves to remain within their lines and others excluded them. In November 1861, General Charles Halleck, Commander of the Military Department of the West, ordered his men to send fugitive slaves already within their lines back to their masters and to receive no others.[6]

Congress, attempting to clarify the issue early in 1861, reaffirmed that slavery in the states was a domestic institution and not within the ambit of federal legislation. As the war progressed, this position became less and less tenable and was eventually discarded. On August 6, 1861, responding to reports that slaves were being used on Confederate defenses, Congress passed the first Confiscation Act. The act freed forever slaves used by rebels to aid or abet the insurrection of the states. The passage of the act was opposed strenuously by congressmen from border slave states but was carried over their opposition.[7] Congress further attempted to clarify federal policy regarding fugitive slaves by passing the Confiscation Act of July 1862, which forbade officers to surrender slaves to rebel claimants and declared slaves of disloyal masters who came within Union lines free forever. The proslavery compromise of the Constitution which required the rendition of fugitive slaves was abrogated. Still, enemies of the act maintained, with some justification, that the act was unconstitutional, since it violated the Fugitive Slave Clause of the Constitution, which had not been amended. In response, supporters of the act declared that the exigencies of war dictated its promulgation. While northern abolitionists had been unable to obtain repeal of the Fugitive Slave Act with the South in the Union, abrogation of the act came quickly with the South in rebellion.[8]

Very early, Union generals in the field were given authority to determine whether slaves belonged to rebels and could offer them freedom on the basis of that determination. Some Union generals, such as David Hunter and John C. Fremont, attempted to move faster than either Congress or the administration by declaring slavery abolished in all areas of their commands, but their orders were countermanded by Lincoln. Late in the summer of 1862, the administration was still not completely ready to change the legal status of blacks or redefine its own position.

With the passage of the Confiscation Act of July 1862, Congress had anticipated President Lincoln in establishing abolition as a war aim. By September 1862, however, Lincoln was finally convinced that the emancipation of slaves in disloyal states was necessary to win the war. But as a tactician and politician, he made a final effort by issuing his Preliminary Emancipation Proclamation, which declared that slaves in those areas in rebellion on January 1, 1863, would be freed. The South had four months in which to decide to surrender and retain slavery or to continue fighting with the knowledge that losing the war would mean the complete destruction of slavery as an institution. The alternative must, of course, be considered from the southern point of view: Southerners believed that even if they did surrender, slavery would inevitably be extinguished and that the South would never regain a place of power and prominence in national affairs. Lincoln explicitly reinterpreted the Domestic Violence Clause of the Constitution in the Emancipation Proclamation, by declaring that the military and naval authorities would "recognize and maintain" the freedom of slaves in the disloyal states and would "do no act or acts to repress such persons [slaves], or any of them, in any effort they may make for their actual freedom."[9] The passage of the Thirteenth Amendment in February 1865, and its ratification the following December, was the final blow to slavery and ended the necessity for protection of slaveholders by federal troops. Slavery was abolished not only in disloyal states, but throughout the Union. The Constitution no longer was a proslavery document.[10]

While Union policy was evolving toward abolition of slavery, the South was left to cope with its blacks, unaided, for the most part, by federal power. Delegates from the seven Confederate states—Alabama, South Carolina, Florida, Georgia, Louisiana, Mississippi, and Texas—met in Montgomery in February 1861 to frame a government for the Confederacy with the awareness that provisions had to be made to deal with domestic slave violence. Faced with the problems of waging war against the Union, they had the additional task of controlling a large black population. The constitution they adopted was similar to the United States Constitution; however, property in black slaves was expressly recognized. The Confederate government pledged to protect each Confederate state against domestic violence, which technically meant that troops would be provided to suppress slave revolts if local patrols proved inadequate. In actuality, with a war in progress and a limited number of men available, each state and community was left to its own devices. The new Confederacy, conceived in the chaos of impending war, was severely challenged; external pressures, internal dissension, and the continuing problem of slave control made forging a unified national policy difficult.[11]

In the first year of the war, many slaveholders reacted to the threat of Union troops disturbing their slaves by simply moving the slaves behind Confederate lines. Initially, this strategy was effective; however, during the latter stages of the war when Union troops were stationed throughout the South, it became impractical. Some planters devised horror stories about the evil "Yankees" in order to frighten the slaves and discourage them from escaping behind Union lines. However, slaves defected in increasing numbers throughout the war.[12]

The threat of widespread slave insurrection demanded more attention than the flight of fugitive slaves to the Union armies. The mobilization of large numbers of white males for the war effort increased apprehension among the population at home. State legislatures responded by tightening restrictions and supervision of slave activities. Patrol duty was made a more regular function with increased fines for the failure to perform such duty, and laws requiring white male supervision of slaves on plantations were stringently enforced. In 1861, the Louisiana legislature increased the fine for permitting slaves to live on plantations without supervision from fifty cents to one hundred dollars a head. The conscription law passed by the Confederate Congress provided an exemption of one adult white male for every twenty adult slaves on a plantation. The "Twenty Negro Law," as it was called, was a source of great irritation and controversy throughout the war. Those southerners who possessed no slaves regarded it as a subterfuge whereby the wealthy could escape military service and complained that some thirty thousand persons evaded the draft in accordance with the provisions of this law. Supporters of the exemption maintained that someone had to remain at home to provide protection against the slaves who might rebel or flee to the Union army if they were unattended.[13]

Additional legislation for slave control was passed by state legislatures during the war; for example, a Texas statute of 1863 provided that a white person convicted of selling, giving, or lending dangerous weapons to slaves would be confined at hard labor in the penitentiary for two to five years. An Alabama law increased the fine for furnishing liquor to slaves from fifty dollars to five hundred dollars, or imprisonment for one to five years. Designed to prevent slaves from wandering about at liberty, a Mississippi act increased the penalty for permitting slaves to sell their own free time, with part payment to the master, from fifty to five hundred dollars and sixty days in jail.[14]

At the beginning of the war, patrol and legislative enactments were rigidly enforced. The situation gradually deteriorated. As the war went badly for the Confederate states, old men and boys were pressed into patrol service to replace the young adult males who were drafted. However, when the militia was called up, old men and boys were drafted as well. Slaves took advantage of the opportunities afforded to rebel. In New Orleans in May 1861, disturbances among the slave population were suppressed by the militia. In October, a Confederate officer wrote to his superior that slaves were in a rebellious mood and that the military must be wary lest the blacks mount a successful revolt. Real or imagined reports of slave plots and rebellions were recorded throughout the Lower South during the war.[15] However, no significant slave revolt took place in the Confederacy as the war progressed. Many discontented slaves simply fled to the Union lines. Fortuitously, the advancing Union forces operated as a safety valve. The repressive measures adopted in the South after the Emancipation Proclamation were rapidly dissipated. There were, however, continuing efforts to insulate slaves from the knowledge of Lincoln's intention to free them.[16]

As the war continued, the position of southerners became more precarious. Many intransigent southerners never yielded the notion that the war itself was of no importance if the slave system was not maintained. Even in 1865, with defeat almost imminent, and the conscription of slaves being seriously considered, still the preservation of the slave system retained a greater priority than the war effort. Some Confederate congressmen claimed that granting freedom to slaves who fought for the Confederacy would subvert their basic contention that slavery was the natural condition for blacks and make victory irrelevant. Rather than compromise in any way on the slavery issue, the South preferred to lose the war. When the Confederate Congress was finally driven to provide for recruitment of slaves in March 1865, no promise of freedom was given; individual states were to decide what reward to give their slaves after the war ended.[17]

Left to their own devices, the Confederates dealt poorly with the management problem of their enormous hostile slave population. The Confederate Constitution provided for assistance from the central government when rebellion occurred, but the central government lacked the resources to provide it. The Confederates considered the large numbers of blacks who defected to the Union to fight against their former masters as criminals. The Confederates threatened these freedmen, and the Confederate army massacred them when they could; but in actuality, there was nothing they could do. Whatever view one takes of the causes of the Civil War, the Confederacy, its resources exhausted, lost the institution of slavery while fighting a war to maintain and extend it.

8

The
Bottom Remains
on the Bottom

HE WAR WAS finally over. With the adoption of the Thirteenth Amendment in December 1865, blacks were at last free from oppression—or so it seemed. Their bright hopes were short-lived. The efforts of the Republican congressional radicals to make freedom for slaves a reality through legislation could not override the established prejudices and suppressive doctrines in order to institute effective reform. Acting under its power to enforce the Thirteenth Amendment, Congress passed the Civil Rights Act of 1866, which remained dormant and unenforced until it was resurrected by the Supreme Court in 1968. According to this statute, black people were citizens of the United States and thus entitled to the same rights within the various states as whites, including the right "to sue, be parties, and give evidence; to inherit, purchase, lease, sell, hold, and convey real and personal property" and the right to "full and equal benefit of all laws and proceedings for the security of persons and property, as is enjoyed by white persons." The act provided that federal courts and officials could invoke army aid for its enforcement. As doubts were spread about the law's constitutionality, Congress passed the Fourteenth Amendment, which reinforced the language of the act by affirming the citizenship of blacks. It also forbade infringement of their privileges and immunities, deprivation of their lives, liberty, or property by the states, without due process of law, and state discrimination in general against black people. Significantly, section five of the amendment allowed Congress to provide military aid, if necessary, to enforce its provisions. Although the language of the amendment guaranteed protection of the rights of "persons," its framers indicated the specific intention to remove all disabilities imposed upon blacks because of their color or previous condition of servitude. Thus, by adopting the Thirteenth and Fourteenth Amendments, implemented by the guarantee of the right to vote in the Fifteenth Amendment enacted in February of 1869, and by the guarantees afforded earlier in the 1866 Civil Rights Act, the radical Republicans believed that they had created a lasting foundation for effectively removing the stigma of servitude from the blacks. Blaming the proslavery compromises of the Constitution for perpetuating slavery, they thought the removal of those compromises would settle the issues arising out of the servitude of blacks. Even preceding events had proven how mistaken they were.[1]

In the aftermath of the war in 1865, the military faced the practical problem of administering the government in southern cities and towns under what was known as Presidential Reconstruction. The army, including the remnants of some one hundred eighty thousand black soldiers who had served the Union during the war, went about the business of occupying, policing, and cleaning the cities, distributing food to the hungry and destitute, and in some areas, setting up schools run by army chaplains. President Johnson delineated the army's role by issuing a proclamation of amnesty on May 29, 1865, which appointed Unionist provisional governors in the southern states and ordered the military to assist the states in organizing elections and registering voters so that peacetime conditions could be restored.[2]

Although the Union Army was ordered to work with the provisional governments, areas of conflict quickly developed. In many southern states, former Confederates requested permission to form militia units to prevent the outrages which they said were being committed against the white populace by the freedmen. The army opposed the formation of these units, believing that former Confederates could not be trusted and that those former rebels who were in fact assaulting and murdering Unionists would be the first to join. The army preferred to keep order without the aid of unreliable military units. However, the provisional governors opposed the army opinion, partly on the grounds that the army could not keep order with such a large number of black troops, whom the white population resented. The southerners, who before the war had used the excuse of threatened slave revolts to gain federal military protection, now complained of alleged plots among the freedmen and black soldiers in order to obtain white militia units. In some cases, President Johnson superseded the decisions of his military commanders and permitted the formation of the white militia units, but he reassured the army by giving them authority to control the militia if they failed to conform to federal law or began attacking black and white Republicans.[3]

The army's relations with the black population during Presidential Reconstruction were no more pleasant than they had been before the war. Officially, the army served as the military arm of the Freedmen's Bureau, set up by Congress in March 1865 to protect the interests of former slaves and destitute whites. Army commanders affected commitment to the principle that blacks and whites were equal before the law, while permitting local authorities almost unlimited latitude in handling the black population unless overt prejudice in law enforcement was demonstrated. The army was receptive to suggestions from white citizens that blacks should be incarcerated for supposedly pillaging and looting indiscriminately. Some generals ordered blacks to remain on the same plantations where they had toiled in slavery; others issued orders declaring that blacks found idle would be imprisoned. For the military, white southerners, and the Freedman's Bureau alike, black vagrancy and idleness were the primary evils that Reconstruction should prevent. Issues involving social equality for blacks revealed that army commanders were as prejudiced as southern white society; some officers opposed integration even in schools set up by the Freedmen's Bureau. In addition, many high-ranking commanders asserted openly that blacks should not be permitted to vote because they lacked the intelligence to exercise the franchise, a view which embraced former slaves as well as the thousands of blacks who had been free before the war.[4] When the state legislatures elected under Johnson's plan of Reconstruction met, they enacted even more restrictive codes than the orders issued by the army or the Freedmen's Bureau regulations. Known as the Black Codes, these statutes were designed to insure that while whites might work or remain unemployed as they saw fit, the freedmen would be kept to the plow lest they plot mischief.[5]

In an effort to alleviate some of the problems of Reconstruction, when Congress met in December 1865, it established the Joint Committee of Fifteen on Reconstruction, which was an expression of disenchantment with Presidential Reconstruction. Congress passed a new Freedmen's Bureau bill which extended federal jurisdiction and protection to cover cases involving blacks in which local authorities could not be expected to act fairly and placed all officers and agents of the bureau under military protection. The same session passed the Civil Rights Act of 1866 and the proposed Fourteenth Amendment. Congress also established the size of the regular army at approximately fifty-four thousand men, believing this would be sufficient to carry out Reconstruction policies as well as the policing of the frontier.[6] On April 2, 1866, after vetoing the Freedmen's Bureau Bill and the Civil Rights Act of 1866, both of which were overridden by Congress, President Johnson issued a proclamation declaring that the rebellion of the southern states had been suppressed and peace restored everywhere except in Texas; on August 20, 1866, the president extended the formal cessation of hostilities to include Texas. When the Supreme Court ruled in *Ex Parte Milligan* that military courts did not have jurisdiction over civilians in areas where civilian courts were open, the role of the military in Reconstruction sank into confusion. Congress indicated that, during Reconstruction, the army's role was superior, not subordinate, to civilian authority. The War Department continued to issue orders directing the army to prevent opposition to federal law and to cooperate with the Freedmen's Bureau in exercising its duties, yet not to interfere with local civilian authorities unless they acted contrary to federal law or attempted to hinder enforcement of federal authority. Unconvinced of the legality of its authority, the army acted cautiously. In some southern states, local officials regarded the president's proclamation as a license to arrest federal officers for minor municipal offenses and to encourage the white population to demonstrate open hostility to the army.[7]

Southerners, perhaps encouraged by the president's antipathy toward the radical congressional program for black equality, expressed their hostility and contempt for the federal programs. Large numbers of blacks were attacked and murdered in the summer of 1866; scattered rioting erupted throughout the South. In Norfolk, Virginia, on April 16, black citizens gathered outside of town to celebrate the passage of the Civil Rights Act with a parade and speeches. White hecklers appeared and a scuffle broke out. When informed that a white man had been killed, the mayor of the city quickly advised the army that his police force was unable to cope with the situation and asked for federal troops to keep order. That evening, the Twelfth Infantry commander dispersed troops in likely trouble spots about the city, but continuing sniper fire resulted in a number of blacks being killed or wounded. The following day, crowds of whites gathered in the streets boasting of plans to attack and kill all blacks and soldiers in the city when night fell. Reinforcements were called in from Fortress Monroe to patrol the city; no massacre occurred. Local officials feebly explained that the blacks had precipitated the disturbance by celebrating the passage of the Civil Rights Act.[8]

Mob violence in Memphis, which followed the Norfolk incident, dramatically illustrates the intense bitterness toward blacks in the former slaveholding states, and particularly toward those who had served in the Union Army. The Third Regiment of the United States Colored Artillery had been organized with blacks from Tennessee who had sought the protection of the Union Army. From the time of its organization, the regiment had been stationed in Memphis and had been employed in routine police duties about the city, bringing the men into frequent contact with the white populace. The circumstances were abrasive. Many black soldiers were arrested from time to time by white policemen, and many whites, including some policemen, were arrested by the black soldiers. On April 30, 1866, the black regiment was officially mustered out of the army, and the men used their pay to celebrate. The following night, the local police arrested two boisterous veterans and were conducting them to the police station when their path was blocked by a group of blacks. After an exchange of words, the police fired into the crowd of blacks, wounding one person; the two arrested blacks escaped. When the blacks returned the fire, wounding one policeman, a large crowd of whites gathered to assist the police. This mob and the entire Memphis police force then began roaming the city, shooting, beating, or arresting any black person who could be found. The carnage lasted until midnight when a small detachment of federal troops intervened and the rioters scattered. Anarchy erupted the next day. Parties of mounted whites rode through the black sections, setting fire to churches, schools, and houses, and beating all who resisted. The violence lasted for four days. At the time, there were only about one hundred and fifty troops stationed in the city after the mustering out of the black soldiers, and they were unable to maintain order. Major General George Stoneham, commander of the troops in the area, tried to contact the mayor to obtain permission to use the police to aid in quelling the disturbance but was informed that the mayor was unavailable for consultation; the police, in fact, formed the hard core of the mob. Subsequently, Stoneham declared martial law, brought in all available troops, and suppressed the disorder. Forty-six blacks and two whites were killed; ninety-one houses, twelve schools, and four churches were burned in the black neighborhoods, the value of property destroyed being estimated at one hundred thousand dollars. A subsequent military investigation placed the blame squarely on city officials. General Ulysses S. Grant suggested that legal proceedings be brought against the city for damages suffered by the blacks.[9] United States Attorney General James Speed opposed the suggestion, however, asserting that since civilian courts were open in Memphis, and the riot was not a violation of the laws of the United States, those who had suffered damages must look to local authorities for redress, an opinion which was quite proper in light of the Supreme Court decision in *Ex Parte Milligan*. Speed was asserting that the blacks who had been attacked under the auspices of the authorities of the city of Memphis had to ask those same authorities for compensation. Before the war, slavery was a matter for local control; after the war, black protection was a matter of local discretion. In the light of Speed's opinion, the Thirteenth Amendment could not be interpreted to offer federal protection, and although the Civil Rights Act of 1866 provided federal protection for the property and persons of blacks, it did not provide monetary compensation for the losses suffered by blacks when sufficient protection was not provided.[10]

Repetition of the violence in Memphis began in August 1866 in New Orleans when several related events culminated in a racial explosion. The reelection of John T. Monroe, who had been mayor of the city in 1862 when Union forces took control from the Confederates, initiated the hostilities. Monroe was an irreconcilable opponent of national policy and a recognized leader of the rebel portion of the white population. Major General Philip Sheridan, Union Commander of the Department of the Gulf, who tried to keep Monroe and his comrades under close surveillance, left for Texas in late July. However, July 30, 1866, was the date set for the proposed reassembling of the Convention of 1864, which had framed the constitution under which Louisiana operated and was adjourned subject to the call of its chairman. The delegates to the convention had been Unionists, and when the chairman pro tempore issued a call to reconvene, former rebels opposed the meeting. Mayor Monroe unabashedly announced his intention to prevent a meeting of this extinct Unionist body and to arrest the members if they did attempt to assemble. The mainstream of white opinion seemed to support Monroe; some suggested undermining the assembly by ridicule, while others considered the possibility of forcibly concluding the convention.

On July 25, Mayor Monroe wrote Major General Absalom Baird, commander of the troops in the city, that the convention was calculated to disturb the public peace and that his duty as mayor was to prevent such assemblies. Baird replied that members of the convention had neither asked, nor obtained military approval, but that he felt citizens should be protected in their right of peaceful assembly. However, if the mayor envisioned the need for troops to avoid a disturbance, he had only to ask, and Baird would provide them. Two days before the convention was to meet, the mayor and the lieutenant governor of the state visited Baird and informed him of their decision to have the sheriff arrest the members of the convention upon grand jury indictments. Baird objected and requested that they wait until he received orders from the War Department; he immediately dispatched a telegram to the War Department, not knowing that the lieutenant governor had already telegraphed the president, informing him that large meetings of black and white Unionists were denouncing the president and insisting that blacks should arm themselves. This purely fictional information partially explains the president's curious response to the lieutenant governor in which he informed him that if the civil authorities arrested members of the convention, they could expect assistance from the military. Johnson also gave the state attorney general permission to call upon General Philip Sheridan for federal

troops to aid in suppressing the convention. Having received no instructions from the War Department, Baird ordered four companies
of soldiers to stand alert on Canal Street.

At noon on July 30, about twenty-five delegates gathered at the
convention site, but since twenty-five did not constitute a quorum,
they decided to recess for an hour. In the galleries and halls of the
building were about twenty black men, women, and children who
came to watch the proceedings. An hour later, a procession of black
men, a few armed with pistols, canes, and clubs, marched up the street
toward the convention waving an American flag. A scuffle which broke
out between the marchers and a group of armed white observers
quickly ended; the white men then pursued the procession to the convention hall where rocks and brickbats were thrown by both sides.
The marchers entered the building, except for a small group which
remained outside. A new scuffle with the police began, and when
someone fired a shot, the police reacted by indiscriminately firing into
the building. The mayor then ordered the police to launch an inten-
sive attack upon the convention. As soon as the convention supporters
inside the building waved a white flag, the firing stopped and the police rushed into the building. Convention delegates were beaten,
stabbed, and shot promiscuously by the police. In some instances,
delegates were driven outside where they were encircled and shot by
the police and an aroused white citizenry. The mob, charged with success, then moved through the city, attacking and beating any black
person they encountered. Although it is not known precisely how
many persons were killed and injured, army medical staff records report thirty-seven blacks found dead, forty-eight severely wounded,
and ninety-nine slightly wounded. Many wounded persons were
treated and hidden by their families, while still other wounded men
fled the city. The federal troops, who did not arrive on the scene until
2:30 P.M., immediately declared a state of martial law, but were ordered by the War Department, upon presidential instruction, to permit the sheriff to arrest members of the convention. Those arrested by
the military were subsequently released without trial. The grand jury
exculpated the local authorities and placed the blame for the disturbances on the convention delegates. In an exhaustive report to President Johnson, the lieutenant governor, the state attorney general, and
the mayor claimed that they had done their utmost to circumvent

trouble but that their efforts had been to no avail. In December 1866, a committee appointed by the House of Representatives visited New Orleans, and after a thorough investigation of the affair, reported in February 1867 that the conditions in the city required the establishment of a provisional government. This report gave impetus to the passage of the Military Reconstruction Act which had been under debate during the Thirty-ninth Congress.[11]

On March 2, 1867, Congress enacted the Military Reconstruction Act, which provided for the displacement of civil authority by military governments in the South. These new governments would protect all people in their persons and their property, suppress insurrection and riot, and supervise all elections until the states framed new constitutions and formally approved the Fourteenth Amendment to the Constitution. The states would then be readmitted to the Union. Along with its amendments of March 23 and July 19, the Military Reconstruction Act became the basis of congressional reconstruction in the South. Dissatisfied with the progress of presidential reconstruction, Congress now legally provided for direct military control over political activity so that the southern states would reconstruct and comply with Congress and with the constitutional reforms resulting from the Civil War.[12] When Military Reconstruction began, one of the first acts of General Sheridan was to relieve Mayor Monroe of his office, as well as other New Orleans city officials responsible for the July 1866 violence. General Sheridan was subsequently relieved of this command by President Johnson, who still controlled military appointments, much to the chagrin of the Congress. It was a small victory for the president over an antagonistic Congress.[13]

Despite the fact that federal military force was used to protect blacks during Military Reconstruction, cessation of open violence against blacks was not achieved in the South. In Mobile, Alabama, in May 1867, rioting broke out at a public meeting held by Republicans at which Congressman William Kelley of Pennsylvania was a leading speaker. During his address, some shots were fired, two men were killed, and several wounded. As the mayor and the police had made no attempt to interfere, the mayor was removed from office and a Unionist was appointed to replace him. Two months later in Franklin, Tennessee, gunfire was exchanged between discharged black soldiers and groups of former Confederates; one person was killed and approximately fifty were wounded. Troops arrived in the city the next day to keep order.[14]

Even after southern states returned to the Union, the military was still required to keep order. Once a state was admitted to the Union, federal commanders expected to operate according to Article IV, Section 4, of the Constitution, in which the national government guaranteed each state a republican form of government and protection against domestic violence. When army officials received requests for aid from state and local authorities, they were usually told by the War Department that local commanders must act on their own discretion when deciding upon the advisability of rendering aid, a delegation of responsibility which was contrary to all constitutional and statutory provisions. Local commanders, acting on their own authority, attempted to keep order according to their interpretations of their duties. Some of the new Republican governments organized state militias for protection not only against former rebels, but also against other Unionist factions who were eager to gain power when, and if, the present governments collapsed. The provisional militias which had been established by the provisional governors under Presidential Reconstruction and later outlawed by the radicals in an act of Congress passed on the same day as the first Reconstruction Act were largely composed of former rebels who opposed the Union Army and all Unionists in the South. When the southern states were readmitted to the Union, the radicals saw the necessity of providing loyal militias to support the newly created radical governments, so a new act was passed allowing the formation of militia units, but only in those states that Congress or the radical governors decided were in need of them. Although large numbers of blacks were enrolled in these units, they were not exclusively constituted of blacks; however, blacks did join the militias freely, because the Republican party was the party of freedom and the pay was equivalent to that of soldiers of the same rank in the regular army. These militia units, reinforced by the presence of regular army units, were used to maintain the Republican governments in the face of continued hostility from unreconstructed southerners and political conservatives who very often formed their own enforcement units such as the Ku Klux Klan. A number of clashes occurred throughout the South between these opposing groups, and one, at

Laurens, South Carolina, in October 1870, resulted in the death of thirteen people and the wounding of many others.[15]

Congress responded to reports of violence and clashes between Ku Klux Klan and state militia units by passing an act on April 20, 1871, which prohibited persons from traveling in disguise on the roads and highways or attempting to overthrow governments by force. Infringements of this act would be considered violations of the Equal Protection Clause of the Fourteenth Amendment, and the army was made responsible for the enforcement of the act. The efforts to suppress extralegal vigilante groups did not relieve black people or white Unionists of their fears since encounters with Klan members characteristically occurred on back roads.[16]

In order for Republicans to maintain political control in a state, it was absolutely necessary that blacks and Unionists counter the votes of white Democrats by being allowed to vote without intimidation. This meant, of course, that white vigilante groups would have to be suppressed by unified Republican state governments, but in many states, the Republicans were rent by internal strife. It was to the advantage of the unreconstructed southerners to see the radical governments divide into factions and hasten their own destruction by engaging in constant war, as they did in South Carolina, Louisiana, and Arkansas. The federal government would be called upon to provide aid according to its constitutional duty, but in each case, the problem really consisted of deciding which Republican faction was in fact the legal government. President Grant was beset by this problem again and again during the 1870s. Federal troops would be sent into an area to settle the dispute and then withdrawn. Thereafter, local militias organized by claimants to office would fight at the bidding of the state governor. Additionally, according to one historian, radical governors did not make use of Union militias to protect black and white Unionists from white terrorists as extensively as they should have, because of their fears of a race war between whites and blacks. By not exercising their military power, they often lost office to the conservatives. When northern public opinion cooled to the idea of enforcing the guarantees of the Reconstruction amendments in the South, when white vigilante groups succeeded in murdering and intimidating blacks so that militia units were practically useless, and when the radical Republican regimes were rendered ineffective by internal friction and tension, the movement for racial political equality was stymied. Military Reconstruction was a failure. The army supervised the elections of 1867 and 1868 and was called in from time to time thereafter to settle scattered disputes. However, most southerners were unreconstructed and, short of continuing military surveillance which the North was unwilling to provide, freedom was a dangerous condition for blacks as well as white Unionists. Conservative southerners needed only staying power, biding their time until the North became weary of the "infernal nigger question." They also successfully exploited northern hypocrisy and resentment to defuse the radical Military Reconstruction.[17]

The compromise settlement resolving the Tilden-Hayes election in 1877 was inevitable; this bargain assured the southerners that the army would not be called upon for civil duty in the South, which was a reconciliation made by the white population at the expense of the blacks. The provisions of the Reconstruction amendments to the Constitution and various related statutes were relegated to oblivion. Although the military had delivered the black vote to the Republican party for a short time, it had done little to protect black persons from injuries committed by angry and bigoted whites. The Thirteenth and Fourteenth Amendments left the Domestic Violence Clause of the Constitution virtually untouched; there was no will to invoke the Constitution to aid the blacks. Federal troops still had to be requested by local authorities; and local authorities were bent on suppressing, not protecting, the black people of America.

9

Changing Modes
of Oppression:
1877-1900

D URING RECONSTRUCTION, the aspirations of the nation concerning black people were in part realized in law, but not in
action. Before the promises made to blacks came to fruition, a
spirit of compromise and reconciliation between the North and
South gripped white America. The Compromise of 1877, resulting
from the Hayes-Tilden election, left the freedman in the custody of
conservative southern Democrats, commonly known as the Redeemers, who pledged to protect the black man in the exercise of his
constitutional rights. Despite these pledges, a new period of black
oppression began. Initially, southern whites attempted to manipu-
late the black vote to their purposes; failing, they turned to repression and disfranchisement, using a multitude of theoretically legal
tactics. Northern whites tolerated this repression and, in fact,
adopted these policies when expedient. Despite the oppression,
some black people attempted to exercise their right to vote and to
make economic progress without the forty acres and a mule it was
rumored the Union would give them. They expected the national
government to provide them with some protection against intimidation and violence, but no assistance was forthcoming. Federal-state
relations were unchanged by the Civil War. As segregation and violence became commonplace, the national government expressed no
willingness to enforce a new racial order. Between 1877 and 1900,
the Constitution and statutes drafted by the Republicans were circumvented or utilized to maintain the racial status quo.

When Rutherford Hayes became the next Republican president of the United States in 1877, there were 24,140 officers and men in the regular army. From 1877 to 1900, there were never more than 29,000 troops enrolled in the army, except during the Spanish-American War when a temporary expansion occurred. These soldiers were expected to police the frontier and control the Indians, as well as man other garrisons and fortifications throughout the country; the War Department repeatedly informed Congress that the military force was inadequate for the tasks but to no avail. At this point, it was as if the nation was reasserting its historic distaste for a standing army, believing it to be inconsistent with democracy. During this period in the South, the area of major racial disturbances, there were no more than 2,500 scattered troops. Another 2,500 troops were stationed along the Atlantic seaboard, and the remainder of the regular army was on duty in the West. The militias, those antiquated, quasisocial institutions, along with all their local prejudices and sympathies, were still the principal force available to quell racial disturbances.[1]

Almost immediately after his election, President Hayes indicated awareness that racial violence might be a continuing problem but that he intended to wait until the 1878 elections to see what action, if any, was necessary. The presence of significant military problems in 1877, as well as the agreement with the southern Democrats that they would be left alone to deal with the blacks, may account for Hayes's unwillingness to commit the small regular army to duty in those states derelict in their constitutional responsibilities. However, Hayes was compelled to use federal troops when, in the summer of 1877, railroad companies, pleading poor economic conditions, reduced the wages of their employees by ten percent. A nationwide railroad strike resulted. Strikers attacked the strikebreakers sent in to replace them. In most cases, members of the state militias sympathized with the strikers and thus failed to break the strike. In the ensuing panic, various governors appealed to Hayes for regular troops to restore order; for about six days, one-half of the army was tied up with policing duty in West Virginia, Maryland, Pennsylvania, Indiana, and Illinois. Hayes was very careful to respond only to those requests which exactly met the conditions required by the statutes passed under Article IV, Section 4, of the Constitution: the state had to exhaust all of its resources, leaving the disorder still uncontained, and the governor had to make a formal request indicating the existence of an insurrection. The regular troops successfully ended the Great Strike within a few days.[2]

During the 1878 political campaigns, white southerners quickly defaulted on their pledge to protect blacks in the exercise of the right to vote. In Sumter, South Carolina, a riot broke out at a political meeting when the Republicans refused to let Democrats address their rally. Two Bourbon leaders, white conservatives whose ploy at the moment was to use the black vote, narrowly averted a black massacre by their pleas for order. In Williamsburg County, South Carolina, the Redeemers disrupted a black meeting and warned a state senator that he would be killed if he did not leave town within ten days. Hayes, however, took no action to end depredations against blacks who wanted to vote. While his party hesitated, believing it could rely upon southern pledges, the election ended their dilemma. The Republicans were soundly defeated in the South, even in places where there were voting black majorities. The whites had not permitted blacks to vote freely; violence, fraud, and intimidation were widespread. Hayes asserted that he had been deceived by the southern promises to maintain order.[3]

Acts of this kind violated the Force Act of May 31, 1870, which was expressly designed to prohibit interference with the voting rights of blacks; interfering or intimidating citizens in the free exercise of their constitutional rights was a federal crime. Violations could also evoke a presidential response under the act of 1871, which provided that unlawful combinations or conspiracies or domestic violence in a state could be suppressed with federal troops if they hindered the execution of the laws and interfered with the right to vote. If the state could not, or would not, provide protection, statutory authority was available if the president chose to assert it.[4]

Attorney General Charles Devens ordered an investigation of the reported violations, and federal marshals arrested a number of people who were later released. James Blaine of Maine demanded and was granted a Senate investigation. The inquiry confirmed commonplace knowledge; black Republicans had been beaten, whipped, and intimidated into either not voting or voting Democratic. Representative Horace Page of California and Senator George Edmunds of Vermont wanted Congress to reaffirm its intention to enforce the Reconstruction amendments and acts; however, Page's proposal was buried in the Judiciary Committee and Edmunds's resolution narrowly passed on a strict party vote. Edmunds's bill to insure enforcement and compliance with those amendments and acts was tabled. Successful Democratic opposition to these measures rallied on the hoary states-rights' position—states, not federal officials, were responsible for enforcing laws involving crimes against the person. Even though Reconstruction statutes had placed that burden squarely on the national government in the absence of state compliance, that view was unpopular. It was most unlikely that state governments representing the forces that kept blacks from voting would undertake their protection.[5]

At this point, the Democrats in Congress, feeling sufficiently confident and daring, attempted open repeal of the enforcement acts of Reconstruction by attaching riders (resolutions unrelated to the subject of the bill) to appropriation bills. As a matter of party principle, Hayes vetoed the bills; at the same time, he made strong public statements assuring the southerners that troops would not be used at the polls. While party leaders congratulated Hayes for standing on principle, that stand was of no immediate comfort to blacks driven from the polls. In his annual message to Congress in December 1879, Hayes cited the race question as central to the peace and prosperity of the nation and demanded action aimed at resolution of the problem. Diplomatically, he placed the burden of responsibility on the state officials, calling upon them to find solutions.[6]

One form of black response to the fraud and violence in the South was a substantial migration of blacks northward. In 1879, a great exodus of blacks began. Senator William Windom of Minnesota introduced a resolution sympathetically supporting this migration from tyranny and violence; he expressed the hope that blacks would be able to buy lands held by the Northern Pacific Railroad in Dakota and other western territories. Southerners hotly contended that no violence necessitating migration existed; the resolution was not passed. The exodus, aided by some leading Republicans, gained momentum. Even President Hayes became involved when he offered federal protection to boats transporting blacks up the Mississippi after white southerners intimidated the owners with threats to sink all the ships.[7]

When the blacks arrived in Indiana, which had Democratic majorities in 1876, accusations were made by congressional Democrats that it was a Republican effort to colonize the state with black voters who were traditionally Republicans. A congressional investigation found that northern Republicans had welcomed black voters, but discovered no evidence of an organized plan or any support for claims that they had contributed money to this cause. Black people themselves insisted that they left the South because of the crop lien and the convict-leasing systems, poor economic conditions, and the outrages perpetrated against them. The exodus soon slowed to a trickle as word reached the blacks in the South that northern weather was cold and that, in some cases, the atmosphere was as inhospitable to blacks as that in the South; furthermore, the land the blacks could acquire was usually unsuitable for farming, and many migrants were homeless and without a source of income. In Kansas, large bands of black aspirants were refused accommodation in hotels and restaurants. Other tentative efforts to initiate black migration or colonization in the North were not supported by the national government. Migration did not subside because blacks thought their destiny lay in the South; on the contrary, the problem was that most black people did not have the financial resources to migrate, and even if they had, there was no place they could go that promised them a better life.[8]

As the election of 1880 approached, the atmosphere of violence in the South still prevailed. James A. Garfield, the compromise candidate of the Republican party, won the election but failed to develop a southern policy before he was assassinated. He seemed to support federal aid to education for blacks as a solution to the race problem. Chester Arthur, who succeeded Garfield, did not support this policy and, in fact, seemed completely uninterested in the race question.[9] As the off-year elections approached in 1882, outrages in the South increased. On August 24, 1882, Jonathan Wright, a black former associate justice of South Carolina's Supreme Court, wrote Attorney General Benjamin Brewster that persons were being murdered at an alarming rate, some in broad daylight. As a basis for federation action, he proposed the Fifth Amendment guarantees that life could not be taken without due process of the law. Instances of violence were not difficult to document. In September 1882, the Greenback candidate for governor of South Carolina in the elections of 1880 was killed in an argument provoked by the charge that he was organizing black voters. At a rally held by blacks in Lancaster, South Carolina, a Democratic representative insisted on speaking in spite of the crowd's protestations. The exasperated blacks finally dragged him out of the meeting. Later that day, whites retaliated by killing four or five blacks and wounding several others. Attorney General Brewster made an attempt to punish the violators by ordering the local district attorney to make arrests. But when the state attorney general defended the alleged criminals and Brewster received no encouragement from the president, he lost interest in the whole problem. Consequently, when blacks wrote Brewster complaining about being prohibited from using public accommodations or being illegally reprimanded or arbitrarily fined, he merely suggested they seek help from state authorities.[10]

As blacks were determined to make the best deal they could under the circumstances, black leaders generally supported President Arthur's policy of forging alliances with independent parties in the South. By not emphasizing the racial issue, the blacks in turn depended on the independents they voted for to protect them. In Virginia, blacks embraced the Readjusters, the William Mahone faction of the Democratic party which supported the repudiation or readjustment of state debts to the national government incurred during the Civil War and Reconstruction. While the Readjusters were in power from 1879 to 1883, black people enjoyed a hiatus from violence. This kind of alliance could work only as long as reactionary Democrats remained divided on some issue other than the racial issue and did not drive blacks out of politics altogether.[11]

This tenuous alliance was in jeopardy when the local elections of 1883 approached in Virginia. In the town of Danville, where the population was slightly more than one-half black, blacks had gained a majority on the twelve-man city council and four of nine policemen were black, as were nearly all the justices of the peace. There was no black domination, however, because the mayor, judge, and police chief were white. In an effort to win the election, whites circulated a broadside alleging that white people were humiliated and unjustly treated in Danville. On November 4, 1883, when a black allegedly jostled a white man on the street, an argument and fight ensued. When the fighting ended, one white and four blacks were dead, and four whites and six blacks were wounded. The ensuing riot lasted for two days. The governor called out the militia, but it arrived too late. It became apparent that blacks were out of politics in Virginia, when only a few blacks voted in the elections, and those who did were Democrats. Although Attorney General Brewster wrote Mahone deploring the mayhem, the Justice Department initiated no action. Congressional committees investigating the riot added nothing to the record. Democrats claimed the incident was exaggerated and that accusations were out of proportion; Republicans maintained that persons elected in such an atmosphere of fraud and violence should not be seated when they came to Congress, but everyone was seated.[12]

The year 1883 became a landmark year in the black struggle, when the Supreme Court declared the Civil Rights Act of 1875, which provided for equal public accommodations, unconstitutional. Black reaction to the decision was not limited to the resolutions of the Civil Rights Congress or the National Convention of Colored Men in Louisville, Kentucky, where Frederick Douglass declared that "who would be free, themselves must strike the first blow." In Gause, Texas, blacks rampaged through the city, destroying property. They were reportedly planning a revolt as a result of the Supreme Court's decision. One thousand state militiamen were sent to control the agitators.[13]

In 1884, when Republicans assessed their record after the election of Cleveland, the first Democratic president since Reconstruction, it was evident that Reconstruction had been abandoned and that the federal government was not interested in proposals that blacks immigrate or any project for blacks that would cost money. Most blacks were illiterate; even those who were educated were oppressed. Those Republicans who regarded themselves as liberals believed that blacks should be eliminated from politics because they were uneducated and easily manipulated; on the other hand, they were unwilling to do anything to educate them. The Republican party, and the nation, marked time; no positive economic or social programs for helping blacks were considered or developed and blacks were in no position to help themselves.

The violence that accompanied Cleveland's election was fast becoming a tradition. In Loreauville, Louisiana, twenty Republicans, mostly blacks, entered the city cheering and shouting profanities at the amassed Democrats. Gunfire was exchanged; fourteen to sixteen blacks were killed. In his inaugural address, Cleveland assured concerned citizens he had no intention of initiating a course designed to limit the freedmen in the exercise of their constitutional rights, a position which inspired confidence everywhere but in the black community. Cleveland failed to break tradition and appointed a few blacks to traditional "Negro jobs," such as Registrar of the Deeds in the District of Columbia.[14]

Black protest continued. The unjustified murder of a Charleston black precipitated a mass meeting of blacks. The participants prepared and published a paper for public distribution which forewarned white people that a revolution such as the one in Haiti might occur if something was not done about the oppression of blacks. But, black protest was not restricted to petitioning. In 1880, when black workers on Louisiana sugar plantations went on strike to demand a wage increase from $.75 to $1.00 a day, the planters broke the strikes by calling up state militiamen who arrested the ringleaders for trespassing. By the fall of 1887, when wages were reduced to $.65 a day as a result of a poor crop in 1886, black workers, who had been unionized by the Knights of Labor, went on strike again, this time demanding $1.00 a day with rations and $1.25 without. When Governor Samuel D. McEnery sent ten companies and two batteries of state militiamen to force the strikers to leave their homes on the plantations, a number of shooting incidents occurred, four blacks were killed and four whites wounded. In Thibodaux where hundreds of evicted blacks had gathered, the violence came to a head. By November 21, the sugar crop was in danger of being completely lost to the cold, damp weather. Although the governor had withdrawn the militia, a local judge, Taylor Beattie, declared martial law be enforced by troops of white vigilantes. Between the night of November 22 and noon the following day, thirty blacks were killed and hundreds of persons were wounded, of whom only two were white. The massacre ended the strike. Henry and George Cox, two black artisans and Union leaders, were taken from jail and never seen again. The strike tactic, along with those of petitioning and migration, did not relieve the suffering of blacks and had no apparent effect on the course of national policy.[15]

In the campaign of 1888, Benjamin Harrison ignored the race question and, as a reward, received more white southern votes than any Republican since Reconstruction. Once in office, even black Republicans were rejected when they came to request the traditional jobs and patronage. Harrison recognized that those blacks who did vote would stay with the party since they had no place else to go; their demands could be ignored while he attempted to fuse the party with some groups of white southerners. His efforts failed; white Democrats, solidified by the ever-present race issue, united and withstood Harrison's entreaties. Violence broke out in Barnwell, South Carolina, in December 1889 when four blacks accused of participating in the murder of a white man, as well as four other unfortunate blacks confined to the same jail, were lynched by a mob of one hundred white men. Aroused blacks gathered in hostile groups, but by this time, the sheriff had gathered a posse and the governor had mobilized the local militia to prevent black retaliation.[16]

Congress was seemingly oblivious to the violent events which formed the backdrop to their debates in Washington and felt no compunction to assert any influence, legal or otherwise, on behalf of the blacks. And yet, in December 1889, the same Congress debated a southern proposal which involved the colonization of blacks outside the United States. The bill proposed that the government finance an expedition and purchase land for the migrants. When Republicans, black leaders, and newspapers opposed the bill, insisting that it was a matter of national pride and responsibility to provide for black people in this country, the bill was not passed. The inherent contradiction is obvious: an immigration bill was defeated on the grounds that "justice must be done to blacks," when, in actuality, there was no evidence of a national will to provide justice for blacks.[17]

The Republicans made two legislative efforts in 1890 to "give justice to blacks." One attempt was made by Senator Henry Blair of New Hampshire whose aid to education bill would have given federal money to public schools, thereby indirectly benefitting the freedmen. If blacks could be educated, at least their antagonists would be forced to seek reasons other than their ignorance as a basis for unequal treatment. Blair had introduced his bill in 1884 and 1885; finally, it was passed in the Senate and defeated in the House in 1888. It was defeated again in 1890 by forces who expressed fear of federal domination, or who thought that money for public schools would weaken private schools, or who believed that taking money out of the federal treasury would support a demand for a higher tariff.

The other legislative attempt to insure "black justice" was the election bill of Representative Henry Lodge, which provided for federal supervisors to inspect registration books, attend elections, and certify the results. This bill would have invoked a federal presence at elections which might have permitted blacks in the South to vote. Its sponsors cited the fact that thirty to sixty working days of each congressional session were taken up with contested elections, as well as questions related to the black vote in the South, as Republicans tried to overturn the election of Democrats. The act was undoubtedly constitutional; in theory, it greatly resembles the 1965 Voting Rights Act which was upheld in *Katzenbach v. South Carolina* in 1966.[18]

Sponsors of the Lodge Bill thought they could pass it with Harrison's support. Harrison, deciding that his attempts to break the solid South to get support for a high tariff would not work but that he might be able to get some mileage out of the race question, stated in his annual message to Congress in December 1889 that blacks should be protected in all relations to the federal government, as litigant, as juror, as witness, as voter, and as traveler in interstate commerce. Harrison's support was not as expansive as some might have wished, but it offered some encouragement. Despite Harrison's lukewarm statements and confirmation in the House by a strict party-line vote, the Lodge Bill failed to pass in the Senate, after being held over until the next session to make way for a vote on the McKinley Tariff of 1890. Interestingly enough, liberal Republican opponents of the bill insisted that education was the answer to the race problem, and if this was accomplished, suffrage would be permitted by state governments. If their thesis was correct, the failure to provide federal aid to education, and the disinterest of state governments in educating blacks, indicated that the racial problem was becoming accepted as a part of the national scene.[19]

Harrison's administration was plagued by labor troubles which seemed to threaten the very foundation of the national economy and which overshadowed such racial disturbances as the one which occurred in March 1892, when black militants and white police clashed in a small community outside Memphis. Calvin McDowell, black manager of a people's cooperative grocery store, and Theodore Moss, a black postman, became upset when a white man, Cornelius Hurst, came into their community and beat a black youth who Hurst claimed had assaulted one of his children. When other blacks tried to interfere, Hurst began clubbing them. A crowd of black people gathered to devise a plan of retaliation. When a white man tried to disperse them, one of the blacks "shot holes into his clothes." Fear spread through the white community; after some of the whites started leaving town, the local judge issued a warrant for the arrest of the black ringleaders. When twelve deputy sheriffs came to serve warrants for arrest of the black ringleaders, they were ambushed in the grocery store. Four deputy sheriffs were seriously injured. A large posse of white people succeeded in capturing twenty-seven blacks. The next day McDowell, Moss, and Allen Stewart, the so-called "ringleaders," were taken from jail and lynched by a mob of seventy-five whites. No action was taken to prosecute the murderers, either by the state or the national government.[20]

Resolution or action on the race question and its legal problems could hardly be expected from the administration of Grover Cleveland, who, capitalizing in part on the threats implicit in the proposed Lodge Bill and the wave of strikes in the country, defeated Harrison in 1892. In 1893, matters worsened. St. George Tucker of Virginia introduced a bill in the House to repeal all laws relating to supervision of elections. During the Hayes administration, southerners had failed in their attempt to accomplish repeal by adding riders to appropriation bills. In 1894, however, Congress passed, and Cleveland signed into law bills repealing those sections of Reconstruction legislation which related to the protection of voting rights. It was suggested by proponents that such legal protection was no longer necessary and was an insult to the South.[21]

Under Cleveland's administration, labor and racial violence continued. The Pullman controversy in 1894 demonstrated the ability of a president to find constitutional authority for the use of federal troops on presidential initiative, with or without a governor's request, and even, as in this case, authority to overrule the governor's specific request that troops not be sent. When Eugene Debs's American Railway Union went on strike, they declared a boycott against Pullman cars; trains were stopped and Pullman cars detached and side-tracked. There is some evidence that the railroad managers had mail cars attached to Pullman cars so that when the strikers detached the Pullman cars, they had to at one point handle the mail cars. Railroad managers then complained that the mails were being interrupted and asked for federal intervention. To keep the mail running, Attorney General Richard Olney ordered thirty-four hundred men, who were hired and paid by the railroad, sworn in as special deputies. When these deputies clashed with the strikers, tumult and the destruction of property followed. On July 2, the managers obtained a blanket injunction from a federal district court forbidding interference with the operation of the mails and prohibiting the union's refusal to perform normal services. At the same time, the court announced its inability to enforce its orders or to quell the riots and suppress the strike. Cleveland, deciding that this strike was outside the states' jurisdiction and involved the enforcement of federal statutes, sent four companies of federal troops to Chicago. The sporadic disturbances spread from Hammond, Indiana, where regular troops fired upon a mob, into the western states as far as California. In each case, federal troops were ostensibly used to prevent interference to the mail. The rioting and the strike subsided rather quickly after Eugene Debs was arrested on July 10. Cleveland's ability to find constitutional justification in this instance resulted from his willingness to defend capital from the threat of organized labor.[22] Cleveland was not, however, interested in finding constitutional authority to insure due process of law when racial violence occurred. In that lack of concern, he was no more or less culpable than his predecessors.

However, some white opposition to lawlessness and lynching was developing. In South Carolina, at the state constitutional convention of 1895, a black delegate, Isaiah Reed, introduced a motion authorizing the governor to remove and replace any official who allowed personal harm to come to a prisoner in his custody and provided that the militia be called out in the case of a threatened lynching. The provision would have been a deterrent, because in many cases, lynchings were publicized in the press to insure that the event was well attended! Reed's motion lost. However, a proposal was approved which provided for the removal of sheriffs who were guilty of negligence, permission, or connivance in giving up prisoners, and provided punitive damages of two thousand dollars to the families of each person lynched. However, there were no reported cases of damage awards or sheriffs removed from office.[23]

McKinley, who was elected in 1896 as the frank protagonist of the conservative classes, stated in his inaugural address that lynching could not be tolerated and that courts, not mobs, would execute the law. No one disagreed with his rhetoric, but two of the most flagrant incidences of racial violence in the period occurred during his administration. It was a long-standing Republican policy to appoint blacks in the South to minor federal posts to insure their support in the Republican nominating conventions in which blacks were free to function as delegates since the party was anathema to southern whites. Frazier B. Baker was appointed postmaster at Lake City, South Carolina. However, the "democratic white majority" of the community did not want their mail handled by a "nigger." On February 21, 1898, while the United States prepared for the Spanish-American War, a mob of approximately four hundred whites gathered outside Baker's home, set it afire, burned him to death, and wounded his wife, a twelve-month-old baby, and three other children.[24]

The tragic circumstances surrounding the Baker incident gain magnitude when the records make the fact clear that the government knew about the threats on Baker's life, yet no federal troops or marshals were sent when a federal function was clearly being subverted. If the national government had seemed perfunctory in its response to the threats against Baker, it seemed oblivious to his death. Although Baker's death had failed to arouse the government, it unified the national black community. A mass meeting was held in Chicago, and a series of resolutions adopted. On March 21, Mrs. Ida Wells-Barnett, a black leader of the antilynching movement, accompanied by a delegation of Chicago congressmen, went to the White House to have an audience with President McKinley. They stated their case and presented their resolutions, which included apprehension of the killer, indemnity for the widow and children, and a national antilynching law. The astute Wells-Barnett reportedly told McKinley she believed that Baker's case was clearly within federal jurisdiction and was not a matter for the state court. From her point of view, failure to act would be a dereliction of governmental duty. Three months later, in June 1898, federal agents arrested and charged eleven persons in the Baker case. Although tried in a federal court, none of the defendants were convicted. Two agreed to testify for the state and were given immunity from prosecution; three were freed on a directed verdict, which means that after considering all the facts as the government insisted they occurred, the judge still did not believe there was cause for legal action. The jury was unable to bring in a verdict on the remaining six defendants.[25]

South Carolina was to be the stage for another bloody incident during McKinley's administration. In November of 1898, T. P. Tolbert, a white man, acting on behalf of his brother who was seeking office, stationed himself outside a polling station in Phoenix to take affidavits from blacks who were refused permission to vote. A white Democrat challenged him; a fight broke out and the Democrat was killed and Tolbert was wounded. Subsequently, a white mob formed, and fighting broke out. An uncle and nephew of the candidate were wounded. Blacks fled the melee and organized for retaliation. Later, one group of blacks ambushed a crowd of white reinforcements on the way to join the mob at Phoenix, wounding several men. As the riot gained impetus, whites roamed the area attacking every black they encountered. Eleven blacks were brought to a church near Phoenix and forced to confess; four were killed on the spot and the others were permitted to escape. The next morning, another black who was allegedly part of the ambush party was brought to the same spot and murdered. The South Carolina press blamed the Tolberts for encouraging black people to be "uppity." One Tolbert was arrested and charged with inciting to riot, but was later released; however, a mass meeting of whites resolved that he should move from the community. Thereafter, white terrorists went around killing and assaulting blacks to eliminate subversives and repulse rebellion. Finally, Senator "Pitchfork" Ben Tillman of South Carolina, an arrant racist, informed his constituency that they should kill the Tolberts and stop all that other "devilment" before the federal authorities intervened. Tillman need not have worried; his concern that the national government might intervene to end wholesale attacks on citizens which the state refused to prevent was misplaced. The national government seemingly could find no constitutional means to intercede to protect its black citizens.[26]

The Tolbert incident had not died down before more violence erupted. In November 1898, the black editor of a local black newspaper in Wilmington, North Carolina, published a retort to an article written by a local white woman in defense of the lynching of blacks to protect white womanhood. Local whites felt that his reply disparaged the white woman, so they called a meeting in which they decided to expel the editor from the city and destroy his press. Fifteen blacks were called in and given this ultimatum. When the black people of the community conferred and agreed that there was nothing they could do except comply, they mailed a letter to the white citizen's committee indicating their compliance. The deadline expired before the committee received the letter, and four hundred armed whites went to the newspaper office to destroy it. Someone set the building afire. A rumor spread that whites were going to burn and attack the black quarter, so the blacks prepared for an invasion. When the uneasy whites ordered the blacks to stop gathering in groups and ordered one crowd to disperse, the panicked blacks fired at the whites. For two days, terrorism, anarchy, and murder prevailed. Many blacks left the city. Officials dispatched letters requesting immediate federal aid; the replies informed the petitioners that the governor had made no request for federal aid. The state militia, as well as a battalion of naval militia which was in the area, tried to end the riot, but peace and order were not restored until the mobs had vented their rage. Later, conciliatory city authorities tried to persuade blacks hiding in the woods to return to their homes.[27]

Black people protested against this violence at a mass meeting in Cooper Union in New York City by demanding an end to the bloodshed in North and South Carolina and deprecating the inaction of the federal government. In Chicago in 1899, a meeting of the Afro-American Council, composed of America's leading black men, considered proposals for radical action in regard to lynching laws, and for migration as a solution to the race question, as well as the proposals of some black politicians who wanted to defend the administration. The resolutions which were eventually passed declared that blacks had the same right to have their lives and liberties protected as whites. The protestors could not understand how the national government could intervene and go to war to protect Cubans and fail to protect American citizens. To this, the administration responded that it was well established in American legal traditions that making war came under the jurisdiction of Congress, while citizens must look to the state for protection. Perhaps the best answer to the administration's reply was made by the Massachusetts branch of the Afro-American Society which convened in October 1899 to consider the Phoenix and Wilmington massacres. In an open letter to McKinley, they explained their understanding that, notwithstanding the plea of constitutional inability to intervene in such cases, ". . . where there is a will . . . there is always a way, and where there is no will there is no way. We well know that you lacked the will and, therefore, the way to meet that emergency."[28]

But the debilitated state of law enforcement and the violence that dominated race relations in the United States between 1877 and 1900 could not establish precedence over the concurrent national issues. The Indians, the new industrialism, the labor movement, agrarian reform movements, the silver and tariff issues, the waves of immigrants, and the new role of the United States as an imperialist power captured the attention of the government and citizens alike. In 1900, the black man's position was not markedly improved over his status as a slave. He stood outside the law; his legal attempts to seek justice, as well as his militant enterprises, were frustrated. There was still no enlightened view of how to solve the problem of racial violence within the framework of the Constitution.

10

Riots, Lynchings, and Federal Quiescence

T HE TURN OF THE CENTURY was an occasion for celebration around the world. Expositions and congresses projected a future wherein human aspirations would be realized through the wonders of technology. The threshold of the century also seemed to mark a quickening in social awareness. In the United States, the Progressives worked to cure social ills ranging from impure food and drugs to housing for urban immigrants. A few white Progressives aided in the founding of the National Association for the Advancement of Colored People (NAACP) and the Urban League, but inside the American government, little attention was paid to the race problem. The Republican party platforms of 1900, 1904, and 1908, which contained planks insisting upon the enforcement of the Fifteenth Amendment and the protection of black voters, afforded a basis for reformers to make an issue of black suppression. Despite the pious platform statements and the general air of reform, twelve more years of Republican control only saw the race problem grow in magnitude, statutes on the subject remain unenforced, and the plight of blacks ignored.[1]

Theodore Roosevelt, who succeeded the assassinated McKinley in 1901, seemed interested enough in the racial problem to invite Booker T. Washington to the White House for dinner. A storm of public protest followed. His interest was short-lived; he became less concerned about blacks and even became sympathetic to racist positions. William

Howard Taft, who succeeded Roosevelt in 1909, was confident that the southern white man was the black's best friend and assured the South that she need not fear the enforcement of "social equality." He saw no inconsistency between disfranchisement techniques and the Fifteenth Amendment. The federal army in the South, in keeping with the 1877 Compromise, largely ignored instances of racial violence. No president, attorney general, or secretary of war commissioned the military to enforce those extant amendments and statutes which enfranchised and protected the blacks.[2]

From 1901 to 1910, 846 persons were lynched in the United States. Of this number, 92 were white and 754 were black. Ninety percent of the lynchings took place in the South. Congress and the president took no action to prevent lynchings, and state governments did not prosecute the perpetrators, even when the event was publicized at least a day in advance. The president could not bring himself to initiate federal action on the basis of the remaining Reconstruction statutes, and no one in the government seemed to care enough to march a few soldiers into these areas, which would have been sufficient to disperse crowds that sometimes gathered to enjoy the lynchings. Senator "Pitchfork" Ben Tillman of South Carolina offered a convenient rationale for lynching; blacks had deteriorated since the beneficial effects of slavery had been removed and the only way to frighten them into submission was to lynch them. Further, if blacks somehow got elected to political office, they must be mobbed and displaced. The major difference between Tillman and his contemporaries in Congress was that he was candid, while many of the others constructed a facade of constitutional theory to justify their inaction or hide their prejudice.[3]

The period of Republican ascendancy was fraught with race riots in the streets, mobbings, and jailhouse disturbances. In Springfield, Ohio, in March 1904, fifteen hundred men stormed the city jail to "liberate" Richard Dixon, a black who had allegedly shot and killed a policeman who interceded in a drunken brawl between Dixon and his woman. The mob shot and hanged Dixon and then moved on to burn the black quarter. No attempts were made to put out or control the fire because the mayor feared the mob would not permit it. The local militia gathered at their barracks, but their officers were reluctant to hurt any members of the mob. The mayor finally asked the governor for assistance, whereupon eight companies were sent in and the saloons ordered closed. The militia, which did not arrive until the mob had spent itself, remained in town five days guarding the public fountain. As a punitive measure, the mayor closed black lodging houses and hotels at public insistence. A grand jury was convened which indicted only two men, not for lynching, but for breaking into the jail.[4]

In August 1904, Paul Reed and Will Cato, two blacks convicted of the alleged murder of a white family, were in the Statesboro, Georgia, jail protected by a local militia company. The militia was armed only with bayonets and unloaded weapons—they did not want to hurt anyone. A crowd broke into the courthouse, pushed past the soldiers, took the prisoners outside town, and then burned them alive. Obsessed, the mob then embarked on the usual pogrom—attacking innocent blacks. At least four additional black people were killed. Five hundred militiamen were sent to the scene, but to no avail. The terror ended only when the weary throng dissipated itself. A commission appointed by the governor concluded that even a regiment could not have controlled the mob. The governor had not asked for federal aid, and none was offered. A Wall Street broker wrote Theodore Roosevelt, asking him to send troops to arrest the lynchers. Attorney General William H. Moody replied that no federal law had been violated.[5]

W. R. Leaken, an assistant attorney general for the district involved, thought there were federal grounds for a conviction. He wrote Moody for authority to ask a grand jury which was in session for an indictment against the mob leaders. The attorney general responded that an indictment under federal law could be invoked only when a federally protected right was violated. In his view, the Constitution did not protect blacks from murder. Leaken responded by sending Moody a press clipping indicating that the "best people" in the state were disgusted with lynching. Leaken also expressed his belief that the Statesboro case paralleled one in Huntsville, Alabama, in September 1904, in which a mob burned a black man, and indictments were brought in federal court. However, the attorney general pointed out the differences between the two cases to Leaken: in Huntsville, when the mob burned the jail, the sheriff let the prisoner out, and the mob captured him outside the jail. The mob leaders were not indicted for murder but for burning the jail and threatening the lives of the other federal prisoners inside.[6] Then, Judge Emory Speer, who was presiding over the jury, wrote the attorney general to ask if Leaken had authority to proceed. He was informed that Leaken had not been given that authority and had, in fact, been reprimanded for his presumptuousness. After the grand jury was discharged, the department had a change of heart and informed Leaken to proceed on his own responsibility, if he so desired. Leaken, angry because now it was too late, wrote a long letter complaining about the department's vacillation. The attorney general explained that the department did not want to issue indictments every time someone was lynched and then be forced to abandon the charges.[7]

The lack of federal response in the Statesboro case was characteristic of post-Reconstruction interpretation of the Constitution, the Thirteenth, Fourteenth, and Fifteenth Amendments, and statutes passed upon their authority. This was an era in which the Supreme Court supported federal police power to regulate lotteries and oleomargarine, yet constricted the use of federal police power in incidences of racial violence. Perhaps the best expression of this judicial leaning was the Supreme Court decision in *Hodges v. United States* (1906). In this case, eight blacks in Arkansas contracted to work for a lumber manufacturer. Three armed white men forced them to leave their jobs for no other reason than their color. The blacks argued that they had been deprived of the protection of the Civil Rights Act of 1866, which asserts in part that blacks have the same right to make and enforce contracts as whites. They reasoned that since the inability to make contracts was a badge of slavery, the Thirteenth Amendment had been violated. The blacks further contended that the white defendants had violated that part of the Civil Rights Act of 1866 which made it a federal crime to deprive persons of federally protected rights. Violation of the act was punishable by a fine of one thousand dollars or imprisonment for one year, or both. Finally, the plaintiffs claimed that the defendants were guilty of a conspiracy to deny federal rights under the Act of May 31, 1870, which was punishable by a five thousand dollar fine or imprisonment for not more than ten years.[8]

Justice David J. Brewer, who wrote the majority opinion in the case, rejected these arguments on the grounds that the Thirteenth Amendment only prohibits forcing someone to work. Brewer felt that if Congress had determined to make blacks aliens, or wards of the nation, after the Civil War, they would be subject to federal protection. However, Brewer stated that whether "this was or was not the wiser way to deal with the problem is not a matter for the courts to consider." According to Brewer, the right to work was not a privilege of national citizenship or a federally created or protected right; the plaintiffs in such cases must look to the states for their protection. Brewer did not think that it was relevant that the plaintiffs were in federal court because the state had refused to give them protection.[9]

Interestingly enough, Justice John Marshall Harlan, the great dissenter in *Plessy v. Ferguson* and the *Civil Rights* cases joined with Justice William Day in asserting that it *was* the purpose of the Thirteenth Amendment to remove all incidents or badges of slavery. Being forced not to hold a job because of color was a badge of slavery. Harlan thought that the majority opinion in the *Civil Rights* cases had asserted that Congress had authority under the second section of the Thirteenth Amendment to remove all incidents of slavery. This was precisely what the court had done under the Civil Rights Act of 1866. Nonetheless, the overruling of the *Hodges* decision did not come until 1968 when the Supreme Court, in *Jones v. Alfred Mayer Co.*, declared the Civil Rights Act of 1866 to be valid legislation under the Thirteenth Amendment. The majority opinion written by Justice Potter Stewart stated that the Civil Rights Act of 1866 was designed to prohibit all racial discrimination with respect to the rights therein enumerated. The blacks in the *Hodges* case, however, received no relief, and for almost fifty years, the case became the rod and staff of those who denied that the federal government had the authority to intervene in race relations.[10]

The year of the *Hodges* decision, 1906, was punctuated with racial violence. In August, black soldiers of the Twenty-fifth Infantry had been stationed in Brownsville, Texas, for three weeks. Even before they arrived, the troops had heard rumors that they would not be sent out on maneuvers with the Texas National Guard because those units had said they would use real cartridges against black troops in war games. Word also circulated that the townspeople had sent letters to their congressmen objecting to the stationing of black troops in their area. When the soldiers arrived, the bars in town refused to serve them or, in some cases, the blacks would be asked to step off in a corner to surreptitiously buy drinks. The townspeople continually complained to the officers about the "uppity" black troops. Black soldiers were accused of not giving way on the sidewalk to whites, of being drunk and disorderly, and of refusing to move on when told to do so. A white woman had also reported that a black soldier threw her on the ground and ran away. White people in the town were infuriated over this incident, and all army passes were cancelled.[11] On the night before the disorder broke out, a search and interrogation was conducted in the barracks for a black soldier who had reportedly assaulted a white woman in her home. One of the soldiers maintained that whites had prompted the woman to make this charge in order to get a soldier lynched and to downgrade black soldiers generally. The blacks bitterly resented being searched and insisted on their innocence.[12]

About midnight on August 13, nine to fifteen armed black soldiers reportedly stole into the town and began shooting, resulting in the death of a bartender who had treated them shabbily and the wounding of a policeman. Later, they allegedly returned to the base, cleaned their guns, and went about their business. In an investigation conducted by the inspector general, threats and intimidations failed to produce informers. The soldiers again insisted on their innocence. The inspector general, relying upon the testimony of white citizens, recommended that the whole unit be given dishonorable discharges. Consequently, President Roosevelt dismissed the entire batallion of approximately 160 men and disqualified them from further military or government employment. Roosevelt was attacked by black groups who cited cases in which blacks were killed in racial assaults without prison sentences being given. They criticized the president for punishing both the innocent and the guilty and for exacting such harsh punishment. Through the efforts of Senator Joseph Foraker of Ohio and other interested members of Congress, a court of inquiry was eventually established, and the soldiers cleared of the charges were reinstated without loss of pay or privileges. No effort was made to reconcile the townspeople and the blacks, either before or after the incident; black troops were simply transferred to Nevada.[13]

In the same month, in the small town of Seaford, Delaware, a disturbance occurred when the news spread that a "strange Negro" had attacked a white boy. White citizens began parading the streets, assaulting any "strange Negro" they encountered. Blacks retaliated by beating whites. In response, the whites formed a squad of "police" and began jailing blacks, which succeeded only in alarming the outraged blacks. Although the town had only five hundred residents, at least two hundred blacks, reportedly from Maryland and Virginia, came to aid their brothers. Whites from out of town also rallied to the cause. When the destruction finally ended, the white community had driven out or jailed most of the blacks.[14]

The Atlanta Race Riot of 1906 was the bloodiest confrontation between the races in the period between 1900 and World War I. That summer, Atlanta was host to a state political campaign. The hotly debated issue of black disfranchisement, dramatized by the newspapers and the contending factions of the Democratic party, exacerbated the race hatred. Charges of black offenses against white women were box-scored in a newspaper for six months before the riot. Tension mounted, and apprehension gripped the city. On the afternoon of the riot, the headlines reported four alleged assaults against white women. Actually, one woman saw a black man outside her house and screamed. The other three assaults were never verified.

Tension, apprehension, and bigotry gave way to maniacal rage, and the purge began. On a Saturday night, September 22, whites indiscriminately began attacking blacks, killing and maiming many of them. Rioters broke into hardware stores and armed themselves, demolished black businesses, and even robbed stores kept by white men. When the mayor, the police force, and the fire department failed to control the rioters, the governor called out the militia, but, as usual, the major damage was already done.

Members of a black citizens' group hastily wrote Roosevelt, explaining the causes of the disorder and requesting prompt federal assistance to prevent further violence. Roosevelt had already demonstrated his reluctance to use federal forces even during the open warfare between the Industrial Workers of the World (IWW), the Western Federation of Miners, and the mine owners in Cripple Creek, Colorado, in 1903-4. He sent no federal troops to Atlanta. Roosevelt's position was traditional—unless a formal request was made from the state indicating its inability to control a situation, no federal troops would be utilized in civil disorders. These requirements were not met in Atlanta.[15]

Although Sunday was quiet in Atlanta, rioting broke out again Monday night. For unknown reasons, a squad of police marched into the black suburb of Brownsville. By this time, the blacks were organized and had established methods of self-defense. The police arrests

of black citizens for being armed threw light on an apparent contradiction: some white citizens aiding the police were armed and were
apparently not deputized. When the whites, with their black prisoners
in custody, approached one group of blacks and began firing to disperse them, the blacks returned their fire. One officer was killed, one
was wounded, and several blacks were killed and injured. As the police
started back to town with their prisoners, two of the blacks were killed
by one or more unknown assailants.

Some twenty-four whites were arrested, found guilty in the rioting
of Saturday night, and sentenced to short terms on a chain gang. Sixty
blacks who were arrested for the shooting of the police officer were
later released for lack of evidence. A grand jury was convened; the jury
condemned the newspapers for creating the atmosphere which instigated the Saturday night riots. A committee of white citizens investigating the riot concluded that two whites and ten blacks had been
killed and some twenty persons wounded. Those who suffered most,
the committee revealed, were the law-abiding citizens.

The Atlanta riot left many questions unanswered. There was no explanation for the failure of the militia to prevent the violence on Monday night, September 24. Although federal troops were not formally
called in, it was known that the commander of the Seventh Infantry at
Camp Chickamauga had come to Atlanta to ask the commander of the
state troops if he needed help. He had been told none was necessary.
On the other hand, military authorities reportedly aided the police
and white citizens in disarming blacks to prevent further violence.
Lewis Douglass, son of the black abolitionist Frederick Douglass, expressed this view in the *New York Age:* ". . . [blacks] must die to be
saved and in dying must take as many along with them as is possible to
do with the aid of firearms and other weapons." However, blacks
found it difficult to rebel, to make revolution, or even to mount successful self-defense when military authorities disarmed them, leaving
them vulnerable to white intimidation and repression.[16]

The 1906 Christmas holidays were also filled with racial disorders.
In the predominately black town of Wahalak, Mississippi, mayhem
erupted when a black killed a white constable and a conductor of the
Gulf, Mobile, and Ohio Railroad. The state militia, fortified with a
Gatling gun and heavy armament, was sent from Meridian to protect
the whites in the town and to keep order. Reports were circulating

that bands of armed blacks and whites were killing each other; twelve persons were known dead. Governor James Vardaman and several staff members, accompanied by twenty-five soldiers, went to Wahalak to examine the situation because the disorder was spreading to surrounding towns. They were reassured when they discovered that the remaining trouble-makers were "tough white elements" who were still killing blacks to avenge the initial murders.[17]

The jailhouse riot in August 1908 in Springfield, Illinois, is a landmark in black history. This perfidy in the birthplace of Lincoln, who was regarded by neo-abolitionists and blacks as the Great Emancipator, led to the formation of the NAACP and the beginning of a new phase of political protest in the black liberation movement. This riot was instigated, as was the Atlanta riot, by reports that blacks had assaulted white women. Before the riot occurred, Joe James, a black man, was in jail awaiting trial; he was accused of fatally stabbing a white man who had allegedly discovered James in his daughter's bedroom. On the way to jail, James had been snatched from the police and severely beaten, but was recovered and placed under protective custody. On Friday, August 14, George Richardson was arrested for allegedly raping a white woman and was put in jail with James. When the word spread of another crime against white womanhood, a white mob gathered outside the jail. The ingenious sheriff arranged to have fire engines race down the street to distract the crowd while spiriting his prisoners to the state prison for safety. When the crowd, now an insurgent mob, demanded the prisoners, the sheriff let them inspect the jail. Finding the prisoners gone, the mob began to search for an object on which to vent its anger.

While the mob was milling aimlessly around the streets, a rumor was circulated that a local restaurant owner had driven the car in which the prisoners were carried to safety. The throng, with a purpose at last, demolished the man's restaurant and overturned his car. The outnumbered police and militia did not interfere. When the mob began burning the car and restaurant, the police fired a few warning shots, but to no avail. The mayor appeared and asked the mob to disperse, but when the mob pushed him aside, he took refuge in a cigar store. With added momentum, the mob turned its vengeance on the black populace. Black porters were beaten at railroad depots, blacks were dragged from streetcars, and the black quarter was sacked, looted, and demolished. Precedents were established when whites flew white handkerchiefs to indicate the ownership of their properties in order to protect them and when mobs refused to let the firemen put out the fires. Many people were killed; four white spectators were unintentionally killed by stray bullets. Blacks were killed indiscriminately. An elderly cobbler, who had been married to a white woman for thirty years, was strung up and his throat cut. The local militia did not, or could not, control the riot, and once again, the state troops arrived after the main surge of violence had passed. By daylight Saturday, the rioters had grown tired and gone home. The eighteen hundred troops who had entered the city busied themselves by clearing the wreckage and patrolling the devastation.

A grand jury investigating the riot was mainly thwarted because too few people were willing to testify against their associates, and most were implicated in some way themselves. The grand jury indicted three of the most vociferous leaders of the mob; one was a woman who had inflamed the crowd to mob violence in the name of the defense of white womanhood and who expressed pride in her own complicity in a number of the homicides. She was the only rioter found guilty, but escaped punishment by poisoning herself on the way to jail. Ironically, the woman whose alleged rape precipitated the riot confessed afterward that a white man whose identity she refused to give had attacked her.[18]

The Taft administration failed to break tradition on the issues critical to the black man. Taft followed the Republican tradition of appointing some blacks to "Negro jobs" and minor offices as patronage for their support as delegates to Republican nominating conventions; he appointed William H. Lewis, a prominent black Bostonian, as one of the assistants to Attorney General George W. Wickersham. In one case, he naively approved the appointment of a one-armed black as a deputy marshal in Houston at a salary higher than that of the marshal. When the deputy was fired because of the difference in salary, he complained to the attorney general, but the attorney general agreed with the marshal that the firing could be justified, without offending black patronage seekers, on the grounds that a one-armed man could not make arrests.[19]

The Taft administration faced its most severe test on the racial issue with an incident that occurred in Palestine, Texas. In August 1910, approximately twenty black plantation workers had been murdered because they had protested against their wages of one dollar a day, and the payment in scrip which they had to spend at the company store. Wickersham was made aware of the event through a letter written to Taft by Cecil Lyon, the chairman of the Texas state Republican committee. Lyon enclosed a letter from a local white man, John Siddon, who asked that his name be kept secret and who asserted that he knew the guilty parties. Siddon said, and Lyon agreed, that since the state of Texas would never undertake the prosecution of anyone for these crimes, a federal investigation was the only hope for ending such incidents. Wickersham replied to Lyon that the matter would receive careful attention. There is no evidence that it did.[20] In addition, a group of black ministers wrote Taft, complaining about the incident and demanding that the government make it clear that blacks were not to be executed without a trial, indictment, and conviction. A staff attorney replied that there was no federal crime involved. However, if the ministers knew of some federal violation, they should submit the facts and an investigation should certainly be made.[21]

When W. H. Ellis, an attorney and concerned citizen, sent a telegram to Taft, he struck at the heart of the issue of constitutional power as it related to the Palestine affair. Ellis thought that if Grover Cleveland could find justification to send troops to Illinois to stop rioting, then Taft should be able to find a means to send troops to Texas to stop the "massacre" of black people, if for no other reason than for the sake of humanity. Taft did not reply; if he had, the answer probably would have reflected all those conventions which had determined federal policy for twenty-five years. Since the national government relied on *Hodges v. United States*, murder was not a matter of federal concern.[22]

As the Republican era drew to a close, is was clear that Roosevelt, who had made progressivism nationally respectable, and Taft, the trust-buster, had failed to develop a program for resolving America's racial problem. They, like the Progressives, must have felt that impure food and drugs, the trusts, corruption in government, and the plight of the immigrants were more important issues. In the meantime, troops and white citizens had rather successfully kept blacks in their place. Perhaps the disorder and violence was not yet profound or continuous enough to grasp the attention of the government or the general public.

11

Moving
Off Dead
Center

T HE ADMINISTRATIONS of Woodrow Wilson were remarkably fruitful in passing reform legislation; the tariff revision, financial renovation, and the "Magna Carta of Labor," the Clayton Antitrust Act, were proud accomplishments of the "New Freedom." But there was no "New Freedom" or reform related to race relations. Many blacks supported Woodrow Wilson in the campaign of 1912, only to find him less interested in their plight than the Republicans had been. Even in federal jobs and office buildings in Washington where black employees had once worked freely with whites, segregation was reestablished. Lynching, pogroms, jailhouse riots, and mob violence continued unabated; racial murder remained a seemingly unpunishable state crime.[1]

Aside from the continuing lynchings of individual blacks, the largest racial disorder in the Wilson era was a riot in East St. Louis in the spring and summer of 1917. The sizeable immigration of blacks into the city resulted in an oversupply of labor; apprehensive whites felt that job competition ought to be eliminated. Pressures mounted, and after a labor dispute in May, groups of disgruntled whites roamed the streets attacking blacks in an attempt to coerce them into leaving the city. The National Guard, which had officially been established in the Dick Act of 1903, was called out by the governor, all saloons were closed, and the violence subsided. Many alarmed blacks left the city.[2] The tenuous peace was shattered when a group of blacks, anticipating further hostilities, fired upon a car which approached them in their neighborhood, believing the car to be full of armed whites. However, the car turned out to be a police car; five policemen were shot, and one was killed. Afterward, the car was parked in front of the police station where crowds gathered to look at this symbol of black perfidy. The purge began; nine whites and thirty-nine blacks were killed.

The racial violence in East St. Louis generated protests across the country. Even Theodore Roosevelt spoke out in support of an investigation of the riot and murders and of the city government's apparent inability to prevent them. Black spokesmen believed federal aid should have been introduced to end the violence, as it had been in the Colorado mining disputes of 1892, 1894, 1899, and 1914, in the railroad strikes of 1877, and in the Pullman dispute. Even businessmen asserted that for the sake of preventing the destruction of plants essential to the war effort, federal force should have been utilized in the absence of state protection.[3]

Despite pressure from the NAACP, concerned citizens, and local businessmen, Wilson refused to intercede. The protests continued, eventually centering upon a request for a federal grand jury investigation to ascertain the causes of the riot and to suggest ways to prevent similar incidents. Lawyers in the Justice Department correctly put forth interpretations of the Civil Rights Act of 1866, which provided a basis for federal punishment of racial violence. However, Wilson and Attorney General Thomas Gregory refused the rationale for intervention provided by their staff attorneys. The governor had not requested federal aid and, in their view, no federal statute had been violated.[4]

In the House, Leonidus Dyer of St. Louis, Missouri, introduced a resolution which requested a committee investigation based on the power of Congress to regulate interstate commerce. Lawrence Sherman of Illinois introduced a similar resolution in the Senate. A committee was set up in August, hearings were held, but access to Justice Department files were denied because Gregory felt that release of the materials would not be in the public interest. No action grew out of the committee report, despite its condemnation of community mores, politicians, labor organizations, and others who had created the environment that precipitated the riot in St. Louis.[5]

Even those blacks who were in the military service were not immune to the infection of violence which spread throughout the country during the summer of 1917. In August, a rebellion involving black soldiers occurred in Houston, Texas. Several companies of the Twenty-fourth Infantry, consisting of about six hundred men, were assigned as guards during the construction of a training base for Illinois National Guard troops. Houston was found to be just as inhospitable to blacks as Brownsville had been in 1906. Jim Crowism and racial insults were common. As the atmosphere became increasingly charged, the commander of the infantry organized an ersatz black military police unit, which was ordered to keep the black soldiers in line, although no arms were issued the unit. Newspaper advertisements placed by local prohibitionists who wanted saloon closing endorsed in the coming election reminded the populace of Brownsville that the presence of black soldiers was an additional reason for prohibiting liquor sales. Conditions were ripe for disorder.[6]

The exact circumstances of the ensuing events are difficult to establish. Reportedly, two Houston police officers arrested a black woman for being drunk and disorderly. A black MP from the base asked the officers to release the woman to his custody. The police refused his request, and when the soldier insisted that they comply, the police struck him and then jailed him along with the woman. Later, another encounter between the same police officers and another black MP heightened the tension. Upon inquiring about the charges made against his fellow officer, the MP was told by one of the police officers that he did not answer questions posed by a black man. When the MP insisted that he needed the information to file a report, the police officer answered him with a pistol butt and an escort to jail. When the MP tried to escape, the police officer shot at him to subdue him. The rumor quickly spread among the black soldiers that other blacks were being brutalized by the police. The vacuum created by the military's apathy was quickly filled. Preparations were made, and arms and ammunition were stolen. That night, approximately one hundred black soldiers marched into town, bent on punishing the police, especially those stationed around the black quarter. On the way to town, the soldiers encountered a group of white policemen and shot two of them. Houston policemen, members of the Texas National Guard, and the Illinois guardsmen who were in town when the trouble started pursued and arrested the black soldiers, wounding five in the process. Six hundred federal troops from Fort Sam Houston were assigned to aid in keeping order. When Assistant Attorney General William Fitts, completely missing the point of the disturbance, simplistically suggested that the opening of grog shops and their availability to the men might have caused the riot, the soldiers involved denied drinking.[7]

Evidence indicates that the army's desire for making an example of the insurrectionaries led the prosecution far afield. To aid in developing their case, the prosecution opened sixty letters addressed to the black soldiers, in an effort to find evidence of a plot, which would have incurred even heavier sentences than the ones given; no such evidence was found. The military believed that insurrections such as this did not occur as an immediate response to provocation, but as a result of a plan or design to create disorder. The black soldiers involved were court-martialed; thirteen were hanged for murder, forty-four were sentenced to life imprisonment for mutiny, and five were acquitted. The Court of Claims was ordered by a Joint Resolution, passed by both houses of Congress in June 1919, to make an investigation and award damages to civilians killed or wounded by the soldiers. Justice was served.[8]

Racial violence on the home front and the war abroad contended for headlines. Amid the lynchings and jailhouse riots in 1918, one event captured the sympathy of the public. In Estill Springs, Tennessee, a black accused of killing two white men was burned at the stake after a confession was forced from him by red-hot irons. The NAACP sent its usual letters of protest to the president and the attorney general, but there was a significantly increased volume of mail from private citizens. A lady who was on a cruise to Europe wrote the president that she was offended by having to explain these barbarities to foreigners.[9]

The most interesting letters from a social and constitutional point of view were those written by Nick Chiles, the editor of a black newspaper, *The Topeka Plaindealer*. Chiles first wrote to the president, who then sent his letter on to the attorney general as was customary. Assistant Attorney General William Fitts sent Chiles the standard *Hodges* response that murder was a state matter. Chiles scathingly replied that he had not asked for legal advice, but rather he had asked the president to make the suppression of lynching and mob violence a war measure. Chiles added that perhaps blacks did not know much, but at least they "know enough to know that the President could demand that the Governors of the several states see to it that their citizens desist from such outrages, as such acts interfere in the prosecution of the war between these countries and the allies against Germany." Chiles continued: "If a local miner's union in Kansas can strike and the Federal officers can be sent to this union to find out the difficulty and trouble and adjust the same, for the reason that it will stop the mining of coal and interfere with the prosecution of the war, the same thing could be done to put a stop to the lynching and burning of colored men who could be used to dig the coal or use guns in the defense of the country." According to Chiles, the *Hodges* decision was not applicable under war conditions. With governmental control of the food supply, railroads, and fuel, states' rights were virtually nonexistent in some areas. Despite Chiles's understanding of the flexibility of constitutional law, his plea had no effect. The department filed his last letter without reply.[10]

In 1919, racial violence escalated. The general strike engineered by the IWW in Seattle in February, the organizing activity of William Z. Foster and steelworkers for a large-scale strike which finally occurred in September, and the increasing militancy of coal workers frightened conservatives who blamed the tensions on a Bolshevist plot. Conservatives were as frightened of black rebellion as they were of strikes and, despite the fact that blacks were used as strikebreakers, sought a Bolshevist link between the two.[11] Federal aid was readily introduced to quell the violence accompanying these disputes, justified in part because the national guard had not yet been demobilized and returned to state control.

In Charleston, South Carolina, when white sailors went on a rampage after an embroilment between a black and two sailors, two blacks were killed and seventeen wounded; seven sailors and one white policeman were wounded. The sailors attacked stores owned by blacks and looted shooting galleries for rifles and ammunition. Blacks and sailors battled each other with clubs and guns. The marines arrived, subdued the sailors, and took them back to the base. Fifty soldiers were sent from North Charleston with orders to arrest only military personnel. The army report on the incident carefully pointed out that their intervention was not official and that any blacks who were killed were killed by the navy. Six sailors were convicted at a court-martial of conduct prejudicial to good order and discipline, and manslaughter, and given short prison sentences. A coroner's jury in the city, where the population was sixty percent black, exonerated the blacks who insisted they fired in self-defense.[12]

Racial violence occurred in Longview, Texas, that year as a result of white response to increasing black sophistication in business transactions. Black efforts to improve their circumstances were met with hostility and suspicion, and finally, open aggression. In order to obtain better prices for their cotton, black businessmen sent it directly to Galveston, thus avoiding local middlemen. A cooperative had also been established where blacks could buy goods more cheaply. In addition, many blacks read the *Chicago Defender*, a newspaper whose militant tone was a source of aggravation to the white community. On July 4, the paper published an article intimating that a black man who had been lynched for raping a white woman was innocent, because the pair were lovers. Whites, suspecting that one of the local black businessmen had written the article, beat him with iron rods and gun butts and ordered him to leave town. A white mob bent on black suppression then marched into the black section and was fired upon; four whites were wounded. Mustering help from other whites, the mob returned to burn houses and shops. The police arrested a number of blacks for rioting; two hundred and fifty national guardsmen called in by the governor arrested a few blacks and whites. The arrested rioters were ultimately released, although the black ringleaders were ordered to leave town.[13]

Just as military intelligence kept labor organizations and black groups under surveillance throughout the country, it kept a careful eye on developments among the black population in Washington, as the epidemic of riots spread into the Capitol. On September 5, 1917, the First Battalion of the District of Columbia, the Negro National Guard, and a battalion of white infantry with two companies of artillery guarded the White House and two squadrons of cavalry were on reserve at Fort Myer to aid the infantries in patrolling Potomac Park.[14] *The Washington Post*, like other newspapers, played-up alleged racial incidents to bolster scare headlines. In July 1919, a story concerning a naval employee's wife who was jostled by two blacks who tried to steal her umbrella led two hundred sailors and marines to attempt the lynching of the two black suspects. Discovering that the blacks had been released by the police, the sailors and marines, joined by white civilians, marched into black neighborhoods, beating any black men and women they encountered. Police and MPs called to disperse the mob held two sailors and eight blacks for investigation. A NAACP request to Secretary of the Navy Josephus Daniels that orders for a cessation of violence be issued to naval personnel elicited no response.

The violence was intensified when a black held in custody on a minor charge was beaten by a crowd of whites. The police recovered the prisoner, but failed to arrest any of his aggressors. Soldiers and sailors then began dragging black citizens from streetcars and beating them. At midnight, the servicemen returned to their barracks, while civilians continued the violence. The Monday morning *Post* called servicemen to assemble at 9:00 P.M. to "clean up the town." A mob of blacks, now thoroughly alarmed, boarded a streetcar, and beat the motorman and conductor, while another group fired on sailors at the naval hospital, and others marched toward the Navy Yard. That night, whites and blacks both raided the other's neighborhoods in automobiles, which resulted in shoot-outs whenever the opposing sides met. Seven hundred Washington police and four hundred servicemen tried to keep order.

On Tuesday, President Wilson, Secretary of War Newton D. Baker, and Secretary of the Navy Daniels ordered additional troops into the city. That night, approximately twelve thousand federal troops were in the city. The NAACP and other organizations had encouraged people to stay at home. Following a rainy night, with only three casualties, one black and two whites, the riot ended. As in many other incidents, military troops did not arrive until after the violence had subsided.[15]

In the congressional debates on the possibility of an investigation of the riot, one southern senator thought that although everyone knew blacks were inferior to whites, whites should set an example by not participating in the riots. Representative Melvin McLaughlin of Nebraska objected to a suggestion made by a congressman from Alabama that the Germans were behind the riot, as there was no evidence of truth in this statement. No investigation was made.[16] However, the police chief naively suggested that hiring more policemen with higher wages would solve the problem. Even military intelligence admitted to the existence of a problem when their undercover man, William H. Loving, who was described as "the best type of white man's Negro," criticized the government for repression and discrimination against blacks. Nonetheless, no positive action to improve race relations in Washington was taken.[17]

A bloodier disorder than the one in Washington broke out in Chicago in July when a young black boy on a raft drifted into the "white" area at a bathing beach; he was reportedly stoned and drowned by the insulted whites. When a white policeman, refusing to arrest the alleged murderers, arrested a black on some minor offense, a mob of enraged blacks attacked the policeman. As news of the incident spread, mobs clashed all over Chicago. The disorders continued for seven days, resulting in the death of fifteen whites and twenty-three blacks.[18]

The biracial Chicago Commission on Race Relations, established by the governor to investigate the riot, reported that the large-scale migration of blacks into the city at the beginning of the war, the efforts of blacks to buy housing outside of traditionally black areas, the hostility between black and white workers, and the tendency of the police to use force when arresting blacks precipitated the riot. Despite the intensity of the riot, no regular army troops were called in; however, on July 30, the third day of rioting, six thousand national guardsmen were called to duty. In the grand jury investigation which had indicted fifty blacks and seventeen whites, the NAACP aided in the defense of the blacks and, at one point, considered placing the responsibility for black violence on those who had created the volatile conditions. However, that position was rejected as being too extreme. Most of the persons arrested, black and white, were acquitted.[19]

Aside from the report prepared by the Chicago Commission on Race Relations, whose conclusions, though valuable to the historian, were left to gather dust, one result of the riot was an increased effort to keep blacks disarmed. Gun retailers refused to sell weapons to blacks. Military intelligence kept Pullman porters under surveillance since it was reported that they were bringing guns and ammunition into Chicago to arm the black population. For the American public and those governmental officials unacquainted with nineteenth-century disturbances and earlier twentieth-century riots in Atlanta, Brownsville, and Houston, the events in Chicago and Washington forced one conclusion—blacks would not simply accept attacks against them without retaliation.[20]

Attempts to lynch black prisoners continued to cause jailhouse riots in 1919. In Knoxville, Tennessee, in August, Maurice Mays, charged with the murder of a white woman, was surreptitiously moved to Chattanooga because a mob had gathered outside the jail. Not believing Mays was gone, the mob ransacked the jail, releasing white prisoners. Having been ordered to move away from the jail by a company of national guardsmen, the mob moved on without purpose or direction, looting stores and stealing weapons. When the rumor circulated that whites were being robbed in black areas, they moved into black neighborhoods and were met with gunfire. Twelve hundred national guardsmen, called in to control the riot, advanced against the blacks. The troopers then fanned out to disarm the blacks; two blacks were shot and two bayoneted in the process. The only two fatalities were national guardsmen who were accidently shot by other guardsmen. The sheriff arrested fifty whites and called a grand jury, despite receiving threats for acting contrary to the interests of the white community; most of the whites were acquitted. The National Guard, in this instance, successfully aided the mob.[21]

Another classic lynching riot occurred that year in Omaha, Nebraska. Again, there had been a plethora of newspaper stories about assaults on white women. On September 28, when a black named William Brown was jailed on the charge of assault, a mob quickly gathered. The mayor, interfering with the lynchers, narrowly escaped hanging. The mob burned the jail and abducted Brown, who was then shot and hanged. Before the lynching, the police had requested aid from the army commander at Fort Crook, but the request was denied, along with one submitted by the federal marshal, on the grounds that troops could be used only to enforce federal law or in response to a formal state request. Red tape in the governor's office had slowed preparation for the official request. Finally, after Brown was killed, the commander at Fort Crook, deciding he could no longer await instructions from Washington, ordered two hundred army troops to disperse the white crowds who had moved into black neighborhoods.

By dawn the following day, the town was quiet. Remaining on guard, the soldiers advised the black population to stay indoors. The machine guns set up by the troops and a heavy rain that evening dampened the enthusiasm of the potential violators. The next morning when General Leonard Wood, Commander of the Central Division of the Army, arrived in Omaha, he began arresting those implicated in the lynching for trial by civilian authorities. Public meetings were prohibited and gatherings of two or more were broken up. Fifty-nine men were arrested for complicity in the lynching. The army remained in the city until early November.

As indicated by the official army report on the incident, the governor's official request for aid went to the chief of staff and secretary of war in Washington where it was approved shortly after the eight hundred troops had already left for Omaha. The War Department did not insist that the governor address himself to the president, which is required by statute, since most National Guard troops were federalized during the war and many states failed to organize volunteer militias as a first line of defense.[22]

While federal troops were still patrolling in Omaha, the last major racial disorder of 1919 broke out in Elaine, Arkansas. Desiring higher prices for their cotton and lower prices for goods, the blacks in Phillips County organized a union and began holding meetings in a black church. Robert L. Hill, a black farmer, emerged as the leader of the union movement, which had followers in several black communities in Arkansas. When the disturbances erupted, the Phillips County group was holding a meeting in the church to decide if they should retain U. S. Bratton as a legal advisor. Bratton was a white lawyer who was known for his efforts to press federal prosecution of white plantation owners who held blacks in peonage in Arkansas.

The account of the events surrounding the violence is punctuated with contradictions. According to the whites, deputy sheriffs had been fixing a flat tire near the church when they were fired upon by the black guards who stood outside the church and then attacked by the union members who feared that the sheriffs had heard of their plans to massacre whites. The blacks said that the whites, fearing the economic organization of the blacks, had fired into the church without provocation and then burned the church to hide any evidence that might contradict the white version of the event.[23]

Colonel Isaac Jencks, commander of the army troops at Camp Pike, did not move in immediately upon receiving word that the secretary of war had approved the governor's request for aid but had awaited further orders. The War Department, perturbed by his hesitancy, issued expanded orders that governors could receive aid from division commanders without informing the adjutant general in Washington.[24]

When Jenck's troops finally arrived in Elaine, they aided the white posses who had formed to scour the countryside in search of blacks. Of the several hundred arrested blacks, a few were released when a white person vouched for their reliability. In the next few days, Jencks, believing he had been ordered into Elaine to suppress a black rebellion, joined the local officials in questioning blacks, in hopes of obtaining confessions of the planned "insurrection." In a report submitted to the military intelligence office in Washington, the district officer indicated that approximately twenty blacks were killed for resisting arrest; in addition, a black guard at the mass meeting had killed a deputy who came to arrest a bootlegger. In his opinion, the incident was caused by the money-making schemes of a few blacks who informed ignorant blacks that whites were cheating them, and that the black masses should arm themselves. Another investigator reported that he could find no Bolshevist or IWW connection with the riot.[25]

The NAACP put up a long and expensive battle to overturn the convictions of blacks who were the alleged leaders of the Elaine insurrection. The effort met with some success in *Moore v. Dempsey* (1923), when the Supreme Court condemned the atmosphere at the trial on the grounds that the defendants lacked proper counsel and that the courtroom was filled with people who were forestalled from lynching the defendants only because guilty verdicts were assured. Another NAACP battle was designed to keep the governor of Kansas from extraditing Robert Hill, who was charged with impersonating a federal officer. In March 1920, after the federal government had dropped charges against Hill, partly because the only evidence submitted was that some of Hill's organizing literature had indicated that the black union had the support of the United States government, the governor of Kansas decided to refuse the request for extradition from the governor of Arkansas.[26]

A spate of letters encouraging intervention on behalf of the Elaine blacks inundated the Justice Department. William Pickens, president of Morgan State College, wrote on November 26, 1919, that blacks would not riot without good cause and that it was peculiar that with all the blacks killed in Arkansas, only blacks were convicted.[27] In Congress, the House listened with great interest as Thaddeus Caraway of Arkansas interrupted Thomas Heflin of Alabama, who was speaking on the evils of anarchy, to give the white version of the Elaine events.

Caraway hoped that President Wilson would ignore the NAACP pleas for intervention on behalf of the black insurrectionaries because to Caraway, the NAACP was an "association for the promotion of revolution and inciting to riot."[28]

The national government remained greatly concerned about black rebellion and possible ties with radical organizations. On August 1, 1919, J. Edgar Hoover, who was appointed Director of the General Investigating Division of the Justice Department, began compiling a report on black radicals. Secretary of War Baker, in a speech reported in the *New York Times* on October 16, 1919, linked race riots with labor disturbances as forces of social revolution and made it clear that the government would suppress every attempted revolt. The War Department prepared an Emergency Plan White, which specified instructions on riot control duty to guarantee effective suppression of revolts.[29]

Military intelligence maintained its surveillance of black organizational activity to determine the extent of black radicalism. On October 13, 1919, when it was reported that the Urban League, a "radical" black organization, would be holding a convention in Detroit at the same time "Big Bill" Haywood of the IWW was scheduled to speak, attention was focused on Detroit. On October 29, a Chicago operative reported that two brothers, Chan and Charlie Jackson, had left October 17 from Philadelphia for New Orleans with instructions from Big Bill to start trouble among blacks. A description would be sent so they could be watched. Incidents such as this one were commonly reported by military intelligence as evidence of black ties with radical groups.[30]

J. Edgar Hoover's report on radicals was issued in mid-November 1919. Attorney General A. Mitchell Palmer, who submitted the report to the Senate Committee on the Judiciary, gave his opinion based on the findings of the report; he asserted that white radicals who tried to use blacks were sometimes successful. He added that major radicalism on the part of blacks was evident in their threats to retaliate for lynchings and in their demands for social equality; they were defiantly making assertions of equality and, in some cases, superiority. The NAACP responded by stating that blacks were not doing anything disloyal by pressing for black equality.[31] Another response to the report came in a letter to the attorney general from Neval Thomas, a teacher at Dunbar High School in Washington D.C., who expressed the view that

black self-assertion had nothing to do with Bolshevism. In another letter on December 29, 1919, Thomas told Palmer that the government
should pay no attention to "the servile Negro patronage hunter who
would tell you that we are contented, and the discontented [are] few,"
as those persons had no following in the black community. He pointed
out that blacks had been drafted disapproportionately to their number
"to fight for a freedom they have never known, and we their blood kin,
regardless of consequences, are going to get the freedom [for] which
we were told to die."[32]

While Hoover diligently pursued his investigation of possible black
ties with radical organizations, racial violence continued. In Wilson's
administration, in Lexington, Kentucky, in February 1920, a white
mob, intent on lynching a black man who had been convicted of raping a ten-year-old white girl, were denied entrance to the jail by state
troopers. Subsequent threats were made by whites that vengeance
would be taken on the authorities and that the tobacco warehouses of
those who interfered would be burned. A riot ensued in which state
troopers killed four whites and wounded eighteen. The governor
asked for federal aid from General Leonard Wood, the division commander at Camp Zachary Taylor, who sent 953 officers and 46 en-
listed men to aid in controlling the disturbance. At this time, military
intelligence was reassured by the officers involved that there were no
outside agitators or foreigners present, that the rioters thought the
black man should have been lynched, and that white civilians had informed them that even the blacks thought he should be lynched. The
officers added that although twenty percent of the federal troops were
foreign born, they all seemed trustworthy. Despite the violence, the
prisoner escaped injury and was sent to the state penitentiary.[33]

Despite the severe attacks on the NAACP, it continued its protest
against the continuing violence. James Weldon Johnson, Executive
Secretary of the NAACP, irately pointed out to President Wilson that
black voter organizations were being brutalized in Florida and that
federal troops should be used to oversee the elections instead of the
unsympathetic state troops. Assistant Attorney General Robert P.
Stewart responded that the government could do nothing since all the
Reconstruction statutes on voting rights had been repealed. However,
although the NAACP was seldom successful in achieving its goals, the
American public could often pressure the national government into

acting on their demands.[34] The increasing public pressure forced Secretary of War Baker to clarify the constitutional basis for supplying federal troops in domestic disorders. In a memo to the chief of staff on December 2, 1920, he stated that troops should be supplied only when the state had exhausted all its resources and was still unable to deal with the disorder. He might have asserted that when the National Guard was federalized during the war, the states could be assumed to have exhausted all their resources. Instead, he admitted that the constitutional rule had been relaxed during the war because the guard had been drafted into federal service. He thought that as enough time had elapsed for demobilization, governors or legislatures should now apply directly to the president as required by the Constitution and the statutes.

The law was now clarified; but the Wilson administration went no further. Even though the Wilson administration had witnessed the most severe racial disorders since Reconstruction, no really positive response was given. The only legislative attempt to curb racial disorders was made by Representative Leonidus Dyer of Missouri who introduced an antilynching bill in Congress. Dyer proposed that the failure to protect a citizen from lynching be made a denial of equal protection under the Fourteenth Amendment and that the act should include a provision that the county in which the violation occurred pay damages to the family of the victim. Dyer's committee took testimony on lynching and the major riots of 1919 to support the necessity for this legislation. Opponents of the bill responded that antilynching legislation was an NAACP tactic to keep black violators from being punished. Dyer's bill passed in the House but was filibustered to death in the Senate. It was apparent that the resolution of the problem of racial violence would again be passed to the next administration.

12

The
Illusion of a
New Era

T HE OPTIMISM of the beginning of the century was not abandoned; the illusive myths of progress and reform and the
American Dream provided a nucleus of aspirations to which
the deprived could cling. The War to End All Wars was over and a
new isolationism emerged, buoyed by "good times" and public indifference, characterized by toleration of the excesses of prohibition
and the deification of Big Business. Treatment of blacks altered
slightly with the great depression of the thirties and the economic
boom of the wartime forties. Still, there was no national antilynching law, and though the number of persons lynched was decreasing,
blacks were still repressed and racial disturbances continued. All the
same, the widening world audience of the new media of radio and
film brought an immediacy to racial situations that heretofore had
been lacking. The trouble was now on Main Street.

The situation of the blacks became increasingly difficult to ignore
because blacks themselves were more vocal in the pursuit of their
rights. The dispersion of the blacks and the improvement of the status of many members of the black community provided a leadership
which challenged the white community in ways that were less sus-
ceptible to direct coercion. Whether the white governmental officials liked it or not, legislation designed primarily to improve the
welfare of white citizens had the incidental effect of improving the
status of some blacks. Yet, the lynchings and the surveillance of

blacks in an effort to prevent the development of rebellion continued. Racial disturbances recurred, reaching a height in the Detroit riot in 1943, which was suppressed by federal troops.

When the segregationist Wilson administration ended in 1920, many blacks welcomed the election of Warren G. Harding; a Republican administration could be no worse, and it was hoped that the party would fulfill the promises of Reconstruction and enforce a solution to the racial problem. The party platform of 1920 resolutely denounced lynching and supported the Dyer Bill, still pending in Congress. Harding's acceptance speech on July 22, 1920, was very sympathetic to the black cause, reaffirming that blacks deserved full citizenship rights. Optimism increased as a result of Harding's speech to a special session of Congress on April 12, 1921, in which Harding asked Congress to pass legislation against lynching, although he did not specifically mention the Dyer Bill. After making these overtures, Harding pressed Congress no further and made no additional public moves to support the Dyer Bill. Attorney General Harry M. Daugherty was asked to prepare a memorandum for the Congress expressing the opinion that the Dyer Bill was constitutional. In response to the memorandum, an attorney in the Justice Department indicated that the Dyer Bill was in clear violation of the Constitution and that the attorney general "advertises his asininity in holding to the contrary."[1]

Although militant interracial leadership, as represented by the NAACP, was disenchanted with Harding, Marcus Garvey of the Universal Negro Improvement Association (UNIA) thought Harding, in his lukewarm response to racial problems, was headed in the right direction. Since Garveyites rejected social integration as unworkable and impossible and proposed a separate homeland for blacks, they could tolerate anti-integrationist politicians and even the Ku Klux Klan. The integrationists feared Garvey's ability to mobilize the masses and ridiculed his lack of sophistication. Garvey's conviction for stock fraud and subsequent deportation in 1927 removed his disquieting influence from their midst. Black leaders who declined to utilize Garvey's ability to organize the masses, or aid him in his programs, continued to optimistically assert integrationist ideals.[2]

Despite the increasing success of the NAACP in bringing more black rights cases to the attention of the government, racial violence continued. In Tulsa, Oklahoma, in June 1921, blacks were killed or ordered to leave town in large numbers for protesting against peonage. In Little Rock, Arkansas, when threats were made to lynch an accused rapist, the governor, reflecting an increased objection to lynching in the state, requested federal troops from Fort Pike to help protect the prisoner. Citing constitutional and statutory grounds, the War Department refused to send aid until the state had exhausted its resources. Senator Joseph Robinson asked the department to honor the governor's request, but received the same reply. State officials wanted to protect the defendant against lynching; even though they knew that national guardsmen drawn from local people could not be trusted to disperse a mob of fellow citizens, their request for aid was denied.[3]

The Justice Department continued to release its *Hodges*-type responses to requests for federal intervention in outrages involving the civil rights of blacks. C. B. Allison, a concerned citizen, wanted to know if the federal government felt there was cause for action when a citizen was forced to leave a state by violence and intimidation. John Shillady of the NAACP wanted to know if federal troops could be used to protect citizens when lynchings were advertised in advance and the state refused to take action to protect the due process of law. Black farmers in Laconia, Arkansas, were unhappy because they were being forced to work cotton crops without pay and were told that if they sought legal relief, they would be killed. In response, the Justice Department stated that these legal problems were all matters under state jurisdiction.[4]

As the election of 1924 approached, disorders resulting from black voters' attempts to register increased. In September, blacks in Oklahoma complained that they could not find the registrars, since they were appointed at the last minute and moved about without advance notice. After looking at the numerous complaints of intimidation and at the devices used to inhibit black voting, Assistant Attorney General Paul Holland prepared a memorandum for Attorney General Harlan Stone, on October 24, 1924, in which he expressed the view that if the suggested plan to have marshals protect the black voters was instigated, whites would be driven from the polls. In his opinion, the problems reflected the old prejudices of the South toward blacks; if the administration attempted to protect blacks, it would incur the enmity of white people. He suggested that the administration should indicate its intention to exercise its constitutional responsibilities and take no other action, a position ambiguous enough to deter the enmity of anyone.[5]

Blacks, as groups or individually, continued the barrage of written complaints during the Calvin Coolidge administration. In a letter to the administration, Charlie Thompson, a house painter in Florida, wrote that blacks were hired to work for pay, but when they finished, all they received was the point of a Winchester to hurry them away. He expressed the belief that the national government had duped blacks during Reconstruction, and although Garfield had offered some hope, he was dead, and promises of justice had been made ever since with no results. He wanted the government to provide protection and compensation for blacks in the South and to aid migration out of the South. The only response Thompson received was a letter from a staff attorney acknowledging his comments.[6]

Even when the information on civil rights violations reaching the NAACP was not always entirely correct, the organization became increasingly successful in obtaining explanations from the government. In September 1926, Executive Secretary James W. Johnson exploded in a letter to the president when he read in the newspapers that, after a hurricane in Miami, blacks were rounded up and ordered to clean up the debris and that marines had shot a black who refused to cooperate. The Justice Department investigated and reported to Johnson that the order was, in fact, directed at blacks and whites, and that no one was forced to work, although many blacks had willingly responded. The marine commander reported that the marines had only helped to clean up the wreckage; they had not shot anyone.[7]

When the Coolidge administration offered no solutions to the race question, black groups continued to make every possible argument to obtain federal intervention when violence occurred. On April 11, 1930, A. Philip Randolph of the Brotherhood of Sleeping Car Porters and Maids wrote Attorney General William Mitchell that a porter named J. H. Wilkins was found hanging a short distance from the track in Locust, Georgia, after the train had been forced to stop between Atlanta and Macon. The state government would not investigate, and Randolph thought that since Wilkins was an employee in interstate commerce, the government had jurisdiction. Although the

Justice Department responded that working in interstate commerce did not invoke federal jurisdiction, Randolph felt that if the department had been sufficiently interested, it could have found a constitutional basis for interference. On the basis of the Supreme Court decision in *Mondou v. New York, New Haven & Hartford R.R. Co.* (1912), which upheld a federal employees' liability statute covering employees in interstate commerce, and a myriad of other cases on the commerce power of Congress, Randolph's opinion was correct.[8]

The search for a means to invoke federal jurisdiction and to rouse state officials continued during the eight depression years of Franklin Roosevelt's prewar administration. The immediate responses to complaints made by Justice Department officials in the new administration seemed cold-blooded and callous. In July 1933, when Corinne Banks wrote to inform the Justice Department of the murder of her brother in Mississippi in the hope that they would investigate, she was told by Patrick Mallory, an assistant attorney general, that "it . . . is believed that if you enlist the aid of your friends among the white people in that vicinity and appeal to the proper state authorities, your cause will receive the consideration it deserves." Mallory's reply was naive at best.[9]

Numerous violations of constitutional rights went unpunished during the thirties. In August 1933 in Tuscaloosa, Alabama, three teenage blacks, Dan Pippen, Elmore Clark, and A. T. Hardin, were accused of murdering an eighteen-year-old white girl. Lawyers from the International Labor Defense (ILD) organization, the legal aid arm of the Communist Party, wanted to defend the three blacks, but were ordered out of town. The state militia guarded the courthouse while the trial was in progress on August 1, but after the trial, it was decided to move the prisoners from Tuscaloosa to Birmingham for safekeeping. The sheriff, three deputies, and a private detective reported that while driving to Birmingham, a group of armed men abducted the prisoners. The four guards and the sheriff were unharmed. The details of the incident were never clear. Later, two of the youths were found dead; one who was left for dead was found in a shanty and returned to jail. His story of the incident was never made known, as he was too frightened to testify. However, questioning the fact that the sheriff and four guards, who were supposed to defend the prisoners, had escaped the confrontation unscathed, the ILD and the NAACP presented a brief to the Justice Department, declaring that the sheriff should be arraigned to explain the episode. The brief asserted that the sheriff was a government official who had denied persons equal protection and due process of the law under the Fourteenth Amendment, thereby negating the state action policy. The Justice Department decided not to prosecute since it was deemed impossible to prove that the sheriff had willfully deprived the victims of their constitutional rights.[10]

Perhaps the most well-known court decision favorable to blacks during this period is the Scottsboro case. Nine black youths were indicted for the rape of two white girls, both of whom were reportedly prostitutes. The National Guard was called out to protect the defendants from lynching during their trials. After long court battles, charges against five of the nine youths were dropped; four were convicted, three of these were later paroled, and one escaped but later died in a Michigan penitentiary. In the final resolution of the cases, the Supreme Court affirmed the constitutional right to counsel in state criminal cases and the right of blacks to serve on juries.[11]

One of several sensational lynchings occurred when attempts to invoke federal jurisdiction were thwarted. In October 1934, when Claude Neal, an accused rapist of a Florida girl, was kidnapped in Alabama by white citizens and brought back to Florida, blacks gathered to protect him from lynching but were driven off by national guardsmen. Federal action was requested when his lynching was forecast in the newspapers. There was no federal response.[12]

The NAACP continued to press for an antilynching law. Three times, in 1922, 1937, and 1940, an antilynching bill was passed in the House, but failed to get by the Senate. The Justice Department files of the twenties and thirties bulge with letters from blacks and whites on the subject. Most of those who wrote in favor of an antilynching law did not expect federal troops to be called every time a lynching was threatened; rather, they hoped that the successful prosecution of a few cases in which troops controlled the mobs would serve as an example to lynchers.[13] The same answer was given each time a reply was made: murder is not a federal crime. For over fifty years, the lawyers in the Justice Department failed to find a connection between the Constitution and issues of civil rights.

Despite the failure to intervene when lynchings were threatened, a new attitude was evident in Franklin Roosevelt's prewar administrations. The president spoke out clearly against lynching and appealed for antilynching legislation, but to protect other legislation, he compromised with southern Democrats. Antilynching legislation invariably died in the Senate. In 1941, he responded to A. Philip Randolph's threat of a march on Washington by issuing an executive order forbidding discrimination in government employment and defense industries.[14] Roosevelt's Attorney General Frank Murphy set up the Civil Rights Section in the Criminal Division of the Justice Department so that civil rights matters might receive greater attention.

For some unknown reason, racial riots during the Depression were almost nonexistent. Crime also reached a national low. Aside from a riot in Harlem in March 1935 in which no troops were used, significant racial disorders did not erupt again until World War II. In May 1943, when the upgrading of blacks to welding jobs caused a rash of beatings at the Alabama Dry Docking and Ship Building Company in Mobile, management ended the disturbances by separating workers on the job and limiting the openings for black welders. In June in Beaumont, Texas, a pogrom in black neighborhoods resulted from a white woman's complaint that she had been raped; two blacks were killed and seventy-three wounded. The Texas Rangers arrived after the damage was done. After an all-white fact-finding committee announced that efforts would be made to compensate innocent black victims, the city manager and other officials met to determine in advance if blacks were planning reprisals.[15]

In June 1943, "Zoot Suit" riots erupted in scattered cities across the country. In Los Angeles, Chicano and black youths wore suits with wide lapels, broad shoulders, fitted waists, and full pants that were tight at the ankles called *zoot suits*. Exaggerated key chains were a standard part of the outfit. The press harped on the irresponsible criminality of the "zoot-suiters." Soldiers and sailors, claiming that military personnel had been attacked by zoot-suiters, roamed through Mexican-American and black neighborhoods beating, kicking, and tearing the clothes of the "guilty." The police did little except to make way for the rioters. Although most of the enmity was directed toward Mexican-Americans, many blacks were attacked.[16]

The most extensive disturbance of the World War II period exploded in Detroit, a city with a long history of racial troubles; for example, in March 1863, a pogrom through black neighborhoods developed as a response to the claim that a black man had raped a white woman. Federal troops were used to disperse a crowd that tried to storm the jail. Five companies of militia marched from nearby Ypsilanti to subdue the mob. In 1925, a mob tried to force Ossian Sweet, a black physician, out of a house he had bought in a white neighborhood. Police watched the mob gather and only acted when Sweet, along with his relatives and friends, fired at the approaching whites. When eleven blacks, including Sweet, were charged with murder, the NAACP hired Clarence Darrow to defend them. Because of Darrow's eloquence and the impartiality of Judge Frank Murphy, the blacks were acquitted by an all-white jury.[17]

In the twenties and thirties, racial tension in Detroit was provoked by the Ku Klux Klan and the Black Legion, a white group which tried to prevent blacks from obtaining employment. The use of black strikebreakers during the sit-down strikes and the increased migration of blacks into the city in the midst of a severe housing shortage during the thirties and forties further inflamed the atmosphere. In February 1942, rioting broke out when whites gathered to prevent blacks from moving into the Sojourner Truth Federal Housing Project, because they felt the project should be occupied by white people. Over two weeks later, when whites realized that the federal government would not give the project to them, the blacks were finally able to occupy the building.[18]

The first massive Detroit riot began on Sunday, June 20, 1943, when a series of affrays occurred between whites and blacks. The incidents increased in frequency and severity, as whites began attacking blacks who happened to be outside their own neighborhoods, especially on Woodward Avenue, the main thoroughfare of the city. In the black neighborhoods, blacks destroyed and looted stores owned by whites and attacked whites whenever they encountered them. The police were apparently more lenient with white violators than black ones, as depicted in one photograph which shows a white man beating a black who is being held by two policemen. Thirty-four persons were killed in the violence, twenty-five blacks and nine whites. Fifteen of the blacks, and none of the whites, were killed by policemen. Of the nineteen hundred persons arrested, three-fourths were black.[19]

By 1:00 A.M. Monday, it was clear to military policemen that the riot was of major proportion. The commander of the military police passed this information on to Colonel August M. Krech, who was the

highest military official in Detroit. Krech alerted a military police battalion and met with Mayor Edward Jeffries and Police Commissioner
John Witherspoon in order to review the procedure for obtaining federal troops. They decided that Jeffries had to ask the governor for assistance, who would request aid from General Henry S. Aurand,
commanding the Sixth Service at Chicago, who would then order
Krech to use the troops in the area. The whole process would take
about forty-five minutes.

No request was made for troops immediately, because Mayor Jeffries thought the riot was over. However, at 9:00 A.M. on Monday,
when the rioting intensified, Jeffries called Governor Harry F. Kelly,
who called General Aurand's office at the Sixth Service Command.
The officials in Detroit thought federal troops would arrive immediately; however, General Aurand's staff in Chicago interpreted Kelly's
call as a *possible* request. While they waited to hear from him again,
Aurand began reading a textbook on aid to civilian authorities, put
troops on stand-by orders, and sent Brigadier General William
Guthner to Detroit to take command when, and if, a formal request
was made.

Meanwhile, Jeffries and black leaders met with no success when
they tried to subdue the rioters. The army staff in Washington received a call from Aurand, who wanted to know if he could use infantry troops in addition to the military police. The staff, recognizing
that the riot was similar to those outlined in Emergency Plan White,
the official army manual for riot control duty, did not bother to inform the president, but decided that military police could be used to
protect stores related to the Defense Department or the war effort.
Aurand ordered troops to guard an outlet where weapons were kept,
while the army staff hesitated in ordering a large number of troops
into Detroit.

On his way to Detroit, General Guthner read the army regulations
and concluded that he could not use troops until martial law was declared by the president and informed Aurand of the regulation upon
his arrival in Detroit. Governor Kelly, who was in Detroit by that
time, did not want martial law declared because he did not wish the
American public to think the situation was as uncontrollable as it was.
As the Michigan National Guard had been federalized for the war effort, the remaining volunteer state troops were asked to mobilize.

However, only thirty-two state troopers were in touch with the governor's office two hours later, and they did not have transportation to the area. Kelly went on the radio and declared a state of emergency in the three counties surrounding Detroit. When Aurand was informed of the developing problems, he called the army staff in Washington, who finally talked to the Secretary of War Henry Stimson about the situation. In accordance with the form in Emergency Plan White, a presidential proclamation extending federal aid was drafted. Aurand authorized Guthner to send military police battalions into action, and they rapidly dispersed the rioters with gas grenades and rifle butts. After the riot was somewhat subdued, Aurand called Washington again and was told that Governor Kelly had to request troops from the president. Kelly telephoned Roosevelt at Hyde Park, whereupon Roosevelt signed the presidential proclamation immediately. More military police and an infantry division was called into action, and the riot was quickly ended the next day.

The usual investigations and expressions of shock followed the riot. The Dies Committee, predecessor of the House Un-American Activities Committee, wanted to pursue claims that Japanese had inflamed blacks into rioting. With Thurgood Marshall as chief interrogator, the NAACP took affidavits and cited examples of police brutality. A citizen's committee composed of the district attorney general, the police commissioner, and the local prosecutor concluded that despite black complaints of prejudicial treatment in their arrest and the disportionate number of blacks convicted, the judiciary, police, and prosecutor had been fair. They concluded that the riot was caused by blacks.

The bungling efforts by city, state, and national authorities to invoke federal assistance in the Detroit situation typify the negligence of authorities in acquainting themselves with the appropriate means for invoking federal aid. The army Emergency Plan White was still available and had been revised from time to time since 1919. Army regulations in force in 1943 outlined the proper constitutional and statutory procedure for obtaining troops, but cited an exception: if public property of the United States was endangered, or an equivalent emergency made it necessary to act immediately, the army commander could take action, reporting the situation immediately to the adjutant general for the information of the president. This was the kind of action initiated in slave revolts, without any express authorization for it, and was in the spirit of the 1919 orders issued by Newton Baker, which were revoked in 1920, but later reissued. In this case, the authorities had plenty of time to inform the president, but apparently were not familiar with the regulations, Emergency Plan White, or Section 333 of the *United States Code* (see Appendix).

After the riot, President Roosevelt wrote to Secretary of War Stimson, stating that he understood from the attorney general that there was confusion on how to obtain federal troops. He ordered that a memorandum explaining the proper procedure be prepared and circulated to service commands. Under Secretary of War Robert Lovett replied that a memorandum had already been prepared and sent to service commands and governors and that Emergency Plan White and the army regulations were already at every command post before the riot. It was believed that at least in the future, officials could obtain federal troops immediately in order to prevent loss of life and property.

While the riot raged, the House of Representatives listened to Clare Hoffman of Michigan explain that while he commended the president for sending troops, Frank Murphy, labor leaders, and the president himself were responsible for the disorders, along with Secretary of Labor Frances Perkins, who had aggravated conditions by supporting sit-down strikes. Hoffman added that the seizure and retention of private property during labor disputes had set the stage for the riot, and that the only remedy was a return to law and order with justice. William Lambertson of Kansas agreed with Hoffman. However, John E. Rankin of Mississippi stated that those congressmen who supported the anti-poll tax amendment were responsible; since riots were caused by "uppity" blacks and race-mixing, the sooner everyone accepted segregation, the sooner it would be more peaceful for all races.[20]

There was, however, some immediate benefit from the lessons learned in the Detroit riot. Mayor Fiorello La Guardia of New York City sent two high-ranking officers to Detroit to see how the riot was handled. When, on August 1, a policeman shot a black soldier who interfered with the arrest of a black woman, New York was prepared for the resulting rumors and disorder. Thousands of blacks swarmed into the streets, attacking policemen, pulling fire alarms, smashing windows, and looting stores. The mayor immediately cut off all traffic to the area, walked the streets with black leaders, kept all policemen on duty, and made a radio speech explaining the incident. Six truckloads of military police were sent by the army to clear out all military personnel so they would not be involved. By the next day, everything was under control. Even though five blacks were killed and four hundred blacks and forty policemen injured, the riot did not become a clash between white and black citizens as had the one in Detroit; no white gangs formed and the area was isolated from white neighborhoods. Even though white persons walked through the ghetto unarmed, they were not touched. During the riots, shops that were owned by blacks or had "colored" scrawled in the windows were spared destruction. Policemen who were, to blacks, symbols of white authority, white-owned ghetto property, and white businesses which refused to employ blacks were the major targets.[21]

A number of other riots and clashes between black and white soldiers and citizens during World War II were caused by Jim Crowism or attempts to put "uppity" blacks in their places, but they were suppressed by local or military police; no further invocation of federal aid was necessary. The American Civil Liberties Union (ACLU) published a pamphlet on riot prevention which suggested that rumor control centers be set up in tension-ridden communities. In addition, the pamphlet discouraged police brutality and described how to obtain federal troops quickly. Its conclusions were left to gather dust with all the commission reports and suggestions accumulated over the past thirty years.[22]

However, there was evidence of a new attitude on the part of the national administration in the wake of the wartime riots. Attorney General Francis Biddle made several public speeches in 1943 and 1944 which underscored the administrative concern about the problems of race and racial violence. On November 11, 1943, he told a meeting of the Jewish Theological Seminary in New York City that the recent disorders were not fostered by Axis propaganda. His greatest concern was the "corroding effect" racial violence had upon the friends of America and the American people. Biddle asserted that under existing law, the federal government could take no action in such cases. However, he rejected the idea of conscious governmental effort to mold public opinion on the subject, believing instead that community action on the local level could create a climate in which states could prosecute violators and remove the causes of racial disorders.[23]

Also in November, Biddle informed a group of black lawyers, meeting at the National Bar Association, that he feared a recurrence of race rioting "at any moment" and that he was "profoundly disturbed by ever-growing racial tension." The attorney general blamed the following five factors for racial unrest: war tension, bad housing, reduced police protection through a manpower shortage, the poor treatment of black servicemen, and the "contradiction between our profession of faith in democracy and our acts." Charles H. Houston, a black member of the District of Columbia Bar, suggested that the Justice Department ought to more actively intervene whenever a citizen's civil rights were unprotected locally. The fruits of a constitutional revolution in federalism, in which the Supreme Court approved the expanded use of federal authority to control the economy after the court-packing fight of 1937, had not yet been used by the Justice Department in the area of race relations. But the administration was willing to speak out publicly on the issue and, in doing so, helped to mold public opinion. Part of this willingness was perhaps in recognition of the unpleasant analogy between American racism and the Nazi attitude toward the Jews.[24]

A more enlightened attitude toward extending federal protection in racial incidents in the absence of state action, was, in fact, emerging. The new departure was in part due to the constitutional evolution of federalism achieved during the New Deal. The national government stepped into the vacuum created by state inability and took responsibility for welfare measures, economic planning, and commercial regulations in an unprecedented manner. Although the exigencies of prosecuting a war against the Nazis partly necessitated this new policy, hope was revived that perhaps the government could find some effective means of dealing with black oppression and racial violence.

13

Toward Federal Protection

HE END of World War II heralded the advent of the atomic age, the cold war, and a revived "red scare" of McCarthyism. As the economic and military influence of the United States enlarged greatly, Americans took on a new and unaccustomed role of responsibility in international affairs. Americans were not particularly comfortable in this new role, nor were they accustomed to the constant international spotlight on their internal problems. It rapidly became evident that the economic prosperity of the war years, as well as new postwar responsibilities, engendered significant social changes. The administrations of Harry Truman and Dwight D. Eisenhower saw the beginnings of an era of reform in race relations. Mounting pressure from black individuals and civil rights groups, as well as increased white sympathy, and the enfranchisement of large numbers of blacks in northern urban areas whose votes aided Truman's victory in 1948, gave impetus to reform. The cold war, the struggle for economic and social development in the nonwhite nations, and the pressure from organizations such as the NAACP which now possessed adequate financial, technical, and legal resources all were factors that made this new reform politically expedient. A new pattern of enforcing old laws and enacting new ones evolved. The constitutional revolution in federalism ushered in by the New Deal provided the national government with a framework in which to utilize federal military power to realize and enforce these new policies.

Initial steps in reform were slow to come. In the Supreme Court case of *Screws v. United States* (1945), the shadow cast by the *Hodges* doctrine was lengthened. The Court refused to affirm the murder conviction of a sheriff in Baker County, Georgia, who had brutally and fatally beaten a black man, Robert Hall, who was accused of stealing a tire. It had been impossible to secure a murder conviction in a state court; the Civil Rights Section of the Justice Department, taking an enlightened view of the statutes, had decided to attempt a federal conviction despite the *Hodges* tradition. The statute under which the sheriff was indicted required proof that the deceased had been *willfully* deprived of his right to trial in a court, not merely evidence that he had been beaten to death. Four justices concluded that, at the federal trial, the instruction on the statute given to the jury had not been clear. However, the justices were not only unsure whether the jury had understood this technical distinction but also unsure whether the sheriff had had the specific intent to willfully deprive the black man of his constitutional rights. Justice Wiley B. Rutledge thought the conviction should be affirmed, but in order to have a majority, he concurred with William O. Douglas, Harlan F. Stone, Hugo L. Black, and Stanley F. Reed in a reversal. Justice Frank Murphy dissented separately and voted to affirm the conviction. He asserted that the sheriff knew he lacked the authority, and was, in fact, forbidden from beating his prisoner to death. Owen J. Roberts, Felix Frankfurter, and Robert H. Jackson dissented because the effect of the majority opinion was to assert federal jurisdiction in such cases, and they reasoned that in enacting the statute, Congress had no intention of interfering with areas of state responsibility; the sheriff, if he was guilty of a crime, was guilty of the state crime—murder. In view of the legacy of the past, the last three dissenters were saying, in effect, that the sheriff should not be punished.[1]

On December 5, 1946, President Truman created the President's Committee on Civil Rights, which was charged to investigate and determine where and how governmental authority could be strengthened to safeguard the civil rights of the people. To redress inequalities, the committee proposed expansion of the Civil Rights Section in the Justice Department, establishment of a permanent Commission on Civil Rights, and a federal antilynching act. A Fair

Employment Practices Commission (FEPC) law and new legislation covering voting rights and criminal procedures were also suggested. In a special message to Congress on February 2, 1948, Truman urged the passage of this recommended legislation. Although Truman's program met strong resistance in Congress, many of the recommendations were effected in the next twelve years. Executive orders, court decisions, and legislation desegregated the armed forces and created fuller opportunity for middle-class and educated blacks in education and some other areas of American life.[2]

Although lynching and jailhouse riots had diminished, three sensational episodes raised the question of federal intervention during Truman's presidency. On February 25, 1946, in Columbia, Tennessee, a black woman and her son were jailed. The son had reportedly knocked a white man, who had slapped his mother, through a plate glass window. A white mob gathered at the jail with the intent to "punish" the two prisoners. Four city policemen were shot when they entered the tense black district. The five hundred state troopers and national guardsmen who were ordered into the area arrested at least one hundred blacks. Thurgood Marshall, then special counsel for the NAACP, alleged that the troopers had roped off the black section and fired indiscriminately at black residents. Two of the blacks arrested were reportedly machine-gunned to death by state troopers at the jail. Walter White, executive secretary of the NAACP, as well as spokesman for other black and white organizations, sent letters and telegrams to Attorney General Tom C. Clark and Truman, pointing to the denial of due process of law and demanding federal intervention to protect blacks in Columbia. Blacks were particularly incensed to discover that Clark had delegated responsibility for an investigation to a local district attorney who was a white resident of Columbia. Apparently, there was no federal intervention.[3]

An even more sensational racial incident in the summer of 1946 was cause for great public and administrative concern. Two black men and their wives were passengers in a car driven by a white farmer who had provided bond for one of the blacks who had been jailed for allegedly stabbing his white employer during a dispute. Near Monroe, Georgia, twenty masked white men surrounded the car, forced the four blacks out, and proceeded to pump approximately sixty shots into their victims, leaving the bodies alongside the road. Black and liberal white individuals and organizations, appalled by this horrifying incident, were skeptical of a prosecution by Georgia state officials, and they wrote President Truman and Attorney General Clark, demanding federal intervention in the case.[4]

President Truman ordered Clark to take every action to apprehend and convict the murderers. Clark began an FBI investigation but turned the results over to state officials, concluding there was no basis for federal prosecution. Fifty black women from the National Association of Colored Women (NACW) began picketing outside the White House. James Carey, secretary-treasurer of the Congress of Industrial Organizations (CIO), sent the president and the attorney general messages urging action to supplement the efforts of "admittedly impotent" local officials. Rewards totaling $12,500 were reportedly offered by various groups.[5]

By October 1946, no criminal proceeding had begun. Attorney General Clark, at a meeting of the *New York Herald Tribune*'s "Fifteenth Annual Forum on Current Problems," said that he would ask that the facts gathered by the FBI be presented to a federal grand jury, possibly permitting conviction for a civil rights violation, since no state indictments for murder had been initiated. Oliver Harrington of the NAACP demanded to know why a federal government capable of tracking down every single spy in World War II was curiously unable to determine who was responsible for or involved in incidents of racial violence in Tennessee and in Georgia. He admonished the government for its lack of convictions in lynching cases over the years and maintained that "the government should spend less time finding legal reasons for not acting and more time acting in behalf of human justice." However, Clark asserted that the government's record for prosecuting civil rights cases was improving; during his sixteen-month tenure, there had been three hundred investigations, twenty-three prosecutions, six convictions, eight acquittals, and nine persons were awaiting trial.[6]

In June 1949, after two years of sporadic racial violence, including the North Carolina lynching of a black prisoner who had allegedly raped a white woman and the acquittal of twenty-eight defendants who had admitted lynching a black man in Greenville, South Carolina, Attorney General Clark urged Congress to pass an antilynching act. Before the House Judiciary Committee, whose chairman, Emmanuel Celler, had drafted a new antilynching bill, Clark said it was imperative that the federal government have the authority to prosecute lynchers, even when no action was requested by the state. According to the Court decisions in the *Hodges* and *Screws* cases, federal prosecution was illegal even for a civil rights violation unless some state action was involved in the violation.[7]

When Clark was elevated to the Supreme Court, the new attorney general, J. Howard McGrath, still faced complaints of lynching and racial violence. In Miami, Florida, in December 1951, Harry T. Moore, state coordinator of the NAACP, was killed when his house was bombed. The bombing was reportedly in retaliation for Moore's efforts to force the prosecution of a sheriff who allegedly shot two handcuffed blacks in his custody. The two black men had been granted a new trial by the Supreme Court after being convicted of rape by an all-white jury. Walter White, executive secretary of the NAACP, the National Council of the Churches of Christ, and numerous veterans' and social organizations wrote McGrath demanding a federal investigation. But no investigation was made.[8]

Although individual acts of violence like the bombing in Miami continued, racial violence during the next few years was largely associated with attempts to desegregate schools and public accommodations. The Supreme Court decision in *Brown v. Board of Education*, which declared that segregated schools violated the Fourteenth Amendment, brought blatant hostility. At first, the NAACP was forced to attack individual school systems on a case-by-case basis. One antagonistic response to these activities came on March 12, 1956, when a group of southern senators and congressmen presented a "Southern Manifesto," largely the work of Senator Sam Ervin, Jr., of North Carolina, which asserted their intention to use every legal tactic to resist desegregation.[9]

President Eisenhower, who had no reputation as a great liberal on the race question, but who was a former army officer with a firm belief in the importance of obeying orders, received reports of numerous civil rights violations in 1955 and 1956. The FBI reported that the Communist Party was trying to curry favor with the NAACP by its assertion that federal troops should have been sent to avenge the murder of Emmett Till for whistling at a white woman in Mississippi in August 1955. The Montgomery, Alabama, bus boycott, led by Martin

Luther King, Jr., in December 1955, resulted in bombing and violence. White Citizen's Councils and the Ku Klux Klan were using
threats and intimidation to prevent blacks from achieving desegregation and equal voting rights. In response to these racial problems, the
administration proposed the Civil Rights Act of 1957, which established the Civil Rights Commission, made the Civil Rights Section a
division in the Justice Department, and gave the government limited
injunctive powers in voting rights disputes.[10]

While the Civil Rights Act was under consideration, the administration's attention turned toward the school crisis in Little Rock, Arkansas. Although federal troops had been used under Section 332 of
the *United States Code* (see Appendix) on numerous occasions to enforce compliance with federal laws, such as the Fugitive Slave Act, and
injunctions in labor disputes, the incident at Little Rock was the first
occasion in American history when federal troops were used to enforce a federal court order favorable to blacks. In 1956, when Autherine Lucy's presence at the University of Alabama set off rioting,
university officials had suspended her, ostensibly for her own safety.
The university and state officials ignored a federal judge's readmission
order. She had been admitted to the school without state interference
and expelled for criticizing the board of trustees. Eisenhower was
asked about the case and explained that it was a matter of state concern. The administration accepted FBI Director J. Edgar Hoover's
warning of Communist influence on the issue.[11]

But in Little Rock, circumstances were different. Eisenhower could
not so easily deflect a response to state defiance. The Little Rock
school board, complying with the Supreme Court's direction, had announced a plan for gradual desegregation, beginning with their senior
high school in the fall of 1957. As desegregation day approached, opponents filed a petition in the Arkansas State Chancery Court to prevent the plan from taking effect. On August 29, Governor Orval
Faubus appeared before the court to express his concern over the possibility of violence if the court refused to order a stay. The chancery
court issued a restraining order forbidding desegregation in September. The federal district court, upon the request of the school board,
ordered noninterference with desegregation. An obvious clash of federal and state authority existed.[12]

On desegregation day, Governor Faubus ordered the Arkansas National Guard to prevent the nine black children from entering the school. The school board responded by asking the black children not to appear. However, the children arrived on September 3 and were turned away. Faubus had defied the federal court. The school board, stymied, asked the federal court for an exemption from contempt proceedings for not executing the court order. Judge Ronald Davies ordered desegregation to proceed. When Faubus continued his defiance, the school board asked Judge Davies to set aside his order. He refused. The United States entered the case as a Friend of the Court and set September 20 as the date for a hearing on whether to enjoin Faubus's behavior. Brooks Hays, congressman from Little Rock, who later lost his seat for his role in the controversy, offered to act as intermediary between Eisenhower and Faubus. A meeting was arranged between the two at Newport, Rhode Island, on September 14. At the conclusion of that meeting, Faubus agreed that upon returning to Arkansas, he would keep the National Guard on duty and admit the black children, but he did not comply. On September 20, without the presence of Faubus or his lawyers, the federal court prohibited him from further interference. Faubus had again thumbed his nose at the judiciary by refusing to appear.[13]

That night, Faubus announced that although he would remove the Guard, he planned to appeal the court order and hoped black parents would keep their children away from the school in the meantime. In effect, this action would have postponed desegregation indefinitely. By Monday, September 23, three weeks of federal irresolution had passed. The National Guard had been removed, and a white mob had gathered at the school to enforce vigilante justice. Nine black children were brought into the school through a side door; when the mob discovered their presence, they attacked the police. The mayor ordered the black children removed in the interest of their safety. At last, the issue seemed clear enough to the president. Attorney General Brownell indicated that since the governor had abdicated his mandatory duty under Article VI of the Constitution to remove obstruction to federal law, the president could use troops to enforce the court orders. Eisenhower persuaded himself that Little Rock was not an issue of racial integration but of insurrection, like Shays's Rebellion. "Well, if we have to do this, and I don't see any alternative," Eisenhower told Brownell, "then let's apply the best military principles to it and see that the force we send there is strong enough that it will not be challenged, and will not result in any clash." Eisenhower issued a proclamation asserting that the events were willful obstruction of the laws of Arkansas and the United States and constituted a denial of equal protection under the Fourteenth Amendment. He commanded all law violators to cease and desist.[14]

When the mob gathered again the next morning, Mayor Woodrow Mann frantically wired that troops were needed. Eisenhower immediately ordered five hundred paratroopers from nearby Fort Campbell, Kentucky, to Little Rock. Another five hundred troops arrived later in the day. Meanwhile, Eisenhower issued an executive order authorizing the use of force and federalizing the Arkansas National Guard. By the next morning, the mob was dispersed with few injuries. The nine blacks entered school and stayed the whole day. The crisis subsided. On October 14, Eisenhower approved withdrawing half the federal troops and defederalizing four-fifths of the guard. On October 23, the students entered the school without military escort; on November 23, the last paratroopers left the city to the protection of the national guardsmen, who remained on duty until the end of the school year.[15]

While Eisenhower acted too slowly to suit some civil rights supporters, who could not understand why he waited three weeks, and too quickly for opponents who thought he should not have acted at all, his broad view of presidential authority under the Constitution and statutes had offered him other alternatives. Even in the face of the *Brown* decision and the federal court orders in the case, he could have asserted that the mob violence outside the high school did not require a federal response. Had he chosen this course, Eisenhower would have found support in a mass of precedents; however, public opinion at home and abroad would not have accepted that interpretation. In a nation greatly concerned about its world image, a new view of old statutes was required. In any event, the Supreme Court affirmed Eisenhower's position in *Cooper v. Aaron* in 1958, when they declared that the constitutional rights of children could not be nullified by state officials or by evasive schemes for segregation. However, Arkansas did not give up the fight for segregation. The legislature closed all high schools in September 1958, only to have them declared reopened by a federal court order in June 1959. Two blacks entered Central High

School in Little Rock that fall after police and firemen dispersed a mob of two hundred and fifty whites.[16]

In Congress, the Little Rock crisis generated contrary views from detractors and supporters of civil rights with little enlightening constitutional debate. In the House, John Bell Williams of Mississippi wanted to know why troops were not sent to Brooklyn when newspapers reported incidents of racial strife in the schools. He thought the Little Rock crisis substantiated arguments for opposing federal aid to public schools, as the government would then have additional authority over the schools. Elijah Forrester of Georgia thought that the soldiers sent to Little Rock should have been used to root out communism around the world. In the Senate, Jacob J. Javits of New York and Richard L. Neuberger of Oregon strongly defended the president's position, while Joseph C. O'Mahoney of Wyoming denounced Thomas H. Kuchel of California for inserting a speech on the subject given by Assistant Attorney General Warren Olney III into the *Congressional Record*. Olney had asserted that James O. Eastland of Mississippi and John L. McClellan of Arkansas, who vitriolically attacked the president, were on the committee that had reenacted Sections 332 and 334 of the *United States Code*, which constituted the legal basis for the president's action. O'Mahoney pointed out that statutes which are only revised and codified are not reenacted at the same time. Moreover, Eastland and McClellan, although appointed to the committee, had taken no part in the revision, which left them free to criticize the president.[17]

The school desegregation crisis persisted after Little Rock, as southern states searched for ways to maintain *de jure* segregation. When the Louisiana legislature attempted interposition in defiance of a federal court order in November 1960, President Eisenhower retreated to the traditional noninterventionist position by asserting that marshals should first be used to enforce court orders. Large numbers of marshals poured into New Orleans. The Supreme Court in 1960 reaffirmed the federal position on interposition and discounted the legal significance of massive resistance as a tactic. The violence against, and harassment of, black students, however, continued.[18]

The Justice Department pursued few racial violence cases, reserving its response for the highly visible episodes. Terrorism was now aimed at blacks seeking to register to vote and at their white sympathizers. By the end of 1958, Justice Department officials had noted six racially motivated killings in the South in the first four years of the administration; twenty-nine other shootings; forty-four beatings; five stabbings; forty-one bombings of homes, churches, and schools; and seven burnings of similar buildings. The lynching of Mack Charles Parker, a black man accused of raping a white woman, was another in a long line of lynching cases. In April 1959, Parker's abduction from an unguarded jail in Poplarville, Mississippi, generated widespread publicity. President Eisenhower, hoping for a quick apprehension of the violators, pledged FBI assistance in solving the case. After seven days of searching, the FBI found Parker's body in the Pearl River.[19]

Seven months later, Attorney General William P. Rogers told a press conference that the handling of the Mississippi case was "a travesty on justice." The FBI had spent eighty thousand dollars investigating the Parker case and had given its report to Mississippi officials to be used in a state murder prosecution. However, the state grand jury adjourned without indictments; none of the FBI witnesses or evidence had been used. Rogers said he believed in states' rights, but state irresponsibility should be remedied by the federal government. The Justice Department attempted to obtain indictments from a federal grand jury in Mississippi on the basis that Parker's civil rights had been violated. From a local jury of one black and twenty white residents, twelve affirmative votes could not be obtained for an indictment. Roy Wilkins, executive secretary of the NAACP, suggested that Rogers make the FBI report public; his request was not honored.[20]

Toward the end, the Eisenhower administration litigated a few cases designed to punish racial harassment of blacks seeking to register and vote. The idea that blacks could protect themselves from violence by electing responsive state and local officials instead of asking for federal help could not be validated if they could not vote. The Justice Department filed four suits, only one of which ended in a conviction, a penalty of two and a half months in prison, and a $5,000 fine.[21]

Police violence against blacks remained a persistent problem. The Justice Department reported that in the first two and a half years after its establishment in 1957 the Civil Rights Division had received 1,328 reports of police brutality. Only 42 civil suits resulted, with *no* verdicts in favor of the plaintiff. Of 52 prosecutions for police brutality, 46 ended in acquittals.[22]

Despite the failure of prosecution in such incidents as the Parker case and despite the continued lynching and racial violence, halting steps toward reform had been taken. The Truman and Eisenhower administrations had responded to increasing public pressure and to the exigencies of maintaining moral leadership in the world with rhetorical commitments to racial equality and sporadic enforcement. Military power had been used to enforce a court order favorable to black people in Little Rock, though resistance to school desegregation elsewhere went unchallenged. Federal officials—though not those in the FBI—suggested that federal intervention and protection might be proper to prevent the indiscriminate murder of black people and, when that failed, to prosecute their killers. There was hope that constitutional authority could be used to equitably adjust black-white relations.

14

The States
Act Despite
Themselves

T HE SHIFT from neglect to grudging intervention in cases of black-white violence and discrimination, already under way when John F. Kennedy was elected president, continued into the 1960s. Government officials in the Roosevelt, Truman, and Eisenhower administrations, however reluctantly, had established precedents for executive action to provide protection for African-Americans when state governments abdicated their responsibilities. The anti-discrimination decisions of the Supreme Court in *Brown v. Board of Education* and its progeny, the increasing influence of liberal ideas in the white community, and the exigencies of moral leadership in international affairs provided a favorable context for a vigorous federal response to racial violence. But political considerations—local officials in the South were Democrats and southerners played key roles in the Congress—always concerned presidents.

On February 1, 1960, when four black freshman from North Carolina Agricultural and Technical State University at Greensboro sat down at a segregated lunch counter and refused to move, the sit-in era began. Countless young blacks were caught up in the proliferating movement on college campuses across the South. White college students joined the movement, out of which the Student Non-violent Coordinating Committee (SNCC) evolved. Southern police responded to sit-ins and civil rights marches with fire hoses, tear gas, beatings, and arrests. When white liberals, as well as blacks in Martin Luther King's Southern Christian Leadership Conference (SCLC) and the Congress of Racial Equality (CORE), joined and supported the movement, the conscience of the nation was stirred. There was no immediate federal response; Eisenhower regarded the sit-ins and the response they engendered as completely within the purview of the states. When the cases of the protesters who were arrested for violation of state trespass and disorderly conduct statutes were appealed to the Supreme Court, the Court did not resolve the issue of whether the use of state law-enforcement officers to protect the property of those who practiced racial discrimination violated the Fourteenth Amendment. The Court decided some cases in favor of the protesters on technical grounds of statutory interpretation and remanded others for reexamination by lower courts. The Court chose not to face head-on the problem of state trespass statutes which conflicted with constitutional prohibitions against racial discrimination.[1]

In 1961, the New Abolitionists focused their attention on segregation in interstate transportation, particularly on passenger buses. Although outlawed by the Supreme Court as being in conflict with the Interstate Commerce Act of 1887, segregation existed as a matter of common practice throughout the South. No administration had directed the Interstate Commerce Commission to order discontinuance of this practice in conformity with the court decisions. In 1947, CORE Director James Farmer had taken a freedom ride to see if the court decisions were being obeyed; he found they were not.[2]

On April 28, 1961, Farmer wrote President Kennedy that freedom rides would be attempted again and asked for federal protection. Although none was given, the rides proceeded. A bus was burned at Anniston, Alabama, and some of the riders were attacked there and in Birmingham. An FBI informant, Gary Thomas Rowe, who was in the local Klavern, warned his FBI contact in advance that the Birmingham police had promised to give the Klan fifteen unmolested minutes to beat up the riders when they arrived. The local special agent in charge informed his office in Washington without mentioning Rowe's name, and then "warned" the police department about the Klan attack, pretending he knew nothing of their involvement in order to protect Rowe.[3]

The police, of course, did nothing. The beatings, in which Rowe participated, proceeded on schedule. After massive press coverage, Attorney General Robert Kennedy asked the state to give the riders protection. Governor John Patterson agreed at first and then changed his mind. He was trying to balance a desire to prevent demands for federal intervention against the political need to avoid protecting the riders. As the riders continued across Alabama, the Kennedys tried to reach the governor, but were not able to do so. On May 20, Patterson announced publicly that he would not protect outside agitators.[4]

As the riders approached Montgomery, the FBI warned the Montgomery police in advance that riots might occur when the bus arrived. The police replied that local authorities could keep peace. When the bus arrived, the freedom riders, as well as sympathetic blacks and whites who had no connection with the protest, were attacked.[5]

Robert Kennedy tried to reach the governor again; when he was unable to do so, the president accepted what he thought was the least politically sensitive way for him to resolve the problem. He sent marshals, Border Patrol, and Bureau of Alcohol and Treasury agents to Alabama and obtained a federal court injunction against the Ku Klux Klan and others who interfered with the riders. Kennedy's action was based on the constitutional obligation of the national government to enforce the right to travel between states if the states failed to do so. The president decided not to use federal troops, which would have needed the governor's request and the issuance of a proclamation. He simply notified the attorney general of a threat to the public peace and asked him to enforce federal law. In molding the enforcement group into place the Justice Department used riot control instructions developed by Attorney General Rogers after Little Rock.[6]

Having take the first step, the administration sent Deputy Attorney General Byron White to Montgomery and assigned more marshals to him. When Martin Luther King, Jr., came to address a black meeting at a church, a mob of white youths, gathered outside, was dispersed by marshals and local policemen. The widespread publicity about the freedom rides and the federal intervention forced state officials to take action if they wanted to insist on their ability to keep order. Governor Patterson proclaimed martial law, called out the National Guard, denounced federal interference, and blamed the disturbance on the federal marshals. The American Nazi Party of George Lincoln Rockwell announced that they planned to protest against the riders by sending a "hate bus" from Washington to New Orleans. When the Nazis arrived in Montgomery, marshals escorted them through town.[7]

As the riders proceeded across the state into Mississippi, Alabama congressmen protested to the attorney general against federal intervention. Kennedy responded that marshals would be removed when state officials kept order and conformed to federal law. Consequently, the riders were escorted to the state line where Mississippi patrol cars took over; Governor Ross Barnett of Mississippi did not want federal marshals to displace his authority. In Jackson, twenty-seven riders, including James Farmer, were arrested for using white facilities. The Justice Department asked the federal district court for an injunction to keep state officials from interfering with interstate travel and also requested black leaders to enforce an end to the rides.[8]

The Kennedy administration wanted urgently to dispose of the whole issue to avoid any further political problems. Attorney General Kennedy agreed to let state officials arrest the freedom riders without interference if the state officials would agree to keep back the mobs. This policy of arrests was designed to undermine the protests. Instead, the publicity brought more and more riders, black and white recruits to the cause, including such figures as Yale University Chaplain William Sloane Coffin.[9]

The attorney general denounced the new riders as not genuine and told the press they would not be protected, winning an expression of gratitude from Alabama Governor Patterson. Although at least two hundred freedom riders were jailed, the press accepted the administration's decision about their nonimportance and stopped reporting the continuing protests. The president and the Justice Department simply abandoned their responsibilities to protect the riders.[10]

In order to end press coverage of the rides, while appearing to be helpful, the attorney general took advantage of a Freedom Riders Coordinating Committee suggestion that the Interstate Commerce Commission issue a ruling clearly establishing the right to ride. At his urging, the commission issued an order forbidding discrimination in interstate travel on September 22, 1961. He then organized a successful effort to channel the energies of civil rights activists into the politically preferable voting rights arena. He explained to the Freedom Riders Coordinating Committee that he would help them to obtain foundation grants to finance their voter registration work and that the federal government could protect them if they were engaged in activities involving the right to vote. Soon direct action civil rights protesters were busily working with the administration to register voters. Blacks had provided significant support to Kennedy's election in 1960 but that had not seemed to lead to the protection of blacks from segregationist violence. The civil rights workers, however, for the moment accepted the theory that black protection would come from exercising the right to vote.[11]

In responding to the freedom rides, the Kennedys showed the same careful concern for the delicate balance between national and local authority in a federal state as had previous administrations. They also exhibited the same sensitivity to the white electorate in the South and discounted the strong motivation of the civil rights activists. The federal government intervened only when repeated efforts to persuade state officials to keep order failed, and it intervened in an extremely limited way.

As whites responded to black voter registration drives with bombings, arson, and shootings, the Justice Department did practically nothing. When the FBI did investigate, they handed over the offenders to the states for enforcement. Robert Kennedy limited his response to statements deploring the violence, apparently forgetting his promises of protection. Assistant Attorney General Burke Marshall, in meetings with civil rights leaders, explained that the Justice Department had limited powers and lacked clear authority and that they must protect themselves. The civil rights workers felt betrayed. They did not expect a national police force but they believed that more aggressive civil rights investigations and prosecutions would deter some of the violence.[12]

Soon, the desegregation of education became front-page news again and forced the Kennedy administration to respond with force. James Meredith, a black Mississippian, decided he wanted to attend the University of Mississippi, the all-white state university in Oxford. Meredith attempted to register at the university in January 1961, but he was turned away. He and the NAACP Legal Defense Fund went to federal court, where they lost at the district level but won in the court of appeals. When the Fifth Circuit Court ordered Meredith's admission, Governor Barnett asserted his intention to defy the court.[13]

When Barnett first announced his position, Attorney General Kennedy pointed out the foolishness of such a course and indicated the willingness of the administration to use marshals to enforce the court order. The state's position clearly defied federal law. On September 20, 1962, when Meredith appeared with marshals to register, Barnett told him that his application for admission had been rejected. On September 23, after repeated efforts to convince Barnett to desist, the Justice Department asked the federal court to have the university officials cited for contempt for failure to comply with the original order to register Meredith. At the hearing, university officials agreed to register him without further delay. Meanwhile, Barnett went into state court and obtained an injunction forbidding university officials to enroll Meredith and issued an executive order directing state police to arrest anyone who tried to arrest or fine a state official in connection with the case.[14]

On September 25, by prearrangement with university officials, Meredith and his marshals appeared in Jackson, Mississippi, where the trustees normally met, to proceed with his registration. Barnett arrived with a group of state troopers and legislators, blocked the doorway, and read a proclamation denying Meredith admission in order to uphold the peace and dignity of the state. By this time, the patience of the administration and the Fifth Circuit Court was exhausted; the court directed the Justice Department to begin contempt proceedings against Barnett and issued a temporary restraining order prohibiting the governor and all others from interfering with its orders.[15]

The next day, when Meredith and his marshals appeared again at the "Ole Miss" campus, state police shoved the marshals back and Lieutenant Governor Paul Johnson denied Meredith admission on the same grounds that Barnett had given the previous day. The Justice Department ordered additional contingents of marshals to the campus and continued negotiation with Barnett.[16]

On September 27, Barnett and Attorney General Kennedy agreed that Meredith and the marshals would confront Barnett and unarmed state policemen at the gate, the marshals would draw their guns, and Barnett would then give way to this show of force. By agreeing to the staged confrontation, Barnett would save face while permitting Meredith to register. However, this little drama was never performed. State police on duty knew nothing of Barnett's negotiation, and a crowd of civilians had gathered to watch the proceedings. Barnett frantically called Attorney General Kennedy saying he had changed his mind because he feared bloodshed might occur. The marshals and Meredith were ordered back to Memphis.[17]

Additional marshals, as well as a support detachment of one hundred army engineers, were ordered into Oxford. On September 28, the court stated that if the governor ignored the order, he would be jailed and fined ten thousand dollars a day until he complied. Meanwhile, the attorney general again stated that Meredith would be enrolled and called attention to federal law which makes it a crime to interfere with the exercise of constitutional rights. Responding to the threat of federal intervention, southern spokesmen referred to the old *posse comitatus* act of 1878, which prohibited the unrestricted use of troops to enforce federal laws. However, the Justice Department correctly pointed out that the act in question applied in all cases, except those in which the Constitution or an act of Congress permitted the use of troops. Article II of the Constitution, which relegates the responsibility for the faithful execution of the laws to the President, as well as the specific powers in federal statutes, was sufficient legal authority for intervention.[18]

While the army engineer troops were on their way to Oxford to set up a tent city and provide food and lodging for the marshals on duty there, Robert Kennedy conferred with Major General Creighton Abrams about the possible use of federal troops, as pressure for federal action was mounting. Meredith's lawyers, Constance Baker Motley and Jack Greenberg of the NAACP Legal Defense Fund, complained about the delay in enforcing the court order; various other black organizations accused the court of being too lenient with Barnett. Citing Mississippi's historical opposition to interposition, Robert Kennedy appealed to Barnett to cease his attempt at nullification.[19]

By Saturday, September 29, the Kennedy administration felt that since all possible alternatives had been exhausted, it was time to use federal force. That afternoon, as they worked on a proclamation, Barnett called with a new plan: while he and his troopers waited at the university in Oxford, Meredith would go to Jackson and be registered; the governor would then complain of federal trickery and the episode would be closed. At 7:00 P.M., the president and Barnett agreed on this subterfuge. Three hours later, Barnett called the attorney general to change the plans and proposed that the marshals and Meredith appear at the university where he would be registered. The administration, rapidly losing confidence in Barnett's promises, agreed with this plan, but ordered army troops to a position nearer the university. The president signed an executive order federalizing the Mississippi National Guard, both for possible service and to prevent Barnett from using them. A cease-and-desist proclamation required by federal law was prepared and signed at the same time. The basis for action cited in the proclamation and order were specific federal enforcement statutes, the necessity for enforcing the court order, and the refusal of Barnett to assure maintenance of law and order.[20]

Early Sunday morning, Secretary of the Army Cyrus Vance telegraphed Barnett that the Mississippi National Guard had been ordered into federal service and informed him of the contents of the proclamation and executive order. Fourteen hundred men, half taken from the 503rd Military Police Battalion at Fort Bragg and the remainder from the 716th Military Police Battalion at Fort Dix, were already ordered to the area. Meanwhile, white people gathered from other parts of the state and the South to defend segregation at "Ole Miss."[21]

When Meredith arrived on campus Sunday evening, he was taken to a dormitory where he was guarded by marshals and state police. Meanwhile, other federal officials on campus worked out registration procedures. An angry crowd gathered, confronting the police, who showed little interest in dispersing them, and began taunting the marshals. By the time President Kennedy went on nationwide television to explain the necessity of federal intervention and ask for peace and order, the marshals on the campus were under heavy attack. They had to use tear gas to drive off the rioters. The students on the campus jeered at the president's plea for calm. Claiming their masks were ineffective against the gas employed by the marshals, the state troopers withdrew from the campus. Paul Guihard, a French reporter, was shot and killed. As the number of marshals injured by shotgun pellets and rocks increased, sixty local national guardsmen were ordered to aid the marshals, but since they had been told by their squadron commander not to bring guns or ammunition, they were largely ineffective. Attempts made by three students and a campus priest to end the riot failed. President Kennedy ordered the army and other National Guard units to move into the campus, but it took them at least two hours to arrive. Meanwhile, Governor Barnett, after his earlier statements indicating acquiescence, went on the air to declare he would never surrender.[22]

However, later that night President Kennedy finally persuaded Barnett to order state troopers to man the roadblocks outside the campus to prevent further incursions of potential rioters. By 3:00 A.M., regular army troops arrived in force, some five hours after they had been ordered to leave Memphis, which was eighty-seven miles away. By morning, twenty-five hundred soldiers were on the campus, and the riot ended. Fifty persons had been injured and a newspaperman and a white bystander killed. After almost two weeks of negotiations between Barnett and the Kennedy administration and several false starts which culminated in violence, Meredith was finally registered without incident. The troops, whose number reached about 23,000, were gradually removed until the last 500 left when Meredith graduated in 1963.[23]

President Kennedy glossed over the racial animus in Mississippi as he let the issue die by moving on to other concerns. In addition to the long-drawn-out negotiations with Barnett, he had tried to placate the sensibilities of Mississippians in other ways. He had black soldiers taken out of the military units sent to Oxford and he, like Governor Barnett, went out of his way to avoid mentioning that Meredith was black. The administration also made sure that the contempt fines imposed on Barnett and Johnson were not collected.[24]

While the Meredith crisis was in process, liberals and conservatives in Congress sparred over the legality of federal intervention in Oxford. In the Senate, New York Republican Jacob Javits described the whole episode as unpleasant, but thought everyone should support the president in the exercise of his duty to uphold the law. Democrat James Eastland of Mississippi inserted a long article in the *Congressional Record* as a definitive statement of the southern constitutional position on the subject; the article outlines one lawyer's opinion that the president cannot use troops to enforce court decisions. Since the laws which he must enforce consist only of statutes, the president, therefore, must rely upon the state for enforcement of court orders, and if the state fails to enforce court orders, the president must have Congress pass a specific law making the court decision law. Then, and only then, would he be justified in interceding.[25]

This argument is easily controverted. The Supreme Court decided in *Erie v. Tompkins* (1938) that the expression *laws* included court decisions as well as statutes. However, in this discussion, it does not make much difference which argument is controlling. If the laws the president must enforce were only statutes, the question of why Congress had not passed laws to outlaw discrimination would arise, instead of why the executive did not enforce the laws already in existence. At the same time, if the president could not use troops to enforce court decisions, the national government would simply have to mobilize enough marshals or let the decision go unenforced.

John C. Stennis of Mississippi, reinforcing his colleague's argument, said that the power to initiate antidiscriminatory actions was not given to the attorney general by the Civil Rights Act of 1957 and that Robert Kennedy was, in fact, initiating Justice Department action in the Meredith case. Javits, responding to the two Mississippians, admitted that ordinarily in Congress, comments could be made about affairs in one's home state without rejoinder from others present. However, he was sponsoring a resolution with Kenneth B. Keating of New York and Paul H. Douglas of Illinois in support of the president's actions. He knew the resolution would be filibustered to death, but thought it should be in the *Congressional Record*. When the resolution was introduced, Eastland intimated it had been prepared by the NAACP. To this, Keating replied that the NAACP had no part in its preparation but he was happy that they were interested. Douglas, in a long speech in defense of Javits's resolution, asserted that he knew southerners were simply prisoners of their institutions, suggesting that once Meredith was in the university, they might discover that he was not so bad. Allen J. Ellender of Louisiana made it known that Meredith had been accepted at other schools, but since he merely wanted to attend a white institution, his motives were suspect. Wayne Morse of Oregon and Hubert Humphrey of Minnesota were concerned that this incident might feed the flames of communist propaganda and mar America's world image.[26]

Once troops were on campus, Morse made a flowery speech commending the president for federalizing the guard before sending in regular troops, an action he thought Eisenhower should have taken in the Little Rock crisis. Herman C. Talmadge of Georgia and Sam J. Ervin of North Carolina felt that although the government had the power to use troops, it was inexpedient to do so. Eastland wished the president would show a similar interest in decontaminating Cuba.[27]

During the discussion, Senator John M. Butler of Maryland demanded the passage of an act which would restrict the jurisdiction of the Supreme Court to giving advisory opinions in cases "the consequence of which will have a serious impact upon the people of a sovereign state, or when the domestic tranquillity is liable to be disrupted and our foreign relations embarrassed." Morse correctly replied that such an act would be unconstitutional, and that the state sovereignty issue had been settled in the Civil War.[28]

In the House, Mississippians and Alabamians castigated the administration while northern liberals defended it. Mississippi's Thomas G. Abernathy said the two states' congressional delegations had asked the Justice Department to wait until Monday when the students would have been prepared for Meredith, but the request was denied. Abernathy made no statement about the abortive negotiations with Barnett. Jamie L. Whitten pleaded that his "poor little Mississippi" had only two hundred state troopers and intimated that it was a shame to ruin a great university for one black. A suggestion was made by Alabama's George W. Andrews that Martin Luther King was the mastermind behind the Meredith incident. Black Congressman Robert Nix of Pennsylvania was not saddened by the plight of "poor" Mississippi, but by the fact that the partial payment on a grievous debt was so long overdue. William F. Ryan of New York agreed with Nix and commended the president for his action.[29]

In April 1963, the administration's difficulties with racial violence escalated when the SCLC began a campaign for jobs and freedom in Birmingham, Alabama. Southern police responded with frenetic repression. When Martin Luther King called for a march on Good Friday, Sheriff Eugene "Bull" Connor procured an injunction forbidding the demonstration. Along with his use of dogs and cattle prods to disband the marchers, Connor arrested King, Ralph Abernathy, and other leaders, who were released after serving fifteen days in jail. As the demonstrations continued, with children taking an active part alongside adults, fire hoses and dogs were increasingly relied upon for crowd control. On May 4, a riveting picture of a police dog held lightly leashed by a police officer so that he could lunge at a demonstrator and bite him in the abdomen was flashed around the world.

President Kennedy, speaking before a group of Americans for Democratic Action (ADA), said that in this situation, the constitution left him powerless; there were no court orders or statutes to enforce. However, Kennedy sent Assistant Attorney General Burke Marshall to Birmingham to mediate a settlement. Meanwhile, the president, Secretary of Defense Robert McNamara, and Treasury Secretary C. Douglas Dillon tried to persuade business leaders to mediate with black leaders on solutions to the crisis. On May 10, an agreement was reached: promotion and hiring would be on a nondiscriminatory basis; black demonstrators would be released on bail or their own recognizance; and a biracial civil rights commission would be established.[30]

Governor George Wallace of Alabama, expressing his dissatisfaction with this agreement, announced that he would never be a party to a compromise on the principle of segregation. On Saturday, May 11, whites responded to his incantations by bombing hotels and houses in black neighborhoods, including the home of King's brother and a motel owned by a wealthy black businessman, A. D. Gaston, where the negotiations for the agreement had taken place. Blacks retaliated by attacking policemen and whites who were in their neighborhoods. The rioting continued until dawn. Wallace finally deployed state troopers, who used shotguns and indiscriminate beating to suppress the blacks.[31]

Disheartened by the precipitous breakdown of the negotiated civil rights settlement and the resulting violence, President Kennedy consulted with his advisors all day Sunday. In the evening, he went on nationwide television to announce that he had alerted army units on bases in the area and had taken preliminary steps to federalize the National Guard. Challenging the president, Governor Wallace stated that as no state request for aid had been made, there was no authority for federal interference. The Justice Department pointed to Section 333 of the *United States Code*, which empowered the national government to intervene when states refused to protect citizens from private violence. The president could use his constitutional powers to move troops about at his discretion. The *Hodges* doctrine, with its limited interpretation of federal power, seemed well on the way to extinction.[32]

On May 13, Birmingham was quiet; threatened with intervention, local police decided they could keep order. President Kennedy assured

Wallace that federal troops would be used only if the state abdicated its responsibilities. Wallace responded by blaming blacks for the trouble. The administration believed events in Birmingham were deplorable but the level of violence had not been sufficient to warrant federal intervention until the rioting on Saturday night. When a new administration took control of Birmingham's city government on May 23, Albert Boutwell, who replaced Connor, expressed his approval of the desegregation agreement. As a result of the crisis in Birmingham, the administration prepared a new, broadly drawn civil rights bill which was sent to Congress on June 19. The bill proposed to expand the use for Section 333 of the *United States Code.*[33]

Events in Birmingham precipitated extended argument in Congress. In the Senate, Keating announced that when the marches began, he had asked Deputy Attorney General Nicholas Katzenbach whether new legislation was needed to enable the administration to deal with attacks on marchers, but had received no reply. Keating wondered if the Justice Department could seek an injunction against those harassing the marchers. Harrison A. Williams, Jr., of New Jersey supported the president for putting troops on a standby basis outside Birmingham, but felt that their use indicated a failure to peacefully resolve the racial problem. Javits of New York opposed the president's initial statements that he lacked constitutional authority to intervene; a state's action or inaction denying the First Amendment guarantee of the right to petition the government constituted a clear basis for federal action. Stennis of Mississippi maintained that the absence of a validating court order or a statute prevented federal interference. Apparently, he now believed that court orders could be enforced with troops, which he had denied during the Meredith incident. He asserted the mere threat of using troops to support demonstrators was the same as using troops. Morse responded by advancing Section 241 of the *United States Code,* which prohibits conspiracies that prevent the free exercise of federally secured rights, as a basis for federal action.[34]

In the House, Armistead Selden of Alabama suggested that if the president had the authority to send troops to Birmingham, he had the authority to send them to Fisk University in Nashville, where students were creating a disturbance. His Alabama colleague, George Andrews, asserted that state officials were keeping order and that Martin Luther King was violating laws with the approval of the president. Joe D. Waggoner of Louisiana chimed in with the observation that the whole situation was a stratagem to raise funds for the NAACP. Despite the congressional criticism, the president's decision to station troops strategically to enforce the peace was effective.[35]

Wallace stubbornly defied federal law again in June 1963, when a federal court ordered the admission of two blacks, James Hood and Vivian Malone, to the University of Alabama. President Kennedy informed Wallace that if he stayed home when the students arrived for registration, there would be no disorder. Wallace insisted on dramatically staging a stand in the schoolhouse door, but retreated when Kennedy sent units of the National Guard to the campus to clear the way for the black students. President Kennedy issued a proclamation and executive order, citing Sections 332 through 334 of the *United States Code* as the basis for his action. Although having to decide whether to intervene in racial crises was becoming a routine matter, the president responded to Robert Kennedy's insistence that any such action ought to be explained to the public.[36]

On June 11, 1963, at 8 P.M. President Kennedy spoke on nationwide television, explaining not only his intervention in Alabama, but giving a stirring address on the problems of blacks in America and the necessity for the passage of his new civil rights bill. A few hours later, Medgar Evers, an NAACP leader in Jackson, Mississippi, was shot by a white assassin at his home and died on June 12, but the controversial bill was not welcomed in Congress.[37]

However, the bombing of a black church in Birmingham on September 15, 1963, resulting in the death of four little girls, and the assassination of President Kennedy in November, along with President Johnson's vigorous support of Kennedy's bill, compelled Congress to pass the broadest civil rights act since Reconstruction. The new act, passed on July 2, 1964, contained provisions outlawing segregation and discrimination in jobs, public accommodations, education, and voting. It established the Equal Employment Opportunity Commission and extended the life of the Commission on Civil Rights. The legislation specifically empowered the attorney general to bring suit against suspected violators in the name of the United States, upon the written complaint of persons that they were being denied access to public facilities or the right to equal protection of the laws on the basis of race.[38]

During Johnson's strong push for Kennedy's civil rights bill, the civil rights movement remained under attack in the South. In the summer of 1964, whites and blacks joined in SNCC's Freedom Summer, which was a concentrated effort to register black voters in the South. More than twelve hundred students, the vanguard of the movement, arrived in Mississippi early in June to get the drive under way. They were greeted with open hostility. The local police frequently arrested students for exceeding the speed limit or other minor infractions of the law. On June 22, one black and two white workers, James Chaney, Michael Schwerner, and Andrew Goodman, were reported missing while traveling from Meridian to Philadelphia, Mississippi, to investigate a church burning. Initial reports indicated that Philadelphia county authorities had stopped the workers for speeding at 5:30 P.M. According to Sheriff Lawrence Rainey, they were released about 10:30 P.M. when Chaney paid a twenty-dollar fine. The sheriff was unconcerned about their whereabouts.[39]

When the trio failed to appear, President Johnson, expressing concern about their fate, sent Allen Dulles and a few FBI agents to organize a search. Administration officials, in keeping with a long Justice Department tradition and concerned about the politics of intervention, vacillated. Although they felt that sending troops all over the South was too provocative and reminiscent of Reconstruction, they did want to take some action to protect student workers. Civil rights groups, as well as Mrs. Medgar Evers, pleaded for federal support.[40]

Although Sheriff Rainey expressed complete confidence in the safety of the three workers, worldwide publicity about the incident dictated a federal response. President Johnson insisted that the FBI must act, despite Hoover's reluctance to get involved in these cases. FBI agents found Chaney's fire-gutted car in a swamp outside Philadelphia on June 23. At this point, the incident was faintly reminiscent of the 1933 Tuscaloosa case in which the sheriff claimed that two carloads of persons had pirated his prisoners away when he, in fact, had conspired in the murder. Over a month later, after the FBI paid an informer $30,000, the bullet-riddled bodies of Goodman, Schwerner, and Chaney were found buried in an earthen dam.[41]

The disposition of these cases differed from the abortive attempts to punish the sheriff in the Tuscaloosa case and to obtain an indictment of the murderers in the Mack Parker lynching. As the facts in the Goodman-Schwerner-Chaney case were coming to light, the parallel case of the murder of Lemuel Penn was being tried in a Georgia state court. Penn was a black educator from the District of Columbia who had been on duty in Georgia as a lieutenant colonel in the Army Reserves when he was shot by Klan members while driving in Colbert. On July 11, 1964, the two Klansmen who were accused of murdering Lemuel Penn were acquitted. Their acquittal made it even more evident how useless it would be to attempt a state prosecution of Deputy Sheriff Cecil Price and the six co-conspirators who were charged with the murder of the three voter-registration workers.

Federal prosecutions were begun in both cases under Sections 241 and 242 of the *United States Code*, which made the deprivation of civil rights through conspiracy a criminal act. Hopes for success were narrowly limited by the traditional disuse of these statutes, except in the *Hodges* and *Screws* cases which the government prosecuted and lost. In the cases growing out of the Chaney, Schwerner, Goodman, and Penn murders, *U.S. v. Price* (1966) and *U.S. v. Guest* (1966) respectively, the lower courts decided against the government, but the Supreme Court reversed the decisions and ordered new trials held in lower courts. In the new trials, all defendants were found guilty and their sentences of three to ten years were upheld by the Supreme Court in 1970.[42]

Sections 241 and 242 were given new vitality in these two cases. The indictment in the *Price* case stated that the deputy sheriff and seventeen others had intercepted Chaney, Goodman, and Schwerner, assaulted and shot them, and then buried their bodies where they were found forty-four days later. The Supreme Court decided there was sufficient state involvement to justify conviction under Section 242 for willfully subjecting the three to a denial of the right to due process of the law which is covered in the Fourteenth Amendment.[43]

In the *Guest* case, Justice Potter Stewart, who wrote the majority opinion, asserted there was sufficient state involvement in the crime to invoke federal prosecution under Section 241. Hugo Black, Abe Fortas, and Tom Clark concurred, but wanted it understood that Congress had the power under Section 5 of the Fourteenth Amendment to punish conspiracies, with or without state action, when they interfered with the rights outlined in the amendment. William Brennan, Earl Warren, and William Douglas concurred with Stewart's finding in that they also felt that there was sufficient state involvement and that a conspiracy to interfere with the right of interstate travel violated Section 241. But they dissented from Stewart's assertion that Section 241 did not cover private action. They thought that Section 241 forbade private, as well as state, action, when that action deprived persons of the right to free interstate travel. Justice John Marshall Harlan dissented on the grounds that the right to interstate travel is not a federally protected right and that the federal government cannot punish private action; he concurred, however, in the view that there was sufficient state action in this case to sustain a reversal. The *Guest* decision was a landmark in the area of civil rights because there was now a clear chance for conviction under federal law if states refused to prosecute or convict. The penalties designated for this crime were much less severe that those for murder, but even the possibility of a short sentence might deter such brutality, especially if the Justice Department brought more prosecutions. Additionally, at least three judges thought that private racial violence could be punished under existing laws, and another three thought Congress could pass a law making such an action a federal crime.[44]

The congressional debates on the Chaney, Schwerner, and Goodman incident foreshadowed the court opinions in *Guest* and *Price*. Apparently, the murder of the lone black, Penn, was unworthy of note. In the Senate, Javits affirmed the right of interstate travel without interference and thought marshals should be used to protect civil rights workers, but Stennis of Mississippi intimated that such persons were nothing but troublemakers. When a group of law professors expressed the view that there was a basis for protection and intervention under the Civil Rights Act of 1866, the 1957 and 1960 Voting Rights Acts, and Sections 332 through 334 of the *United States Code*, Javits had these comments inserted in the *Congressional Record*.[45]

After President Johnson authorized FBI agents and sailors to join in the search for the bodies, Stennis complained that he and Eastland had not been informed of the president's decision to move into their state. Stennis had asked Hoover about the situation and when he was told that these men had simply constituted a searching party, Stennis suggested that the government could have used the Mississippi National Guard for the search.[46]

In the House, John Bell Williams of Mississippi said communists were demanding that the president send troops to Mississippi. The president, he incorrectly reported, had already assigned two hundred Marines to aid in the search for persons who had come to Mississippi looking for trouble. William Colmer of Mississippi agreed with Williams and expressed the view that the president ought to send troops to find missing persons in New York.[47]

The federal government's response to the Chaney-Goodman-Schwerner murders remained exceptional. Segregationist violence, arson, and murders of civil rights workers for trying to exercise constitutional rights continued unabated. The studied indifference of the federal government increased disaffection among civil rights workers. Black activists especially became increasingly alienated. Hoover maintained his position that the FBI was an intelligence agency and not prepared to protect the civil rights workers. In fact, the FBI agreed with the Southern devotion to white supremacy. FBI agents spent more time investigating the white students and black activists, who were considered a threat to national security, than worrying about the segregationist violence. Also, in a successful effort to deflect liberal criticism of its inaction, the FBI implemented a campaign against the Klan. This campaign involved extra-legal intelligence operations, as well as an occasional legal investigation for civil rights violations if it could generate newspaper, television, and magazine coverage favorable to the agency. Hoover thought the Klan, by its high-profile activities, undermined the white supremacist cause. Other organizations, the White Citizens Council, and Klan fronts would be left to operate covertly.[48]

The murders of Chaney, Goodman, and Schwerner, and the killing of three additional civil rights workers were part of a chain of events which led to the enactment of the Voting Rights Act of 1965, as was a march from Selma, Alabama, to Montgomery. In March 1965, Governor George Wallace's police harassment of persons attempting to register and vote led to the protest march from Selma to the state capital. Attorney General Nicholas Katzenbach asked the FBI to become a little more active because he did not want civil rights sympathizers to call for the federal government to send troops. When the marchers were beaten and gassed, out-of-state black and white supporters came to join the effort. In the case of *Williams v. Wallace*, Federal Judge Frank Johnson decided that the march could continue as a reasonable exercise of the right of petition. At this point, Governor Wallace asked President Johnson for aid, claiming his force was inadequate to curtail the potential violence. Wallace probably knew he could not prevent intervention and wanted the national government to bear the responsibility. The march continued. President Johnson sent seventy deputy marshals to cooperate with the Alabama National Guard and the military police in providing protection for the marchers. As grounds for his action, Johnson cited the necessity for enforcing the court decision and also the states' inability to provide for the safety of the marchers; he claimed the authority was his to exercise under Sections 332 through 334 of the *United States Code*.[49]

On March 25, after the march to Montgomery, the FBI had seventy agents in the area when Viola Liuzzo, a white activist from Detroit, was killed as she transported marchers from Montgomery back to Selma in her car. On Highway 80 in Lowndes County a car with four Klansmen drove past and one shot her. In the public furor, Johnson demanded, as he had done in the Chaney-Schwerner-Goodman case, that the FBI immediately find the murderers. They had little trouble complying by the next day because their informer, Gary Rowe, was one of the Klansmen in the car. Johnson used the announcement of the offenders' arrests to further encourage passage of the Voting Rights Act of August 6, 1965.[50]

Not surprisingly, Mrs. Liuzzo's assailants were acquitted of murder charges in state court. The Justice Department prosecuted them in federal court for violating Section 241 and the three Klansmen were convicted and given the maximum ten-year sentence. The court of appeals upheld the sentences for the two remaining after one died of a heart attack.[51]

Congress took note of the events surrounding the march and the Liuzzo murder. In the Senate, Javits deprecated the violence which occurred during the voter registration drives and hoped federal troops would be used to deter it. Walter F. Mondale of Minnesota and Joseph S. Clark of Pennsylvania asked that the Justice Department prepare the Voting Rights Act for immediate passage; they felt that if federal enforcement supported the registration and voting efforts, such marches would become obsolete. Despite the protestations of Southern congressmen and senators that outside agitators were responsible for their civil rights problems, the sweeping Voting Rights Act of 1965 was passed. It suspended literacy tests in states where less than 50 percent of the adults had voted in 1964 and provided for federal supervision of registrations and elections.[52]

The terms of the Voting Rights Act were similar to those of the Lodge election bill of 1890, which was labeled unconstitutional by its opponents. However, this bill was saved from the onslaught of Southerners by the Supreme Court decision in *South Carolina v. Katzenbach* (1966), in which the act was determined to be a valid exercise of constitutional power under the Fifteenth Amendment. By the end of the year, nearly 250,000 new black voters had registered and blacks won seats in the Georgia legislature and in several Southern city councils.[53]

By enacting the 1964 and 1965 civil rights acts, the national government indicated its willingness to provide a basis for the achievement of full equality for blacks. The legislation resulted from pressure generated by a civil rights movement that had taken to the streets. Events pressed the Kennedy and Johnson administrations into acting more vigorously than previous administrations in cases of racial violence, and into using the authority provided in Sections 241, 242, and 333 of the *United States Code*. The states and the federal government found it more difficult to use the facade of states' rights to abdicate their duties.

15

Riots, Rebellion, and Repression

I
N THE LAST HALF of the 1960s, the national government was faced with an expanded, but significantly transformed, black liberation movement. Black and white "togetherness" was challenged by black activists who recognized violence as one tactic for achieving their goals and whose thinking was greatly influenced by cultural black nationalism. In reflecting on his actions as assistant attorney general for civil rights in the Kennedy administration, Burke Marshall explained that his behavior and the FBI's, which he considered justified in the name of federalism, caused a loss of faith in law among "Negro and white civil rights workers. The consequences in the future cannot be foreseen."[1]

The tepid federal response to the assault and murder of civil rights workers engaged in nonviolent activities fomented distrust. Martin Luther King's assassination made even nonviolence as a strategy seem ridiculous to some activists. The agreement of white liberals to the rejection of Fannie Lou Hamer and the Mississippi Freedom Democratic Party delegates in favor of a regular delegation of white racists completed the alienation of many black civil rights workers. Black activists began to think of economic and social revolution, of black power, and of forging alliances with white radicals and with nonwhite people in developing nations as a means for gaining equality of opportunity in American society. The black masses continued to lash out at "whitey" through his person and his ghetto property, while some militants devised plans and projects to move African-Americans from reform to revolution.[2]

Successive presidents turned their attention to constitutional means of suppressing rebellious black masses and supporting state and local law enforcement, while searching for a means to meet the needs or thwart the anger of hostile African-Americans, without too much change in the social and economic status quo. Congress, even as it put the finishing touches on civil rights legislation, was perplexed by the new problems arising out of the violence perpetrated by blacks who seemed ungrateful for congressional beneficence.

Joblessness, bad housing, bad education led to despair that festered in poor African-American communities. However, the surface issue that most often sparked violence and retaliatory repression by the federal government in the 1960s was police brutality. African-Americans had complained about police harassment for generations. In many of the incidents leading to riots, police action was a precipitant. In 1959, Robert F. Williams, then director of the Monroe, North Carolina, branch of the NAACP, asserted that African-Americans should respond violently when attacked by whites, since justice could not be expected in local court systems. His caustic expression of bitter disillusion reflected the verdicts of a local county court which handed an acquittal to two white men accused of brutally assaulting two black women but gave a jail sentence to a mentally retarded black man for having had an argument with a white woman. Williams asserted that African-Americans must understand that a liberation struggle had to be flexible; there was a place for violence as well as nonviolence. In August of 1961, during an outbreak of racial violence in Monroe, Williams was falsely accused of kidnapping a white couple. Fearing for his life, Williams fled the United States to seek asylum in Cuba and later in China. Williams returned to the United States in 1969 to live in Detroit and to fight extradition and the charges against him. The prosecution dropped the charges in 1976, announcing that the principal witness was too ill to ever testify.[3]

It was in 1959, too, that Malcolm X, the most articulate spokesman for Elijah Muhammad's Black Muslims, gained national attention for his analysis of the shallowness of earlier civil rights movements and leadership and his own program for black nationalism. Malcolm frightened whites and bourgeois blacks as he ridiculed integration and called for African-Americans to maintain their cultural identity as they worked for economic and political self-sufficiency in American life. While whites castigated Malcolm for preaching hatred, the black masses, weary of promises, believed he accurately described the "Man" and his injustice to African-Americans. Many blacks, even when ignorant of the Muslim organization, believed that the rhetoric of organization and manliness made good sense. Malcolm modified his views toward integration shortly before his assassination on February 21, 1965.[4]

The new era of riots overlapped the nonviolent phase of the black liberation struggle. Even while the Civil Rights Act of 1964 was being passed, disturbances surfaced in Harlem and to a lesser degree in Rochester, New York, in Elizabeth and Jersey City, New Jersey, and in Philadelphia, Pennsylvania. The Harlem riot erupted when an off-duty policeman killed James Powell, a teenage boy who had allegedly attacked him. Blacks moved in protest, demanding establishment of a police precinct in Harlem. The police tried to restrain the marchers and arrest the leaders. Instead of acquiescing, as most blacks had done in the nonviolent marches in the South, the crowd attacked the police. By the next morning, one black had been killed by the police, twelve policemen and at least one hundred blacks had been injured, dozens of shops had been looted, and more charges of police brutality were made by James Farmer of CORE. Intermittent violence continued for the next few nights. Worried about the political consequences for the 1964 election and unsure what his response should be, President Johnson announced an FBI investigation of the riots. The FBI reported that it had found no evidence of systematic organization or planning, although it claimed that communist organizations had tried to exploit black unrest. Johnson persuaded Thomas Dewey to prepare a report on the role of the FBI. The report made clear that Johnson's Great Society programs had not encouraged the riots.[5] Hoover endorsed the report's conclusions.

Black Americans such as Roy Wilkins, A. Philip Randolph, and Whitney Young tried to maintain their leadership positions and to help the administration. They embarked on the policy they would follow for the next few years: blacks would make their voices heard in the political process. Denouncing the riots as well as nonviolent demonstrations, they insisted on a moratorium on sit-ins and other confrontational tactics in order to win the presidential election of Lyndon Johnson. However, other black leaders, such as James Forman of SNCC and James Farmer of CORE, dissented and articulated the seething black resentment against police brutality, which unsympathetic whites regarded as simply black objections to "law and order."[6]

Black leaders, counseling temperance, were unheeded by African-Americans in the ghettos. The Watts riot in Los Angeles in August 1965 exploded when a highway patrolman stopped an apparently intoxicated black man for speeding. A crowd of African-Americans gathered. The crowd believed they were witnesses to an incident of police brutality. When a patrolman struck a bystander with a billy club, the crowd began throwing objects at the police. The next night, looting and burning of ghetto businesses, many of which were white-owned, began. As the conflagration grew, the chief of police asked for National Guard assistance. When the guard arrived, they and the police made heavy use of firearms. Four thousand persons were arrested, thirty-four were killed, and hundreds were injured. Property damage was estimated at thirty-five million dollars. Despite the enormous casualty figure, a major concern of governmental officials was that insurance cover property losses.[7]

During the riot, Congress, having just appropriated some $950 million in August 1964 for President Johnson's War on Poverty, was in a dither. During the nonviolent phase of the civil rights movement, liberals and conservatives in Congress knew where they stood; now liberals were confused, while conservatives blamed liberals for the disturbance. While insisting that the movement toward equality should continue, Senator Javits of New York expressed horror at the "hoodlums" of Los Angeles. Richard Russell of Georgia intimated that civil rights leaders had pushed lawbreaking too far, setting the example for rioters. Walter Mondale of Minnesota denounced his colleagues who were blaming civil rights leaders for the riots. Then, Senator Robert C. Byrd of West Virginia proposed that planned parenthood be introduced to blacks so that they would not have so many children who would grow up and be unemployed. Michael Mansfield of Montana, defending the police against charges of brutality, insisted that mass defiance of law could not be justified by this charge. Strom Thurmond of South Carolina knew that communists and agitators were responsible for these racial problems.[8]

In the House, Selden of Alabama was pleased with the discomfort of his northern colleagues. He commented that even though the northerners had run to the South to investigate her racial problems and to advise southerners on solutions, he was not going to meddle in their communities. By now, he stated, the public must recognize that racial problems were nationwide, that the encouragement of law violation by demonstrators in Alabama had led to lawlessness in northern communities, and that the passage of civil rights bills would not eliminate racial friction. George Hansen of Idaho thought Martin Luther King and other leaders should put an end to the riots since their example had caused them. James Roosevelt of California felt that the House should investigate and make recommendations for riot prevention. At this time, Adam Clayton Powell of New York correctly enumerated the causes of the riots for his colleagues: blacks were angry and furious because the white power structure chose to work with "Uncle Toms." As a result, the "natives" were ready to take matters in their own hands. Civil rights legislation had absolutely no meaning to blacks in the North who were fed up with police brutality, de facto segregation, unemployment and underemployment, inferior education, political tokenism, and Jim Crow justice. Powell predicted that Los Angeles would be only the first of a long series of riots and episodes of lawlessness. Ignoring Powell's impassioned and accurate explanation, Richard H. Ichord of Missouri insisted that it was a simple matter of keeping the peace, as exemplified in Selma. James D. Martin of Alabama was heartened by the fact that newspapers, by speaking out in favor of law and order, were finally assuming their responsibility for action when demonstrators were violating local segregation and trespass statutes.[9]

In the summer of 1966, there were approximately forty-three disorders, all initially precipitated by some incident between blacks and the police. Commentators stated that the country was in for a succession of long hot summers without realizing that racial disorders had characterized every American summer for years.[10]

When rioting and violence erupted in 1966, liberals in Congress were understandably disturbed, while conservatives felt vindicated. In the previous two years, legislation had been passed before the summer rebellions. But in 1966, when the riots came early, Javits feared that the Civil Rights Act of 1966 might not be passed. He was correct; the bill, containing a fair housing section, did not pass. Javits tried to explain the positive side of black power and to subvert the argument that blacks were not like other immigrant groups who simply had to work hard and who would someday become assimilated in the melting pot. In the first place, he said, there was no melting pot, and in the second place, blacks came in chains and had been subjected to accumulated oppression. Undismayed, conservatives, such as Byrd of West Virginia, called for strong repressive measures to end the riots.[11]

In the House, where northerners were, for the most part, silent, Abernathy of Mississippi rose to ask why those who were so vocal when racial troubles plagued the South had nothing to say now. Convinced, as were his fellow southerners, that outside agitators caused the riots, William C. Cramer of Florida introduced an amendment to the Civil Rights Act under consideration which would provide for punishment of those who crossed state lines to cause riots. His bill was intended to supplement the efforts of those state governments which were passing repressive legislation. The amendment passed the House on August 9 by a vote of 389–25. Interestingly enough, southerners who argued against federal intervention and for local control between 1962 and 1965 now wanted federal legislation, and northerners, such as Don Edwards and James Corman, both of California, who had supported federal intervention previously, opposed the bill on the grounds that law enforcement was a local matter. However, both groups were consistent; southerners wanted outside agitators suppressed, and northerners were opposed to the suppression of civil rights activists and civil liberties in an effort to end racial disturbances. In any case, the amendment was lost when the bill failed to pass.[12]

President Johnson concerned himself not with police brutality or other grievances of the rioters but the political considerations. He expressed confusion about why African-Americans who were the beneficiaries of his programs would rebel on his watch. He encouraged Hoover's surveillance of black rioters and investigations into whether any were benefiting from Great Society programs. While helping Johnson to deflect criticism from conservatives, Hoover expanded the mission of his agency in the domestic arena. He explained that if a national pattern of black violence developed, his office would take responsibility for containing it instead of deferring to local police. Johnson did not expect the riots to continue, believing blacks were basically content. Hoover disagreed. He published a manual called "The Prevention and Control of Riots" that included information about using intelligence to identify those inclined to cause urban violence. Prior to its publication, Hoover also insisted that the Justice Department's Civil Rights Division review and approve each word in the document. After the Watts rebellion, Johnson asked Hoover to expand his intelligence operations to include riot prediction.[13]

In the spring of 1967, when disorders began again, ignited by police attempts to make arrests on minor charges, there were actually about 150 episodes, ranging from minor clashes to widespread arson, looting, and sniping. Hoover had predicted 8 or 9. In April and May, disturbances broke out at several black colleges in the South where SNCC had been organizing youthful militants. In Tampa, Florida, riots occurred in June after policemen shot a black man held on a robbery charge as he was attempting to escape. Police, with the aid of a hastily organized black youth patrol, restored order. That same month, in Cincinnati and in Atlanta, police encounters with blacks—as well as accumulated grievances—set off rioting. In Newark, New Jersey, the allegedly brutal arrest of John Smith, a black cab driver, for driving without a license and assaulting a police officer, set off retaliatory rioting in July. National guardsmen and police suppressed the violence, which spread to other New Jersey cities; in Plainfield, national guardsmen and police further antagonized the black community by making a warrantless house-to-house search for arms that had allegedly been stolen from a manufacturing plant.[14]

The most extensive racial disorder of 1967 grew out of a police raid on a "blind pig," an illegal after-hours drinking establishment, in Detroit on Saturday night, July 22. A crowd gathered outside the after-hours club, vocally criticizing the police for the way in which they made the arrests, charging they used excessive force. Window-breaking and looting spread. Early Sunday morning, Mayor Jerome Cavanaugh asked Governor George Romney for National Guard support; Romney complied. When the violence increased, a request was made for federal troops and 4,700 paratroopers arrived in Detroit that evening. On Thursday, the rioting had almost completely subsided and the paratroopers left on Saturday. National guardsmen remained in town until August 1. Of the forty-three persons killed, thirty-three were black; 7,200 citizens were arrested, most of whom were also black. One white national guardsman, one white fireman, and one black private guard lost their lives, all three being mistakenly killed by policemen and guardsmen. Claims of police brutality, wholesale violations of civil rights, illegal arrests, and unreasonable bail were commonplace. Seventeen of the persons killed were reportedly looters, two of whom were white. Some twenty million dollars in damage was done, most of which was covered by insurance.[15]

Considerable discussion and controversy arose over the roles played by President Johnson and Governor Romney in introducing federal troops to suppress the disorder. Realizing that state troopers and the National Guard were virtually all-white units who might further aggravate the rioters, Mayor Cavanaugh reluctantly called the governor for aid. Romney, who began discussing the disorder with Attorney General Ramsey Clark about 3:00 A.M. on July 22, was told that he should use the specific language required by statute in order to obtain federal aid; he was to assert that there was a state of "insurrection." Romney, fearing that insurance companies would not cover the property damage involved if that language was used, refused to use that term. In later conversations, Romney said that Clark told him there was a statute which permitted troop use in cases of domestic violence, so he could substitute that term in his request. At 10:00 A.M., Clark informed President Johnson that Romney thought he would definitely need troops and that the governor had been informed that he must send a written request. Romney charged that Clark first indicated that an oral request was sufficient, but changed his mind at 4:00 A.M. and stipulated that a written request was required. Although Romney said he had a telegram prepared by 8:00 A.M., he waited to send it until Clark agreed that he did not have to indicate the existence of an insurrection. At 11:00 A.M., President Johnson received the telegram in which Romney asserted that there was a reasonable doubt that looting and disorder could be suppressed without the use of federal troops.[16] At 11:20 A.M., Johnson ordered Secretary of Defense Robert McNamara to start sending troops to Detroit. He also decided to send Cyrus Vance as his personal emissary to study the situation. He then conferred with Clark and three Justice Department civil rights attorneys, Warren Christopher, Roger Wilkins, and John Doar, to draft a reply to Romney and a presidential proclamation and executive order. At 11:42 A.M., a reply was sent to Romney that troops would be landing at Selfridge Air Force Base. Shortly after 1:00 P.M., Vance and other federal officials flew to Detroit.[17]

When Vance arrived in Detroit that afternoon, he toured the riot areas with local officials and met with Cavanaugh, Romney, and a dozen black leaders. Everyone, except Representative John Conyers, agreed that troops should be sent into the riot areas at once. At 8:30 P.M., Vance reported to the president that the need was not critical enough to send the troops into the streets. Representative Charles Diggs called the White House, threatening to denounce the administration's behavior as being politically motivated in an effort to discredit Governor Romney, who was being considered as a Republican presidential candidate, unless troops were used immediately. Shortly before midnight, federal troops moved into the city and the president went on nationwide television to explain the reasons for their use.[18]

Newspaper accounts and official reports from both sides correlated substantially. The administration, admitting they were reluctant to use federal troops, did not want to establish a precedent for sending regular troops all about the country whenever civil disorders occurred. Apart from the economics of the situation, it was not a tactic that would win favor at the polls. No troops had been used in Newark or Watts, and no request had been made for them. Romney, however, blamed the president for his own ignorance of the statutory and constitutional means for invoking the use of federal troops. Romney should have been familiar with the procedures. After the 1943 riots, instructions were reiterated and sample requests were sent to all states. The information on how to proceed was also available in any law library. Based on his own account as published in the newspapers and outlined in the statutes, Romney did not proceed in the proper manner.[19]

There was considerable confusion in the administration over the correct procedure. In his proclamation and executive order giving the basis for troop use, Johnson cited all of Chapter 15, Title 10, of the *United States Code* (see Appendix). However, a Justice Department memorandum, written to explain the federal grounds for the Detroit action, cited only Sections 331 and 333 of the same chapter. If the administration was relying upon Section 331, which is the only part of the statute that provides for action upon a state request, Johnson was correct in insisting upon the word *insurrection*, because that is the only situation in which the statute permits him discretionary authority to use troops. The statute is based upon Article IV, Section 4, of the Constitution, which provided that the United States shall, upon application, protect the states from domestic violence. It was decided by the Supreme Court in *Luther v. Borden* (1849), that Congress, by statute, must decide how Article IV, Section 4, shall be enforced. The presidential authority comes only from Section 331, which Congress enacted in response to the court decision. Since Romney refused to state there was an insurrection, technically troops should not have been sent. In addition, it is well accepted that as the President has discretionary authority under Section 331, he can make his own investigation before determining whether to send troops. Sending Vance under those circumstances, especially since riots earlier in the year had been suppressed without federal troops, seems quite proper.[20]

Since Romney never said there was an insurrection, perhaps the president was relying upon Sections 332 and 333 as authority for sending troops. Congress had passed these two sections to give the president authority to enforce federal law without a state request. If that was the case, he did not need a state request. Section 332 requires a rebellion against federal law before troops can be sent; however, no assertion was made that federal law was being opposed in Detroit. Section 333, which was used as a basis for action in Birmingham, Selma, and the investigatory stages of the Schwerner-Chaney-Goodman cases, is the best statutory basis cited by the president. That section requires only that domestic violence hinder the execution of state or federal law so as to deprive persons of constitutional rights secured by law, along with evidence of state failure to provide protection. Again, no state request is necessary. It is very likely that neither Clark nor the president knew what constitutional authority they would use when the rioting was first reported; however, when Romney refused to aver that there was an insurrection, but insisted he needed help, and after politicians threatened to condemn the president's inaction as a political ploy, the president probably decided in haste to cite all of Title 10.[21]

The president and the attorney general must have become aware that their refusal to send troops upon Romney's first request could only be based on the theory that they thought Section 331 covered riot situations. In a letter from Clark to the governors on August 7,

1967, the law on the subject is correctly explained. Clark cites only Article IV, Section 4, and Section 331, which requires a state request, and Section 334, which requires that the president issue a proclamation ordering citizens to cease and desist when troops are introduced upon state application. The sticking points in the Detroit riot situation seemed to be Romney's unwillingness to say that there was a state of insurrection or of domestic violence which he was unable to suppress and the administration's unwillingness to send troops, despite the seriousness of the riot, without Romney making these assertions when both were relying upon statutes which seemed to require very specific language. In cases of state requests for troops before 1967, references had been made to either domestic violence or insurrection existing in the state. In cases in which a reference was made to domestic violence in the state applications, it was clear from the language that the reference was to Article IV, Section 4, and, by extension, to Section 331. In his wire to the president, Romney referred only to looting, arson, and sniping, and the necessity for federal troops to assist local authorities in restoring order. If any blame must be given for the delay in acquiring federal assistance, it should probably fall on the governor.[22]

In Congress, the same jockeying for political capital, of which Johnson and Romney were accused, was evident. In the House, southerners, such as Joe D. Waggonner, Jr., of Louisiana, repeated the 1965 and 1966 charges that communists were initiating the riots. F. Edward Hebert, also from Louisiana, thought action should be taken to make the National Guard more effective so that the use of federal troops would be unnecessary. Speaker of the House John McCormack of Massachusetts inserted Johnson's explanation of the sequence of events in the *Congressional Record*. Republican Gerald Ford of Michigan sparred with Wayne B. Hayes of Ohio and Democratic Whip Carl Albert of Oklahoma over the roles played by Romney and Johnson in the disturbances. Chet Hollifield of California and Hale Boggs of Louisiana supported the president. L. Mendel Rivers of South Carolina, the chairman of the Armed Services Committee, commended the military, but emphasized the responsibility of the guard to keep order. Abernathy of Mississippi could not resist needling the northerners again, and addressing them, he said that every time racial disturbances occurred in the South, they would all "pack [their] shabby old valises and head down to revel in the activity. Ike and Kennedy sent the military at the drop of a hat. But President Johnson sort of held back until Detroit was on its knees." He stated that the National Guard could have handled the situation, but Romney, "another Civil Rights expert, piddled around" before releasing the full force of the National Guard.[23]

In the Senate, Republican Robert P. Griffin of Michigan supported the view that Johnson was attempting to make Romney appear incapable of handling affairs in his state, while Philip A. Hart, his Democratic colleague, opposed Griffin's charges. Robert Byrd of West Virginia, remaining consistent with his positions on disturbances in the South, said he was opposed to the use of federal troops except as a last resort. Asserting it was necessary for future historians and scholars to have material available from which to form an opinion about the dispute, Hart helpfully inserted a memorandum prepared by the attorney general, the proclamation and executive order signed by the president, the president's speech, and Romney's telegram all into the *Congressional Record*.[24]

A number of strange circumstances and controversies grew out of the intense apprehension which followed the riot. One of these resulted in the death of three black youths at the Algiers Motel in Detroit on July 26, 1967. The police, responding to a report that there were snipers in the motel, discovered ten black males and two white females in the building annex. No guns were found. An hour later when the police left, three youths were dead; they had been shot at close range. The other people, including the two women, had been beaten. There was no immediate acknowledgement or explanation of the incident. Later, one of the policemen, Ronald August, admitted shooting one of the youths, but claimed he had acted in self-defense. He was acquitted by an all-white jury in June 1969. Since a white judge ruled his confession inadmissible because it was made without proper constitutional warning, no trial was possible in the case of a second policeman, David Senak, who admitted shooting another one of the youths. Senak, August, and Robert Paille, a third white police officer, and Melvin Dismukes, a black private guard, were charged under the same statute used in the *Guest* and *Price* cases—conspiring to violate the civil rights of the three youths by murdering them. All four were acquitted by an all-white jury in February 1970.[25]

President Johnson expressed a sense of betrayal as a result of the riots. Blacks had brought him political trouble and showed their ingratitude after all he had done for them. Black nationalists denounced liberalism because they were fed up with paternalism and no power and too much emphasis on gradualism and control and too many black people having died with no response. In the North, the problems of overcrowded housing, a black unemployment rate twice as high as that of whites, and the segregation of black children in inferior schools seemed not to change much as a result of African-Americans' voting and holding office. The embrace by Martin Luther King, Jr., and other blacks of the anti–Vietnam War movement further angered Johnson.[26]

Johnson described disaffected blacks as radicals or criminals and Republicans depicted them as Johnson's wards, created by the anti-poverty programs of the Great Society which undermined responsibility. Concerned that persons funded in the poverty programs might be participating in the riots, Johnson asked Hoover to step up his investigations on July 25, in the midst of the Detroit riots. Hoover, who favored the Republicans, began to give aid and comfort to conservatives who blamed the riots on Johnson's too-favorable attitude toward blacks. Hoover accurately reported that riots grew out of incidents of police brutality, but now focused blame on the exhortations of Rap Brown and others for fanning the flames. Johnson became committed to discrediting the civil rights movement and asked Hoover to provide the ammunition.[27]

Johnson appointed the Kerner Commission to investigate the causes of the riots with the hope that it would provide political cover as the Dewey Report on the 1964 riots had done. The final commission report, issued in February 1968, ignored Johnson's concerns for the most part and focused on the corrosive effects of race discrimination in creating two separate societies in which domestic disorders occurred. Johnson ignored the report's recommendations for employment, education, and other reforms, claiming budgetary problems in the midst of the Vietnam War. However, he asked local police to act on one minor recommendation contained in the report's appendix by creating intelligence units to channel information to the FBI. The units expanded domestic intelligence operations and led to the designation of countless people as subversives or radicals in the FBI files.[28]

After the Detroit riot, the army organized a directorate for civil disturbance policy and operations and issued new riot control instructions to insure rapid response in an expected succession of long, hot summers. If no major disorders had occurred in the next few years, those plans and preparations would probably have been forgotten. However, the assassination of Martin Luther King, Jr., on April 4, 1968, set off a wave of rioting in black ghettos across the country, resulting in the use of federal troops in Chicago, Washington, and Baltimore. Troops were dispatched without problems. In the Washington riots, the president cited not only Sections 331 through 334 as authority, but also his position as commander-in-chief of the local National Guard in response to a request for aid from Mayor Walter Washington, Chief of Police John B. Layton, and Commissioner of Safety Patrick V. Murphy.[29]

Racial violence became widespread after King's assassination, with disturbances occurring in 36 states and 138 cities. Deaths and injuries in the King assassination riots, however, were not as great as those in the summer disturbances of 1965, 1966, and 1967. In Chicago, 9 were killed and 500 injured; in Washington, 11 deaths occurred with 1,113 injuries, mostly minor. There were 6 deaths and 900 injuries in Baltimore, and 6 more deaths in Kansas City. The decrease in casualties can perhaps be explained by the training given National Guard and the police after 1967 in which they were instructed to use tear gas and curfews rather that arms and ammunition, except in the most severe circumstances.[30]

The summer violence of 1968 continued into the fall and spring semesters on college campuses, and into the summer of 1969. The murder of three black college students by highway patrolmen in Orangeburg, South Carolina, in February was reminiscent of many previous cases. The incident grew out of student efforts to integrate the local bowling alley. When no state charges were filed, Attorney General Ramsey Clark sought federal indictments for civil rights violations of the nine highway patrolmen responsible for the murders. A South Carolina jury refused to convict the patrolmen. In the fall of 1970 one of the wounded protestors, Cleveland Sellers, was convicted

by a state court of participating in a riot two nights before the Orangeburg massacre. The occurrence of violent confrontations on campuses and on the streets was no longer primarily confined to the summer months. By April of 1969, more racial violence and use of
National Guard and federal troops had already taken place that year
than in all of 1967. Militarism, too, was fast becoming a common occurrence; in Wilmington, Delaware, National Guard troops occupied
the city from April 1967 to January 1969.[31]

For the first time, in 1968, there was evidence of planned strategic
acts of violence and conspiratorial warfare by blacks. In Cleveland in
July, three policemen were ambushed and killed by black snipers.
Black militant Fred Ahmed was later convicted of murder in the case.
There were several attacks on policemen in Brooklyn late in the summer; in August, two policemen were wounded by shotgun fire; in early
September, two policemen were hit by sniper fire as they waited for a
traffic light; and in mid-September, a police communications truck
was fire-bombed, slightly injuring the policemen. Also in mid-
September in Harlem, two policemen, sitting in a parked patrol car,
were shot and wounded, reportedly by two black men. Two attacks on
policemen occurred in Illinois in September; in Kankakee, a policeman was wounded in an ambush in the black community; in Summit,
black youths reportedly fired shotguns at two police cars, injuring two
policemen. In the same month, eighteen black militants were arrested
in St. Louis following a series of attacks on the police, including one
incident in which shots were fired at a police station and at the home
of a police lieutenant. Organized violence, involving Black Panther
confrontations with police in Oakland, California, and other cities developed into significant methods of racial confrontation in 1968.[32]

Some political science theorists and commentators assumed that as
the black liberation struggle had changed its tactics to selected strategic violence, the era of the riot was at an end. Events in early 1969
seemed to support their opinion. In Detroit in March, black separatist
members of the Republic of New Africa allegedly fired on policemen
outside the New Bethel Church, wounding one officer and killing another. The police then stormed the church in search of the sniper and
arrested 142 black adults and 5 children. Black Judge George Crock-
ett, who began releasing the prisoners a few hours later since there was
no evidence of their complicity, enraged the police department. How-

ever, these commentators seem to have forgotten that the level of consciousness of different groups of black people varies. Police brutality
would still cause an outbreak of rioting and property destruction in
the ghettos, while other members of the black community would react
with guerrilla warfare. This theory was borne out in the summer of
1969 by the Omaha, Nebraska, rioting and looting precipitated by the
killing of a young black girl by a white policeman investigating a robbery and incidents such as the one at New Bethel Church and the
shooting of policemen in Kokomo, Indiana. There were approximately 683 race-related disorders in 1968 and 688 in 1969. The 1969
disturbances, unlike those of 1967 and 1968, occurred, for the most
part, in smaller communities that had not experienced such disturbances before. Some black people still chose marching, picketing, or
other nonviolent methods as evidenced in Resurrection City in June
1968, in the Charleston Employees' strike in the summer of 1969, and
the Cairo, Illinois, movement of 1969. All of these protests were coordinated by the SCLC, with Ralph Abernathy, Jesse Jackson, and others maintaining the tradition of Martin Luther King, Jr. The NAACP
found a new cause in trying to insure that the Nixon administration
would not bargain away recent civil rights legislation in a second
Compromise of 1877.[33]

Congressional conservatives, urged on by the FBI, aggressively defended the public from manifestations of civil violence. During the
disorders of 1968, Congress was faced with the resubmitted Cramer
anti-riot bill, which from the congressional debates on the subject
might more accurately have been titled the "Stokely Carmichael and
H. Rap Brown Bill." Cramer and his supporters were convinced that
agitators, such as Carmichael and Brown, who traveled from place to
place around the country, were responsible for the riots and that the
national government must take action to end their ubiquitousness.
The bill, based on the commerce power of Congress, provided that
persons who traveled in or used facilities of interstate commerce with
intent to incite a riot or to aid or abet a riot could be fined ten thousand dollars or imprisoned for five years, or both. Supporters, demanding assurance that the law would be enforced, added a section
requiring the attorney general to prosecute speedily and to exhaust all
possible appeals, or explain to Congress in writing why action was
delayed. According to the bill, a riot is any public disturbance involv-

ing acts of violence by one or more persons as part of an assemblage of three or more persons.[34]

Assertions by proponents of the bill that Rap Brown and Stokely Carmichael were the demons of the riot era filled page after page of the *Congressional Record.* Opponents of the legislation, such as John Conyers of Michigan and Don Edwards of California, pointed out that the bill was too simplistic to stop riots, but to no avail. Robert Nix of Pennsylvania was not convinced that the section of the bill that excluded punishment of mere oral or written expression of ideas advocating violence would not prevent infringements of First Amendment rights. Joseph Resnick of New York pertinently asked whether the legislation could be labeled as a Bill of Attainder, which is prohibited by Article I of the Constitution, since its framers had gone on record by stating that the bill was designed to "get" the two former SNCC chairmen, Carmichael and Brown.[35]

The Riot Control Act received its first court test in the conviction of eight defendants for allegedly conspiring to incite the riots that erupted during the Democratic Convention in Chicago in 1968. Bobby Seale, national chairman of the Black Panther Party, was indicted along with seven white protestors. Seale was gagged and shackled to his chair in the courtroom to prevent his outcries and protests over not having preferred counsel. Seale was found guilty on sixteen counts of contempt and sentenced to four years imprisonment by the judge sitting without a jury. The seven whites, also indicted for violating Section 231 of the *United States Code* by teaching persons techniques of resisting and obstructing the police, were found innocent of both charges but were convicted of contempt of court at the trial. All of the charges were reversed on appeal three years later. The federal courts, in 1981, refused the defendants' requests to expunge their convictions because documents from the FBI and Chicago police files disclosed communications during the trial between the trial judge, the government's prosecutor, and the FBI. These discussions and the infiltration of the defense camp by government agents, the defendants claimed, tainted the trial so as to deprive it of its character as a judicial proceeding. Therefore, they argued, their contempt citations for interfering with the trial process were invalid. The federal appeals court decided that since the defendants did not know of the misconduct at the time, it could not have motivated their contemptuous behavior.

Essentially, what this comes down to is that the defendants' protests against the unfairness of the trial that led to their contempt charges did not count—because they did not know *at the time* that the trial was indeed unfair![36]

While passing the Riot Control Act in 1968, Congress, moved by King's assassination, enacted some of the civil rights legislation which had been left over from 1966. The Fair Housing Act reaffirmed the principle expressed in the Civil Rights Act of 1866 that the purchase of housing on a nondiscriminatory basis was a matter of national policy. Persons convicted of violating the act could be subjected to a ten thousand dollar fine or not more than ten years imprisonment, or both. The bill's enforcement provisions were so weak, however, that it made practically no dent in the housing discrimination problem. Amendments to Sections 241 through 244, as well as the new Section 245 of the *United States Code*, were also enacted (see Appendix). The new legislation was designed to close loopholes which had been pointed out by the Justice Department and the Supreme Court in the *Price* and *Guest* cases of 1966.[37]

The new Section 245 made it a federal crime for any individual, whether acting under authority of law or not, to interfere with the right to vote or the right to participate in any activity administered by the United States government or under federal financial assistance. The act also made it a crime to interfere with anyone engaged in interstate commerce during a riot. The punishment for violators was a one thousand dollar fine or imprisonment for one year, or both; if bodily injury resulted, the fine was increased to ten thousand dollars or a prison sentence of not more than ten years, or both; and if death resulted, the punishment could be a term of years at the judge's discretion or life imprisonment. The penalties under Section 241 were similarly increased. The penalty under Section 242, when only one individual acted, was still not entirely satisfactory. This section covered police misconduct and the maximum sentence was one year in jail. This provision meant that if a police officer beat an individual, no matter how seriously, unless death resulted no other punishment was possible. These changes could have significant impact if prosecutions were brought and convictions achieved. Previously, the killers of Chaney, Goodman, and Schwerner, Viola Liuzzo, and the three blacks in the Algiers Motel incident, if successfully convicted under federal law, could only be subjected to short prison sentences. Now, in cases involving civil rights, life imprisonment was a possible punishment for murder, even when a state refused prosecution. The section on injury to persons in interstate commerce during a riot was intended to provide a basis for prosecuting looters and rioters who attacked businessmen on the grounds that such business was federally protected and secured.[38]

The majority of the Senate committee that conceived the bill indicated that the measure was directed against brutal acts of violence done to blacks and whites, such as the Chaney-Goodman-Schwerner incident, and allowed the government to prosecute offenders without the necessity of proving a conspiracy when states failed to act. Its scope was based on the Fourteenth Amendment and the Commerce Clause of the Constitution. The minority on the Senate committee, consisting of Sam Ervin, George Smathers, Everett Dirksen, and Roman Hruska, ignoring the slavery and discrimination against African-Americans that motivated the enactment of the Fourteenth Amendment, complained that the act was not in the American tradition, since it referred to acts done to people on account of race or color. Apparently oblivious to the violence perpetrated against African-Americans without state protection for 179 years, they asserted that there was no evidence that states had refused to provide protection for their citizens. Eastland of Mississippi and Thurmond of South Carolina filed a separate report in which they articulated the new tactics of the southern conservatives in the light of recent northern riots; they asserted that the bill would protect roving "fomenters of violence," such as Carmichael and Brown. Eastland offered an example: if Rap Brown, while making a speech, was yelled at and hit by a white man, the white man could be convicted of interfering with Brown's constitutional rights, while Brown would not be guilty of any violation. In Eastland's opinion, there was no reason for Brown not to be hit while making speeches.[39]

While the passage of the Fair Housing Act and Section 245 seemed to be a high-water mark at the end of the brief period in which the executive grudgingly protected some African-Americans trying to exercise their civil rights, at least one part of the legislation could be used to suppress black militancy. The Nixon administration considered using Section 245 to obtain injunctions against black and white radicals who used disruptive tactics to gain their objectives. They seemed to have in mind black students who demanded that universities offer Black Studies and power in the academic community, or white radicals protesting against the war in Vietnam. Any governmental suppression of students under Section 245, would presumably be "in the public interest" as required by the terms of the bill.[40]

In the spring of 1969, Congress had its attention more and more drawn to the Students for a Democratic Society (SDS) and such groups as the Black Panthers and the Revolutionary Action Movement (RAM). The FBI had placed these groups on its Rabble-Rouser lists and targeted them for counterintelligence activities in 1966. Many members of Congress seemed to believe that either there were no iniquities that could generate radical liberation efforts, or that even if such inequities did exist, the oppressed could not possibly consider revolutionary action unless some group or individual encouraged them. The groups or individuals responsible must be communist-backed or actual communists. The Nixon Republicans, elected on a law-and-order platform in the midst of growing black militancy, increased the repressive stance that had come to characterize Johnson's behavior. They made great use of the FBI's expansive intelligence operation, targeting black radicals as well as anyone involved in civil rights by the time they took office. The FBI embarked on a wide-ranging campaign of counterintelligence. They used charges of anti-Semitism against black nationalist leaders in an attempt to persuade liberal Jews and other whites to withhold their support, sent disinformation to each side whenever FBI surveillance reported ego or ideological conflict between groups of black nationalists, and used informers to foment violence in the organizations and to fabricate charges for criminal prosecution. The purpose was to destroy any possibility of a coherent movement.[41]

The government responded to militancy in the traditional ways. The House Un-American Activities Committee (HUAC) continued its thorough investigation of subversive influences in riots, looting, and burnings begun after the riots in 1967. The committee heard a variety of testimony which was used to place the blame for the riots on communist influence: words of admiration for revolutionists such as Che Guevara; comments about the imperatives of people to attain freedom by any means necessary; statements expressing the refusal to discountenance violence; the enumeration of trips to communist countries; and comments by communists in support of riots.[42]

In 1968–69, Senator John McClellan's permanent investigation subcommittee, working hand-in-glove with Hoover, investigated the same organizations HUAC had probed, but this time, the Black Panthers and the SDS drew more attention. McClellan stated that a year-long study by his investigators indicated that there was an anarchistic movement, operating under different labels, which was dedicated to the objective of overthrowing the government. Vice President Spiro Agnew aided the governmental effort by sending the committee a copy of coloring books reportedly circulated to black children, depicting white policemen and merchants as "pigs" and urging black children to "off" (kill) them. The Panthers had organized a "feed breakfast to the children" program across the country for ghetto youngsters and, according to the committee, were preaching violence as part of the program. Panther Chairman Bobby Seale told a press conference that the coloring book was unauthorized and that they had taken it out of circulation after only twenty-five copies were printed. Seale took this opportunity to state that Larry Powell, a star witness at the committee hearings who said he had been a Panther and who had charged the group with conducting robberies and having venal leadership, was a paid government agent who joined the group for the express purpose of finding a means to undermine its image with the people. While the committee determined what legislation was needed to suppress such groups, a Catholic priest in whose church some of the books had reportedly been circulated said he did permit the distribution of the books, but in a society where "the only good Indian was a dead Indian" and "the only good nigger was a dead nigger," he was not alarmed when the victims of police brutality said "the only good pig was a dead pig."[43]

In late 1969 and 1970, attacks on policemen continued. These assaults were usually attributed to urban guerrillas, including the Black Panthers, even when there was no evidence of their complicity. In 1969, 86 policemen were reported killed, a 34 percent increase over the casualties of 1968, and by mid-October 1970, 67 were reported killed, 16 of them murdered in allegedly unprovoked attacks. In each case, investigations were made and charges were brought against alleged attackers. The Panthers engaged police in more than a dozen firefights from October 1967 to December 1969, and at least 2 policemen and 10 Panthers died in that two-year period. In 1969 law enforcement officers arrested 348 Panthers on murder, armed robbery, rape, bank robbery, drug trafficking, burglary, and dozens of other charges. Congress responded predictably to these events. Hearings were held by the Senate Internal Security Subcommittee chaired by Senator Eastland. Law enforcement officials testified to threats and attacks made on policemen, and the subcommittee proposed the passage of a federal law, based on the Commerce Clause of the Constitution, which would make the murder of a policeman a federal crime.[44]

In this climate the traditional federal disinterest in protecting African-American lives from white violence while showing great concern for controlling blacks took a different turn. Federal officials began to violate the civil rights laws in addition to refusing to enforce them. The government acted under Section 242's "under color of law" provision designed to punish police abuse to harass blacks who demanded civil rights enforcement. They worked closely with local officials and stooped to withholding evidence in trials of black militants charged with offenses and even simulating evidence to gain convictions.[45]

Many members of black revolutionary groups, particularly the Black Panthers, were killed or injured in confrontations with policemen in late 1969 and 1970. The FBI infiltrated their organizations with informants to target them for police action. On December 4, 1969, two Panthers, Mark Clark and Fred Hampton, were killed in a police assault on Hampton's apartment in Chicago. An FBI informant, William O'Neal, gave the FBI the floor plans and indicated when the occupants would be most vulnerable. In January 1970, a county coroner's jury ruled that the slayings were justifiable homicide. A federal grand jury reported in May 1970 that the police fired eighty-three shots into the apartment while only one shot was fired toward the police. They shot and killed an unresisting Hampton in his bed. Clark had reportedly fired one shot but it could not be shown whether he fired before or after the police began shooting. Witnesses testified that Hampton was probably drugged with secobarbital at the time, which explains why he did not rise from his bed. The grand jury, however, did not believe there was enough evidence to sustain the indictment of any of the police for violating the civil rights of the victims under the statute used in the *Price* and *Guest* cases.[46]

Three weeks after the killing O'Neal received a special payment from the FBI of $300.00 for "uniquely valuable service which he rendered over the last several months." In 1972, following the longest civil rights trial in U.S. history, the survivors of the massacre and the families of Hampton and Clark agreed to accept a settlement of $1.85 million from the federal, county, and city governments. The U.S. Attorney said they settled to avoid a long and expensive trial. A commission of inquiry chaired by Roy Wilkins and Ramsey Clark concluded in 1973 that the raid on December 4, 1969, was not handled in compliance with the Fourth Amendment guarantee against unreasonable searches and seizures and that the grand jury erred in not finding probable cause to believe that Sections 241 and 242 of the *United States Code* were violated by the "summary punishment" of the Panthers in the raid.[47]

Aside from reported attacks on individual police officers, there was at least one black revolutionary action against the court system in the late summer of 1970. In August, Jonathan Jackson, a seventeen-year-old Black Panther, carried weapons into the Marin County courthouse in San Rafael, California, tossed them to three black prisoners who were awaiting trial, and set off a kidnapping and shooting incident which led to the murders of Judge Harold Haley, Jackson, and two of the prisoners. Two of the weapons were found to be registered in the name of Angela Davis, a twenty-five-year-old former philosophy professor at UCLA and an avowed Communist. The FBI started a nationwide manhunt for Davis, who was charged with kidnapping and homicide, even though she had not been present when the incident took place. Under California law, if Davis had given the guns to Jackson to be used in the slaying, she would be guilty of the actual crime.[48]

Davis went into hiding and was arrested in New York City after the FBI named her as one of the ten most wanted criminals for murder, kidnapping, and conspiracy. She remained in jail for sixteen months while a massive international campaign demanded her release. In this setting, on June 4, 1972, a California jury declared her innocent on all charges.[49]

The FBI and police war on the Panthers succeeded. By the mid-

1970s when the hearings of the Senate Select Committee to Study Governmental Operations With Respect to Intelligence Activities documented the abuse of FBI surveillance, the Panthers were all either dead, in jail, or announcing they were reformed. The committee focused on the FBI and their investigations of racial matters. FBI surveillance of blacks, including militants and Martin Luther King, Jr., was an old story. On March 8, 1971, an antiwar group, the Citizens Committee to Investigate the FBI, burglarized an FBI agency in Media, Pennsylvania. The committee made some material from the burglary available to the press, including documentation of FBI surveillance and the ghetto informants' program.[50]

Before and after Hoover died in May 1972, the FBI, which was supposed to investigate crimes and prevent criminal conduct, engaged in lawless tactics and responded to the race problem by inciting violence and disorder, with the support of the president and the entire Justice Department. They continued to recruit informers, collect information on Black Student Unions, report on black studies programs and personnel, and spread disinformation to undermine the programs and organizations. The FBI kept an index not just on activists but also on teachers, writers, and lawyers whom they believed influential in espousing revolutionary philosophies. In the name of suppressing terrorism and violence, wiretaps on suspected militants' homes and offices continued.[51]

The federal government's suppression of black revolutionary activity may be justified practically as an appropriate response to the violence advocated by black nationalist groups. The contrast, however, between the behavior of the Justice Department and the FBI toward black groups and toward white segregationists who burned, bombed, maimed, and killed black citizens and civil rights activists was stark. The theories of federalist limitation which Burke Marshall and other Justice Department lawyers threw so eagerly at civil rights workers who demanded protection were nowhere in evidence. Suppressing black resistance and rebellion was not a job reserved primarily for the local police, although the latter were considered strong enough to handle white violence against blacks. Furthermore, protecting African-Americans and vindicating injury done to them was not a priority of the federal government.

The Community Relations Service (CRS) of the Justice Department, established under the Civil Rights Act of 1964, reported police brutality and other violence against blacks that went unpunished throughout the 1970s while the FBI and the Justice Department's Civil Rights Division spent their time in surveillance of black individuals and groups. The CRS was mandated to conciliate tense civil rights incidents but did not include the names of alleged offenders and victims in their reports. Among the occurrences they reported, on October 15, 1971, three black youths in Memphis accused of stealing a truck were severely beaten by police and one died. Eight officers charged with the murder were acquitted on December 7, 1974, by an all-white jury, setting off a week of protests and racial disturbances.[52]

In 1972, the CRS reported several protests by blacks against police violence in the North and the South. In a southern city on a second day of demonstrations a young black man was stopped by police and arrested for driving without a license. After being released from jail he told protestors the police beat and shot at him. When marchers gathered on a third day of protest, violence erupted and buildings were burned.[53]

In 1973 and 1974, the Justice Department and the White House monitored the violence growing out of the busing of black students into South Boston but did little to alleviate the crisis. African-American community leaders Ruth Batson and Mel King and others became upset because white schools had better resources, were not overcrowded, and employed permanent teachers. In 1963 they began meeting with the school committee to demand better racial integration and quality education for black children but got nowhere. They received little support from the city or state government as they continued the struggle over the years. In 1972 they filed a lawsuit in federal district court, and a court order sent black children to South Boston and Charlestown in 1974. A white antibusing group called Restore our Alienated Rights, or ROAR, operated throughout the city under the leadership of Louise Day Hicks, who was a member of the city council.[54]

On the first day of busing in 1974, at the end of the school day buses carrying black elementary school children out of South Boston were stoned. Boston's Dorchester High also had an influx of black students. The South Boston assailants thought they were protecting their neighborhood by protesting in the tradition of the civil rights protestors in the South—although they used violence. The Boston troubles were among the 959 alerts to racial trouble that CRS reported in 1974, an increase of 369 from the previous year. There were over four hundred orders in the federal case filed in 1972, as opponents tried to overturn the busing order, but the U.S. Supreme Court never accepted an appeal. President Gerald Ford supported a brief opposing Supreme Court intervention upon the plea of NAACP Washington lobbyist Clarence Mitchell, who explained to Ford that otherwise he would be supporting lawlessness. Mitchell told Ford that he had to be as strong as Eisenhower on Little Rock; it did not matter that he was opposed to busing personally. In November 1977, Louise Day Hicks lost her seat on the city council and John O'Bryant became the first black member of the council. Desegregation, however, remained stalled.[55]

Between 1965 and 1976, the "We Shall Overcome" principles of the Black Liberation movement were merged with and, in some cases, overwhelmed by an increased emphasis on violence as a tactic and strategy. Where the Kennedy administration had been forced by the movement to use federal military power to protect African-Americans within the framework of constitutional law, the Johnson and Nixon administrations found themselves using governmental power against blacks, who seemed to be law violators. Liberals in Congress who had fought for civil rights bills with great moral fervor were dismayed. While they supported the War on Poverty as one solution to ghetto ills, their programs lacked the breadth to deal adequately with the problems. Liberals were inundated by the law-and-order protagonists, led by the conservative southerners who were pleased to be able to say, "I told you so." Meanwhile, militant blacks, in unvarnished rhetoric, demanded economic and social revolution, making it clear that they did not believe America had the capacity to reform itself, as racism was fundamental in American life, in its foreign policies, and in its profit system. The response of the federal government, reflecting the Nixon administration's conservative position, seemed to be that police and military power would be used to suppress those who refused to submit to the system, a position which required no real alteration in constitutional theory; the techniques for instituting local and federal suppression of rebellion and disorder had always been in the Constitution and had always been effectively utilized when considered necessary.

Conservatives and black militants, as well as white radicals, seemed to have come full circle and to have all reached the same conclusions. Militants and radicals asserted that the Constitution was a property-minded instrument which failed to provide equality and justice for the masses; therefore, they wanted to change or subvert it. Conservatives agreed with them about the nature of the Constitution, but asserted that such change was undesirable and that militant efforts to "radicalize" the framework of government would be suppressed.

As the black nationalist rebellion was suppressed, African-American leaders directed the masses toward political participation as the route to equality of opportunity and an end to black subordination. The results would determine the future course of black resistance and the federal role in controlling African-Americans.

16

Protests
and Renewed
Violence

D URING THE LATE 1970s and the 1980s African-American leaders promoted electoral politics as the route for black empowerment. However, voting did not appear to many African-Americans to eliminate economic and social constraints on their opportunities. Consequently, nonviolent direct action as a strategy endured. Resistance movements that demanded positive government action and an end to police brutality and racially motivated intimidation and violence remained central to the struggle for justice.

By 1977 black revolutionary organizations, including those emphasizing black nationalism, had been largely suppressed or had receded in visibility. Those blacks who had been best positioned to benefit from the civil rights movement, urban rebellions, and the social programs they inspired enjoyed their new economic and political opportunities.

From one perspective, not much needed to be resisted. Enormous change had occurred since the beginning of the civil rights movement. By 1977, whites were still twice as likely as blacks to complete college but the college attendance rates of African-American high school graduates had increased substantially. Eleven percent of African-Americans had completed college, compared to less than 2 percent in 1940. African-American men, women of all races, and other racial minorities experienced increased state and local government employment, including jobs in municipal fire and police departments, and began to make a dent in private sector professional and white-collar jobs. Many poor African-Americans moved into better jobs as police officers, firefighters, clerks, and other kinds of employment from which they were excluded before the movement.[1]

Many of the poor, however, did not benefit from the civil rights movement before it ended. Some were not born, others were too young, or the under-funded programs never arrived in their neighborhood. The class divide which had always existed in the community appeared even greater as some African-American scholars and activists joined in the growing political backlash against the race relations changes of the 1960s. They began to insist that the civil rights movement had benefited middle-class African-Americans who abandoned the black poor. Their analyses downplayed the diminution of government support to those left behind. Instead, they agreed with political opponents of social programs and civil rights that the poverty resulted from an emphasis on civil rights, the availability of welfare payments, and black middle-class negligence.[2]

White conservative writers, policymakers, and elected officials, whose emerging political coalition opposed government spending and civil rights, embraced those African-Americans who agreed with their emphasis. The shift in focus from discrimination, and the accent on class division, created internal conflict in the African-American community. The disagreement weakened efforts to demand positive government policy and to insist that perpetrators of racially motivated violence against blacks be punished. It also distracted attention from the continued effects of racism. Mobilization became more difficult but community-based resistance against police violence, racial harassment, and other problems continued.[3]

In the years after the passage of the Voting Rights Act in 1965, elected black and white law enforcement officials publicly discouraged acts of police brutality. The police abuse, however, often continued even when discouraged. Furthermore, the economic problems of the masses that Martin Luther King, Jr., had tried to address in the Poor People's Campaign remained unaddressed and in some cases worsened. Once blacks saw that voting seemed to have limited effectiveness, black political participation steadily declined from 1968 through 1975.[4]

African-American access to the vote increased the total number of black elected officials. In 1975 there were 3,503 black elected officials of the more than 500,000 elected officials in the whole country. In 1966 there was no black mayor of any major American city but by 1975 blacks had served as mayors of Gary, Newark, and Los Angeles, as well as a number of small southern towns. One black sat in the Senate, Edward Brooke of Massachusetts, and 17 sat in the Congress, including 4 women, Shirley Chisholm, Barbara Jordan, Yvonne Burke, and Cardiss Collins. After Nixon resigned for the crimes of Watergate, Gerald Ford, in January 1975, appointed William T. Coleman, Jr., the secretary of transportation, the second time an African-American Cabinet member had been named since Robert C. Weaver ran HUD in the Johnson administration.[5]

Noting the continual decline in black political participation, in May 1976 a group of black leaders who represented major civic, fraternal, labor, and religious groups decided to work together to increase the black vote. In addition, early in the presidential primary season Andrew Young, a congressman from Georgia, became a highly visible campaigner for Jimmy Carter who was seeking the Democratic nomination. In 1976 about 57 percent of whites who were eligible voted, but only 49 percent of blacks did so. Of the estimated nine million blacks registered to vote in the November 1976 election, about 64.1 percent voted and most of them opted for Jimmy Carter, giving him a crucial margin of victory over Gerald Ford. When Carter took office, he appointed more blacks than ever before to posts in his administration.[6]

Discontent grew, however, when elected black mayors found that they had few economic resources to command. The economic power of cities was controlled by whites even as white flight, followed by the exodus of the black middle class to the suburbs, depleted the cities' resources. Mayors inherited an eroding tax base and the loss of jobs. Newly elected black officials tried to give their black constituencies greater equity, in access to city contracts, appointments, and other ingredients of political patronage. They were met with draining legal challenges from whites who used the equality arguments blacks had honed in the civil rights struggle to claim that it would be discriminatory to force them to relinquish these valuable resources.[7]

In searching for alternative routes to betterment, some blacks joined James Jones, a white Indianapolis preacher based first in Ukiah, California, and then San Francisco. He became a leader in local politics, although behind-the-scenes corruption, drugs, rape, aberrant sexual behavior, and torture suffused his cult. In 1976–77 he moved his following to Jonestown in Guyana. Rumors grew about the organization. After a visiting congressman, Leo J. Ryan of California, was murdered in November 1978, Jones's followers submitted to his order to commit mass suicide. Nine hundred and twelve bodies were recovered, two-thirds of whom were black.[8]

President Carter seemed committed to civil rights and economic justice. However, in 1978, he publicly agonized over the case of *Bakke v. California*. Allan Bakke, a white student who was denied admission to the University of California at Davis Medical School, claimed that less qualified minority students were admitted instead. Carter pondered long and hard before announcing that the Justice Department would support the university's affirmative action plan in the case, which had become a symbol for those who saw affirmative action as reverse discrimination. Carter did not defend the university's aim of building diversity in its student body or the qualifications of the students who were admitted. Before his decision, he stated publicly that their admission "contravenes the concept of merit selection." The concern for Bakke contrasted sharply with presidential and congressional disinterest in the distress in poor black communities or in remedying the effects of discrimination against African-Americans. A lack of remedies and high unemployment and economic deprivation in the black community caused Jesse Jackson, in May 1980, to lead a March for Jobs on Washington.[9]

President Carter had appointed his friend Griffin Bell as attorney general. They named as assistant attorney general for civil rights a former NAACP Legal Defense Fund attorney, Drew Days, the first African-American in that job. He served for the entire four years of the administration. Carter and his appointees confronted one major riot and several instances of rebellions and police violence during their tenure. They established a more aggressive record than the Nixon-Ford team in responding to police violence but on other issues their record was spotty. The civil rights changes of the 1960s and the fact that there was a black assistant attorney general for civil rights did not end the use of the states' rights argument as a barrier to federal enforcement. The emphasis on suppressing black resistance and the theme of reluctant federal intervention when violence interfered with civil rights did shift somewhat, however, in the Carter years.[10]

The Justice Department was concerned about the problem of police abuse. In 1979, Days reported that the Civil Rights Division (CRD) had a high of 12,000 complaints of interference with the civil rights of citizens in 1977 and a low of 10,000 complaints during his time in office. He reported that "investigations into complaints alleging summary punishment by law enforcement officials continued to account for much of the Section's activities." In addition, the conviction rates for cases that went to trial were very good, except in cases involving police and law enforcement officers, which were most often reversed. His division had filed no more than 73 police cases each year after investigations, mostly through grand jury indictments. Many of these cases involved multiple defendants.[11]

Episodes of police violence which African-Americans thought unnecessary sparked civil disturbances, which led to community protests and more violence. The Justice Department's Community Relations Service (CRS) routinely helped local officials to conciliate. In 1978, in Providence, Rhode Island, disturbances broke out after an unexplained murder of a black man by police. In Cincinnati, after the police killing of a mentally disturbed black man, continuing community tensions surfaced over a four-month period in 1979 during which four black citizens and four white policemen were killed. In Oakland, California, police killed nine black males in 1979 alone, one of whom was a fifteen-year-old boy.[12]

The Civil Rights Division found no basis for federal charges in most of the CRS cases. In 1979, however, the division set what Days called "a modern-day record," prosecuting 118 persons for violations of federal civil rights criminal laws. Thirty-seven of the 39 cases tried involved violations by police or other law enforcement officials.[13]

The extensive and persistent reports and complaints of police brutality received from the regions and at commission headquarters led the U.S. Commission on Civil Rights to hold a series of hearings around the country and in Washington, D.C., in 1979. Days explained to the commission that the small number of convictions gained by the Civil Rights Division reflected several constraints. The absence of sufficient testimony or other evidence to gain conviction, or insufficient proof that the federal government had jurisdiction, inhibited the Civil Rights Division's efforts. Furthermore, Days noted that technicalities in the criminal civil rights laws made conviction difficult. Section 241 only covered conspiracies and not individual action; and Section 242 required a specific intent to deprive a person of his or her constitutional rights. Conspiracies and "specific intent" were both difficult to prove or explain to a jury. Juries often failed to understand that beating someone, in itself, constituted a specific intent to administer summary punishment by a police officer, without due process, which was impermissible under the Constitution. Jurors were inclined, incorrectly, to think that specific intent required the police officer to think, while he beat the victim, "I am beating you to deprive you of your constitutional right to due process."[14]

Also, Days explained that police officers convicted under Section 242 of acting under color of law or authority could receive only one-year sentences unless death resulted. Many of the cases involved severe beatings whose victims survived. Drew also underscored the prosecution problem by noting that in police cases, the conviction rate was only between 45 and 70 percent, while in cases against private citizens or organized groups the percentage of convictions was in the nineties.[15]

Days echoed the attitude of his predecessors in expressing reluctance to bring charges in police brutality cases. He told the commission, "it is neither proper nor feasible for the federal government to become the law enforcement body of first resort" in police abuse cases. The department's policy required that federal civil rights charges against a state police officer be undertaken only if, after a state prosecution for the same act, there is "a compelling Federal interest." The policy applied when a prior state proceeding had led to an acquittal, conviction, or other termination on the merits, and not before the state proceeding was concluded. The Civil Rights Division weighed whether the outcome has left "substantial federal interest demonstrably unvindicated."[16]

The division would consider such factors as whether the prosecution was ineffective, whether the court or jury had nullified the verdict in blatant disregard of the evidence or the failure of the state to prove an element of the offense, or whether significant evidence had been unavailable in the state proceeding. Days believed it was better not to bring cases than to lose them. The failure to achieve conviction, he thought, would encourage others to continue their abuse. Administration critics believed, to the contrary, that no prosecution meant acquiescence and that at least prosecution which had some likelihood of success might discourage police brutality. From their perspective, the discretion used by federal officials produced reluctant justice at best.[17]

Despite Days's expression of caution the CRD took the unprecedented action of suing the city of Philadelphia in 1979, alleging a pattern and practice of police abuse on racially discriminatory grounds. They asked the courts to terminate federal funds and to enjoin the abusive practices. The department lost at every stage as the courts rejected the complaint on the grounds that no direct statutory authority existed for the attorney general to sue on behalf of third parties. Days explained that he and Attorney General Bell filed the charges because they believed an institutional problem existed in Philadelphia. When a police officer who brutalized persons believed that "he or she is going to be shielded and protected by the institution from an investigation and from prosecutions, that the counsel is going to be provided, and even when damages are awarded that not the officer but the city is going to pay, then I think what we have is a situation where even prosecuting individual officers is not going to change the environment." The city of Philadelphia's victory in the case meant that the police brutality problem remained unresolved.[18]

In May 1980 the work of the Civil Rights Division went beyond the usual complaints and prosecutions for police violence to confront a large-scale riot which originated in police abuse. In December 1979 in Miami, Florida, white policemen arrested Arthur McDuffie, a black man, after they chased him on his motorcycle at high speed. While in police custody he was beaten and died four days later. McDuffie was a U.S. Marine Corps veteran and the black community counted him as yet another black man killed unnecessarily by the police. When the case came to trial, the judge agreed that the defendants could not receive a fair trial in Miami and moved the case to Tampa. In May 1980, when the defendants were acquitted by a nonblack jury, rebellion and angry rioting in the Miami black community erupted. Seven whites were among the fifteen killed as a result of the riot. In response to the rebellion, white police used billy clubs, rifles, and steel pipes to destroy the automobiles of blacks whom they suspected of rioting.

Automobiles were spray-painted with the words "Looter," "Thief," and "I am a cheap no good looter."[19]

President Carter dispatched Days, CRS staff, and FBI investigators to Miami. State national guardsmen subdued the riot, without a call for federal troops. The Carter administration promised social and economic help to the alienated black residents, and local and state government officials promised reforms in the criminal justice system. The U.S. Civil Rights Commission held hearings and recommended changes in the prosecution system and positive policies to increase black economic empowerment and relieve racial tensions.[20]

The commission noted that McDuffie's experience was not that unusual. Other cities routinely reported police abuse. The underlying causes ranged from police department employment practices to inadequate police training and evaluation. The Miami Police Department, for example, screened applicants for the department with an allegedly biased test. Dade County established an independent review panel to investigate complaints against the police but the panel was given few resources and had no subpoena power. The problems in Miami and elsewhere were not seriously addressed by either the federal government or local communities. In 1980, the Justice Department recorded riots, incited most often by police brutality, not only in Miami, but also in Orlando and Tampa; Chattanooga, Tennesse; Nampa, Idaho; Flint, Michigan; and Wichita, Kansas.[21]

In addition to police abuse and individual acts of racial harassment, organized violence and intimidation by white supremacists continued to plague African-Americans in the Carter years. The Ku Klux Klan, still very much in existence after J. Edgar Hoover's highly publicized war against the organization, tripled its membership between 1971 and 1980. So bold was the Klan that in January 1977, 250 Klansmen held a demonstration in Plains, Georgia, the hometown of incoming president Jimmy Carter. In November 1978, Klansmen and Okolona, Mississippi, police cooperated in an ambush of members of the United League, a black rights organization. In the shoot-out one Klansman was killed, and five others were seriously wounded. United League leader Skip Robinson stated later, "Over one hundred rounds were fired." Neither the Klan nor the police publicized the incident but he said, "after that we never saw no more Klan in Okolona."[22]

In 1978 and 1979, Klansmen fired shotguns into the homes of several NAACP leaders in the South. The CRD successfully prosecuted ten of the Klan members in Alabama, charging them with conspiring to intimidate NAACP leaders. Eight of the ten Klan members were also convicted of intimidating biracial couples. The Klan firebombed black homes, churches, and schools in over one hundred towns and rural areas.[23]

In Greensboro, North Carolina, on November 3, 1979, seventy-five Klansman and Nazis attacked an antiracist "Death to the Klan" rally organized by local black and white activists, leaving five protestors, all members of the Communist Workers Party and heavily involved in labor organizing, dead, and eleven other demonstrators wounded. Only six of the murderers were tried. An all-white jury acquitted the defendants, despite videotaped evidence which documented the killings in detail. Nine were acquitted of conspiracy charges in federal court four years later. Eight of the demonstrators in Greensboro were arrested by local police and charged with fire-bombing and conspiracy to fire-bomb. Black Marxist Nelson Johnson, who received severe knife wounds during the attack, was charged with felony riot and later jailed for twenty days on contempt charges.[24]

The shooting of a black woman in Birmingham on June 22, 1979, by the Klan ignited protest marches and countermarches. Decatur, Alabama, exploded on May 26, 1979, when sixty African-Americans, some of whom were armed, demonstrated in support of Jimmy Lee Hines, an apparently retarded black man who had been convicted earlier and given thirty years for allegedly raping a white woman. The African-Americans were intercepted by one hundred Klansman; after the encounter two Klansmen and two blacks lay wounded in the street. The Southern Christian Leadership Conference vowed to have a nonviolent march to protest the events on June 9 and asked for national support. CRS helped local law enforcement to conciliate in the effort to maintain order. The marches took place without further incident. A CRD suit against local city officials for failure to provide protection and engaging in a conspiracy to intimidate participants in the parade ultimately failed on technicalities. The court of appeals found that the Justice Department failed to prove that the parade was "provided by" or "administered" by the city. The number of incidents involving the Klan which the CRS reported in 1979 increased by 450 percent over the previous year.[25]

One Klansman, "Grand Dragon" Thomas Metzger, organized a fascist-oriented, black-uniformed security force in California which led violent attacks against progressive and interracial groups. In 1980 Metzger's support among conservative southern California white voters led to victory in the state's forty-third congressional district Democratic primary. His program of white rights included promises to end affirmative action, foreign immigration, and school desegregation. The Democratic Party officials and machinery mobilized against him after his surprise primary victory and he lost overwhelmingly in the general election. Metzger continued his political and organizational efforts, regarding the primary victory as a real sign of his strength.[26]

A scuffle between black demonstrators and a group of whites broke out in front of the county sheriff's office in Wrightsville, Georgia, on April 8, 1980. Nine persons were reportedly injured. Blacks were demonstrating against employment discrimination and a lack of political representation. Wrightsville, a segregated town, still restricted its cemetery to whites only. They reported that a group of one hundred or more whites, including sheriff's deputies, charged into the group. The Johnson County sheriff denied that the charge had occurred or that he or other police officers were involved. Governor George Busbee sent state troopers to the town of 2,100 people after the incident. They dispersed a crowd of whites and seized weapons in the black section of town. Buildings were set ablaze in the black neighborhood; whites and blacks exchanged gunfire. Invisible Empire KKK members wounded a nine-year-old black girl on April 19, by a shotgun blast into a mobile home. The Southern Christian Leadership Conference held a peaceful demonstration that day. The following month a twenty-two-year-old black man was shot and seriously injured by a carload of white men. Racial violence began again when law enforcement officers brutalized peaceful civil rights protestors. The Klan established a local Klavern. Mob assaults upon blacks and street fights continued.[27]

Shootings and other racially motivated violence perpetrated by private citizens continued to the end of the Carter years. National Urban League President Vernon Jordan was shot in the back by a gunman in Fort Wayne, Indiana, on May 29, 1980. Police arrested an avowed racist, Joseph Paul Franklin, for shooting him and the CRD brought charges under Section 241 after consulting with local officials. During the trial, witnesses testified that Franklin talked to them about killing Jordan. An all-white jury declared him innocent on August 17, 1982.[28]

CRD prosecuted Klan members for violations of federal civil rights in addition to the charges brought against the Klan for intimidating NAACP leaders in the South. In 1979, prosecutors charged Klan members in Detroit with conspiracy against the rights of citizens and interference with federally protected activities. The offenders had made shotgun attacks upon a black victim and harassed and threatened a black family living in a white neighborhood. Four Klan members admitted their culpability. In California, two Klan members entered guilty pleas to charges of interference with housing rights after having fired a sawed-off shotgun into the mobile home of a black family.[29]

In other Klan-related prosecutions, two defendants were convicted of civil rights violations and two other defendants tendered guilty pleas; three defendants were convicted for cross burnings. A Massachusetts defendant indicted for harassing a black family for living in her neighborhood admitted her actions.[30]

In addition the CRD, which had failed to convict Joseph Paul Franklin for shooting Vernon Jordan, succeeded in gaining his conviction in 1983 under Section 241 for fatally shooting two black men who were jogging with two white women near a municipal park in Salt Lake City. Franklin ended up serving four life sentences on dual state and federal charges. The Justice Department also obtained guilty pleas in several cases. Four Klansmen were convicted for abusing a black male and his white wife who were engaged in "enjoying their rights to interstate travel between Tennessee and Alabama."[31]

As the Carter administration came to an end with Ronald Reagan's landslide victory in 1980, black voters who were disenchanted with the president but could not support an openly hostile Reagan gave Carter 85 percent of their vote. When Reagan took office, African-Americans did not expect him to emphasize enforcing their civil rights. Candidate Reagan had begun his campaign in August 1980 with a speech delivered in Philadelphia, Mississippi, where Chaney, Schwerner, and Goodman had been killed. He pledged that his administration would defend the principle of states' rights, which augured poorly for civil rights enforcement.[32]

For the first time since the CRD was established in the Eisenhower administration, during the first Reagan term the number of racial violence complaints filed with the division steadily diminished. From a high of 11,064 criminal complaints in the last year of the Carter administration and the first nine months of the Reagan administration the numbers decreased each year. In 1984 there were only 8,617 complaints. The complaints decreased, while the CRS reported increasing numbers of incidents of racial harassment, police abuse of African-Americans, and complaints that state and local officials refused to punish the perpetrators. Aggrieved African-Americans were less likely to complain to what they regarded as an unsympathetic Justice Department.[33]

During Reagan's first term a number of black conservatives, who downplayed the existence of racism, became increasingly visible in the media. Continued racial animus alongside economic problems, however, engendered widespread alienation among African-Americans. Reagan's rhetoric and policies, which blamed blacks for reverse discrimination against white men, who were encouraged to see themselves as victims, contributed to a climate in which racially motivated violence increased substantially. In addition, hopelessness among poor African-Americans contributed to an increase in crime in the black community. The drug culture, along with the law enforcement crackdown on drug users and dealers, caused increased incarceration of African-Americans. The prison system became, by default, a major enforcer of repression. Ever larger numbers of African-American men were in prison serving long sentences for drug offenses. The policy response of the administration was to increase repression rather than improve economic conditions, education, the treatment of drug addicts, or other solutions that were denounced as liberal. Poor African-Americans perceived the twin faces of oppression, the unavailability of legal jobs, increased racial harassment, and few helpful responses.[34]

Reagan appointed his personal attorney and friend, William French Smith, as attorney general. As assistant attorney general for civil rights they chose William Bradford Reynolds, in the mold of Burke Marshall in the Kennedy administration, a corporate lawyer with no previous civil rights record. The administration opposed civil rights as defined in the statutes and by Supreme Court decisions in almost every area of enforcement. The Civil Rights Division also gave scant attention to police abuse of black citizens. When asked about their record the administration followed the example set by former FBI Director J. Edgar Hoover. They changed the subject by noting their prosecution of some highly publicized cases against the Klan and other white supremacist organizations. Hoover used a similar tactic to defend his policy of not investigating the clandestine murder of civil rights workers and of instructing FBI agents to stand aside and watch workers being assaulted. Reynolds spent a great deal of energy in public debate demonizing blacks and canonizing white males, attacking affirmative action in court and in the media. The administration's rhetoric did nothing to deter a rising tide of violence and racial harassment.[35]

Throughout the Reagan first term, the Justice Department's Community Relations Service (CRS) continued to report on racially motivated violence by groups and individuals as well as police abuse, and to engage in conciliation efforts. The CRS reported in 1982 that such harassment and violence constituted "the fastest growing body of cases" handled by the agency. The service monitored news reports and local government requests for assistance and exercised a federal role restricted to suppressing community outrage. In 1982 the CRS was involved in 961 racial hate crime incidents, compared to 691 in 1981. Alleged acts of racial harassment by the Ku Klux Klan and other groups accounted for a majority of the new alerts of trouble the agency received.[36]

Some alerts involved only the possibility of trouble. The CRS consulted with state officials "when it was feared that a gathering of 1,200 black motorcyclists in Colorado might lead to violence." Black motorcycle clubs held their annual gathering on federal property near Silver Plume, Colorado, in August 1982. They arrived on Thursday for a stay through Sunday. Clear Creek County Undersheriff David Benson worried about trouble especially if the bikers stayed around after Sunday. The Hell's Angels planned to gather the next week for their national meeting about fifty miles away. Benson used 6 extra patrol cars to patrol the area where the black bikers met. He planned to gather 100 deputies and additional weapons from around the state to monitor the activities of the Hell's Angels. No violence occurred.[37]

Also, "disputes related to environmental issues" became "a growing CRS concern." In Warren County, North Carolina, black protestors failed to prevent state officials from establishing a dump site for soil contaminated with polychlorinated biphenyls (PCB) in their neighborhood. Daily protests involving hundreds of arrests were made as blacks tried to block the trucks.[38]

The Civil Rights Division (CRD) filed eight cases against fourteen hate-crime defendants in federal court in 1982. They succeeded in convicting a Memphis defendant for harassing a black family who purchased a home in a predominantly white neighborhood. The family's car and home were repeatedly vandalized and finally fire-bombed. In addition a South Williamsport, Pennsylvania, juvenile was convicted for a rock-throwing and cross-burning incident directed at a black family. They also gained an indictment of four defendants for fire-bombing a black family's home in Muncie, Indiana.[39]

In Savin Hill, a predominantly white Roman Catholic neighborhood in Boston, in March 1982, a black nursing-home maintenance man, William (Frankie) Atkinson, thirty, was found dead from a fractured skull in a subway station. He and a white friend, William Grady, had been chased into the station by white youths throwing bottles and stones. As the youths chased them into the station Atkinson ran down the rails to escape the rocks and bottles. Grady was knocked unconscious near the stairway. The original police report said the whites chased Atkinson while others waited for him on the tracks and beat him to death. Fear of retaliation which might ignite other serious incidents led community leaders to mobilize, urging calm and cooperation with the police in their investigation of the death. The CRS brought community leaders together with police officials, the district attorney, and U.S. attorney to share information and deter anger. Five white teenagers were later arrested and charged with manslaughter. Two of the youths, Francis X. Devlin, twenty, and William M. Joyce, nineteen, were convicted and sentenced to six to twelve years imprisonment. Paul MacGregor, twenty, Edward J. Tuffo, nineteen, and Michael Nowacki, twenty, were acquitted of manslaughter but convicted on assault charges and sentenced to one year in a house of correction and one year of probation.[40]

Soon after the Atkinson killing, fire-bombing and harassment of black families in the Savin Hill area and nearby neighborhoods began. Some whites tried to help black families by aiding in guard duty. Soon, however, attempts at interracial cooperation broke down into blame-casting and shouting matches.[41]

A Detroit hate crime incident in 1982 sparked demonstrations by

African-Americans, along with Hispanics and Asian-Americans, and led to a federal prosecution. In June 1982, Vincent Chin, a twenty-seven-year-old Chinese-American, and three friends out celebrating his upcoming marriage became racial abuse victims. They became involved in an altercation with two white men, Ronald Ebens and Michael Nitz, at a topless club. Ebens and Nitz followed them to their car and after taking a baseball bat from their car severely beat Chin, who was hospitalized but later died from his injuries.[42]

Tried and convicted on manslaughter charges early in 1983, the two whites were sentenced in Wayne County Circuit Court to $3,000 fines and three years' probation. The city's Chinese-American community, in outrage, quickly organized to protest the sentences. They charged that the whole affair displayed a callous disregard for the lives of Asian-Americans. Leaders organized demonstrations which received the support of Detroit's black and Hispanic communities. The CRD prosecuted under Section 241. In June 18, 1984, Ebens was convicted and sentenced to twenty-five years in prison but Nitz was acquitted. The Sixth Circuit Court of Appeals reversed Ebens's conviction, ordering a change of venue. He was retried and acquitted in April 1987.[43]

In June 1982 also, a white mob in the Gravesend section of Brooklyn murdered Willie Turks, a thirty-four-year-old black Transit Authority maintenance worker. Two of his coworkers also were injured by the gang of ten to thirty whites who dragged Turks from his car and beat him to death. Turks and his friends usually stopped at a bagel shop in the predominantly white Brooklyn neighborhood at the end of their shift in the late evening. The bagel shop was about five blocks from the subway repair yard where they worked. No evidence of previous hostility existed but when they drove up, a white youth began shouting racial slurs and berating the men for being in the neighborhood. They attempted to drive away but when their car stalled the angry youth opened the car door and struck the driver on the head with a beer bottle. Between ten and twenty other youths, said to be between eighteen and twenty years old, joined the fight. They dragged Turks from the car, pulling him through the intersection, and beat on his head "with a blunt instrument," according to the police.[44]

There were numerous witnesses, some of whom called the police. Mayor Edward Koch called the crime "an outrage against all New

Yorkers, a despicable and unconscionable act," and hundreds of demonstrators marched repeatedly through the neighborhood in protest. No one was convicted of murder in the case. Three eighteen-year-olds received jail sentences. Paul Mormando and Anthony Miccio were convicted on misdemeanor assault and discrimination charges. Mormando was sentenced to two years in jail and Miccio from three to nine years. Gino Bova was convicted of manslaughter and sentenced to five to fifteen years in prison. Nineteen-year-old Joseph Powell was convicted of assault and sentenced to three to nine years in prison. Another assailant, Antonio Bermudez, was killed in 1983 in an unrelated incident and charges against nineteen-year-old Daniel Stoli were dropped.[45]

In addition to unorganized individual and mob action, the Klan continued to foment racial violence. In Meriden, Connecticut, the Klan repeatedly paraded through the town in 1981 and 1982 after the fatal shooting of a black man by police in 1981 incited a series of protests against police violence in the black community. Marches, counter-marches and confrontations between anti-Klan activists and the Klan developed.[46]

In the original incident, Officer Gene Hale, twenty-seven, shot and killed Keith Rakestrau, twenty-four, on February 24, 1981. The police claimed that Rakestrau and his two brothers, suspected of shoplifting, were chased by Hale's wife, a guard at the Meriden Square Mall. They claimed she was punched in the face by one of the suspects. Hale, who was meeting his wife for dinner and was off duty, reportedly fired at Rakestrau when he drove toward him at high speed in a shopping mall parking lot. The black and Hispanic community mobilized in the belief that the shoplifting charges and the shooting were unjustified. Klan Imperial Wizard Bill Wilkinson of Louisiana came to Meriden to lead the Klan's demonstration. In September 1980 Wilkinson had held cross-burnings and rallies in a cow pasture in rural Scotland, Connecticut, the first public Klan gathering in the state in seventy years. Meriden Police Chief George Caffrey asked the Klan not to demonstrate but Connecticut Klan Kleagle William Bohndorff of North Haven said, "We must take a stand for all this nation's police departments."[47]

When the rally took place on March 22, 1981, about two dozen hooded Klansmen were pelted with rocks and bricks in a violent confrontation with about two hundred counter-demonstrators. At least eight people were injured, none seriously. The counter-demonstrators, a self-avowed violent anti-Klan group, consisted of young blacks and Hispanics from the inner city. After this incident, the Klan continued low-key recruitment in the state, avoiding rallies.[48]

The Klan and other white supremacists were suspected by blacks of being responsible for at least twelve separate lynch murders of African-Americans in 1980 and a number of others in the early part of the decade. In Walton County, Georgia, Lynn Jackson, a black soldier, was found hanging from a tree on December 8, 1981. He was the seventeenth person murdered in the county for apparently racial reasons since 1946. Despite indications that he was lynched, the coroner ruled he had committed suicide. About five hundred blacks marched from Social Circle to Monroe on Saturday, February 20, 1982, as part of a series of continuing protests against what they regarded as murder. Supporters joined the marchers as they approached Monroe. When they arrived they were met by one thousand cheering blacks and some one thousand angry Klansmen. About one hundred state troopers wearing bulletproof vests kept the groups well separated after a fistfight broke out in the afternoon. Two blacks and two whites were arrested during the march and four handguns and a shotgun were reportedly taken by the police. By Sunday, the towns were quiet again but the blacks believed the issues remained unsettled. Also, in February 1982, Frederick York, a thirty-eight-year-old black man, was found hanging from a tree in downtown Atlanta.[49]

The CRD investigated repeated episodes in the 1980s in which Klansmen beat white women or threatened arson to their residences because they had black friends. For example, on November 23, 1982, Mailon Paul Wood, Kenneth E. Davis, and William L. Deering, along with Lyndon Terrell, all of whom were members of a Ku Klux Klan Klavern in Haralson County, Georgia, decided to "serenade" a white woman for associating too often with African-Americans. That evening, the four men drove to the home of Mrs. Peggy Jo French, who lived with her two children, Lori and Michael Roper, aged fifteen and nineteen, in Waco, Georgia. The men, all masked with the exception of Mailon Wood, forcibly entered the French residence with guns. They told Mrs. French that they were looking for "niggers" and guns and that if they found any it was "going to be bad." They searched the house, emptying drawers and kicking in a wall in the process. One of the masked men grabbed Mrs. French, saying he knew she was a "nigger lover." Deering threw her across a coffee table and beat her with a leather strap "eight to ten times across her back, arms, buttocks, and the back of her legs." Wood forced Lori Roper from her bedroom at gunpoint to witness the attack on her mother.[50]

Wood asked Lori if anyone in the household had been sleeping with "niggers." Threatening to "blow" off Michael Roper's head, one of the men forced him to watch Deering beating his mother with a strap. Deering also hit Roper with the strap and ordered him to avoid drug use and being friendly with blacks. Wood told the family that he was concerned about Lori Roper's upbringing and that if they did not "straighten out," he would come back to take Lori away. Before leaving, Wood reiterated his threats and warned Mrs. French that the house would be kept under surveillance. If they saw any black people there the Klansmen would return to "tar and feather" her.[51]

After the men left, Mrs. French and her children went outside to drive to the police station, but found the tires on her car slashed. The assailants had also cut her telephone lines. After replacing the tires, she reported the attack to the police, who were unable to find the suspects. Wood and his associates were captured because months later Mrs. French and Lori Roper saw a news segment on television of a Ku Klux Klan rally and recognized one of the men participating in the rally as the unmasked man from the group that had terrorized their family. After Mrs. French informed the FBI, the agency obtained a copy of the videotape to replay for her and her children. As a result, the FBI identified the unmasked man as Mailon Wood.[52]

Before Mrs. French's identification, the same Klansmen, joined by a fellow Klavern member, Kent Adams, had terrorized Warren and Peggy Cokley, a black man and a white woman in Tallapoosa, Georgia, because of their interracial relationship. Wood tried to cut the Cokleys' telephone line but expressed little concern when he failed because the Klansmen had designed a strategy to avoid police interference. They had had a woman call the Tallapoosa Police Department, which was about half a mile from the Cokleys', saying that three black males were chasing a white female near a church on the other side of town. They timed the call to coincide with the attack on the Cokleys'.

The two officers who went to the scene found nothing. As a result, when a call came from the Cokleys' saying that masked men had invaded their house, the police were two or three miles away. Terrell and Deering entered the front door. Deering, whom Warren Cokley knew, entered pointing a gun at him. Deering told him, "You think you're a smart-ass nigger," and the two began to scuffle. By this time the other three men entered at the back door. As they did so, Peggy Cokley ran out the front door to the home of Warren Cokley's mother, Georgia Wise, who lived next door. Wood and Deering then beat Warren Cokley.[53]

Cokley managed to remove a small pocket knife from his pocket and cut Deering on the leg. Cokley's mother arrived at the house and screamed at Wood, Deering, and the others to stop beating her son. The Klansmen left the premises to "rendezvous" with the rest of the group as Mrs. Wise aided Cokley, who was bleeding profusely. Sure enough, when Warren Cokley tried to call the Tallapoosa Police Department, he could not find the officers. He then called the Haralson County sheriff and reported the incident, identifying Deering, despite the stocking mask he wore. Mrs. Wise took Warren Cokley to the hospital.[54]

The conviction of the Klansmen arose from Warren Cokley's recognition of Deering and blood sample evidence. The state crime laboratory determined that Cokley's blood type was similar to three of the four samples taken from the Cokley residence. The fourth sample, however, was consistent in every respect with Deering's. His blood group and enzymes were uncommon enough to appear in only about .02 percent of the population.[55]

On August 8, 1984, the grand jury returned a seven-count indictment against Mailon Wood, Davis, Billy Wood, Deering, and Adams. They were charged with violating Section 241 and for conspiring to interfere with the right of Peggy Jo French and her children to associate with blacks in and around their dwelling, in violation of the Federal Fair Housing Law. Mailon Wood, Davis, Billy Wood, and Adams were also charged with the same offenses in the Cokley incident. Adams entered a guilty plea. In exchange for immunity from prosecution, Terrell agreed to cooperate with the government's investigation. Wearing a body recorder and transmitter, he engaged in several conversations with the offenders in which they incriminated themselves.

These tapes were played for the jury at the trial. The remaining defendants were found guilty on all charges and their convictions were upheld on appeal.[56]

The CRD announced a stepped-up emphasis on "increased Ku Klux Klan activities around the country" in 1984. The division brought charges against thirty-six Klan defendants in thirteen cases, resulting in fifteen guilty pleas. Successful prosecutions included the attacks on the Cokleys and Roper-French family in Georgia.[57]

Along with hate crimes, police violence and abuse continued to incite racial disturbances in the early 1980s. In the first two years of the Reagan administration the Civil Rights Division completed cases begun in the Carter administration. Local and state officials continued to ask for CRS help in suppressing racial tensions that resulted from the police abuse. The CRS noted that the demographic changes in the country were reflected in increasing reports of police misconduct involving Hispanics and Asian-Americans, in addition to African-Americans. Most of the cases, however, still involved police abuse of blacks. In 1982, CRS noted that "Although minority citizens are disproportionately the victims of crime, conflict with the police over the use of deadly force and other issues has often impeded the cooperation needed to do something about it."[58]

The use of excessive force remained a matter of great African-American community concern. The *Black Scholar* devoted extensive space to the subject in early 1981, noting that by the early 1980s for every white person killed by the police in any year, twenty-two black persons were killed. As an example of police violence, the magazine discussed the New Orleans police response when a white policeman was killed in New Orleans on November 8, 1980. White officers retaliated by beating witnesses to the shooting. They also vented their anger and intimidated the black community by assassinating four blacks in five days.[59]

Police violence in every region of the country led to black community protests. In Norwich, Connecticut, on October 13, 1981, the shooting death of a black burglary suspect by a private security guard who was trying to handcuff him stimulated a disturbance in the black community. A state's attorney ruled the killing accidental amidst calls for a federal investigation. Complaints of police harassment of black youths in Council Bluffs, Iowa, also generated tense conditions.[60]

The fatal shooting of a black youth in December 1982 incited another rebellion in the Overtown district of Miami where the 1980 McDuffie killing and subsequent disorders had taken place. This was only one of several controversial police shootings in Miami and Dade County. Some victims of police abuse received compensation in local civil trials. Chester, Pennsylvania, paid $7 million in judgments in civil suits for police abuse in a period of eighteen months. They subsequently asked CRS for help in training officers to avoid such behavior. In Milwaukee, numerous civil rights lawsuits led to monetary damage awards to victims of police actions. Despite lawsuits some police departments remained indifferent, because the city, and not individual officers, had to pay the costs.[61]

In Baker County, Georgia, in October 1982, sheriff's deputies were accused of routinely beating a number of African-Americans they encountered. A young man was beaten on two occasions but never arrested for anything. Also, deputies were accused of harassing local citizens for no reason. African-Americans found that some black police officers also abused black victims. A black officer in Des Moines, for example, shot and killed a black man he stopped for questioning under circumstances that local blacks thought were suspicious.[62]

Most police abuse cases, however, continued to involve white officers. In 1984 a coalition of minority organizations in Springfield, Ohio, staged a sit-in to protest the alleged excessive use of force in the arrest of a black woman, who was charged with battery by the arresting officer. In Stamford, Connecticut, black parents who called the police because their son was behaving strangely had reason to regret their action. Their son, "an architect, had been taking his clothes, putting them in plastic bags and sleeping with them in the family car." At the end of three days the mother called the police for assistance. Within a short time, three police officers arrived and seconds later the man was killed. The CRS was called in to help defuse the community's anger.[63]

Along with the decrease in racial violence complaints received by the Justice Department during Reagan's first term, CRD police brutality prosecutions declined and became a reduced percentage of the cases investigated and prosecuted. Despite the increase in incidents of police abuse, the department showed disinterest in prosecuting police officers for brutality. As White House counselor, Edwin Meese, who was an ex-prosecutor, strongly criticized the U.S. Civil Rights Commission for issuing a report on police brutality in 1981, based on hearings at several sites in the country on the subject. The criticisms of police violence in the report constituted one grievance that led President Reagan to fire the chairman and other members of the commission.[64]

In the Justice Department's 1981 report, which covered cases filed by the Carter administration, forty-one charges were filed against a total of seventy-eight defendants, including fifty-six law enforcement agents. Thirty-one cases were tried, many with more than one defendant, resulting in thirty-one convictions and seventeen acquittals. Twenty-one of the thirty-one cases tried involved law enforcement officials.[65]

In the department's 1982 report, fifty-six charges were filed, charging a total of ninety-eight defendants, including sixty law enforcement officers. Forty-three cases were tried, in which there were twenty-seven convictions and thirty-four acquittals. In 1983, only thirty-nine charges were actually filed, some of which had been under investigation since the Carter administration. The prosecutors charged eighty-five defendants, including forty-four law enforcement officers. Twenty-one cases were tried, resulting in the conviction of twenty-eight defendants and fourteen acquittals. Twenty-three defendants, ten of whom pleaded guilty, were law enforcement officials. Investigations into law enforcement officers' behavior were reduced, though they still constituted a large part of the case load. In fiscal 1984, the division charged ninety-four defendants, but only forty-seven law enforcement officers, including ten Puerto Rican policemen indicted on forty-four counts for their involvement in the unlawful killing of two independence advocates. Media accounts and CRS alerts belie any conclusion that the decline in charges against law enforcement officers meant the existence of fewer incidents.[66]

The slight improvement in the Justice Department's response to police abuse and racially motivated violence during the Carter administration lost momentum during the first Reagan term. Organized violence from the Klan received highly publicized attention but police abuse or interference with the rights of African-Americans to seek housing or education was of little concern to the Reagan Justice Department. However, the Reagan retrenchment gave new energy to civil rights groups, which had seemed largely ineffective and fragmented when he was first elected.

17

More
Rebellion and
Repression

FROM RONALD REAGAN'S reelection in November 1984 to the end of the Bush presidency, racial polarization, hate crimes, and reports of police brutality increased across the nation. High-profile black Reaganites continued to preach against civil rights and civil rights leaders and to de-emphasize the role of government in resolving social problems. Alienation born of the contrast between the country's affluence and the poverty African-Americans experienced grew apace in black urban communities. Drugs, crime, homelessness, and the specter of AIDS also afflicted the poor.[1]

Government reports of mortgage lenders' refusing to make loans to qualified blacks exacerbated despair even among well-off African-Americans. Studies reported that restaurant owners preferred to hire immigrants instead of young blacks for jobs as waiters or janitors, graphically demonstrating discrimination. Andrew Brimmer, former governor of the Federal Reserve Board, calculated the enormous costs in community resources and alienation and economic productivity from employment discrimination against African-Americans. Even the lag in educational attainment that continued to mount from the late 1970s did not account for the differences. As Brimmer put it, many blacks "continue to be employed in jobs well below what their actual education and skills would justify."[2]

Social policy during the Reagan-Bush era elicited a resurgent emphasis on racial solidarity and the black nationalist tendencies that always exist in the black community. Pride in Jesse Jackson, who as the head of his Rainbow Coalition ran for president in 1984 and 1988, receiving over seven million votes in the 1988 primaries, reinforced community solidarity. Support also grew for the Black Muslims, and such regional and local leaders as Al Sharpton in New York. Rap music, which articulated mass social and economic concerns, also expressed the inward turning, the alienation, and the deep resentment at the stagnation of positive change in poor black communities. On campuses and in black communities, the mood was underscored by the popularity of Afrocentricism and its proponents, including Leonard Jeffries, a professor and head of the black studies department in City College, City University of New York, and Louis Farrakhan, as well as by the resurgence of Malcolm X as a hero.[3]

The Civil Rights Division (CRD) continued to neglect the problem of police brutality and to respond gingerly to hate crimes. Racial intimidation and violence complaints filed with the CRD continued to diminish. From the previous low in 1984 of 8,617 complaints, the number dropped, by 1986, to only 7,500. The Justice Department report, after Edwin Meese's appointment as attorney general in 1985, became an unabashed propaganda document, including little statistical information on the department's work. By the end of the Bush administration Attorney General William Barr's report included no separate section on civil rights activities.[4]

The Community Relations Service (CRS) continued to mediate local conflicts and to collect information on the incidence of racial harassment and violence. In 1985, the Pocatello, Idaho, Klan spray-painted the car of an African-American family who moved into a white neighborhood. Also, assailants fire-bombed the home of a black family in a white Philadelphia neighborhood.[5]

In other 1985 incidents, a Wren, Mississippi, black man suffered cross burnings, threats, and the arson of his home in November 1985 after he ignored warnings to leave a white area. In Dallas in October 1985, a black woman was abducted by four white men wearing hoods. The homes of two African-American families who moved into white neighborhoods were fire-bombed. Some of these offenders were convicted and others acquitted or not even arrested.[6]

In 1985, Columbia, Missouri, violence erupted when police shot and killed a black teenage girl who officers said ignored their order to stop and tried to run them down in the car she had allegedly taken without a friend's permission. A Cedar Rapids, Iowa, disturbance arose after an African-American black man died of injuries sustained while in the custody of the county sheriff's department. He had been arrested for public drunkenness. There were strong protests in both cities. Columbia experienced minor rock- and bottle-throwing incidents before black youths responded to African-American leaders' call for calm. Also, the Cape Verdean community in Pawtucket, Rhode Island, and the NAACP chapter in Beaumont, Texas, complained of police brutality. Confrontations arising from police violence occurred in dozens of other cities in the same year.[7]

The CRD continued to prosecute Ku Klux Klan and white supremacist group violence. In 1985, the CRD prosecuted the Klan and associated groups in North Carolina for successive acts of intimidation and violence. A two-year grand jury investigation of cross-burnings and shootings into residences in Iredell and Alexander counties, North Carolina, led to the conviction of three members of the White Knights of Liberty, as well as the indictment of nine other members. Paralleling Klan activity in other states, the defendants aimed to intimidate white women and black men from associating with each other. The incidents included placing a cross in front of the home of a black teenager who was dating a white girl and cross-burnings at a high school and at the homes of interracial couples. Kenneth Ray Blankenship, Jerry Douglas Suits, Mary Vestal Suits, and Jerry Albert Henderson all pleaded guilty of a conspiracy to violate civil rights in the cases. Glenn Miller, leader of the White Patriot Party, insisted proudly that extremism was on the rise and that people were "flooding into" the party. He claimed 2,600 members in six southern states. In Montgomery, Alabama, three persons associated with the Klan admitted setting fire to the offices of the Southern Poverty Law Center, which maintained files on Klan activities. Another Klansman received a year's imprisonment for the burning of a cross on the residential property of a black county commissioner who had been urging African-Americans to boycott a local bar for its alleged discriminatory hiring practices.[8]

The CRS reports of hate crimes and conciliation efforts in the late

1980s began to include racial harassment and intimidation on college campuses. In the 1986–87 academic year at The Citadel in Charleston, South Carolina, the University of Michigan in Ann Arbor, the University of Missouri at Columbia, the University of Wisconsin at Madison, Pennsylvania State University at State College, Pennsylvania, and Oklahoma State University in Stillwater, racially motivated incidents disturbed the campus scene. At The Citadel, the West Point of the South, white students harassed Kevin Nesmith, a black cadet, repeatedly. On October 23, 1986, five whites wearing white sheets and what looked like Klan headdresses entered his room shouting obscenities, leaving a burned cross made of newspapers. The CRS mediated an agreement between the school and a group representing the black community that included NAACP leaders and black ministers to find ways to reduce tensions by promoting multicultural sensitivity, including inviting prominent blacks to visit the campus to mingle with students and faculty. The white students were reduced in rank, confined to campus for six months, and ordered to walk 195 additional marching tours. Black leaders asked unsuccessfully that the offenders be expelled. Incidents on other campuses ranged from black-facing by white fraternities, and eggs thrown at black students by white students to professors making racial slurs and refusing to give black students grades above D.[9]

The Civil Rights Division continued to emphasize the prosecution of hate-group racial violence in 1986. The department pursued a three-year grand jury investigation into cross-burnings and shootings by members of the White Knights of Liberty of the Klan. Of twenty-one individuals charged, nineteen were ultimately convicted, including three statewide leaders of the Klan. Sentences included prison terms of up to seven years and a total of $17,000 in fines.[10]

In Philadelphia in 1986, the CRD prosecuted four whites, one a juvenile, who burned down the house of a black couple who moved into a white neighborhood in order to intimidate the family and others who might wish to move in. They received prison terms and were ordered to pay restitution. Harassment of blacks on the job continued also. In North Carolina a white state prison guard, a member of the Carolina Knights of the Ku Klux Klan, admitted to interfering with the employment rights of a black correctional officer, who had filed a grievance after he failed to get a promotion at the facility. The Civil Rights Division prosecuted the offender after he sought to intimidate the victim by burning a cross near his home.[11]

Georgia remained a hotbed of Klan violence. Forsyth County had been a whites-only enclave since 1912 when an eighteen-year-old white woman was raped and beaten to death allegedly by a black man. A black suspect was lynched and about one thousand African-American residents were forced to abandon their homes. In August 1987, when Hosea Williams led a civil rights march through Forsyth County, the marchers were pelted with rocks and bottles. He returned a week later, after widespread publicity, with more than twenty thousand marchers, who demonstrated peaceably. Five years later, Morris Dees of the Southern Poverty Law Center finally settled a Federal Civil Rights damage suit forcing the Klan to relinquish its name, mailing lists, and all assets for perpetrating the 1987 violence.[12]

In New York a series of events caused blacks to mobilize against racially motivated violence and exacerbated race relations in the city. On the night of December 16, 1986, four African-American men were driving through the all-white community of Howard Beach in the New York City borough of Queens when their car broke down. By the early morning, Michael Griffith, who had left the car to find help, had been struck and killed by a car as he fled, and Cedric Sandiford, who lay beaten nearly to death with a tree limb and a baseball bat, had been attacked by a dozen white teenage pursuers. Blacks mobilized in anger to demand convictions in the case. On December 21, 1987, African-Americans, led by Al Sharpton and Vernon Mason and other community leaders awaiting a verdict in the case, tied up traffic, closing the Brooklyn Bridge and all subway service to Brooklyn. State charges against Jon Lester and Scott Kern for second-degree murder and against Jean Ladone and Michael Pirone for second-degree manslaughter were rejected by the jury. Instead they convicted Kern, Lester, and Ladone of second-degree manslaughter and assault and acquitted Pirone of all charges. The judge sentenced Lester to ten to thirty years, Kern to six to eighteen years, and Ladone to five to fifteen years in prison.[13]

Racial tensions in New York City had already worsened with episodes of police violence, the Bernard Goetz incident in 1984, and other highly visible attacks, which African-Americans perceived as still unavenged. Blacks noted the fatal police shooting of Eleanor Bumpurs, a Bronx grandmother, during a 1985 eviction and a series of allegedly false arrests of blacks on the subways by transit police officers who were striving to fulfill arrest quotas. Many of the blacks were charged with "jostling" or sexually abusing other passengers, although some of the victims said they were unaware of any offense. The police were also found to be conducting undercover surveillance of a radical black group and of monitoring broadcasts of New York City's major black-oriented radio station.[14]

In response to the Howard Beach incident and mounting racial tensions in New York, Governor Mario Cuomo established a Governor's Task Force on Bias-Related Violence on February 6, 1987. The task force was designed to thoroughly explore the problem, including public education and the role of the judiciary. By June the task force had recommended legislation mandating the collection of data on hate crimes and stiffer criminal penalties for bias-related incidents. On August 11, 1988, Cuomo directed the state attorney general to investigate thoroughly bias-related crimes.[15]

The Tawana Brawley incident also led to increased consternation among African-Americans. On November 24, 1987, Brawley, a black fifteen-year-old teenager from Wappingers Falls, was found dazed and curled up in the fetal position in a trash bag. Her family contacted CBS News and broke the story, claiming a white assailant. Widespread publicity and tensions resulted until the incident was determined to be a hoax.[16]

Racial tensions and hate-group intimidation and violence existed in every region of the nation. In the Northwest, the strength of the violent neo-Nazi group known as the Aryan Nation and of other white supremacist groups led to the formation of local coalitions of citizens concerned about hate-violence in 1987. These groups coalesced into a regional association of state and local coalitions in Idaho, Montana, Oregon, Washington, and Wyoming.[17]

Hate-group violence persisted. The Klan begin routinely applying for parade permits. On April 20, 1988, a man identifying himself as member of the Ku Klux Klan requested a parade permit at the Parkside, Pennsylvania, Borough Council meeting. The permit allowed two hundred Klan members to march on May 21, clad in Klan robes and Army fatigues.[18]

The CRS continued to report the problem of police abuse, as well. In 1986, CRS reported that an Irvington, New Jersey, policeman crossed over into neighboring Newark and shot a black seventeen-year-old Newark youth. A Lawton, Oklahoma, police detective shot and killed a black man wanted for questioning in a rape case, inspiring protests of unnecessary use of deadly force.[19]

In San Diego, California, a policeman was killed and another seriously wounded in March 1985. Shortly thereafter, six officers with shotguns decided unilaterally to find the killers. They marched through a predominantly African-American neighborhood in Southeast San Diego on a hunch that the suspect had fled to a house used by a local gang. They surrounded the house, kicked in the door, and found no one, according to neighbors who saw the police actions. About the same time, Sagon Penn, a black man who belonged to no gang, turned himself in as the shooter. Testimony at Penn's trial reported that the police had barged into the house of Carlton Smith, who they knew had seen the confrontation between Penn and the police before the shooting. They turned off a television set, isolated his six children in one room and four adults in another, and held them for three hours until detectives arrived. Penn was found innocent twice of the killing of police agent Thomas Riggs and of attempted murder in the shooting of agent Donovan Jacobs. He was first acquitted of murder after spending a year in jail and then prosecuted for manslaughter and acquitted again. The jury each time concluded that Jacobs had provoked Penn by beating him repeatedly and using racial slurs. In addition, witnesses testified that the police emergency operators disregarded pleas from African-American residents calling for help and that patrol officers stormed into several houses and held black occupants against their will. Assistant Police Chief Bob Burgreen responded that "If there was any misconduct it has not been brought to our attention."[20]

On Christmas Day, 1987, police severely beat a black man, Loyal Garner, Jr., in the Sabine County jail in Hemphill, Texas. Garner, who lived nearby in Louisiana, was driving near Hemphill with two companions. The town's white police officers were notorious for their brutality toward African-Americans. Hemphill police officers stopped the car and arrested the men. They were taken to jail and placed in a detox room even though there was no evidence that they had been drinking. Police Chief Thomas Ladner and his deputies for some reason took Garner into a room alone, where they beat him, and left him on a concrete ledge all night. A doctor examined him the next day and determined he was brain dead. Taken to a hospital in Smith County one hundred miles away, he was pronounced dead of massive head injuries on December 27. A Hemphill grand jury indicted the officers but a local jury acquitted them of violating Garner's civil rights. A Smith County jury, however, found them guilty of murder. Ladner was sentenced to twenty-eight years in prison; the other two officers were given shorter sentences. Garner's widow and children filed a civil damage suit against the officers and the town of Hemphill; it was settled out of court, for, reportedly, $300,000 outright and trust funds for his children.[21]

The Garner murder case was unusual in that the officers were convicted. Colorado City, Texas, police shot and killed a Hispanic man wanted for questioning in a rape case. A long-standing conflict between the police and the Hispanic and black community activists escalated into a tense dispute. The officer was not prosecuted.[22]

Civil Rights Division activity seemed unrelated to the violence the CRS noted. In 1985, the department charged 106 defendants, including 67 law enforcement officers. Thirty cases were tried, resulting in conviction for 41 defendants and acquittal for 21 defendants. In 1986, 112 individuals were charged, including 70 law enforcement officers. Trials were held in 34 cases, resulting in conviction for 55 defendants and acquittal for 20 defendants. The law enforcement officers included a number of cases of correctional officers who beat inmates to death. The Department of Justice's abbreviated report filed in election year, 1988, claimed that the 101 convictions obtained as a result of FBI efforts more than doubled the previous year's totals. However, information made public by the CRD after the Rodney King incident noted that there were 71 individuals charged, 49 of whom were law enforcement officials. Trials were held in 30 cases, and there were 21 convictions and 26 acquittals.[23]

When George Bush became president in January 1989, he had just finished a campaign in which he emphasized racial issues, following in Reagan's footsteps. His attorney general, former Pennsylvania governor Richard Thornburgh, ignored the CRS reports of increasing racial violence in stating his priorities. He stated summarily in 1989 that the CRD would emphasize litigation on housing rights, voting rights, and rights of the disabled. He did not mention hate crimes or police abuse. Bush appointed former New York legislative leader John Dunne as assistant attorney general for civil rights. Bush highlighted racial quotas as an issue throughout his administration, opposing a civil rights employment bill on those grounds. Unemployment and the overall economy in continued recession, weighed down by Reagan's deficit and tax-cut measures, further exacerbated class and racial tensions. Former Klansman and legislator David Duke's unsuccessful campaign for governor of Louisiana in 1990 further emphasized white supremacy as an issue in American politics. Thornburgh and Dunne avoided public discussion of racial issues and Dunne, unlike his predecessor, Reynolds, kept a very low profile.[24]

The reticence of Dunne and the departure of Reynolds had an effect. Aggrieved persons began turning to the Justice Department hoping for assistance again. CRD complaints gradually rose in the Bush years but did not reach the levels experienced before the Reagan ascendancy, despite the increases in disturbances and the increased population of the country. From October 1, 1990, to October 1, 1991, the Department of Justice received 9,800 civil rights complaints, in comparison to the 7,500 received from October 1, 1985, to October 1, 1986.[25]

The Community Relations Service continued to receive alerts and to attempt conciliation. The CRS noted a continued "upward trend in racial conflicts between minority groups." In 1988, gays reported being attacked by black and Latino gangs in New York City. The reports of racial disputes between African-Americans and Hispanics increased from sixty-one in 1988 to seventy-five in 1989. This trend was most dramatically displayed by a series of violent and deadly racial clashes in Miami during the 1980s between blacks and Hispanics. Repeated episodes of racial tension and violence between Korean merchants and black customers took place in South Central Los Angeles.[26]

Race relations in New York further deteriorated when in May 1989 a gang of black youths raped and beat a white woman jogging in Central Park. They were convicted of rape and assault or attempted murder. One of the suspects said they were targeting "white people." In August 1989 three black teenagers from the East New York section of Brooklyn walked off a subway train in the predominantly white

Brooklyn neighborhood of Bensonhurst. One of the black youths, sixteen-year-old Yusef Hawkins, had asked his two friends to accompany him while he went to Bensonhurst to look at a used car. As they walked down the main street of the neighborhood, a gang of white boys carrying baseball bats attacked them, calling them "niggers" and demanding that they get out of the neighborhood. During the attack one of them shot and killed Yusef Hawkins. When black demonstrators marched through Bensonhurst to protest the shooting, whites yelled obscenities at them and held up watermelons in ridicule. No one was ever convicted of murder in the Hawkins case. Black activists pointed to the disparity in treatment as fresh evidence of the ability to murder blacks without retribution.[27]

These incidents, as well as disputes between blacks and Koreans and Jews and blacks, represented a sharp increase in the number of racial incidents in New York. Also, protracted demonstrations by blacks against a Korean grocer in Flatbush, Brooklyn, began in January 1990. A clash between a black customer and a Korean greengrocer prompted a month-long boycott. These were among the 192 incidents of racial incidents that CRS reported.[28]

The Civil Rights Division continued to focus not on the urban tensions that were tearing the nation but on organized white supremacist groups, mainly the Klan. In 1989 and the first months of 1990, the Civil Rights Division filed sixty-eight cases, charging 129 individuals with racial violence—the largest number in a single year since 1971. Fourteen Klan members in Shreveport were indicted on conspiracy charges in a series of cross-burnings following the sentencing of a Klan leader on a federal firearms offense. In Seattle, 3 white supremacists connected to the Aryan Nation were convicted of plotting to firebomb a minority discotheque. In an ongoing investigation of hate crimes in Nashville, Tennessee, 8 people were convicted on charges of criminal conspiracy, obstruction of justice, vandalism, and intimidation. Among those convicted was the leader of the Nashville area Confederate Hammerskins, a neo-Nazi skinhead organization. In Tulsa, Oklahoma, 17 defendants, including several juveniles, all of whom were associated with the Oklahoma Skinhead Alliance, pleaded guilty to conspiring to interfere with the rights of minorities to enjoy the use of public accommodations, such as public parks and live music clubs. The defendants received sentences of up to nine years in prison.[29]

In the Northwest, the Ayran Nation and other white supremacist groups continued their activities. Tom Metzger and John Metzger of the White Ayran Nation were subjected to a $12.5 million judgment in Portland, Oregon, for inciting three skinhead followers of the White Ayran Resistance to the murder by bludgeoning of Mulugeta Seraw, a twenty-seven-year-old Ethiopian. Morris Dees of the Southern Poverty Law Center brought the action on behalf of Seraw's family for the 1988 murder. The judgment came on October 25, 1990. Mr. Seraw's father flew from Ethiopia to hear the verdict announced. The Ayran Nation members' property would be sold and 25 percent of their wages could be garnished so long as the judgment remained unpaid. The judgment was expected to at least restrict their activities.[30]

Attorney General William Barr, who took office in 1990 when Richard Thornburgh left for an unsuccessful Senate race in Pennsylvania, included hate crimes as a priority under his administration. He reported after his first year that "an outstanding record was achieved by the Civil Rights Division in the prosecution of hate crime defendants, 100 percent of whom were convicted for acting out their racial, ethnic, and religious hatreds with violence and acts of intimidation." Prosecutors in the Northern District of Alabama successfully convicted six men charged with the intimidation of a black man who moved into an all-white neighborhood. Each defendant received a prison sentence and was ordered to pay for the damage to the victim's apartment when they set fire to an automobile driven into the dwelling. In another case in the northern district of Georgia, the much-publicized mail-bomb murders of U.S. Appeals Court judge Robert S. Vance and civil rights attorney Robert E. Robinson resulted in a seventy-count indictment charging the defendant with murder and a series of related criminal and civil offenses.[31]

Congress, in response to the flood of hate-crime incidents, enacted legislation to require regular reports of their occurrence from police departments. The Hate Crimes Statistics Act, passed over the objections of law enforcement officials who thought it was too difficult to determine whether a crime was bias-motivated, ordered the attorney general to report for 1990 and four succeeding years "crimes that manifest evidence of prejudice based on race, religion, sexual orientation, or ethnicity." The FBI would begin including hate crimes, including murder, rape, and arson and other attacks upon persons and property, as part of the Uniform Crime Report on May 9, 1990. More accurate data collection might encourage greater prosecution and investigatory efforts. Additionally, the legislators hoped to silence their colleagues who challenged the data and downplayed the existence of bias whenever CRS and private organizations reported the hate-crime statistics they had collected. Congress passed the act only after adding conservative amendments unrelated to the purpose of the act. The extraneous amendments included a section expressing Congress's view that "the American family is the foundation of American society," which should be promoted by schools and federal policy, and that no funds appropriated under this data collection bill should be used to "promote or encourage homosexuality."[32]

The president announced, at his signing of the Hate Crimes Act on April 30, 1990, that CRS would initiate a hotline for reporting incidents of racial, color, and national origin harassment as well as those based on sexual orientation and religion. In the first six months of operation the Hate Crimes hotline received over 2,140 calls. Seven hundred and one reported incidents were targeted at people instead of property, the majority of which involved verbal or physical attacks. Twelve cross-burnings and ten occurrences of swastika graffiti were reported. Fifty-seven percent of the reported offenders were white, 27 percent were African-American, 8 percent Latino, 3 percent Asian or Asian Indian, and 1 percent Native American. CRS began working with the Uniform Crime Reporting Unit of the FBI to prepare training for law enforcement agencies on the procedure for reporting hate crimes through the Uniform Crime Report System. Police departments expressed continuing dismay about, for example, when to categorize an assault as a hate crime or simply as an assault.[33]

Hate violence reported to CRS continued to increase. In 1991 the CRS reported trying to alleviate community tensions involving hate crimes in 277 localities, an increase from 187 in 1990. The agency also noted that the number of communities in which hate groups were active continued to grow and "a considerable number of minorities, particularly African-Americans, are being identified as perpetrators of racial incidents in retaliation for incidents against them."[34]

In Brooklyn, a traffic accident involving the motorcade of a prominent Hasidic rabbi in mid-August 1991 resulted in the death of a seven-year-old black child, Gavin Cato, and serious injury to another black child. This incident sparked several nights of violent tensions among blacks, Hasidic Jews, and the police who tried to quell the violence. Afterward an Australian rabbinical student, Yankel Rosenbaum, was stabbed to death by someone among a group of black youths in apparent retaliation for the death of Cato. Lemrick Nelson was charged with the crime. His acquittal on October 29, 1992, exacerbated the animosity between the Hasidim and the black community in Crown Heights. The Justice Department began an investigation of possible civil rights violations in the case.[35]

The Klan remained active throughout the country, with widely visible manifestations in the South. On August 22, 1992, Hosea Williams led a march of about forty people from Atlanta about fifty miles to the Forsyth County courthouse to replicate the 1987 march that had been stopped by the Klan. The Klan and others shouted epithets from behind police barricades. Earlier that day, approximately fifty white supremacists shouting "white power" demonstrated to protest the march. Jerry Lord, a Klansman and county organizer for the white supremacist movement, made a speech featuring racial name-calling. Williams noted that those who said there was no more "Klan activity" in the county were obviously wrong.[36]

The first FBI report issued under the Hate Crimes Act in January 1993 indicated widespread abuse even though the statistics were problematic. The data covered calendar year 1991. There were 4,558 hate-crime incidents, involving 4,755 offenses. Intimidation was most frequent, with racial bias motivating six of ten offenses. Anti-black offenses counted for the highest percentage, 36 percent of the total; and 65 percent of the crimes were committed by whites. Antiwhite offenses were 19 percent and anti-Jewish, 17 percent of the totals respectively. The reporting was voluntary and fewer than one in five law enforcement agencies reported. Some blamed tight budgets and lack of sensitivity to the problem. Others indicated continued confusion about the nature of hate crimes. Alaska, Montana, Wyoming, Utah, North and South Dakota, Nebraska, Michigan, Alabama, North and South Carolina, Florida, West Virginia, Maine, New Hampshire, Vermont, and Rhode Island did not report. The nonresponsiveness limited the usability of the data. The information appeared compatible, however, with the pattern of random incidents to which CRS responded and included in the agency's reports.[37]

While CRD began to emphasize hate crimes, police abuse cases festered unattended. The department's response to police abuse and violence remained weak and ineffectual in the Bush administration. The CRD's response contrasted sharply with the prosecution of hate crimes. From October 1990 to October 1991, for example, the Department of Justice received 9,835 civil rights complaints, investigated 3,583 cases and prosecuted 134 people, 64 of whom were police officers. The majority of the defendants were convicted either through jury trials or guilty pleas. Twenty-six police officers were convicted, twenty-four entered guilty pleas, and twelve were acquitted.[38]

CRS reports contained ample evidence of the continued problems of police abuse that augmented the weak enforcement record in CRD reports. In many instances, no state or federal prosecution resulted. In Orange, Texas, on February 10, 1989, a black man suspected of being a drug dealer was shot and killed by the police after he allegedly lunged at an officer with a knife. The shooting occurred in a housing project rumored to be rife with drugs and youth gang problems. The NAACP and unorganized black community protesters, at a council meeting, denounced what they regarded as an unnecessary shooting. African-American leaders expressed concern about the deadly force used by the police as well as the lack of social services being offered the residents of the housing project. The residents believed the increased drug gang problems which occasioned an increased police presence created an unsafe environment. The local government responded by establishing an alcohol and drug treatment program and a drug treatment program in the housing project. They also implemented a Human Relations course for the police.[39]

In 1989, Labor Day Greekfest activities in Virginia Beach precipitated widespread confrontations between black college students and the police. The black community of the Norfolk-Tidewater area strongly protested what they regarded as a hostile reception and continued hostility to the students who felt they should be tolerated as well as white students who went to Fort Lauderdale, Virginia Beach, or other beach resorts on vacation. The city of Virginia Beach began planning for the 1990 Labor Day almost immediately after the 1989 riot. The city officials, law enforcement agencies, and the black community coordinated their plans. The city established black community-designated marshals and organized rumor control mechanisms to avert violence. The CRS sent in a nine-person team to help.[40] Few black students bothered to visit the resort in 1990 and subsequent years.

Complaints of violence, abuse, and excessive use of force by police continued to increase. In New Jersey, a white Teaneck police officer fatally shot a black male teenager on April 10, 1990. The police department said that the officer was responding to a report that among a group of African-American youth gathered at a playground one was brandishing a gun. The police officer allegedly shot the youth in the leg and back as he ran from police. Subsequent to the shooting, community residents massed in front of the municipal complex. They dispersed without incident only after the chief of police and leaders from the local NAACP addressed the crowd, promising to take ameliorative action. After a series of conciliatory meetings between city officials and community leaders, a crowd gathered, became angry and began looting. Some businesses were destroyed before order was restored. A serious disorder involving blacks and Hispanics occurred on Sunday, May 5, 1991, in a riot in the Mt. Pleasant section of Washington, D.C., following the shooting of a Hispanic male by a black police officer during an arrest.[41]

The pall of racism also affected law enforcement agencies internally. There were tensions among black and white officers in departments in which blacks became a presence for the first time. In Oak Park, Illinois, black police officers complained of being harassed by white officers of the police department. The community relations service reported fistfights between black and white police officers, intended to harass the black officers into leaving the force. In the FBI, which began hiring black agents in the seventies, reports of harassment of black agents began to surface. In January 1990 the FBI reached significant out-of-court settlements with black employees in major discrimination cases. Donald Rochon, an African-American agent, sued the agency in Chicago in the mid-eighties, charging death threats by white colleagues. The bureau settled racial discrimination suits brought by two other blacks who had worked with Rochon, one in Chicago and another in Omaha.[42]

The Department of Justice record in Los Angeles graphically illustrated the difficulties and lack of enforcement in police cases. Between 1982 and 1991 the department conducted 720 investigations of the police and sheriff's department. Only four cases resulted in indictments and only three cases, one involving the border patrol, resulted in convictions. From 1985 to 1991 the department presented no cases of police misconduct.[43]

One of the most significant episodes of racial violence during the Reagan-Bush era, however, arose from police abuse. In Los Angeles on March 3, 1991, Lake View Terrace resident George Holiday videotaped the police beating Rodney King, a black man, whose automobile they had pursued in a high-speed chase. A Los Angeles jury indicted Sgt. Stacey Koon and officers Laurence M. Powell, Theodore J. Briseno, and Timothy E. Wind but the trial was moved to Simi Valley, a conservative, overwhelmingly white area outside of Los Angeles. The jury consisted of ten whites, one Asian, and one Hispanic member. The announcement of the verdict acquitting the police officers on April 29, 1992, set off the worst urban riot in United States history. The five days of rioting resulted in at least 60 deaths, more than 16,000 arrests, and nearly $1 billion in property damage in Los Angeles alone. A number of Hispanics were involved in the rioting and looting, and blacks attacked Koreans as well as looting and smashing property and attacking whites. In overall terms the rebellion resembled the 1965 Watts disturbance, the McDuffie riot in 1989 in Miami, and others earlier sparked by police violence. This time the violence waited until the acquittal. The black community hoped that the legal system would exact punishment. When it did not, they responded.[44]

President Bush, like his predecessors when confronted with riot and rebellion, vacillated and tried to assess the most beneficial political response. He at first said he thought an appeal would clarify the situation. After he was told an acquittal could not be appealed he expressed shock at the verdict and announced the beginning of a federal investigation. Two days after the riots began, when thirty-eight people were dead and untold damage had occurred, he ordered in one thousand federal law enforcement officers to help the police and National Guard. In addition, four thousand Army and Marine troops were encamped outside of Los Angeles awaiting possible orders to join in quelling the rebellion.[45]

The federal law enforcement officials sent into Los Angeles included agents from the FBI, the United States Border Patrol, Bureau of Prisons, federal marshals, and the Bureau of Alcohol, Tobacco, and

Firearms in a strike team patterned after the group organized by the Justice Department for duty in the South during the civil rights movement. The department had maintained a force trained and ready since those days for such marshal duty. They could be introduced without the president having to follow the constitutional procedure for calling out troops. Helping the local authorities, they would operate under a separate command.[46]

The riots focused public attention on the grievances of the poor black community, including police brutality, homelessness, joblessness, violence, drugs, lack of education, and economic opportunity. Polls showed that most whites agreed with the overwhelming African-American sentiment that the verdict was wrong. The entire nation had seen the videotaped beating. However, fewer whites understood the rebellion in response to the verdict. Political analyst Kevin Phillips, who had predicted the Republican ascendancy to the presidency in the 1970s, in part by using the race issue, told *The New York Times* that the liberals failed to solve major social problems including race and they "were repudiated and the Republicans moved into a 25-year-period of executive hegemony." However, the "twelve years of Reagan and Bush has not cured the problems either. It hasn't given us the morning in America. It's produced more columns of smoke rising from our inner cities." He did not think increased public financial support for addressing the plight of cities directly was likely. However, the Democrats should make the cities "part of a larger discussion of the Republicans' failure to address things most voters do care deeply about, like education and health care for everyone."[47]

Rodney King, appalled by the violence, counseled peace, saying, "People, I just want to say, can we all get along. Can we stop making it horrible for the older people and the kids." King, an unemployed twenty-six-year-old construction worker, continued: "We'll get our justice. They've won the battle, but they haven't won the war. We'll have our day in court and that's all we want."[48]

President Bush met with an array of civil rights leaders on May 1, 1992, including Executive Director Benjamin Hooks of the NAACP and John Jacob, president of the National Urban League. Afterward, the president gave a nationally televised address, in which he spoke of blacks who had saved a white truck driver who was being beaten by the rebels. The president asked for peace and promised justice. Satisfying the constitutional requirement, he announced that "at the request of the governor and the mayor," he was ordering the federal troops to help restore order and was federalizing the National Guard. Federal troops had last been sent to prevent looting after Hurricane Hugo in the Virgin Islands in 1989. Federal troops were also sent to Washington in 1972 to help control riots protesting the Vietnam War. Bush told the nation: "What we saw last night and the night before in Los Angeles is not about civil rights. It's not about the great cause of equality that all Americans must uphold. It's not a message of protest. It's been the brutality of a mob pure and simple. And let me assure you I will use whatever force is necessary to restore order."[49]

The president also detailed Justice Department involvement in investigating the King beating. In a statement which belied the emphasis in the reports submitted by the Justice Department to Congress, he announced that "since 1988, the Justice Department has successfully prosecuted over one hundred law enforcement officials for excessive violence." The president first blamed the Great Society for the rioting, but then decried blame-casting, or the idea that money could solve the Los Angeles problems, asking instead for ". . . an honest, open national discussion about family, about values, about public policy, about race."[50]

As one reaction by legal officials to the riot, Dade County, Florida, Circuit Judge W. Thomas Spencer moved the retrial of police officer William Lozano from Orlando to Tallahassee in May 1992. In January 1989 Lozano had shot and killed a black motorcyclist in a predominantly African-American neighborhood in Miami. He claimed that the man had tried to run over him while fleeing from another police officer. A passenger was thrown from the motorcycle and later died. The incident led to three days of rioting in the Overtown district of Miami, in which 136 buildings were burned, 1 person was killed, and 372 people were arrested. In December 1989 Lozano was convicted of two counts of manslaughter in 20-percent-black Dade County, by a jury with black, white, and Hispanic members. The court of appeals reversed the verdict and the judge moved the retrial to Orlando. Judge Spencer decided, however, in view of the Los Angeles disturbances, to move the trial again, to Tallahassee, which has a 20 percent black population, rather than Orlando, where blacks formed only 10 percent of the population.[51]

President Bush visited Los Angeles after the mobilization of fed-

eral troops to tour the riot area. While in the city, he announced a
$19 million aid program, including more money for Head Start,
health and drug treatment clinics, housing for about 175 low-income
families, worker retraining, and law enforcement to combat drug dealers. A *New York Times* poll showed that most people wanted to increase education and pay more attention to the plight of blacks. More
than half, however, thought the problem was not necessarily money
but little understanding of how to solve the problems. As soon as the
riot dissipated, Congress and the president did very little for Los Angeles or any of the other hard-pressed cities. During the 1992 presidential campaign, Bill Clinton promised some rebuilding of
infrastructure and more education and training which might help
blacks.[52]

On May 13, 1992, Los Angeles District Attorney Ira Reiner and
U.S. Attorney Lourdes Baird announced the prosecution of the three
black men who were accused of beating the white truck driver, Reginald Denny. When the prosecutors were asked why charges against
three black men were filed so quickly when nothing had happened to
punish the assailants of King, they answered that the case was simpler
and they had more evidence.[53]

On May 15, 1992, the prosecutor announced a retrial of Laurence
Powell, who had had a hung jury on one of the charges in the first
trial. Thereafter federal charges were filed on July 31, 1992. Then, on
August 5, 1992, three months after a state jury acquitted the four police officers on nearly all charges, a federal grand jury indicted the
same four men. The indictment under Section 242 stated that "while
acting under color of the laws of California," they "did willfully strike
with batons, kick, and stomp Rodney Glen King." They thereby deprived King of "the right to be kept free from harm while in official
custody." The indictment, U.S. Attorney Baird stated, did not mention racial animus because "Racial motivation is not an element of any
of these charges. It is not needed under the statute." Alan Dershowitz,
a Constitutional law professor at Harvard, thought that federal
charges after state acquittals were inappropriate. He noted that while
the Constitution prohibits double jeopardy, "unfortunately the Supreme Court has held that if a second jurisdiction frees them, it's a
different act."[54]

In the meantime the pre-trial proceedings went forward in the case of Damian Williams, Antoine Miller, and Henry Watson, the three black men accused of beating white driver Reginald Denny during the riots. Anthony Lamar Brown pleaded guilty to spitting on Denny, after pulling another motorist from a car and beating him. He was sentenced to six months for the spitting and two years for the assault. Ira Reiner, the district attorney, removed from the case the only black judge trying cases in criminal courts in the district, Roosevelt Dorn. In late August 1992 Reiner explained at first that Judge Dorn did not have time for the case. When Dorn insisted he had ample time Reiner said he wanted the removal because of Dorn's "intemperate behavior."[55]

While further proceedings in the Rodney King and Reginald Denny beating cases continued, the nation's attention was drawn to an incident of alleged police abuse in Detroit. On November 5, Malice Green, an unemployed thirty-five-year-old black man, was stopped in his car outside a suspected crack house by three Detroit police officers. Larry Nevers and Walter Budzyn, known on the streets of the west side as "Starsky and Hutch," began to beat him when he "reached into the car's glove compartment and pulled out a clenched fist that they thought contained an unidentified object, possibly cocaine." Green died as a result of the beating. Michigan District Court Chief Judge Alex Allen, Jr., ordered Nevers and Budzyn to stand trial for second-degree murder and the third officer, Robert Lessnau, for assault with intent to commit great bodily harm. Judge Allen dismissed an involuntary manslaughter charge against Freddie Douglas, a black sergeant who arrived after the beating started but while Green was still alive and who stood by and observed. He was charged instead with neglect of duty.[56]

Witnesses testified at the preliminary hearing that Green suffered twelve blows to the top and sides of his head from heavy metal flashlights, including at least four blows after Douglas arrived. According to the evidence, these four blows could have been enough to kill him. Douglas publicly charged that his inclusion among the defendants was a racially motivated attempt to diminish parallels between Green's death and the King beating. He said that the prosecution, having in mind the Los Angeles riots, did not want "the tragic incident to be seen as another case of white police officers versus a black motorist."[57]

The city suspended the officers without pay immediately after the incident and as the hearing continued all four were fired. The city, reportedly, also agreed to pay about $5 million to Green's family to settle a wrongful death suit.[58]

In a case of police violence disturbingly similar to events in Detroit and Los Angeles, in December 1992 in Nashville the victim and witnesses accused five white officers of roughing up a black motorist who turned out to be an undercover vice squad officer. Police Chief Robert Kirchner at first dismissed two of the officers, David E. Geary and Jeffrey Blewett, after a three-hour closed hearing in his office. The black officer was Reginald D. Miller. There was an altercation outside the chief's office between a group of black ministers and white officers who had gathered outside the chief's door.[59]

Reverend James Thomas of the Jefferson Street Missionary Baptist church said that the department acted promptly because the victim was an officer. "Had it been anybody else, I don't think that it would have ended so quickly. And perhaps it wouldn't even have been reported." Chief Kirchner told the press that other undercover officers ran to stop the beating, unlike the event in Los Angeles. "This was not a sustained beating, and that is what the Rodney King incident was." Miller said there were five officers involved; he thought race was at the root of the incident and that he would not have been beaten if he had been white. "Let's just say that I am two-fifths satisfied," he concluded. "I still feel that I was a piece of meat thrown to a pack of dogs and everybody got a bite out of me." After public controversy, the department insisted that Miller take a lie detector test. He refused, saying that he was a victim and not an offender. The chief reinstated the accused officers after Miller's refusal, prompting continuing protests in the black community. A grand jury refused to indict the five white officers, deciding that Miller himself had caused the incident because he refused to identify himself or respond to their commands.[60]

As the federal trial of the three Los Angeles officers and one former officer in the Rodney King beating went forward in 1993, Willie Williams, the city's new police chief, an African-American from Philadelphia, reassured everyone that he would maintain order. The prosecution adopted the strategy of having King testify. His testimony included inconsistent statements about whether racial slurs had been used by the officers during the beating. However, experts, including

Laurie Levenson, a former federal prosecutor and now a professor at Loyola Law School in Los Angeles, noted of the defense: "I think they [the prosecution] neutralized some of his testimony but I don't think they neutralized the overall impact of his testimony." His testimony was effective because "the jury has seen Rodney King and he is not a drug-crazed monster, he is not a slick liar, he is not a rehearsed actor, he is a victim."[61]

Hate crimes against African-Americans as well as incidents of police abuse continued to occur. On New Year's Day, 1993, three white men hijacked Christopher Wilson's car at gunpoint and forced him to drive to a remote area about twenty miles southeast of Tampa, Florida. They doused him with gasoline and set him afire. Wearing only biker shorts, with burned flesh covering his neck and back, Wilson ran screaming for help along a rural road. He ran to the gate of a cattle farm where he encountered Kathy and Omer Surface. They ran water from a hose over him and called the police. Wilson, a clerk at a Fort Lee, New Jersey, stock brokerage firm, was visiting his white girl-friend in the Tampa suburb of Valrico at the time of his New Year's Day abduction in a shopping center. Wilson had skin graft surgery for the burns covering 40 percent of his body. He told police—who found a note at the burning site: "One less nigger, one more to go," signed KKK—that the assailants leveled racial slurs at him. On January 6 the police announced the arrest of three white males: Jeff Ray Pellet, Mark Kohut, and Charles Rourk. They were subject to assault charges, possible charges under the Florida Hate Crimes law, as well as federal carjacking and civil rights violations.[62]

In April 1993, residents of South Central Los Angeles waited to see the fate of the defendants in the Denny trial and the Rodney King trial, respectively. The Denny trial was put off for months. Judge John Ouderkirk responded to defense complaints that they had been per-mitted to talk to their clients only through Plexiglas and over a phone by ordering face-to-face contact in February 1993, thereby further delaying the trial. The defense wanted the trials to take place after the Rodney King federal trial concluded. African-Americans in South Central were as concerned about the Denny trial as they were about the Rodney King trial. Compton councilwoman Patricia Moore warned that the decisions could either "ignite further injustice and bias in the courts" or "serve as the catalyst to restore confidence." Los

Angeles Urban League President John Mack stated that "if the officers are allowed to take a walk again, and if the book is thrown at these
young black men, in the minds of most black people that will again
confirm the hypocrisy of the criminal justice system. It's going to be
hard to keep the faith."[63]

In early 1993, the defense in the Miami officer William Lozano
manslaughter trial challenged Judge W. Thomas Spencer's decision to
move the trial from Orlando to Tallahassee to make it more likely that
blacks would be on the jury. His attorneys argued that the judge's decision, taken after the Los Angeles riot, made it less likely that Hispanics would be included, giving them a basis for an appeal if Lozano,
a Hispanic, were convicted. The prosecution agreed with the defense
and the district court of appeals ordered the trial moved first back to
Tallahassee and then to Miami, where Lozano was acquitted.[64]

On Saturday, April 17, 1993, the jury in the federal Rodney King
beating case—eight men and four women, including two African-
American members—reported a verdict. The police, fully deployed in
riot gear, and the National Guard, on stand-by, prepared for the
worse. The jury convicted Koon and Powell and acquitted Briseno
and Wind. Judge John Davies set sentencing for August 4, 1993, as the
two convicted officers remained free on bail. The 1988 amendments
to Section 242 made a maximum sentence of ten years possible. However, under federal sentencing guidelines enacted in 1987, the penalty
for Powell was expected to be between one and six years and for Koon,
probation or up to two years. They had not decided whether to appeal.[65]

President Clinton and his attorney general, Janet Reno, the first
woman to hold this office, expressed satisfaction with the verdict as
many Angelenos celebrated. Some African-Americans thought all of
the officers should have been convicted and worried that the promises
to rebuild the city after the riot remained unfulfilled. Clinton said the
verdict represented an opportunity "to reaffirm our common humanity and to make strength of our diversity." Reno had been Dade
County, Florida, prosecutor for six terms. She had tried unsuccessfully to achieve a conviction in the McDuffie police murder case and
was involved in the Lozano prosecution.

Also in April, President Clinton, with Reno's strong approval,
nominated University of Pennsylvania law professor and former

NAACP-LDF attorney Lani Guinier, who had attended Yale Law School with the Clintons, as assistant attorney general for civil rights.[66] Two months later, over Janet Reno's objections, President Clinton withdrew Guinier's nomination. He asserted that her views on the rights of African-Americans were racially polarizing. The president scorned her scholarly writings as seeming to suggest "that minority rights cannot always be guaranteed under majority rule and calling for more effective ways to ensure minority political power."[67]

What the King beating, the Los Angeles rebellion and similar incidents of police abuse, and hate crimes all underscored was how little change had occurred in the relationship of African-Americans to the legal system in the decades since the 1960s. And for those who had not followed the Justice Department reports over the years, the incidents also gave ample evidence of the continued existence of police violence and racial harassment. Whether the Clinton administration's policies would decrease racial tensions and stem the tide of racial violence remained to be seen.

18

Still the ''Disquieting'' Presence

WHITE OPPRESSION and black resistance have been a part of the American scene since the colonial period. The response of the government in its effort to suppress racial disorder has reflected the tension between the lofty ideals expressed in the documents on which constitutional government is based and the tendency of the white majority to desire summary disposition of those they regard as marginal or powerless. The predilection of the white majority to suppress efforts by African-Americans to acquire real freedom and equality in the United States as a *group*, even when white repression means resorting to illegal violence and brutality, has added to that tension. Of course, not all white Americans believe in black repression and African-Americans have not been the only oppressed group in American society. But while single individuals may achieve some recognition of rights, it remains true that African-Americans were subjected to group oppression upon enslavement in Africa and from the day they first set foot on English-American soil. The Constitution was designed and has been interpreted to maintain the racial status quo. Class and lack of economic wherewithal have clearly affected the lives of the black poor. But the possession of wealth and high economic status has not insulated African-Americans from race discrimination. Racism, the promotion of white supremacy, is the primary reason why African-Americans have served as the mudsills of American society. The need to respect constitutional government has been so twisted and perverted in the name of this objective that it is no wonder that many African-Americans long regarded law and order as an instrument for their repression.

Racial tensions and the justification for their suppression originated in the theory and practice of law developed before the Civil War. The constitutional history of military power, as it relates to rebellion and black-white relations in the United States, indicates that the use of troops and the threat of force against blacks in large measure effectively prevented widespread slave revolts. The United States used the regular army to return slaves to their masters, to execute a twenty-year war against blacks and Indians in Florida, and to keep the slaves in "awe" by the strategic stationing of troops. On the other hand, the government refused to oppose the suppression of the civil liberties of antislavery activists. Dominated by southerners and "doughfaces," the executive branch of the government ignored the mobbings and beatings of abolitionists, even when state officials were among the perpetrators. The national government chose to interpret its powers in such a way as to weaken and inhibit the development of the antislavery movement. This inaction was another phase of legal racism.

At the beginning of the Civil War, the behavior of the Union government reinforces the view that the emancipation of slaves was not among the Union's war aims. Troops, in fact, protected and defended slaveholders, as they had done before the war. Although the Union was forced to issue the final Emancipation Proclamation, the fact that the proclamation was only a war measure made it still uncertain whether there was a national will to end the use of military power to suppress the newly freed blacks.

Because military power was not used effectively to protect blacks and suppress white violators, even during Reconstruction, the status of African-Americans remained in doubt. One indication of this continuing doubt was that the government was still unwilling to use force against whites for the injury or murder of blacks. However, after Reconstruction, the intentions of the government in cases of black-white confrontations and racial violence became somewhat clearer. From 1877 to 1957, federal troops or marshals were not used to prevent pre-advertised lynching or other kinds of violence directed against African-Americans when state officials refused them protection. The government's oft-asserted declaration that it lacked the power to intervene was based on disinterest, rationalized as statutory or constitutional incapacity. Even though African-Americans were nominally free, government officials were unwilling to interpret broadly that status and reluctant to insure blacks the opportunity to achieve the freedoms granted the American whites. On the other hand, the national government's pattern of inaction in cases of white violence against African-Americans indicated its certainty about the status of white Americans and its unwillingness to punish whites for murdering and assaulting blacks.

These conclusions were reinforced when, between 1957 and 1965, national power was used to enforce court orders and protect African-Americans from racial violence. The widespread social upheaval generated by a civil rights movement across racial lines made a governmental response necessary. It now became clear that the problem had not been a constitutional one after all; the Constitution had merely been interpreted to support the disinclination of whites to regard blacks as persons.

The use of troops to suppress black riots and rebellions after 1964 was a return to the policy utilized before the Civil War. Federal force was used to defend white persons and property from African-Americans when state forces were inadequate or when states requested federal help. In such cases, black rioters and rebels were in the same position as slaves who attempted to revolt before 1865. They were outside the law, and federal military force has always been used to enforce the "law," whether it be the law of slavery, segregation, or disfranchisement.

After the decline of the civil rights movement and the riots and rebellions of the 1960s and early 1970s, the Voting Rights Act remained as a central achievement of the civil rights movement. Some African-American leaders became politicians and promoted electoral politics as the route for black empowerment. Quickly, however, many African-Americans saw that voting did not eliminate economic and social constraints on their opportunities. Consequently, unheralded by major media attention, nonviolent direct action endured as a strategy. Demands for positive government action and an end to police brutality and racially motivated intimidation and violence from organized groups and individuals remained central to the struggle for justice.

Many African-Americans benefited from the civil rights changes. Job opportunities increased and the middle class burgeoned. Educational attainment and college attendance increased. Many poor blacks moved into better jobs as police officers, firefighters, clerks, and into other areas of employment that were racially segregated before the movement. Those poor African-Americans who did *not* benefit from the social policy generated by the civil rights movement before it declined, however, increased in number. Poverty rates, the large-scale infusion of drugs into the African-American community, and the perpetuation of separate but unequal education in segregated poor black communities increased alienation.

Efforts by newly elected politicians to achieve social policy to relieve poverty were impeded by resistance not just from whites but by many African-Americans. Even though they had benefited from the civil rights enforcement and social programs generated by the civil rights movement, they opposed, on ideological grounds, affirmative government efforts targeted to African-Americans.

Years of unimpeded, festering racism encouraged racially motivated violence against blacks and police abuse unavenged and unpunished. The justice system, even in cities with black mayors, remained largely unresponsive to the problems of police abuse. The Justice Department's response to police abuse and racially motivated violence during the Carter administration slightly improved over the record of preceding years, but retreat became the byword in the Reagan-Bush years. The Klan, skinheads, and other organizations received attention but not the police abuse or individual intimidation shown to African-Americans seeking housing or education. The result during the Reagan-Bush years was increased racial polarization, hate crimes, and reports of police brutality.

Throughout our national history, governmental action in response to the problem of black-white violence and black rebellion has been slow and uneven until some great cataclysm threatening white Americans has occurred. If alienated African-Americans are to be an integral part of American society, the removal of racial discrimination directed at them should have the highest priority. Although racism may not be erased by legislation, educational techniques and even-handed justice as positive government programs might prove effective. Since Americans are apparently enamored of the profit motive, perhaps a government policy for paying grants or giving tax credits for efforts designed to end racial antagonism might be useful. Even if those ideas seem utopian, one superficial indicator of prejudice—continued racial violence—is amenable to solution. The enforcement of laws designed to make contact between whites and blacks less abrasive and a willingness on the part of the government to respond *as quickly and as equitably* when African-Americans are the victims as when the persons or property of white Americans are at a stake would be a good beginning.

This study also supports the view that the government allocates military power, as everything else, to defend those who are its friends and to injure those who are its enemies. So long as the government possesses a virtual monopoly of military power and is unencumbered by widespread internal disorder, such as that which occurred during the Civil War, white Americans apparently see no need to deal seriously with the factors that cause black rebellions. Surely, the lack of motivation that afflicts many people of all races also affects some African-Americans, but opportunity as well as motivation are required to achieve upward mobility. Rebellions and protests will continue to occur because of continued racial and economic inequity, unfair administration of justice, and our failure to use the Constitution to effect needed social, economic, and political reforms.

Notes

CHAPTER 1

1. For information concerning the establishment of slavery and other aspects of black history, see any number of general surveys. E.g., John Hope Franklin, *From Slavery to Freedom* (New York: Alfred Knopf, 1988); Andrew C. McLaughlin, "The Background of Federalism," *American Political Science Review* 12 (May 1918), pp. 215–40.

2. John R. Western, *The Militia in the Eighteenth Century: The Story of a Political Issue, 1660–1802* (London: Routledge & K. Paul, 1965), pp. xii–xv; Louis Morton, "The Origins of American Military Policy," *Military Affairs* 22 (1958), pp. 75–82; John W. Shy, *Toward Lexington: The Role of the British Army in the Coming of the Revolution* (Princeton: Princeton University Press, 1965), chap. 1, *passim*; Herbert Osgood, *The American Colonies in the Eighteenth Century*, 4 vols. (Gloucester, Mass.: P. Smith, 1958), 1:99, 151; 2:349.

3. John Russell, *The Free Negro in Virginia 1619–1865* (Baltimore, 1913), chap. 2, *passim*; Leslie Fishel and Benjamin Quarles, eds., *The Negro American: A Documentary History* (Glenview, Ill., 1967), pp. 18–20; A. Leon Higginbotham, *In the Matter of Color, Race and the American Legal Process* (New York: Oxford University Press, 1978), pp. 20–2, 31, 316–7.

4. Osgood, *American Colonies*, 2:218; Franklin, *From Slavery to Freedom*, pp. 54–5; Herbert Aptheker, *American Negro Slave Revolts* (New York: International Publishers, 1963), pp. 14, 176–7.

5. Shy, *Toward Lexington*, pp. 12, 33; Franklin, *From Slavery to Freedom*, pp. 56–9. *See* Thomas W. Clarke, "Negro Plot, 1741," *New York History* (April, 1944) and Joshua Coffin, *An Account of Some of the Principal Slave Insurrec-*

tions (New York: The American Anti-Slavery Society, 1860) for information concerning conspiracies in the north.

6. Lord John Campbell Loudon to Lord William H. Lyttleton, April 24, 1757, MS, Clements Library, University of Michigan, Ann Arbor, Michigan.

7. Aptheker, *Slave Revolts*, pp. 74–8; Robert Taylor, "Slave Conspiracies in North Carolina," *North Carolina Historical Review* 5 (1928), p. 20; Howell M. Henry, *The Police Control of the Slaves in South Carolina* (New York: Negro Universities Press, 1968), pp. 28–34; Edgar J. McManus, *A History of Negro Slavery in New York* (Syracuse: Syracuse University Press, 1966), pp. 79–99; Ralph B. Flanders, *Plantation Slavery in Georgia* (Chapel Hill: University of North Carolina Press, 1933), pp. 23–31.

8. Aptheker, *Slave Revolts*, pp. 18–23; Benjamin Quarles, *The Negro in the American Revolution* (Chapel Hill: University of North Carolina Press, 1961), pp. 111–9; John S. Lofton, *Insurrection in South Carolina: The Turbulent World of Denmark Vesey* (Yellow Springs, Ohio: Antioch Press, 1964), p. 32; Report of Secretary of War Henry Knox, 1789, *American State Papers, Military Affairs*, 7 vols. (Washington, 1832–1860), 1:5.

9. *Articles of Confederation* (1781), art. II, VI: Mary S. Locke, *Anti-slavery in America from the Introduction of African Slaves to the Prohibition of the Slave Trade* (Gloucester, Mass.: P. Smith, 1965), pp. 112–29.

CHAPTER 2

1. *American State Papers, Military Affairs*, 7 vols. (Washington, D.C.: Gales and Seaton 1832–1860), 1:5–6; Max Farrand, ed., *Records of the Federal Convention*, 4 vols. (New Haven: Yale University Press, 1911), 2:220–2; Henry Wilson, *History of the Rise and Fall of the Slave Power in America*, 3 vols. (Boston: Houghton Mifflin, 1875), 1:47–8; John S. Lofton, *Insurrection in South Carolina: The Turbulent World of Denmark Vesey* (Yellow Springs, Ohio: Antioch Press, 1964), p. 54; Ernest M. Lander, "The South Carolinians at the Philadelphia Convention, 1787," *South Carolina Magazine of History* 57 (1956), p. 316.

2. Farrand, *Records*, 2:220–2; *Constitution of the United States*, art. I, sec. 2.

3. A. Leon Higginbotham, *In the Matter of Color, Race and the American Legal Process* (New York: Oxford University Press, 1978), pp. 20–2, 31, 316–7; James Madison, *Journal of the Federal Convention* (New York: G. P. Putnam, 1908), pp. 460, 631.

4. Jonathan Elliot, ed., *The Debates in the Several State Conventions on the Adoption of the Federal Constitution,* 5 vols. (Philadelphia: J. B. Lippincott Co., 1861), 3:427.

5. Farrand, *Records,* 3:84; Elliot, *Debates,* 3:254, 325. See also Isaac Kramnick, ed., *The Federalist Papers* (New York: Penguin Books, 1987), Federalist Number 43.

6. *Constitution of the United States,* art. IV, sec. 4, art. I, sec. 8; Andrew C. McLaughlin, "The Background of Federalism," *American Political Science Review* 12 (May 1918), pp. 215–40.

7. The 840 soldiers stationed at Springfield, Massachusetts arsenal and at West Point comprised the small military contingent which was created by a resolution of the Confederation Congress in October 1786 and was continued by act of April 1787. See *American State Papers, Military Affairs,* 1:5, 6; 1 *United States, Statutes at Large* 95 (hereafter cited as *Stat*); 1 *Stat* 222; 1 *Stat* 264 (1792); *see also* 2 *Stat* 443 (1807); 1 *Stat* 424 (1795). *See* Appendix, Title 10:332.

8. *Annals of Congress,* 1st cong., 2nd sess. (1790–1), pp. 1413, 1415, 1456; Herman Ames, *State Documents on Federal Relations* 5 (Philadelphia: University of Pennsylvania, 1904), pp. 1–2.

9. *Annals of Congress,* 4th cong., 2nd sess. (1796–7), p. 1895.

10. *Annals of Congress,* 4th cong., 2nd sess. (1796–7), p. 2021; John Hope Franklin, *The Free Negro in North Carolina 1790–1860* (Chapel Hill: University of North Carolina Press, 1943), pp. 22–5. Herbert Aptheker, *A Documentary History of the Negro People in the United States,* 2 vols. (New York: Citadel Press, 1969), 1:40–4, contains a copy of the black petition, which may also be found in *Annals of Congress,* 4th cong., 2nd sess. (1796–7), pp. 2015–8.

11. *Annals of Congress,* 5th cong., 1st sess. (1797–9), pp. 292–3.

12. Ibid., p. 661.

13. *Annals of Congress,* 6th cong., 1st sess. (1799–1801), pp. 229, 231, 234, 242, 244–5; Harper and Rutledge were Federalists and anti-French. *See also* Henry Aptheker, *American Negro Slave Revolts* (New York: International Publishers, 1963), p. 44.

14. *Annals of Congress,* 8th cong., 1st sess. (1803–4), pp. 995, 1015; Lofton, *Denmark Vesey,* pp. 104–7.

15. 1 *Stat* 264 (1792). This act had three sections designed both to enforce federal law and suppress insurrections against state governments. Sections 2

and 3 were at issue in the Fries and Whiskey rebellions: 1 *Stat* 424. *See* Appendix, Title 10:331, 332.

16. Leland D. Baldwin, *Whiskey Rebels: The Story of a Frontier Uprising* (Pittsburg: University of Pittsburgh Press, 1939), pp. 56–60; Bennett Rich, *The Presidents and Civil Disorder* (Washington, D.C.: Brookings Institution, 1941), pp. 2–20, 22–6. *See also* Frederick T. Wilson, *Federal Aid in Domestic Disturbances*, Senate Document 209, 57th cong., 2nd sess. (1903), pp. 34–42 (hereafter cited as *Sen. Doc.*).

CHAPTER 3

1. Howell M. Henry, *Control of Slaves in South Carolina* (New York: Negro Universities Press, 1968), pp. 36–8; Ralph B. Flanders, *Plantation Slavery in Georgia* (Chapel Hill: University of North Carolina Press, 1933), pp. 276–9; Joe G. Taylor, *Negro Slavery in Louisiana* (Baton Rouge: Louisiana State University Press, 1963), pp. 170–1, 204; Orville W. Taylor, *Negro Slavery in Arkansas* (Durham: Duke University Press, 1958); James Sellers, *Slavery in Alabama* (Birmingham: University of Alabama Press, 1950), p. 247.

2. Correspondence between Secretary of War Henry Knox and Captain Thomas Holt, commanding at New London, Virginia, October 17, 1793; General Accounting Office Record Group (hereafter cited as R.G.) 217, 3rd Auditor's Report, National Archives; Henry Aptheker, *American Negro Slave Revolts* (New York: International Publishers, 1963), pp. 209–19, *passim*; F. Roy Johnson, *The Nat Turner Slave Insurrection* (Murfreesboro, N.C.: Johnson Publishing Co., 1966), pp. 35–8; Roland McConnell, *Negro Troops of Antebellum Louisiana* (Baton Rouge: Louisiana State University Press, 1968), pp. 45–6; John S. Lofton, *Insurrection in South Carolina: The Turbulent World of Denmark Vesey* (Yellow Springs, Ohio, Antioch Press, 1964), pp. 72–4; John Hope Franklin, *Free Negro in North Carolina 1790–1860* (Chapel Hill, University of North Carolina Press, 1943), pp. 60–2.

3. Aptheker, *Slave Revolts*, pp. 219–23.

4. Ibid., pp. 234–9; Henry, *Control of Slaves*, pp. 35–9; John Russell, *The Free Negro in Virginia 1619–1865* (Baltimore: Johns Hopkins University Press, 1913), pp. 66–7, 96–7; Henry Ames, *State Documents on Federal Relations*, 5 *American State Papers, Military Affairs* (Philadelphia: University of Pennsylvania, 1904, 1900), 2:464–7; *Annals of Congress*, 9th cong., 2nd sess. (1804–5), pp. 994–1000; Leon Litwack, *North of Slavery: The Negro in the Free States, 1789–1861* (Chicago: University of Chicago Press, 1960), p. 16; Aptheker, *Slave Revolts*, p. 226; John Hope Franklin, *From Slavery to Freedom* (New York: Alfred Knopf, 1988), p. 137.

5. McConnell, *Negro Troops*, pp. 48–9. Aptheker, in *Slave Revolts*, pp. 249–51, says that sixteen more were executed in New Orleans shortly afterward. Dunbar Rowland, ed., *Official Letter Books of W. C. C. Claiborne, 1801–1816*, 6 vols. (Jackson, Miss.: State Department of Archives and History, 1917), 6:17, 20; *Constitution of the United States*, art. IV.

6. Lofton, *Denmark Vesey*, pp. 81–2, 94–5, 125–6; Aptheker, *Slave Revolts*, pp. 268–72; Franklin, *Free Negro in North Carolina*, p. 193; Ames, *State Documents*, pp. 3, 11–12, 18–19; Litwack, *North of Slavery*, pp. 20–9.

7. Ames, *State Documents*, pp. 4–10.

8. *Annals of Congress*, 16th cong., 1st sess. (1820), pp. 1398, 1415, 1427, 16th cong., 2nd sess. (1820–1), p. 98. Samuel E. Morison, in *Harrison Gray Otis, 1765–1848: The Urbane Federalist* (Boston: Houghton Mifflin 1969), pp. 424–32, puts Otis in perhaps a more favorable light but does not contradict the view that he accepted federal responsibility for the suppression of slave revolts.

9. James Hamilton, *Negro Plot, an Account of the Late Intended Insurrection Among a Portion of the Blacks of the City of Charleston, South Carolina* (Boston: Joseph W. Ingraham, 1822); Lionel H. Kennedy and Thomas Parker, *An Official Report of the Trials of Sundry Negroes Charged with an Attempt to Raise an Insurrection in the State of South Carolina* (Charleston: James R. Schenck, 1822); Lofton, *Denmark Vesey*, chap. 12; Richard Wade, "The Vesey Plot: A Reconsideration," *The Journal of Southern History*, 30 (May 1964), pp. 143–61.

10. Thomas Bennett to John C. Calhoun, July 15, 1822, Register of Letters Received, file no. 30B (16), War Records Branch, National Archives, July 30, 1822; Calhoun to Colonel A. Eustis, July 22, 1822, file no. 55B (16), item 324, R.G. 107, National Archives; Calhoun to Major James Bankhead, July 22, 1822, item 446, 408, R.G. 107, National Archives. *See also* Lofton, *Denmark Vesey*, pp. 172–3, and *Sen. Doc.* 209, 57th cong., 2nd sess. (1903), pp. 32–3, 50.

11. *Elkinson v. Deliesilline*, 8 *Federal Cases* 493 (1823) (hereafter cited as *Fed. Cases*); Philip Hamer, "Great Britain, the United States and the Negro Seaman Acts, 1822–48," *The Journal of Southern History* 1 (1935), pp. 3–28; *Annals of Congress*, 17th cong., 2nd sess. (1822–3), p. 1055; Ames, *State Documents*, pp. 12, 45; *Constitution of the United States*, Sixth Amendment.

12. *American State Papers, Military Affairs*, 7 vols. (Washington, D.C.: Gales and Seaton, 1832–1860), 3:393, 414–5, 443, 1823.

13. Aptheker, *Slave Revolts*, pp. 290–310; *Sen. Doc.* 209 (1903), p. 56.

14. Aptheker, *Slave Revolts*, pp. 293–309; *Richmond Enquirer*, September 2, 3, 6, and 16, 1831; *Sen. Doc.* 209 (1903), pp. 261–2. Aptheker believes that troops helped to massacre blacks but does not say whether they were federal or state forces; *see Slave Revolts*, pp. 300–1.

15. *Richmond Enquirer*, September 16, 1831; *see also Sen. Doc.* 209 (1903), app. p. 262.

16. *Sen. Doc.* 209 (1903), app. pp. 263–4. The Virginia legislature responded with a brief flurry of interest over whether slavery ought to be maintained. The legislature did nothing tangible except to conclude that slavery could not be abolished unless compensation was paid to owners which no one apparently was willing to do; *see* Theodore M. Whitfield, *Slavery Agitation in Virginia 1829–33* (Baltimore: Johns Hopkins University Press, 1930).

17. Lofton, *Denmark Vesey*, pp. 211–37. William Freehling, *Prelude to Civil War: The Nullification Crisis in South Carolina* (New York: Harper and Row 1965), *passim*. Chapter 2 indicates that the economic decline was not all pervasive and that some proponents of nullification were prospering.

18. Bennett Rich, *The Presidents and Civil Disorder* (Washington, 1941), pp. 45–50; Freehling, *Prelude to Civil War*, pp. 280–96. Richard E. Ellis, *The Union at Risk: Jacksonian Democracy, States' Rights, and the Nullification Crisis* (New York: Oxford University Press, 1987), reaches similar conclusions.

19. *Annals of Congress*, 22nd cong., 2nd sess. (1832–3), pp. 132–3.

20. *Register of Debates in Congress*, 23rd cong., 2nd sess. (1833–4), pp. 1394–5; Francis B. Heitman, *Historical Register and Dictionary of the United States Army* (Washington, D.C.: Washington Government Printing Office, 1903), p. 626; *House Document 2*, 22nd cong., 2nd sess. (1832), p. 19 (hereafter cited as *House Doc.*).

CHAPTER 4

1. William Jay, *On Slavery*, miscellaneous writings (Boston: J.P. Jewett and Company, 1853), pp. 245, 249, 311–9.

2. Herbert Aptheker, "Maroons Within the Present Limits of the United States," *The Journal of Negro History* 24 (1939), pp. 172–3; Kenneth Porter, "Negroes and the Seminole War, 1817, 1818," *The Journal of Negro History* 36 (1941), pp. 249–80.

3. *American State Papers, Military Affairs*, 7 vols. (Washington, D.C.: Gales and Seaton, 1832–1860), 1:748–9.

4. Herbert Osgood, *The American Colonies in the Eighteenth Century*, 4 vols. (Gloucester, Mass.: P. Smith, 1958), 2:218; John W. Shy, *Toward Lexington: The Role of the British Army in the Coming of the Revolution* (Princeton, Princeton University Press, 1965), pp. 12, 33, *passim;* Charles Mowat, *East Florida as a British Province, 1763–84* (Berkeley: University of California Press, 1934), pp. 113–4, 120–1.

5. Peter Force, ed., *American Archives*, consisting of a collection of *Authentick Records, State Papers, Debates, and Letters and Other Notices of Publick Affairs*, 9 vols. (Washington: Prepared and Published under Authority of an Act of Congress, 1837–53), 5th ser., p. 1; Worthington C. Ford, ed., *Journals of the Continental Congress*, 33 vols. (Washington: U.S. Government Printing Office, 1909–37), 13:385; Aptheker, *American Negro Slave Revolts* (New York: International Publishers, 1963), p. 22.

6. *American State Papers, Indian Affairs*, 2:15, 5:25; *Articles of Confederation*, art. IX.

7. Loc. cit.; *Constitution of the United States*, art. IV, sec. 2 and 4; art. VI; art. I, sec. 8; art. II, sec. 3.

8. Anthony Wayne to Henry Knox, December 25, 1789, MS, Clements Library, University of Michigan, Ann Arbor, Michigan.

9. Anthony Wayne to James Wilson, July 4, 1789, MS, Clements Library.

10. *Annals of Congress*, 1st. cong., 1st sess. (1789–91), pp. 1068–74; *American State Papers, Indian Affairs*, 1:73–4, 304–5, 320, 336, 387, 792; Laurence Foster, *Negro-Indian Relationships in the Southeast* (Philadelphia: Published by author, 1935), p. 23.

11. *American State Papers, Indian Affairs*, 1:586–7.

12. Ibid., p. 813.

13. Rembert W. Patrick, *Florida Fiasco: Rampant Rebels on the Georgia-Florida Border, 1810–15* (Athens: University of Georgia Press, 1954), p. 170 ff.

14. Ibid., pp. 199–207.

15. *House Exec. Doc.* 119, 15th cong., 2nd sess. (March 1819) contains letters and reports to and from the War Department describing the events leading up to the destruction of the fort.

16. Loc. cit.; *see also: American State Papers, Indian Affairs*, 1:714, 748 et seq.; *Sen. Doc.* 172, 15th cong., 1st sess. (March 24, 1818). Cf. James Parton, *Life of Andrew Jackson*, 3 vols. (New York: Mason Brothers, 1860), 2:402,

who asserts that the Spanish wanted the fort destroyed. There is a letter written under threat of attack from the commander of Pensacola to Jackson, which indicates that the commander agreed with Jackson's viewpoint about the fort.

17. *House Exec. Doc.* 173, 15th cong., 2nd sess. (March 1819); *American State Papers, Military Affairs*, 1:681–2, 712, 714, 764.

18. *American State Papers, Military Affairs*, 1:680, 687, 700, 739; *American State Papers, Indian Affairs* 2:4, 16; *Sen. Doc.* 173, 15th cong., 1st sess. (25 March 1818).

19. *American State Papers, Military Affairs*, 1:690–1, 700–8, 735–40; 754–7.

20. *Sen. Doc.* 35, 15th cong., 2nd sess. (November 1818), contains letters to and from Jackson, Gaines, and the War Department.

21. *House Doc.* 100 (February 24, 1819); *Sen. Doc.* 82 (January 12, 1819).

22. Loc. cit.; *American State Papers, Military Affairs*, 1:735, 754–5.

23. Fugitive Slave Act of 1793, 1 *Stat* 302 (1793); *Constitution of the United States*, Fugitive Slave Clause, art. 14, sec. 2.

24. *American State Papers, Indian Affairs*, 2:248–9, 253, 429, 665.

25. Ibid., 2:69–71, 433–4, 439, 440.

26. Loc. cit.

27. *House Exec. Doc.* 271, 24th cong., 1st sess. (December 1835), contains documents, letters, and reports on Seminole difficulties.

28. Loc. cit.

29. *House Doc.* 17, 19th cong., 2nd sess. (December 1826), contains letters transmitted from War Department relative to Seminole Affairs; *House Doc.* 82 (January 1825) contains letters from Indian agents concerning condition of Indians and blacks.

30. 4 *Stat* 411–12 (1830); *Constitution*, art. II, sec. 2; art. VI.

31. *Sen. Doc.* 142, 24th cong., 1st sess. (December 1835), contains letters and papers tracing the origin and evolution of Seminole hostilities. The cases involving the Cherokees were *Cherokee Nation v. Georgia*, 5 Peters 1 (hereafter cited as Pet.) (1831); *Worcester v. Georgia*, 6 Pet. 515 (1832).

32. Loc. cit.; Treaty of Indian Springs, 1821, supra.; *American State Papers, Indian Affairs*, 2:248–9, 253, 429, 665.

33. Loc. cit.; *American State Papers, Military Affairs*, 6:466, 478.

CHAPTER 5

1. John K. Mahon, *History of the Second Seminole War, 1835–42* (Gainesville: University of Florida Press, 1967), pp. 96, 98, 103–6; Kenneth Porter, "Relations Between Negroes and Indians Within the Present Limits of the United States," *Journal of Negro History* 17 (July 1932), pp. 287–367.

2. *Congressional Globe,* 24th cong., 1st sess. (1835–6), pp. 290–1.

3. *Sen. Doc.* 224, 26th cong., 1st sess. (December 1839), pp. 38–41, 47, 48, 347–50.

4. *House Doc.* 225, 24th cong., 2nd sess. (December 1836); *House Doc.* 78, 25th cong., 2nd sess. (December 1837), pp. 76–7; *American State Papers, Military Affairs,* 6:561, 7:724, 834.

5. *House Doc.* 225, 25th cong., 3rd sess. (December 1838), pp. 2, 7, 13; Joshua A. Giddings, *The Exiles of Florida: Or, the Crimes Committed by Our Government Against the Maroons, Who Fled from South Carolina and Other Slave States, Seeking Protection Under Spanish Laws* (Columbus, Ohio: Follett, Foster and Company, 1858), p. 148. An abolitionist, Giddings set out to prove that slavery was the cause of the Seminole hostilities. He was biased but there is much useful source material in his book and much validity to his point of view; *see also* Mahon, *Second Seminole War,* p. 216.

6. *House Doc.* 225, 25th cong., 3rd sess. (December 1838), pp. 30–9.

7. *Register of Debates in Congress,* 25th cong., 1st sess. (1837), pp. 640–4, 667, 702–3, 738, 764, 770–1, 1290–6, 1326, 1682; *Sen. Doc.* 512, 23rd cong., 1st sess. (1837).

8. *Loc. cit.;* Grant Foreman, ed., "Report of the Cherokee Deputies in Florida, February 17, 1838, to John Ross, Esq.," *Chronicles of Oklahoma,* 9 (1931), pp. 423–38.

9. *House Doc.* 78, 25th cong., 2nd sess., pp. 33, 35.

10. *Congressional Globe,* 25th cong., 2nd sess. (1836), pp. 357–8, and app., pp. 453, 478, 536–8, 559, 566, 574–8, 1480.

11. Charles Kappler, *Indian Affairs, Laws and Treaties,* 2 vols. (2nd ed.) (Washington D.C.: Government Printing Office, 1904), published as *Sen. Doc.* 319, 58th cong., 2nd sess., 2:249, 290; *Congressional Globe,* 25th cong., 2nd sess. (1838), app., pp. 353–4.

12. *Congressional Globe,* 26th cong., 1st sess. (1839–40), and app., pp. 73, 75, 79, 84, 98, 99. In August 1842, Benton's efforts succeeded and Congress enacted an Armed Settler's Bill. By this time, the Seminoles and blacks had

largely been exterminated or removed. The bill did encourage settlement in Florida, however, since under its provisions a head of a family could acquire 160 acres of land at no cost. *See* James Covington, "The Armed Occupation Act of 1842," *Florida Historical Quarterly* 40 (1961), pp. 41–52.

13. *House Doc.* 225, 25th cong., 3rd sess. (1838), p. 30; John T. Sprague, "Macomb's Mission to the Seminoles: John T. Sprague's Journal Kept During April and May, 1839," Frank F. White, ed., *Florida Historical Quarterly* 35 (1956), pp. 130–93.

14. *House Doc.* 225, 25th cong., 3rd sess. (1838), pp. 1–99, *passim;* James W. Covington, "Cuban Bloodhounds and the Seminoles," *Florida Historical Quarterly* 33 (1954), pp. 111–9.

15. *House Doc.* 262, 27th cong., 2nd sess. (1842), pp. 27, 34–5.

16. Loc. cit.; *House Doc.* 200, 27th cong., 2nd sess. (1842), pp. 10, 41, 53, 63.

17. *Opinions of the Attorney General* 4 (1848), pp. 720–9; *House Doc.* 15, 33rd cong., 2nd sess. (1854) and *House Doc.* 58, 34th cong., 1st sess. (1855) contain letters and reports gathered by the War Department explaining the Creek-Seminole difficulties and the flight by Seminoles and blacks to Mexico.

18. *Opinions of the Attorney General* 3 (1838), pp. 370–1. *Opinions of the Attorney General* 6 (1854), pp. 302–12.

19. *House Doc.* 15, 33rd cong., 2nd sess. (1854–5), includes army report of October 16, 1854, which indicates that a group of Seminoles and approximately 60 blacks were living near Eagle Pass in Mexico on a plane of "perfect harmony and equality."

CHAPTER 6

1. See Chapter 2 supra for information on how the doctrine was already established before the intensified abolition movement of the 1830s; *Barron v. Baltimore*, 7 Pet. 243 (1833).

2. 1 *Stat* 424 (1795), 2 *Stat* 443 (1807).

3. Howell M. Henry, *Police Control of Slaves in South Carolina* (New York: Negro Universities Press, 1968), pp. 154–64; Russell Nye, *Fettered Freedom: Civil Liberties and the Slavery Controversy 1830–1860* (East Lansing: Michigan State University Press, 1963) pp. 177–92, 217–8. *See also* Leonard Richards, *"Gentlemen of Property and Standing": Anti-Abolition Mobs in Jacksonian America* (New York, 1970).

4. Kempes Schnell, "Court Cases Including Slavery: The Application of Anti-slavery Thought to Judicial Controversy, 1830–1860" (unpublished doctoral dissertation, University of Michigan, 1955), pp. 24–32 and notes there cited. *See* W. E. B. Du Bois, *The Philadelphia Negro* (New York: Schocken Books, 1967), pp. 27–31 and notes cited for other early urban riots; Richards, *Gentlemen of Property*, pp. 159–65.

5. Merton Dillon, *Elijah P. Lovejoy: Abolitionist Editor* (Urbana: University of Illinois Press, 1961), pp. 159–70; Schnell, "Court Cases," pp. 33–4, 42–3.

6. Letters from Conrad to Commanding Officer at Fort Independence, February 17, 1851, R.G. 109, National Archives, Sec. of War, Letters Sent: *Sen. Doc.* 209 (1903), p. 75; Marion Gleason McDougall, *Fugitive Slaves, 1619–1865* (Boston, 1891, reprinting, 1967), p. 48; there were some fugitive slave riots under the 1793 Fugitive Act also. In 1833, for example, two fugitives in Michigan, Thornton Blackburn and his wife, evaded a slavecatcher in an interesting fashion. Mrs. Blackburn fled to Canada after a woman visitor exchanged clothes with her and took her place in jail. Mr. Blackburn joined her after escaping just outside the jail while a crowd of approximately five hundred blacks pushed the sheriff back. Arthur Kooker, "The Antislavery Movement in Michigan, 1796–1840: A Study in Humanitarianism on an American Frontier" (doctoral thesis, University of Michigan, 1940), p. 63.

7. Dunbar Rowland, ed., *Jefferson Davis Constitutionalist, His Letters, Papers and Speeches*, 10 vols. (Jackson, Miss.: State Department of Archives and History, 1923), 1:29; *Congressional Globe*, 31st cong., 2nd sess. (1851–2), p. 828.

8. Schnell, "Court Cases," pp. 284–8. Benjamin Quarles, *Black Abolitionists* (New York; Oxford University Press, 1969), pp. 211–2; McDougall, *Fugitive Slaves*, p. 51.

9. Henry Wilson, *History of the Rise and Fall of Slave Power in America*, 3 vols. (Boston: Houghton Mifflin, 1875), 2:435–44; *see also* letters and papers collected in *House Doc.* 30, 44th cong., 2nd sess. (1876), pp. 89–91, *Sen. Doc.* 209 (1903), pp. 76–7.

10. Loc. cit.; Hazel Wolf, *On Freedom's Altar: The Martyr Complex in the Abolitionist Movement* (Madison: University of Wisconsin Press, 1952), p. 106; *Ableman v. Booth*, 21 Howard 506 (1859), concerning trial of newspaper editor who aided Glover's escape; *Sen. Doc.* 209 (1903), p. 78; *Liberator* (April 1854), pp. 7, 24.

11. *Register of Debates in Congress*, 24th cong., 1st sess. (1835–6), pp. 86, 89–90, 207, 711, 723, 730.

12. Nye, *Fettered Freedom*, chap. 2, *passim*.

13. 9 *Stat* 462 ff. (1850); *Sen. Journal*, 31st cong., 1st sess. (1850), pp. 118 ff.; *Dred Scott v. Sandford*, 19 Howard 393 (1852).

14. *Senate Committee Report* 278, 36th cong., 1st sess. (1859). There are numerous works available on John Brown and the Harpers Ferry incident; *see*, for example, W. E. B. Du Bois, *John Brown* (Philadelphia: G. W. Jacobs and Company, 1909); *Sen. Doc.* 209 (1903), p. 101.

CHAPTER 7

1. James Blaine, *Twenty Years in Congress: From Lincoln to Garfield* (Norwich, Conn.: The Henry Bill Publishing Company, 1889–86), 1:253; Dunbar Rowland, ed., *Jefferson Davis Constitutionalist, His Letters, Papers and Speeches*, 10 vols. (Jackson, Miss.: State Department of Archives and History, 1923), 5:33; *South Carolina, Declaration of Causes of Secession*, Frank Moore, ed., *The Rebellion Record*, 11 vols. (New York: G. P. Putnam, 1861–63; D. Van Nostrand, 1864–68), 1:3 ff.

2. James Richardson, *Messages and Papers of the Presidents* (Washington D.C.: Government Printing Office, 1896–99) 6:1–61.

3. 12 *Stat* 329 (1861); 12 *Stat* 331 (1861); 12 *Stat* 333 (1861); *The Prize Cases*, 4 Miller 878, 2 Black 667 (1863).

4. Richardson, *Messages and Papers*, 6:5 ff.

5. Moore, *The Rebellion Record*, 2:437; U.S. War Department, *The War of the Rebellion: A Compilation of the Official Records of the Union and Confederate Armies*, 128 vols. (hereafter cited as *O.R.*) (Washington, D.C.: Government Printing Office, 1880–1901), ser. I, 2:52–3, 649–52.

6. *House Exec. Doc.* 72, 37th cong., 3rd sess., pp. 1–6; *O.R.*, ser. II, 1:778, 808–9, 812; ser. I, 3:370; ser. III, 1:243; ser. I, 17:470, 5:301–2, 20:439–42, 14:33–4, 15:618–9; ser. III, 2:43; *see also* Bell Wiley, *Southern Negroes, 1861–65* (New Haven: Yale University Press, 1938), pp. 183–90; Moore, *The Rebellion Record*, 7:33, 2:437.

7. *Confiscation Act of August 6, 1861*, 12 *Stat* 319 (1862).

8. 12 *Stat* 592 (1862); *Congressional Globe*, 37th cong., 2nd sess. (1862), pp. 3087, 3102–9, 3121–4.

9. 12 *Stat* 1269–79 (1863).

10. Thirteenth Amendment, *Constitution of the United States*.

11. Richardson, *Messages and Papers of the Confederacy*, 2 vols. (Nashville, Tenn., 1906), 1:37 ff.; *Confederate Constitution*, art. I, sec. 9, art. IV, sec. 4, same language as in art. IV, sec. 4, of the *Constitution of the United States*.

12. Wiley, *Southern Negroes*, pp. 5–6; *O.R.*, ser. I, 1x:477, 24:681; John W. DeForest, *A Volunteer's Adventures: A Union Captain's Record of the Civil War*, James Croushore, ed. (New Haven: Yale University Press, 1946), pp. 26–7.

13. "Journal of the Confederate Congress," *Southern Historical Society Papers*, new series. X whole no. 65, 48 (1941), pp. 1958–9; Albert Moore, *Conscription and Conflict in the Confederacy* (New York: Macmillan, 1924), pp. 68, 70, 74; *Laws of Florida* (1861) reg. sess. 34.

14. *Acts of Louisiana* (1861–2), reg. sess. 130; *Public Acts of Georgia* (1862), p. 40; *General Laws of Texas* (1861–62), 9th leg., p. 80.

15. Moore, *Conscription*, pp. 70, 74; *General Laws of Texas* (1863), extra sess., p. 15; *Laws of Mississippi* (1861), called sess., p. 30; Wiley, *Southern Negroes*, pp. 35–7.

16. Herbert Aptheker, in *American Negro Slave Revolts* (New York: International Publishers, 1963), pp. 362–5, believes there were frequent disruptions; despite his viewpoint, it is true that no general rebellion occurred.

17. *O.R.*, ser. IV, 3:1161; "Journal of the Confederate Congress," 7:542, 4:526, 528.

CHAPTER 8

1. Thirteenth, Fourteenth, and Fifteenth Amendments, *Constitution of the United States*; 14 *Stat* 27 (Civil Rights Act of 1866). James Sefton, *The United States Army and Reconstruction 1865–77* (Baton Rouge: Louisiana State University Press, 1967), pp. 8, 9.

2. James Richardson, *Messages and Papers of the Presidents* (Washington D.C.: Government Printing Office, 1896–99) 6:310–4.

3. *Sen. Doc.* 26, 39th cong., 1st sess. (1866), p. 231; Sefton, *Army and Reconstruction*, pp. 25–8.

4. *Sen. Doc.* 6, 39th cong., 2nd sess. (1867), pp. 170–230; *House Doc.* 70, 39th cong., 1st sess. (1866); *see* Theodore Wilson, *Black Codes of the South* (Tuscaloosa: University of Alabama Press, 1965), pp. 81–95, and Sefton, *Army and Reconstruction*, p. 43, fn. 49, for similarity between codes, army orders, and bureau regulations.

5. *O.R.*, ser. I, 47:427, 461; Sefton, *Army and Reconstruction*, pp. 42–5.

6. *House Report* 30, 39th cong., 1st sess. (1866), p. 123; Benjamin B. Kendrick, *The Journal of the 39th Congress, 1865–1867: Joint Committee of Fifteen on Reconstruction* (New York: Columbia University, 1914), pp. vii–xxii.

7. *Ex Parte Milligan*, 4 Wallace 2 (1866); Richardson, *Messages and Papers*, 6:431–2, 438; Sefton, *Army and Reconstruction*, p. 80.

8. *House Doc.* 72, 39th cong., 2nd sess., Letter of Secretary of War, January 21, 1867; *Sen. Doc.* 209, 57th cong., 2nd sess. (1903), pp. 108–9.

9. *House Report* 101, 39th cong., 1st sess. (1866), p. 36; *Sen. Doc.* 209 (1903), pp. 110–1; Sefton, *Army and Reconstruction*, p. 82.

10. *Opinions of the Attorney General* 11 (1866), pp. 531–2.

11. *House Doc.* 68, 39th cong., 2nd sess., pp. 43, 151–3, 166 et seq.; *House Report* 16, 39th cong., 2nd sess. (1866); *Sen. Doc.* 209 (1903), pp. 42, 130; Sefton, *Army and Reconstruction*, pp. 84–8.

12. 14 *Stat* 428 (1867); 15 *Stat* 2 (1867); 15 Stat 14 (1867).

13. *House Report* 16, 39th cong., 2nd sess. (1867); *Sen. Doc.* 209 (1903), p. 142 ff.

14. *Sen. Doc.* 14, 40th cong., 1st sess. (1868), p. 131; *Sen. Doc.* 209 (1903), pp. 113–4.

15. 14 *Stat* 485 (1868); Otis Singletary, *The Negro Militia and Reconstruction* (Austin: University of Texas Press, 1957), pp. 9, 24, 129; *Sen. Doc.* 209 (1903), p. 119.

16. 17 *Stat* 13 (1871); *The Ku Klux Conspiracy: Testimony Taken by the Joint Select Committee to Inquire into the Condition of Affairs in the Late Insurrected States*, 42nd cong., 2nd sess., *House Report* 22; and *Testimony as to the Denial of the Elective Franchise in South Carolina at the Elections of 1875 and 1876*, *Sen. Misc. Doc.* 48, 44th cong., 2nd sess. (1876), as well as other house and senate reports written during Reconstruction which describe in detail the violence of the period.

17. Singletary, *Negro Militia*, pp. 145–6. There were also election riots and violence against blacks in the North during Reconstruction; for example, in Philadelphia in 1871, there was so much disorder associated with efforts to prevent blacks from voting—several blacks were killed—that the marines were called in to keep order; *see* W. E. B. Du Bois, *The Philadelphia Negro* (New York: Shocken Books, 1967), pp. 38–40 and notes there cited; *see also* "Conclusions" in Sefton, *Army and Reconstruction*, pp. 251, 253–4.

CHAPTER 9

1. Russell F. Weigley, *History of the United States Army* (New York: Macmillan, 1967), app., pp. 566–8; U.S. War Department, *Annual Reports of the Secretary of War, 1877–1900* (Washington, 1878–1901).

2. James A. Dacus, *Annals of the Great Strikes* (Chicago: L. T. Palmer and Company; Philadelphia: W. R. Thomas, 1877); *Sen. Doc.* 209, 57th cong., 2nd sess. (1903), p. 189 ff.

3. Stanley Hirshson, *Farewell to the Bloody Shirt: Northern Republicans and the Southern Negro, 1877–1893* (Bloomington: Indiana University Press, 1962), pp. 44–6, 49–50, *passim.*

4. 16 *Stat* 140 partially survives as Section 241, Title 18, of the *United States Code;* 17 *Stat* 13 ff. survives as Section 333, Title 10, of the *United States Code* (see Appendix). The *posse comitatus* act of 1878 forbade the use of regular troops to execute the laws except in cases where Congress authorized their use; this was an exception.

5. *Sen. Report* 855, 45th cong., 1st sess. (1877), 1:xxiv–xxvi; xiv–xvi; *Congressional Record*, 45th cong., 3rd sess. (1878–9); Hirshson, *Farewell to the Bloody Shirt*, pp. 49–51.

6. *Congressional Record*, 46th cong., 1st sess. (1879), pp. 418, 801–7, 837, 504–511, 593–600; James Richardson, *Messages and Papers of the Presidents* (Washington, D.C.: Government Printing Office, 1896–99), 10:4475–87, 4512–13.

7. *Sen. Report* 683, 46th cong., 2nd sess., pt. 2, p. 39; pt. 3, p. 438; Hirshson, *Farewell to the Bloody Shirt*, chap. 3; Herbert Aptheker, ed., *Documentary History of the Negro People in the United States* (New York: Citadel Press, 1951), pp. 713–7.

8. Vernon Wharton, *The Negro in Mississippi 1865–90* (Chapel Hill: University of North Carolina Press, 1947), pp. 115–6; Aptheker, *Documentary History*, pp. 724–6; Hirshson, *Farewell to the Bloody Shirt*, p. 77.

9. Richardson, *Messages and Papers*, 10:4598–9; Rayford Logan, *The Betrayal of the Negro* (New York: Collier Books, 1965), pp. 48–51; Hirshson, *Farewell to the Bloody Shirt*, pp. 93–94.

10. Hirshson, *Farewell to the Bloody Shirt*, pp. 100–1; J. J. Wright to Brewster, Justice Department, Letters Received, R. G. 60, August 24, 1882; Brewster to Niles, 28 September 1883, Letterbook P., Letters Sent, National Archives.

11. Aptheker, *Documentary History*, pp. 727–33; *Congressional Record*, 47th cong., 1st sess. (1881–2), pp. 3384–7; Hirshson, *Farewell to the Bloody Shirt*,

pp. 117–8; Charles Wynes, *Race Relations in Virginia, 1870–1902* (Charlottesville: University of Virginia Press, 1961), pp. 25–6.

12. Wynes, *Race Relations*, pp. 31–2; Hirshson, *Farewell to the Bloody Shirt*, pp. 119–20; *New York Times*, November 4, 5, 6, 1883. Report of the Special Committee to Inquire into Alleged Election Outrages at Danville, Va., *Sen. Report 579*, 48th cong., 1st sess. (1883), 1:xlii, 2:lxxii. For other incidents, *see* Report of the Special Committee to Inquire into the Mississippi Election of 1883, *Sen. Report 512*, 48th cong., 1st sess. (1883), 1:xxv–xxxvi, 2:lxxiii.

13. *New York Times*, October 30, 1883; Aptheker, *Documentary History*, pp. 658–9, 665.

14. Richardson, *Messages and Papers*, 5:302; *New York Times*, November 4, 1884.

15. George B. Tindall, *South Carolina Negroes, 1877–1900* (Baton Rouge: Louisiana State University Press, 1966), p. 246; William I. Hair, *Bourbonism and Agrarian Protest: Louisiana Politics, 1870–1900* (Baton Rouge: Louisiana State University Press, 1970), pp. 172–184.

16. Hirshson, *Farewell to the Bloody Shirt*, pp. 166, 182–3; *New York Times*, December 29, 1889, pp. 1, 6; Tindall, *South Carolina Negroes*, pp. 239–40.

17. *Congressional Record*, 51st cong., 1st sess. (1889–90), pp. 155, 157, 802, 628–30, 802–7.

18. Hirshson, *Farewell to the Bloody Shirt*, pp. 192–200; *Congressional Record*, 51st cong., 1st sess. (1889–90), pp. 100, 102, 3760, 6079; *Katzenbach v. Carolina 383*, *U.S.* 301 (1966).

19. Richardson, *Messages and Papers*, 12:5490–1, 5562–4; *Congressional Record*, 51st cong., 1st sess. (1889–90), pp. 6507–8, 6538–44, 6548–52, 6596, 6599–6601, 6688–92, 6772–3, 6940–1, 7792, 8306–7; 2nd sess. (1890–91), pp. 1323–4, 1564, 1739–40. *See also* Vincent P. DeSantis, "Republicans Face the Southern Question, the New Departure Years, 1877–97," *Johns Hopkins Studies in Historical and Political Science 76* (1959), pp. 198–214.

20. Foster Rhea Dulles, *Labor in America, A History* (New York: Crowell Books, 1949), pp. 168–71; *New York Times*, March 7, 1892, p. 1; March 9, p. 1.

21. *28 Stat* (1894); Logan, *Betrayal*, note on pp. 61–71.

22. *United States v. Debs*, 64 *Fed. Report* 724 (1894), *In Re Debs 158 U.S.* 564 (1895); Dulles, *Labor in America*, pp. 171–82; *Sen. Doc.* 209, 57th cong., 2nd sess. (1903), pp. 347–50.

23. *Journal of the Constitutional Convention of the State of South Carolina* (Columbia: State of South Carolina, 1895), pp. 122–30; *Constitution of the State of South Carolina*, ratified in state convention, December 4, 1895 (Columbia: State of South Carolina, 1909), art. VI, sec. 6; Tindall, *South Carolina Negroes*, p. 254.

24. Tindall, *South Carolina Negroes*, pp. 255–6; Aptheker, *Documentary History*, p. 798.

25. Loc. cit.

26. Tindall, *South Carolina Negroes*, pp. 257–8; Appleton's *Annual Cyclopaedia* (1898), p. 700.

27. *New York Times*, November 11, 12, 13, 15, 16, 1898, p. 1.

28. Aptheker, *Documentary History*, pp. 242–7, 788, 790.

CHAPTER 10

1. Kirk H. Porter, comp., *National Party Platforms* (New York: Macmillan, 1924), pp. 232, 263, 305; Rayford Logan, *The Betrayal of the Negro* (New York: Collier Books, 1965), pp. 346–7; Leslie Fishel and Benjamin Quarles, *The Negro American: A Documentary History* (Glenview, Ill.: Scott, Foresman, 1967), pp. 359–62.

2. Seth M. Scheiner, "President Theodore Roosevelt and the Negro, 1901–8," *Journal of Negro History* 47 (July 1962), pp. 169–82; William Howard Taft, *Political Issues and Outlooks: Speeches delivered between August, 1908, and February, 1909* (New York: Doubleday, Pope and Company, 1909), pp. 231, 237, 350; *Annual Report of the Secretary of War for 1900*, p. 134.

3. Logan, *Betrayal*, p. 348; NAACP, *Thirty Years of Lynching, 1889–1918* (New York: Arno Press, 1969). (*See* Sections 241, 242, 332, and 333 of the *United States Code* in Appendix.) *Congressional Record*, 57th cong., 2nd sess. (1902–3), pp. 2511–5, 2559, 2558–64; Francis Butler Simpkins, *Pitchfork Ben Tillman* (Baton Rouge: Louisiana State University Press, 1944), pp. 394–401.

4. *New York Times*, 8–12 March 1904, p. 1; Ray Stannard Baker, *Following the Color Line: American Negro Citizenship in the Progressive Era* (New York: Harper and Row, 1964), pp. 204–9.

5. *New York Times*, August 17, 1904, p. 1; August 18, 19, and 27, p. 2. Fred Gordon to Theodore Roosevelt, Department of Justice, R.G. 60, National Archives, Letters Received, August 19, 1904, Letters Sent, August 26, 1904,

file no. 40036. *See also* U.S. Commission on Civil Rights, *Freedom to the Free: A Century of Emancipation, 1863–1963* (Washington, D.C.: Government Printing Office, 1963), pp. 75–6.

6. *See* entire file no. 40036, Department of Justice, R.G. 60, Statesboro, Georgia, 1904.

7. Department of Justice, file no. 40036, R.G. 60; Baker, *Following the Color Line*, pp. 187–201.

8. *Hodges v. United States*, 203 *U.S.*, 66, 70, 71 (1906). (*See* Sections 240 and 242 of the *U.S. Code* in Appendix.)

9. Ibid., p. 70.

10. Ibid., pp. 73–5; *Plessy v. Ferguson*, 163 *U.S.* 537 (1896), separate but equal facilities on passenger trains are constitutionally permissible; *Civil Rights Cases* 109 *U.S.* 3 (1883), the Fourteenth Amendment does not permit Congress to outlaw individual acts of racial discrimination, but only state discriminatory action. *Jones v. Alfred Mayer Co.*, 392 *U.S.* 409 (1968).

11. Department of Justice, file no. 88139, R.G. 60, 1906.

12. *New York Times*, August 15, 1906, p. 1; Department of Justice, file no. 88139, R.G. 60.

13. *New York Times*, August 16, 1906, p. 3; August 18, p. 1; August 20, p. 1; August 21, p. 2; Department of Justice, file no. 88139, R.G. 60.

14. *New York Times*, August 19, 1906, p. 1; August 22, p. 11.

15. Charles S. Crowe, "Racial Massacre in Atlanta, September 22, 1906," *The Journal of Negro History* 54 (April 1969), sheds little new light on the subject; however, Crowe's paper (copy in my possession), "Race Riots in the Progressive Period," delivered at the Association for the Study of Negro Life and History in October 1969, was much more informative. *See also* Letter from J. E. Sistrunk to President Roosevelt, Department of Justice, file no. 67459, R.F. 60.

16. Baker, *Following the Color Line*, chap. 1; *New York Times*, September 24, 1906, pp. 1, 2; September 25, p. 1; September 26, pp. 1, 5; September 28, p. 1; *see* Aptheker, *Documentary History*, p. 868, for the speech of Lewis Douglass. Crowe believes that if blacks had engaged in serious retaliation, the federal troops would have aided the militia in repressing them: *see* fn. 15 above.

17. *New York Times*, December 25, 1906, p. 1; December 26, p. 1; December 27, p. 3; December 28, p. 3.

18. The following account of the Springfield riot is based on James L. Crouthamel, "The Springfield Race Riot of 1908," *The Journal of Negro History* 45 (1908), pp. 168–81; *New York Times*, August 15, 16, 17, 1908, p. 1; August 18, p. 5; August 19, p. 2; August 20, p. 14; Mary White Ovington, "The Founding of the NAACP," *The Journal of Negro History* 9 (1924), pp. 107–116; Herbert Aptheker, *Documentary History of the Negro People in the United States* (New York: Citadel Press, 1951), pp. 915–28.

19. Department of Justice, file no. 9282–02, R.G. 60, 1909.

20. Department of Justice, file no. 152961–1, R.G. 60, 1910; file no. 152961–2, 1910.

21. Department of Justice, file no. 152961, R.G. 60, 1910; file no. 152961–3, 1910.

22. Department of Justice, file no. 152961–1, R.G. 60, 1910.

CHAPTER 11

1. Kathleen Wohlgemuth, "Woodrow Wilson and Federal Segregation," *The Journal of Negro History* 44 (April 1959), pp. 158–173; Arthur Link, *Woodrow Wilson and the Progressive Era, 1910–17* (New York: Harper and Row, 1954), pp. 64–6.

2. Elliott M. Rudwick, *Race Riot at East St. Louis, July 2, 1917* (Carbondale: Southern Illinois University Press, 1964), pp. 39–40; *New York Times*, May 29, 1970, p. 3; May 30, p. 6; May 31, p. 1.

3. Department of Justice, Glasser File Box 14, R.G. 60, East St. Louis, July 3, 1917.

4. Ibid.; Rudwick, *Race Riot*, p. 137.

5. Department of Justice, Glasser File Box 14, East St. Louis, October 1917; Letters Received, file no. 186835–55, R.G. 60, December 1917.

6. Edgar Schouler, "The Houston Race Riot, 1917," *The Journal of Negro History* 29 (July 1944), pp. 300–38, is based on a report in the *Houston Daily Post* during the riot.

7. Department of Justice, file no. 196821, R.G. 60, National Archives; *New York Times*, August 24, 1917, p. 7; August 25, p. 1; August 26, p. 3; August 27, p. 7.

8. Department of Justice, file no. 196821-x, R.G. 60; *Sen. J. Res.* 51, 10 June 1919.

9. Department of Justice, file no. 190267-1 through 4, R.G. 60; *see also* 158260, February 1918.

10. Department of Justice, file no. 190267-5, R.G. 60, February 1918.

11. Foster Rhea Dulles, *Labor in America, A History* (New York: Crowell Books, 1949), pp. 231–40; Robert Kerlin, *The Voice of the Negro, 1919* (New York: E.P. Dutton, 1920), pp. 68–70; Allen A. Holland, Jr., "The Negro and the IWW" (unpublished seminar paper, 1942), Michigan Historical Collections, University of Michigan, Ann Arbor, Michigan.

12. Arthur Waskow, *From Race Riot to Sit-In—1919 and the 1960's* (Garden City, N.Y.: Doubleday, 1966), pp. 13–6, is a useful study, although based primarily on NAACP files; Waskow does not include the riots between 1919 and 1960. Department of Justice, Glasser File Box 14, R.G. 60, Charleston, S.C., May 10, 11, 1919.

13. *New York Times*, July 12, 1919, p. 20; July 14, p. 2. Peonage (debt slavery) was endemic in the South despite the federal law of 1867 outlawing it. It was one means used by some southerners to continue their exploitation of black labor. Justice Department efforts to enforce the law were feeble at best; *see* Pete Daniel, "Peonage in the New South" (unpublished doctoral dissertation, University of Maryland, 1970).

14. Department of Justice, Memo for Chief of Staff, Glasser File Box 14, Washington, D.C., and Virginia, September 1917.

15. Department of Justice, Memo for Chief of Staff, Glasser File Box 14, Washington, D.C., September 1917; War Department, A.G.O. 370, p. 6; Department of Justice Glasser File Box 14, Washington, D.C., Executive Branch, Military Intelligence, "Negro Agitation"; *New York Times*, July 21–24, 1919, p. 1, Waskow, *Race Riot*, chap. 3.

16. *Congressional Record*, 66th cong., 1st sess. (1919), pp. 3367, 3646, 8979.

17. Department of Justice, Glasser File Box 14, Office of Chief of Staff, Executive Branch, Military Intelligence, August 1919.

18. Chicago Commission on Race Relations, *The Negro in Chicago* (Chicago: The University of Chicago Press, 1922), pp. 4–5; *New York Times*, July 28–August 1, 1919, p. 1; August 3, p. 9; August 4, p. 6; August 5, p. 1.

19. *New York Times*, dates cited in fn. 18; Waskow, *Race Riot*, chap. 4.

20. Waskow, *Race Riot*, p. 57 and notes there cited; Department of Justice, Glasser File Box 5, Chicago Riot, 1919.

21. *New York Times*, August 31–September 1, 1919, p. 1; Waskow, *Race Riot*, pp. 105–10.

22. Report of Lt. Col. Jacob West, commanding troops in Omaha, to War Department, Department of Justice, Glasser File Box 14, October 1919; *see also* telegram from General Leonard Wood to the Adjutant General, October 1919.

23. *New York Times*, October 3, 1919, p. 6; October 4, p. 7; October 5, p. 10; Waskow, *Race Riot*, p. 125.

24. Memo for Adjutant General, War Department, File A.G.O. 370, p. 6, September 29, 1919, Box 15, Use of troops, Memo from Major General Jery to the Adjutant General, October 1919.

25. Passailogue to Ass't. Chief of Staff G-2, 3rd div., Eugene Bates Intelligence Officer, Camp Pike to Acting Intelligence Office Army, Department of Justice, Glasser File Box 14, Elaine Riots, 1919.

26. Waskow, *Race Riot*, chap. 8, discusses the difficulties involved.

27. Department of Justice, file no. 158260-1-12, R.G. 60, 1919.

28. *Congressional Record*, 66th cong., 1st sess. (1919), p. 8818.

29. Department of Justice, Glasser File Box 10, War Plan White, May 27, 1920.

30. Department of Justice, Code Military Staff in Chicago to Chief of Staff, Executive Division, Military Intelligence, Glasser File Box 14, Chicago, October 29, 1919.

31. *Sen. Doc.* 153, 66th cong., 1st sess. (1919), ser. no. 7607, p. 162.

32. Department of Justice, file no. 158260-119, R.G. 60, 1919.

33. Department of Justice, Office of Chief of Staff, Executive Division, Military Intelligence, Glasser File Box 14, Lexington, Ky., February 19, 1920; Department of Justice, file no. 158260-1-20, R.G. 60, 1920.

34. Department of Justice, Baker to Chief of Staff, Glasser File Box 15, December 2, 1920; Russell F. Weigley, *History of the United States Army* (New York: Macmillan, 1967), p. 396; *Congressional Record*, 67th cong. 1st sess. (1921), p. 81; Waskow, *Race Riot*, p. 206-7.

CHAPTER 12

1. Richard Sherman, "The Harding Administration and the Negro, An Opportunity Lost," *The Journal of Negro History* (1964), Department of Justice, Letters Received, file no. 158260-18-5, R.G. 60, 1921.

2. Edmund David Cronon, *Black Moses, The Story of Marcus Garvey and the Universal Negro Improvement Association* (Madison: University of Wisconsin Press, 1962), pp. 74, 110, 194–5; NAACP, *Crisis* (July 1921), pp. 115–6.

3. Department of Justice, Glasser File Box 14, Elaine, Ark., March 1921. For a rare case in which a white man was convicted of murdering a black person in a state court, *see* Pete Daniel, "Peonage in the New South" (unpublished doctoral dissertation, University of Maryland, 1970), chap. 10. John Williams and his black foreman killed more than eleven peons, some for attempting to escape from Williams's Georgia plantation, others after an FBI investigation into peonage on the plantation caused Williams to fear that they might testify against him.

4. Department of Justice, file no. 158260-95, 158260-135, 158260-1-29, R.G. 60, 1923.

5. Department of Justice, file no. 72-59-1-21, R.G. 60, 1924.

6. Department of Justice, file no. 50-18-6-1, R.G. 60, 1925.

7. Department of Justice, file no. 50-18-7-13, R.G. 60, 1926.

8. Department of Justice, file no. 158260, R.G. 60—Lynching, April 1930.

9. Department of Justice, file no. 158260, R.G. 60, July 1933.

10. Department of Justice, file no. 158260, R.G. 60, 1933. Lynching, Memo from Assistant Attorney General Kennan to Parrish.

11. Dan T. Carter, *Scottsboro, A Tragedy of the American South* (Baton Rouge: Louisiana State University Press, 1969), pp. 123, 174. Carter's book is a comprehensive study which discusses the clash between the NAACP and the ILD over who would defend the youths; the ILD won. Carter also describes communist efforts to organize black sharecroppers which led to white terrorism and rumors of a black uprising in Camp Hill and Tallapoosa County, Alabama, in 1931 and 1932.

12. Department of Justice, file no. 158260, R.G. 60, October 1934.

13. Department of Justice, file no. 158260, R.G. 60, and its subdivision contain an abundance of letters and other material on the subject of lynchings.

14. U.S. Attorney General, *Annual Report*, 1939; *Congressional Record*, 74th cong., 1st sess. (1935), pp. 5750, 6292, 6350–73, 6520–47; Exec. order 8802, 6 *Fed. Reg.* 3109 (1941); Exec. order 9346, 8 *Fed. Reg.* 7183 (1943); Robert K. Carr, *Federal Protection of Civil Rights: Quest for a Sword* (Ithaca: Cornell University Press, 1947).

15. *Report of the Commission on Conditions in Harlem*, E. Franklin Frazier et al., eds. (New York, 1935); Foster Rhea Dulles, *Labor in America, A History* (New York: Crowell Books, 1949), pp. 301–6; *New York Times*, June 17, 1942, p. 1; June 18, 1943, pp. 8, 27.

16. Charles R. Lawrence, Jr., "Race Riots in the United States, 1942–1946," *Negro Year Book* (Tuskeegee, Ala., 1947), pp. 236–7.

17. David E. Lilienthal, "Has the Negro the Right to Self-Defense," *Nation* 121 (1925), pp. 724–5; Langston Hughes, *Fight for Freedom, the Story of the NAACP* (New York: Norton, 1962), p. 43; *A Thrilling Narrative from the Lips of the Sufferers of the Late Detroit Riots, March 6, 1863* (Detroit, 1863), Burton Historical Collections, Detroit.

18. Walter White, "What Caused the Detroit Riots," Frank Murphy's Papers, Box 109, Michigan Historical Collections, Detroit.

19. This account is largely based on Alfred McClung Lee and Norman D. Humphrey, *Race Riot* (New York: Dryden Press, 1943); Robert Shogan and Tom Craig, *The Detroit Race Riot—A Study in Violence* (Philadelphia: Chilton Books, 1964); *see The Detroit News, Free Press*, and *New York Times* for the dates indicated and Harvard Sitkoff, "The Detroit Race Riot 1943," paper read at the Association for the Study of Negro Life and History, October 1969 (copy in my possession); War Department, Adjutant General's Office; R.G. 319/209, 207 Office of the Provost Marshal General.

20. *Congressional Record*, 78th cong., 1st sess. (1943), pp. 3180–1, 6344, 6554, A3463, 6303, 6371.

21. *New York Times*, August 2, 3, 1943, p. 1; Walter White, "Behind the Harlem Riot," *New Republic*, August 10, 1943; Shogan and Craig, *Detroit Riot*, pp. 91–4; Lawrence, "Race Riots in the United States, 1942–6," *Negro Year Book*, p. 245; according to official police reports in the La Guardia papers, 6 men were killed and 172 were injured.

22. *New York Times*, February 27, 1946, p. 44; March 1, p. 2; Lawrence, "Race Riots in the United States, 1942–6," pp. 246–56. *New York Times*, June 11, 1943, p. 122—the riot of black soldiers at Camp Stewart, Georgia; Winifred Rashenbush, *How to Prevent A Race Riot in Your Home Town* (New York: ACLU, 1943).

23. *New York Times*, November 12, 1943, p. 9.

24. Ibid., November 28, 1943, p. 34. For the decline of dual sovereignty and the affirmation of federal responsibility in critical areas of national economic concern during the New Deal, *see* any textbook; for example, Kermit Hall, *The Magic Mirror: Law in American History* (New York: Oxford University Press, 1989), pp. 272–84.

CHAPTER 13

1. *Screws v. United States*, 325 *U.S.* 91 (1945): see memo of Justice Robert Jackson on this case in Frank Murphy's Papers, Box 133, Michigan Historical Collections, in which he states that the Justice Department had received eight to fourteen thousand complaints of violations of civil rights a year since 1939, but relied heavily on state officials to punish violators. No more than seventy-six cases a year were even investigated.

2. Exec. Order 9808, 11 *Fed. Reg.* 14153 (1947); U.S., Congress, Senate, *Congressional Record*, 80th cong., 2nd sess. (1948), p. 929. U.S. Commission on Civil Rights, *Freedom to the Free* (Washington, D.C.: Government Printing Office, 1963), pp. 122–55.

3. *New York Times*, March 2, 1946, p. 26.

4. Ibid., July 27, 1946, p. 1; July 29, p. 36.

5. Ibid., July 31, 1946, pp. 1, 48.

6. Ibid., October 29, 1946, p. 1; John Elliff, "Aspects of Federal Civil Rights Enforcement: The Justice Department and the FBI, 1939–1964," *Perspectives in American History*, 5 (1971), pp. 605–73.

7. *New York Times*, May 24, 1947, pp. 1, 32; June 17, 1949, p. 6.

8. Ibid., December 27, 1951, p. 1; December 29, 1951, p. 1.

9. *Congressional Record*, 89th cong., 1st sess. (1965), pp. 4460–61, 4515–16; *Brown v. Board of Education*, 347 *U.S.* 483 (1954).

10. Dwight D. Eisenhower, *Waging The Peace 1956–61* (Garden City, N.Y.: Doubleday, 1965); 71 *Stat.* 634, 42 *U.S. Code* 1975c (1958); *New York Times*, January 12, 1957, p. 38.

11. Anthony Lewis, *Portrait of a Decade: The Second American Revolution* (New York: Random House, 1965), pp. 91–2.

12. Eisenhower, *Waging the Peace*, pp. 163–65; Virgil T. Blossom, *It Has Happened Here* (New York: Harper and Row, 1959), pp. 62–3.

13. *Faubus v. United States* 254 F.2d 797 (1958).

14. Opinions of the Attorney General 41 (1957), p. 67, Proclamation 3204, September 23, 1957; Taylor Branch, *Parting the Waters: America in the King Years 1954–63* (New York: Simon and Schuster, 1988) p. 224.

15. Exec. Order 10730, 22 *Fed. Reg.* 7628 (1957); Eisenhower, *Waging the Peace*, pp. 162–75. Troops could be used without a governor's request because federal law was being violated; *see* Section 332 of *U.S. Code* in Appendix.

16. Eisenhower, *Waging the Peace,* pp. 162–75; U.S. Commisssion on Civil Rights, *Freedom to the Free,* pp. 154–5; *Cooper v. Aaron,* 385 *U.S.* 1 (1958).

17. *Congressional Record,* 85th cong., 2nd sess. (1958), pp. 763, 1388, 3825, 5090, 18872, 19975.

18. *United States v. Louisiana* 364 *U.S.* 500; Robert Burk, *The Eisenhower Administration and Black Civil Rights* (Knoxville: University of Tennessee, 1984), pp. 175–99; Numan V. Bartley, *The Rise of Massive Resistance: Race and Politics in the South During the 1950's* (Baton Rouge: Louisiana State University Press, 1969); Michael Belknap, *Federal Law and Southern Order: Racial Violence and Constitutional Conflict in the Post-*Brown *South* (Athens: University of Georgia Press, 1987).

19. U.S. Commission on Civil Rights, *Freedom to the Free,* pp. 184–5 and notes there cited; *New York Times,* April 26, 1959, p. 1; April 29, pp. 1, 23; Howard Smead, Jr., *Blood Justice: The Lynching of Mack Charles Parker* (New York: Oxford University Press, 1986), pp. 55–6, 107–17.

20. *New York Times,* November 18, 1959, pp. 1, 25; January 15, 1960, pp. 1, 16; Smead, *Blood Justice,* pp. 173–6, 196–8.

21. Burk, *The Eisenhower Administration,* pp. 194, 247–8.

22. U.S. Department of Justice, *1960 Annual Report,* pp. 331–9; Burk, *The Eisenhower Administration,* pp. 249–50.

CHAPTER 14

1. By the end of 1960 there were about 50,000 blacks engaged in direct-action campaigns, including sit-ins, walk-ins, and pray-ins. About 3,600 protestors were arrested; *see Bell v. Maryland,* 378 *U.S.* 226 (1964); *Garner v. Louisiana,* 368 *U.S.* 157 (1961); *Peterson v. City of Greenville,* 373 *U.S.* 244 (1963); *Bouie v. City of Columbia,* 378 *U.S.* 347 (1964); *Barr v. City of Columbia,* 378 *U.S.* 146 (1964); and Monrad G. Paulsen, "Sit-In Cases of 1964, But Answers There Came None," *Supreme Court Rev.,* 1964, p. 137; the issue became moot with the enactment of Title II of the Civil Rights Act of 1964, insofar as the facilities in question are covered by the terms of that act; Robert Burk, *The Eisenhower Administration and Black Civil Rights* (Knoxville: University of Tennessee Press, 1984), pp. 254–5.

2. *Crandall v. Nevada,* 6 *Wallace* 35 (1868); *Mitchell v. United States,* 313 *U.S.* 80 (1941); *Morgan v. Virginia,* 328 *U.S.* 373 (1946); *Boynton v. Virginia,* 364 *U.S.* 454 (1960); Robert G. Dixon, "Civil Rights in Transportation and the ICC," *George Washington Law Review* 31, 1962, p. 198.

3. Taylor Branch, *Parting the Waters: America in the King Years 1954–63* (New York: Simon and Schuster, 1988), pp. 420, 427, 434, 435.

4. Ibid.

5. Ibid.

6. Ibid.

7. Ibid.

8. Ibid.

9. Ibid.

10. Ibid., pp. 469–70.

11. Arthur Waskow, *From Race Riot to Sit-In—1919 and the 1960's* (Garden City, N.Y.: Doubleday, 1960), pp. 231–2; *New York Times*, May 21, 1961, pp. 1, 78; Louis Lomax, *The Negro Revolt* (New York: Harper and Row, 1962), pp. 135–33. As Dixon points out in "Civil Rights in Transportation," op. cit., this was a good example of the executive branch taking the initiative in requesting specific action from an independent regulatory commission which possesses rule-making power; Branch, *Parting the Waters*, pp. 478–9; Mary Frances Berry and John W. Blassingame, *Long Memory: The Black Experience in America* (New York: Oxford University Press, 1982), p. 182.

12. Branch, *Parting the Waters*, p. 640.

13. Michael Dorman, *We Shall Overcome* (New York: Delacorte Press, 1964), pp. 15–16, 142–3; this eyewitness account by a reporter provides a useful chronology of events. Burke Marshall, *Federalism and Civil Rights* (New York: Columbia University Press, 1964), discusses Justice Department attitudes.

14. Dorman, *We Shall Overcome*, pp. 25, 27, 30–2; *see* Section 332 of the *U.S. Code* in Appendix.

15. *New York Times*, September 26, 1962, pp. 1, 22; Dorman, *We Shall Overcome*, pp. 30–1.

16. *New York Times*, September 27, 1962, pp. 1, 28, 29.

17. Dorman, *We Shall Overcome*, pp. 34–6.

18. *New York Times*, September 27, 1962, pp. 1, 28, 29; *see also* sections of the *U.S. Code* in Appendix.

19. *New York Times*, September 28, 1962, p. 22.

20. *New York Times*, September 30, 1962, p. 1, 68; Arthur Schlesinger, Jr., *A Thousand Days: John F. Kennedy in the White House* (Boston: Houghton

Mifflin, 1965), p. 946; Dorman, *We Shall Overcome*, pp. 53–5; *see also* sections of the *U.S. Code* in Appendix.

21. Dorman, *We Shall Overcome*, pp. 56, 58–9.

22. *New York Times*, October 1, 1962, p. 23; U.S., *Public Papers of the Presidents of the United States*, John F. Kennedy, January 1–December 31, 1962 (Washington, D.C. 1963), pp. 726–8.

23. *New York Times*, October 1, 1962, pp. 1, 23; October 2, pp. 1, 24.

24. Branch, *Parting the Waters*, p. 671.

25. *Congressional Record*, 87th cong., 2nd sess. (1962), pp. 19622, 19649; Alfred J. Schweppe, "Enforcement of Federal Court Decisions: A Recurrence to Fundamental Principles," *American Bar Association Journal* (February 1958).

26. *Congressional Record*, 87th cong., 2nd sess (1962), pp. 19622, 19649, 19876, 20114, 20115, 20117–8, 20144.

27. *Congressional Record*, 87th cong., 2nd sess. (1962), pp. 20250, 20251, 20262–3, 20310, 21404, 22569.

28. Ibid., p. 20523.

29. Ibid., pp. 20346, 20347–8, 20523, 20649, 21329, 21552.

30. *New York Times*, May 11, 1963; Schlesinger, *Thousand Days*, p. 959; Dorman, *We Shall Overcome*, pp. 181, 192.

31. *New York Times*, May 13, 1963; Dorman, *We Shall Overcome*, pp. 194–7.

32. *New York Times*, May 13, 1963, pp. 1, 25; U.S., *Public Papers of the Presidents*, John F. Kennedy, January 1–November 22, 1963, pp. 397–8; *see* Section 333 of the *U.S. Code* in Appendix and Constitution of the United States, Article II. See also *State of Alabama by and through Wallace v. United States*, 373 *U.S.* 545 (1963) in which the Supreme Court refused to permit Alabama to sue the national government for damages arising from the general adverse effects on the state created by the president's threatened use of troops in Birmingham.

33. *New York Times*, May 14, 1963, pp. 1, 26.

34. *Congressional Record*, 88th cong., 1st sess. (1963), pp. 8291–3, 8322, 9115, 9140, 9293. *See* Section 241 of the *U.S. Code* in Appendix.

35. Ibid., pp. 8501, 8613.

36. Exec. Order 11111, Proclamation 3542, 28 *Fed. Reg.* 5209, 5707 (1963); *New York Times*, June 11, 1963, pp. 1, 20; June 12, pp. 1, 21; U.S.,

Public Papers of the Presidents, John F. Kennedy, January 1–November 22, 1963, pp. 406, 468, 477; *see* sections of *U.S. Code* in Appendix.

37. Schlesinger, *Thousand Days*, p. 966; Dorman, *We Shall Overcome*, pp. 251–2; U.S., *Public Papers of the Presidents*, John F. Kennedy, January 1–November 22, 1963, pp. 468–71; Branch, *Parting the Waters*, pp. 823–8.

38. 78 *Stat* 241 (1964), Title 42, USC Sec. 2000A; Kenneth O'Reilly, *Racial Matters: The FBI's Secret File on Black America* (New York: Free Press, 1989), pp. 887–9.

39. *New York Times*, June 21, 1964, p. 21; June 22, p. 15; June 23, p. 1; June 23, p. 13.

40. *New York Times*, June 24, 1964, p. 21; June 25, p. 18; U.S., *Public Papers of the Presidents*, Lyndon B. Johnson, November 22, 1963–June 30, 1964, p. 808.

41. *New York Times*, June 24, 1964, p. 1; *United States v. Price*, 383 *U.S.* 787 (1966), *United States v. Guest*, 383 *U.S.* 745 (1966); O'Reilly, *Racial Matters*, p. 162 et. seq.

42. *United States v. Price*, 383 *U.S.* 787 (1966), *United States v. Guest*, 383 *U.S.* 745 (1966); *Guest v. United States*, 414 *U.S.* 831 (1973).

43. *Price*.

44. *Price* and *Guest*; *see also* sections of *U.S. Code* in Appendix.

45. *Congressional Record*, 88th cong., 2nd sess. (1964, pp. 14813, 15645, 15851, A3626; *see* sections of *U.S. Code* in Appendix.

46. Ibid., pp. 15005–6, 15158.

47. Ibid., 15005–6; 30 *Fed. Reg.* 3739, 3743 (1965).

48. O'Reilly, *Racial Matters*, pp. 177, 180–85; James Forman, *The Making of Black Revolutionaries: A Personal Account* (New York: Macmillan, 1972), p. 380.

49. U.S., *Public Papers of the Presidents*, Lyndon B. Johnson, January 1–May 31, 1965, pp. 274–6, 296, 299. Governor Wallace tried a new twist: he asked for aid, claiming his peacekeeping forces were insufficient. *Race Relations Law Reporter* (1965), pp. 218–34; see also sections of the *U.S. Code* in Appendix.

50. O'Reilly, *Racial Matters*, pp. 215–17.

51. Ibid., pp. 214–17, 218–23.

52. *Congressional Record*, 89th cong., 1st sess. (1965), pp. 4311, 4350, 4545, 4563, 5178.

53. *79 Stat* 437, 42 *U.S.* 1973 (1965), *South Carolina v. Katzenbach*, 383 *U.S.* 301 (1966); Berry and Blassingame, *Long Memory*, p. 184.

CHAPTER 15

1. Burke Marshall, *Federalism and Civil Rights* (New York: Columbia University Press, 1964), p. 81; Kenneth O'Reilly, *Racial Matters: The FBI's Secret File on Black America 1968–72* (New York: Free Press, 1989), p. 192.

2. James Forman, *The Making of Black Revolutionaries: A Personal Account* (New York, Macmillan, 1972), pp. 390–405.

3. Robert F. Williams, *Negroes With Guns* (New York: Marzani and Munsell, 1962); Julian Mayfield, "Challenge to Negro Leadership," *Commentary* 31 (April 1961), pp. 297–305; NAACP, "The Robert F. Williams Case," *Crisis* 46 (June, July, August, September 1959), pp. 325–9; 409–10; Elliot Rudwick and August Meier, "Negro Retaliatory Violence in the Twentieth Century," *New Politics* 5 (Winter 1966), p. 42. This latter article is reprinted in Rudwick and Meier, eds., *The Making of Black America: Essays in Negro Life and History*, 2 vols. (New York: Atheneum, 1969), pp. 407–17, and in Staff Report of the National Commission on the Causes and Prevention of Violence 3, *Violence in America: Historical and Comparative Perspectives* (Washington, D.C.: Government Printing Office, 1969), pp. 307–16. The North Carolina Supreme Court voided indictments against four blacks charged with Williams in the alleged 1961 kidnapping: *Detroit Free Press*, November 2, 1969, p. 3a; November 21, p. 4; *Facts on File World Digest*, January 31, 1976, p. 79 A1.

4. C. Eric Lincoln, *The Black Muslims in America* (Boston: Beacon Press, 1961); Malcolm X, *The Autobiography of Malcolm X* (New York: Grove Press, 1964, paperback ed., 1965), pp. 237–44.

5. *New York Times*, July 17, 27, 1964, p. 7; September 27, 1964, p. 81; Arthur Waskow, *From Race Riot to Sit-In—1919 to the 1960's* (Garden City, N.Y.: Doubleday, 1960), pp. 255–60; U.S. National Advisory Commission on Civil Disorders Report (Washington, D.C.: Government Printing Office, 1968), pp. 19–20 (hereafter cited as Kerner Report); U.S., *Public Papers of the Presidents*, Lyndon B. Johnson, July 1–December 31, 1964, p. 938; O'Reilly, *Racial Matters*, p. 235.

6. *New York Times*, September 30 and October 1, 1964, p. 1.

7. *New York Times*, August 13–15, 1965, p. 1; Governor's Commission on the Los Angeles Riots, *Violence in the City: An End or a Beginning* (Los Angeles, 1965).

8. *Congressional Record*, 89th cong., 1st sess. (1965), pp. 20518, 20560–7, 20610, 20625, 20672, 20681, 20825, 21372, 22046.

9. *Congressional Record*, 89th cong., 1st sess. (1965), pp. 20488–9, 20490, 20793.

10. Ibid., pp. 20754–6.

11. Ibid., pp. 14765, 20825; 89th cong., 2nd sess. (1966), pp. 16764–6.

12. *Congressional Record*, 89th cong., 2nd sess. (1966), pp. 17652, 17654, 17659, 17669.

13. O'Reilly, *Racial Matters*, pp. 236–38.

14. Kerner Report, pp. 21–47.

15. Ibid., pp. 47–61; *New York Times*, July 24–29, 1967, p. 1; July 30, p. 52; July 31, p. 17; August 1, p. 17; August 2, p. 16; *Detroit Free Press*, July 24–30, 1967, p. 1; at that time Hubert Locke, administrative assistant to Police Chief Girardin, said that troops were in fact needed immediately since there were never more than eleven hundred policemen on the street during the riot. Interview on WJR Detroit, "Focus," November 12, 1969.

16. *Detroit Free Press*, July 26, 1967, p. 1; Allen Sultan and Richard Howard, in "The Efficient Use of Military Forces to Control Riots, Some Proposals for Congressional Action," *Journal of Urban Law* 45 (1968), p. 847, point out that standard insurance policies also included riots and civil commotions, a statement which could lead one to question the justification given by the governor for not calling for federal troops at an earlier time.

17. *Detroit Free Press*, July 25, 1967, p. 1.

18. *Detroit Free Press*, July 26, 1967, pp. 1a, 10a.

19. Ibid., July 30, 1967, pp. 1b, 4a; July 25, p. 2a; *New York Times*, July 26, 1967, p. 38; July 20, p. 1.

20. *Luther v. Borden*, 7 Howe 1 (1849); Sultan and Howard, "Efficient Use of Forces," p. 861; 32 *Fed. Reg.* 10905, 10907 (1967). *See* sections of *U.S. Code* in Appendix and *Martin v. Mott*, 12 *Wheat* 19 (1827), for affirmation of president's power to decide when to use troops; conversation with Ramsey Clark, September 18, 1969.

21. *Sen. Doc.* 209, 57th cong., 2nd sess. (1903), p. 256; U.S. Civil Rights Commission, *Law Enforcement: A Report on Equal Protection in the South* (Washington, D.C.: Government Printing Office, 1965), pp. 150–4.

22. *Congressional Record,* 90th cong., 1st sess. (1967), pp. 21391–7; Ramsey Clark's press conference, p. 21396; Ruthanne Gartland and Richard Chikota, "When Will the Troops Come Marching In?: A Comment on the Historical use of Federal Troops to Quell Domestic Violence," *Journal of Urban Law,* 45 (1968), p. 881, ignores Romney's refusal to allege either domestic violence or an insurrection in pressing the argument that the president should have acted more quickly.

23. *Congressional Record,* 90th cong., 1st sess. (1967), daily edition, H9256–9.

24. Ibid., pp. S10854–9.

25. Kerner Report, p. 59; John Hersey, *The Algiers Motel Incident* (New York: Bantam Books, 1968); *New York Times,* June 15, 1969; *Detroit Free Press,* February 26, 1970, p. 1.

26. O'Reilly, *Racial Matters,* pp. 242–5.

27. Ibid.

28. O'Reilly, *Racial Matters,* p. 250.

29. Ben W. Gilbert, *Ten Blocks from the White House* (New York: F. A. Praeger Co., 1968); Staff Report, National Commission on Causes and Prevention of Violence 2, *Violence in America: Historical and Comparative Perspectives,* p. 330; as example of army proposals, see Army Field Manual 119–25, *Civil Disturbances and Disasters* (March 1968); *see also Detroit Free Press,* July 9, 1969, p. 6d, on the unveiling of an enlarged fully manned operations center; *see also* sections of *U.S. Code* in appendix.

30. Staff Report, National Commission on the Prevention and Causes of Violence 2, *The Politics of Protest, Violent Aspects of Protest and Confrontation,* p. 128, quoting from Lemberg Center for the Study of Violence, *Riot Data Review* 2 (Waltham, Mass., 1968), p. 60; Army Field Manual 119–25 (1968).

31. Violence Commission, Staff Report, 2:128, 2:332. When three black college students were killed by state troopers during a South Carolina State College protest against segregation in a local Orangeburg bowling alley, state officials refused to bring charges. Attorney General Ramsey Clark attempted to obtain prosecution for a civil rights violation under Sections 241 and 242, but a grand jury refused to indict. Clark believed the policemen

were literally getting away with murder. *New York Times*, February 10, 1968, p. 23; November 9, 1969, p. 25; conversation with Ramsey Clark, September 18, 1969; *see also* Jack Nelson and Jack Bass, *The Orangeburg Massacre* (New York: World Publishing Co., 1970); O'Reilly, *Racial Matters*, p. 257.

32. Violence Commission, Staff Report, 2:129; Lemberg Center, *Riot Data Review* 3 (Waltham, Mass., February 1969), p. 1–38; *New York Times*, July 24, 1968, p. 1; September 13, p. 1; September 20, p. 37; March 13, 1969, p. 22; May 29, p. 1; *St. Louis Post Dispatch*, September 12, 1968; Civil Violence Research Center, Case Western Reserve Univ., National Commission on Prevention and Causes of Violence, *Shoot-Out in Cleveland, Black Militants and the Police, July 23, 1968* (Washington, D.C.: Government Printing Office, 1969).

33. *New York Times*, June 15, 1969, p. 40; July 6, pp. 1, 30; *Detroit Free Press*, July 1, 1969, p. 1; July 12, p. 10a; *Newsweek*, July 7, 1969, p. 19; *New York Times*, September 6, 1970, p. 1.

34. Title 18, *U.S. Code*, chap. 102, Riots (1968), *see* section of *U.S. Code* in Appendix.

35. *Congressional Record*, 90th cong., 1st sess. (1968), pp. 19347–19433.

36. *Detroit Free Press*, October 30, 1969, pp. 1a, 4a; November 5, 1969, p. 16; November 20, 1969, p. 20b; the other defendants were David Dellinger, Rennard Davis, Thomas Hayden, Abbott Hoffman, Jerry Rubin, Lee Weiner, and John Froines; *United States v. Seale*, 461 F.2d 345 (7th Cir. 1972). Subsequently, the government dismissed both the substantive charges and the contempt charges against Seale. *United States v. Dellinger*, 68 CR 180 (N.D. Ill. 1969); *In re Dellinger*, 461 F.2d 389 (7th Cir. 1972); *United States v. Dellinger*, 472 F.2d 340 (7th Cir. 1972), cert. denied, 410 U.S. 970, 93 S.Ct. 1443, 35 L.Ed.2d 706 (1973). The government also thereafter dismissed the remaining substantive charges; *U.S. v. Dellinger*, 657 F.2d 140 (1981).

37. Title 42, *U.S. Code* 3601 (1968), 82 Stat 81; *see* sections of *U.S. Code* in Appendix.

38. 18 *U.S. Code* 241–5 (1968); *see* sections of *U.S. Code* in Appendix; Section 242 was changed in 1988 to provide the same penalties as section 241.

39. 2 *U.S. Code*, Congressional and Administrative News, 1837–1854 (1968), Senate Report 721 (9168).

40. 245 *U.S. Code* (1968); *see* sections of *U.S. Code* in Appendix; *New York Times*, May 21, 1969, pp. 1, 28.

41. O'Reilly, *Racial Matters*, p. 316.

Notes

42. Ibid., p. 268; Hearings Before House Un-American Activities Committee, 90th cong., 1st sess., *Subversive Influences in Rioting and Looting and Burning*, 6 pts. (1969).

43. *Detroit Free Press*, June 27, 1969, pp. 10, 13; *New York Times*, June 15, 1969, p. 57; "CBS Evening News," June 25, 1969; *San Francisco Chronicle*, June 25, 1969, pp. 1, 10.

44. *New York Times*, July 19, 1970, p. 50; September 6, p. 3c; October 11, p. 4e; September 20, p. 60; *Los Angeles Times*, July 19, 1970, p. 3; *Washington Post*, September 1, 1970, p. 3; October 27, p. 2. These are examples of alleged attacks on police by revolutionaries. Investigation and prosecution were certain and conviction practically assured.

45. O'Reilly, *Racial Matters*, p. 280.

46. *Detroit Free Press*, December 5, 1969, p. 1a; December 21, p. 1a; May 16, 1970, p. 1a.

47. O'Reilly, *Racial Matters*, p. 315; *New York Times*, December 21, 1969, p. 47; Henry Hampton et al., comp., *Voices of Freedom: An Oral History of the Civil Rights Movement from the 1950's through the 1980's* (New York: Bantam Books), p. 538. For a discussion of FBI counterintelligence actions against the Panthers, *see* "Hearings Before the U.S. Congress, Select Committee to Study Governmental Operations With Respect to Intelligence Activities of the United States Senate," 94th cong., 1st sess., 7 vols., VI (Hearings in 1975), published 1976, U.S. Government Printing Office, Washington, D.C., 1976, pp. 76–77, 94–95.

48. *Los Angeles Times*, August 8, 13, 14, 17, 1970; *New York Times*, October 13, 1970, p. 1.

49. Angela Davis, *Angela Davis: An Autobiography* (New York: Random House, 1974), p. 15.

50. O'Reilly, *Racial Matters*, p. 346.

51. Ibid., p. 350.

52. Community Relations Service (CRS) *Annual Report*, 1974, pp. 18–19.

53. CRS *Annual Report*, 1972, p. 24.

54. Hampton et al., comp., *Voices of Freedom*, pp. 587–619.

55. Ibid., CRS *Annual Report*, 1974, pp. 13, 17.

NOTES

CHAPTER 16

1. U.S. Department of Commerce, Bureau of the Census, *The Social and Economic Status of the Black Population in the United States: An Historical View, 1790–1978* (Washington, D.C.: Government Printing Office, 1979), pp. 60–1, 86–7.

2. *See*, for example, three works by Thomas Sowell: *Ethnic America: A History* (New York: Basic Books, 1981); *The Economics and Politics of Race: An Interracial Perspective* (New York: Morrow, 1983); *Civil Rights: Rhetoric or Reality* (New York: Morrow, 1984); and Walter Williams, *The State Against Blacks* (New York: McGraw-Hill, 1982).

3. Don Wycliff, "Black Conservatives Have Their Own Ideas and the Ear of the President," *New York Times*, April 12, 1981, p. E5; Lee Daniels, "The New Black Conservatives," *New York Times Magazine* 131 (October 4, 1981), pp. 20–23.

4. "Black Voting Percentage Drops Lower than Whites," *Jet* 45 (December 13, 1973), p. 26; "Black Attitudes Toward the Political System in the Aftermath of the Watts Insurrection," *Midwest Journal of Political Science* 13 (1969), pp. 515–44; The percentage of the voting-age black population that voted was 58 percent in 1968, 52 percent in 1972, and 49 percent in 1976; the percentage of the registered black population that voted was 87 percent in 1968, 80 percent in 1972, and 83 percent in 1976; U.S. Department of Commerce: Bureau of the Census.

5. Mary Frances Berry and John W. Blassingame, *Long Memory: The Black Experience in America* (New York: Oxford University Press, 1982), pp. 187–88.

6. Joint Center for Political Studies, *The Black Vote: Election '76* (Washington, D.C.: Joint Center for Political Studies, 1977).

7. Berry and Blassingame, *Long Memory*, pp. 187–8.

8. David Chidester, *Salvation and Suicide: an Interpretation of Jim Jones, the People's Temple and Jonestown* (Bloomington: Indiana University Press, 1988).

9. Paul Delaney, "U.S. Brief to Support Minority Admissions," *New York Times*, August 24, 1977, p. A1.

10. Berry and Blassingame, *Long Memory*, p. 189.

11. Seventy-three defendants were charged. Twenty-five cases were tried, nineteen of which involved complaints against police or other law enforcement officials. Thirty-three of the defendants were convicted and seventeen

acquitted; *The Annual Report of the Attorney General of the United States 1977*, p. 153.

12. Community Relations Service (hereafter cited as CRS), *Annual Report*, 1978, pp. 4–5, 8.

13. *The Annual Report of the Attorney General of the United States 1979*, p. vi. During fiscal 1979 the division's criminal section reviewed approximately 11,000 complaints of criminal interference with the civil rights of citizens. More than 3,100 of these were investigated by the FBI. Forty-nine cases, involving 118 defendants, were filed after an indictment or information was received. Of the 49 cases filed, 43 involved Section 241 and/or 242.

14. *Annual Report of Attorney General 1979*.

15. U.S. Commission on Civil Rights, *Who Is Guarding the Guardians? A Report on Police Practices* (Washington, D.C.: Government Printing Office, 1981), pp. 112–114.

16. Ibid., Days's testimony, pp. 116–17.

17. Ibid.

18. U.S. Commission on Civil Rights, *Who Is Guarding the Guardians?*, p. 135.

19. U.S. Commission on Civil Rights, *Confronting Racial Isolation in Miami* (Washington, D.C., Government Printing Office, 1982); Manning Marable, *Race Reform and Rebellion* (Oxford, Miss.: University Press of Mississippi, 1984), p. 189.

20. U.S. Commission on Civil Rights, *Confronting Racial Isolation*, pp. 317–39.

21. Ibid.; CRS *Annual Report*, 1980, p. 3.

22. Marable, *Race Reform and Rebellion*, p. 188.

23. *Bettis v. United States* 615 F.2d 672 (1980); they were convicted under Section 245 of violating the right to be free of housing discrimination, a federally protected activity; *Annual Report of Attorney General 1979*, p. 111.

24. Ibid., p. 188.; David Treadwell, "Klan Foes to March Again in City Where 5 Died," *Los Angeles Times*, June 6, 1987, p. 23. After a thirteen-week trial in 1985 a federal jury ordered eight Klansmen, Nazis, and police officers to pay damages to Martha Nathan, wife of Dr. Michael Nathan, one of the five killed; Bill Peterson, "Anti-Klan Rally Case Goes to Third Jury," *Washington Post*, June 6, 1985, p. A10.

25. *U.S. v. Creekmore* 648 *F. Supp.* 1369 (N.D. Ala., 1986); CRS *Annual Report,* 1979, pp. 10–11.

26. Reuters wire, "Klan San Diego," November 5, 1980; Marable, *Race Reform and Rebellion,* p. 188.

27. Chris Lutz, comp., *They Don't All Wear Sheets: A Chronology of Racist and Far Right Violence—1980–1986* (Atlanta: Center for Democratic Renewal, 1987), pp. 40–41.

28. Douglas Kneeland, "Vernon Jordan Shot at Motel in Indiana: Wounds Are Severe," *New York Times,* May 30, 1980, p. A1; "Federal Jury Returns Verdict of Not Guilty in Jordan Shooting," *New York Times,* August 18, 1982, p. A1.

29. *Annual Report of Attorney General 1979; U.S. v. Bishop,* E.D. Mich. 1992, WL 189244; *The Annual Report of the Attorney General of the United States 1981,* pp. 123–4.

30. *The Annual Report of the Attorney General of the United States, 1980,* pp. 126–7; *Annual Report of Attorney General 1981,* pp. 123–4.

31. *U.S. v. Franklin* (D. Utah), 704 F.2d 1183 (1983), 1185–91; *Annual Report of Attorney General 1981,* pp. 123–4.

32. Lou Cannon, *Reagan* (New York: Putnam, 1982), pp. 269, 303.

33. *Annual Report of Attorney General 1981,* p. 123; *The Annual Report of the Attorney General of the United States 1986,* pp. 127–8; *The Annual Report of the Attorney General of the United States 1984,* p. 145.

34. Marable, *Race Reform and Rebellion,* pp. 92–95; 195–97 for social conditions; *see* note 3 above on black conservatives.

35. Marable, *Race Reform and Rebellion,* pp. 205–6 (1991 ed.); *Report(s) of the Attorney General of the United States* (for the years 1981 through 1988).

36. CRS *Annual Report,* p. 5; in fiscal 1982 the agency received 1,996 new alerts of race-related incidents. It conducted in-depth assessments of 1,476, eliminating the "unfounded, non-jurisdictional or for other reasons"; 101 actual cases were added from these alerts.

37. UPI wire, "Silverplume Colorado," August 7, 1982.

38. CRS *Annual Report,* 1982, pp. 8, 18.

39. *U.S. v. Redwine* 715 F.2d 315 (1983); *The Annual Report of the Attorney General of the United States 1982,* p. 157.

40. CRS *Annual Report,* 1983, pp. 18–19; AP wire, "100 Told Break Due in Slaying," March 17, 1982; Mary Thornton, "Monster That's Always

Around; Deadly Assault Stokes Boston's Racial Tensions," *Washington Post*, April 8, 1982, p. A1; News services and staff reports, "2 Convicted in Black's Death," *Washington Post*, March 30, 1983, p. A15; UPI wire, "Boston, Subway," January 31, 1985.

41. CRS *Annual Report*, 1983, pp. 18–19.

42. U.S. Commission on Civil Rights, "Civil Rights Issues Facing Asian Americans," (Washington, D.C., 1992), pp. 25–26; CRS *Annual Report*, 1984, pp. 12, 16; CRS *Annual Report*, 1983, p. 12.

43. U.S. Commission on Civil Rights, "Issues Facing Asian Americans," pp. 25–7.

44. CRS *Annual Report*, 1982, pp. 18–19.

45. Joseph P. Fried, "Jurors Find Slaying of Black in Brooklyn Was Manslaughter," *New York Times*, March 9, 1983, p. A1; "3d Youth Guilty in Black's Death," UPI wire, *New York Times*, August 25, 1983, p. B3; "Youth Ends Term for Racial Attack," *New York Times*, March 15, 1984, p. B13.

46. CRS *Annual Report*, 1982, p. 22.

47. 1982 UPI wire, "Meriden, Ct., Klan," March 16, 1981; "The News Briefly," *Christian Science Monitor*, March 23, 1981, p. 2.; "Connecticut Klan Rally Erupts in Violence," and Robert E. Tomasson, "School Program to Counter the Klan," both in *New York Times*, July 19, 1981, p. 1 of Conn. Weekly.

48. "The News Briefly," March 23, 1981, p. 2; "Connecticut Klan Rally Erupts in Violence," and Tomasson, "School Program to Counter Klan."

49. Lutz, *They Don't All Wear Sheets*, pp. 22, 26, 34–40; Rhonda Cook, "East Georgia Town Quiet After Racial Confrontation," UPI wire, February 21, 1992.

50. *Wood v. U.S.* 780 F.2d 955–56 (1986).

51. Ibid., p. 957.

52. Ibid.

53. Ibid., p. 958.

54. Ibid., pp. 958–9.

55. Ibid.

56. Ibid., pp. 960–3; 42 *U.S.C.* § 3631 (1982). Deering was named in count one as an unindicted coconspirator.

57. *Annual Report of Attorney General 1984*, pp. 145, 147.

58. CRS *Annual Report*, 1981, p. 5.

59. John Conyers, "Police Violence and Riots," pp. 2–6; Damu Smith, "The Upsurge of Police Repression," pp. 35–58; Herb Boyd, Brenda Payton, Kalamu Ya Salaam, and Jean Damu, "The *Black Scholar* Forum on Repression," *Black Scholar* 12 (January 1981).

60. CRS *Annual Report*, 1982, pp. 9–12.

61. CRS *Annual Report*, 1983, pp. 11–12; *Annual Report*, 1984, p. 13.

62. CRS *Annual Report*, 1983, pp. 11–12.

63. CRS *Annual Report*, 1984, p. 13.

64. U.S. Commission on Civil Rights, *Who Is Guarding the Guardians?*; *Berry v. Reagan* 732 F.2d 949 (1983), U.S. Court of Appeals District of Columbia Circuit; personal recollections.

65. *Annual Report of Attorney General 1981*, p. 123; *see*, for example, *U.S. v. McKenzie* E.D. La.524 F. Supp. 186 (1981).

66. *Annual Report of Attorney General 1983*, p. 134; between October 1981 and October 1982, 56 charges were filed, charging a total of 98 defendants, including 60 law enforcement officers. Forty-three cases were tried, in which there were 27 convictions and 32 acquittals.

CHAPTER 17

1. Manning Marable, *Race Reform and Rebellion* (Oxford, Miss.: University Press of Mississippi, 1984), pp. 92–95, 195–97; Gerald Boyd, "President Meets With 20 Blacks," *New York Times*, January 16, 1985, p. A1; "Black America Under the Reagan Administration: A Symposium of Black Conservatives," *The Heritage Foundation Policy Review*, Fall 1985, p. 27.

2. Joel Glenn Brenner, "Regulators Are Called Lax on Bias; Senators Study Mortgage Lending," *Washington Post*, October 25, 1989, p. C1; David R. Sands, "Poll Finds Poor White Gets Loan OK'd Easier than Wealthy Black," *Washington Times*, October 22, 1991, p. C1; Jason DeParle, "Conversations—William Julius Wilson: Responding to Urban Alarm Bells at Scholarship's Glacial Pace," *New York Times*, July 19, 1992, sec. 4, p. 7; Rudolph Pyatt, "Racial Discrimination Has Become a Major Drain on the U.S. Economy," *Washington Post*, January 7, 1993, p. D13.

3. Laurie Goodstein, "CUNY Virtually Puts Professor on Probation; Board Limits Term of Black Studies Chairman," *Washington Post*, October

29, 1991, p. A4; Michel Marriott, "Afrocentrism: Balancing or Skewing History?" *New York Times*, August 11, 1991, p. A1; John J. O'Connor, "Blacks on TV: Scrambled Signals," *New York Times*, October 27, 1991, sec. 2, p. 1.

4. *The Annual Report of the Attorney General of the United States 1981*, p. 123; *The Annual Report of the Attorney General of the United States 1986*, pp. 127–28; *The Annual Report of the Attorney General of the United States 1984*, p. 145; *1991 Annual Report of the Attorney General of the United States.*

5. CRS *Annual Report*, 1986, p. 15.

6. Chris Lutz, comp., *They Don't All Wear Sheets: A Chronology of Racist and Far Right Violence—1980–1986* (Atlanta: Center for Democratic Renewal, 1987), pp. 22, 26, 34–40.

7. CRS *Annual Report*, 1985, pp. 2, 6, 7, 9, 10, 11; alerts in the fiscal year increased from 1,772 to 2,165.

8. *Annual Report of Attorney General 1984*, pp. 145, 147. *U.S. v. Suits* (WD NC); *U.S. v. Garner* (M.D. Ala.); *U.S. v. Stoner* (M.D. Ala.), 751 F.2d 1535 (1985); *The Annual Report of the Attorney General of the United States 1985*, pp. 164–5. Eleven racial violence cases were filed, charging 30 defendants. Six of these 11 cases involved Klan activity and 16 defendants in those cases were charged. Seven defendants were convicted and the remaining 9 were awaiting trial; AP wire, "2 Klansmen and 2 others Plead Guilty in Carolina," *New York Times*, December 19, 1985, p. A17.

9. CRS *Annual Report*, 1987, p. 3.; U.S. Commission on Civil Rights, "Bigotry and Violence on American College Campuses" (Washington, D.C., 1990).

10. *U.S. v. Earp* (W.D. N.C.); 812 F.2d 917; *U.S. v. Stewart et al.* (E.D. Pa.), 806 F.2d 64 (1986); *Annual Report of Attorney General 1986*, pp. 127–28.

11. *Annual Report of Attorney General 1986*, pp. 127–28.

12. AP wire, "Civil Rights Marchers Hold Rally in White Georgia County," *Boston Globe*, August 23, 1992, p. 12; Lynne Duke, "Klan Unit Gives Up Assets in Rights Suit Settlement," *Washington Post*, May 20, 1993, p. 1.

13. Charles Hynes and Bob Drury, *Incident at Howard Beach* (New York, 1990), pp. 295–305.

14. Howard Kurtz, "New York Racial Tensions Run High Since Verdict in Howard Beach Case," *Washington Post*, January 18, 1988, p. A3. Goetz shot four youths he said were about to rob him on a subway on December 24,

1984. He was acquitted of attempted murder, assault, and other charges but convicted of gun possession. He was sentenced to one year in jail, served eight months, and was released on September 20, 1987; Gannett News Service, February 1, 1989; Leonard Buder, "Police Kill Woman Being Evicted; Officers Say She Wielded a Knife," *New York Times*, October 30, 1984, p. B3.

15. CRS *Annual Report*, 1988, pp. 8–10, 12–13; editorial, *New York Times*, June 14, 1987, sec. 4, p. 24.

16. CRS *Annual Report*, 1988, pp. 8–10, 12–13.

17. CRS *Annual Report*, 1987, pp. 3, 16, 17, 24, 67.

18. CRS *Annual Report*, 1988, pp. 12–14. In fiscal 1988, CRS reported a 47 percent increase in Klan and hate group cases; CRS *Annual Report*, 1989, pp. 6–9.

19. CRS *Annual Report*, 1986. *U.S. v. Garner*.

20. Glenn Bunting, "Police Conduct in the Handling of Penn Case Raises Questions," *Los Angeles Times*, July 13, 1986, part 2, p. 1; CRS *Annual Report*, 1986, p. 15.

21. CRS *Annual Report*, 1988, p. 11; *see also* Howard Swindle, *Deliberate Indifference: A Story of Murder and Racial Injustice* (New York: Viking, 1993), pp. 286–8.

22. CRS *Annual Report*, 1988, p. 11.

23. In 1985, the FBI investigated 3,000 cases; there were 35 indictments and 13 proceedings by information filed, charging a total of 106 defendants, including 67 law enforcement officers. *The Annual Report of the Attorney General of the United States 1985*, pp. 164–5; *Annual Report of Attorney General 1986*, pp. 127–8; *The Annual Report of the Attorney General of the United States 1988*, p. 20. Congress increased the penalties under Section 242 as part of the comprehensive crime bill of 1988, the Anti-Drug Abuse Act of 1988, 100th cong. 2nd sess., 1988. *See Code* in appendix. Report of Linda K. Davis, chief, Criminal Section, Civil Rights Division, to U.S. Commission on Civil Rights, April 16, 1993.

24. *1989 Annual Report of the Attorney General of the United States*, p. 15; *1990 Annual Report of the Attorney General of the United States*; Marable, *Race Reform and Rebellion*, 2nd ed. (1991), pp. 205–6.

25. "Hearings on Police Brutality Before the House Subcommittee on Civil and Constitutional Rights," 102nd cong., 1st sess., March 20 and April 17, 1991, p. 320.

26. Ibid.; CRS *Annual Report*, 1989, pp. 6–9;

27. Craig Wolff, "Youths Rape and Beat Central Park Jogger," *New York Times*, April 21, 1989, p. B1; Ronald Sullivan, "Genetic Tests 'Inconclusive' in Jogger Rape," *New York Times*, October 10, 1989, p. B1; Ronald Sullivan, "Last Sentencing in Jogger Attack," *New York Times*, March 14, 1991, p. B4. Hynes and Drury, *Incident at Howard Beach*, pp. 295–305; Ralph Blumental, "Black Is Killed by Whites; Brooklyn Attack Is Called Racial," *New York Times*, August 25, 1989, p. A1; Nick Ravo, "Marchers and Brooklyn Youths Trade Racial Jeers," *New York Times*, August 27, 1989, sec. 1, p. 32.

28. CRS *Annual Report*, 1988, pp. 8–10, 12–13; CRS *Annual Report*, 1990, p. 14.; CRS Draft Report, 1991

29. *1990 Annual Report of Attorney General*, p. 20.

30. CRS *Annual Report*, 1987, pp. 3, 16, 17, 24, 67; Robb London, "Sending a $12.5 Million Message to a Hate Group," *New York Times*, October 26, 1990, p. B20.

31. *U.S. v. Moody* 762 F. Supp. 1485 (1991); 763 F.Supp. 589 (1991); 762 F. Supp. 1491 (1991). *Annual Report of Attorney General 1988*, p. 20; *1990 Annual Report of Attorney General*, p. 22.

32. "Hate Crimes Statistics Act," 28 *U.S.C.* 534 104 Stat 140 Public Law 101–275– April 23, 1990, 101st cong.

33. CRS *Annual Report*, 1990, p. 5. Forty-one percent involved victimization of whites; 32 percent involved blacks, 10 percent Hispanics, 6 percent Asians or Asian Indians, and 5 percent Native Americans. Eight percent reported the cause of victimization as sexual orientation and 1 percent as religion; 1991 CRS Draft Report; Joseph Fernandez, "Bringing Hate Crime Into Focus—The Hate Crimes Statistics Act of 1990," *26 Harvard Civ. Rights and Civ. L.L. Rev.* 261 (Winter 1991).

34. CRS Draft Report 1991, pp. 25–26;

35. CRS Draft Report 1991, pp. 25–26; Raymond Hernandez, "Crown Heights Standoff: A Routine of Animosity," *New York Times*, November 1, 1992, p. 51.

36. AP wire, "Civil Rights Marchers Hold Rally in White Georgia County," *Boston Globe*, August 23, 1992, p. 12.

37. CRS Draft Report 1991, pp. 25–26; U.S. Department of Justice, Federal Bureau of Investigation, "Report from the FBI's Statistical Program on Hate Crimes," January 1993; Stephen Labaton, "Poor Cooperation Deflates FBI Report on Hate Crime," *New York Times*, January 6, 1993, p. A10.

38. "Hearings on Police Brutality Before the House Subcommittee on Civil and Constitutional Rights," 102nd cong., 1st sess., March 20 and April 17, 1991, p. 320; Report of Linda K. Davis, April 16, 1993.

39. CRS *Annual Report*, 1989, pp. 5–6.

40. CRS Draft Report 1991, on 1990 activities.

41. CRS *Annual Report*, 1990, pp. 10–11; Draft Report 1991.

42. CRS *Annual Report*, 1978, pp. 4–5, 8; CRS *Annual Report*, 1989, pp. 6–9; Phillip Shenon, "FBI Settles Suit by Black Workers On Discrimination," *New York Times*, January 12, 1990, p. A1, and "FBI Agent Remains Silent in Racial Harassment Case," *New York Times*, January 16, 1990, p. A16.

43. "Hearings on Police Brutality Before the House Subcommittee on Civil and Constitutional Rights," 102nd cong., 1st sess., March 20 and April 17, 1991, p. 320.

44. Leef Smith, "Jury Was Asked to See Events as Police Did," *Washington Post*, April 30, 1992, p. A25; Robert Reinhold, "U.S. Jury Indicts 4 Police Officers in King Beating," *New York Times*, August 6, 1992, p. A1.

45. Eric Schmitt, "Elite U.S. Forces Sent In to Perform Rare Role," *New York Times*, May 2, 1992, p. 8.

46. Ibid.

47. R. W. Apple, Jr., "Riots and Ballots," *New York Times*, May 2, 1992, p. 9.

48. King made this statement on May 1; Paul Taylor and Carlos Sanchez, "Bush Orders Troops Into Los Angeles," *Washington Post*, May 2, 1992, p. A1.

49. Andrew Rosenthal, "Bush Says Verdict 'Stunned' Him But Vows to Put an End to Rioting," *New York Times*, May 2, 1992, p. A1.

50. Ann Devroy, "Bush Links Rioting to 60's Policy," *Washington Post*, May 7, 1992, p. A1; R. W. Apple, Jr., "Bush Says Largess Won't Help Cities," *New York Times*, May 7, 1992, p. A22.

51. Larry Rohter, "Trial of a Miami Policeman in Death of Blacks Is Moved," *New York Times*, May 7, 1992, p. A23.

52. Andrew Rosenthal, "Bush Finds 'Horror' on Los Angeles Tour," *New York Times*, May 8, 1992, p. A1; Andrew Rosenthal, "Bush Pledges Help to Riot-Torn Area," *New York Times*, May 9, 1992, p. A1; Robin Toner, "Los

Angeles Riots Are a Warning Americans Fear," *New York Times*, May 11, 1992, p. A1; Clifford Kraus, "Bush and Congress Return to Urban Politics as Usual," *New York Times*, May 14, 1992, p. A20.

53. Amy Stevens and Milo Geyelin, "Charges Brought in Riot Beating Incident," *Wall Street Journal*, May 14, 1992, p. B8.

54. Robert Reinhold, "U.S. Jury Indicts 4 Police Officers in King Beating," *New York Times*, August 6, 1992, p. A1.

55. Penelope McMillan, "Man Given 6 Months for Spitting on Denny," *Los Angeles Times*, March 3, 1993, p. B3; "Judge in L.A. Beating Trial Denounces His Removal," *Washington Post*, March 27, 1992, p. A12.

56. Edward Walsh, "Three Detroit Officers to Stand Trial, But Charge Against Fourth Dismissed," *Washington Post*, December 24, 1992, p. A3.

57. Ibid.

58. Ibid.

59. Ronald Smothers, "2 Nashville Officers Dismissed in Beating," *New York Times*, December 19, 1992, p. 7.

60. Darryl Fears, "Tennessee Blacks Protest Ford Jury, Disposition of Nashville Police Case," *Atlanta Constitution*, March 2, 1993, sec. H., p. 4; from news services, "Around the Nation, White Officers Not Charged," *Washington Post*, May 29, 1993, p. 2.

61. Seth Mydans, "Los Angeles's New Police Chief Gains Good Will But Even More Difficulties," *New York Times*, January 5, 1993, p. A8; Seth Mydans, "Rodney King Admits Doubts on Beating," *New York Times*, March 12, 1993, p. A18.

62. Lynne Duke, "With Guns and Flame, a Hate Crime Begins," *Washington Post*, January 7, 1993, p. A3.

63. Haya El Nasser and Richard Price, "In L.A., This Country Is on Trial," *USA Today*, February 3, 1993, p. 3A; *Bee* staff and news services, "Trucker Beating Trial Delayed," *Sacramento Bee*, March 5, 1993, p. B3; William Hamilton, "King, Denny Cases: To Many, a Contrast in Black and White," *Washington Post*, February 25, 1993, p A3.

64. "Miami Officer's Retrial Moved Yet Again," *New York Times*, March 11, 1993, p. A18; Larry Rohter, "Miami Police Officer Is Acquitted in Racially Charged Slaying Case," *New York Times*, May 29, 1993, p. 11.

65. Lou Cannon, "Jury Convicts 2 Los Angeles Officers in King Beating," *Washington Post*, April 18, 1993, p. A1; Seth Mydans, "2 of 4 Officers Found Guilty in Los Angeles Beating," *New York Times*, April 18, 1993, p. A1.

66. Mydans, "2 of 4 Officers Found Guilty," p. A1; AP wire, "Clinton, Reno Announce 7 Justice Dept. Nominees," *Washington Post*, April 30, 1993.

67. Ruth Marcus, "Clinton Withdraws Nomination of Guinier," *Washington Post*, June 4, 1993, p. A1.

Bibliographical Note

All sources utilized are sufficiently described in the notes to enable readers to consult them. This essay comments on some of the most useful materials.

MANUSCRIPTS AND PRIMARY DOCUMENTS

Of the manuscript collections consulted, letters received and sent in the Justice Department Record Group 60 were most informative both for governmental policy and for the grievances of black people. Correspondence on the subject of lynching, mobbing, racial violence, and requests for federal aid was forwarded to the Justice Department by the president and other officials in the executive and congressional branches of the government. Also, many letters were sent to the Justice Department directly. War Department records and files in the National Archives were most useful for the period of an actual riot or major disturbance. Typescript from manuscript records for most of the earlier disturbances are collected in the Glasser File of the Justice Department Records.

Public documents such as the *Annals of Congress* (1789–1824), *The Register of Debates in Congress* (1824–37), *The Congressional Globe* (1833–73), and the *Congressional Record* (1873–) were relied upon for official congressional response to racial disorder, comment upon the president's power to intervene in domestic crises, and for the development of legislation on the subject. These same materials also contain many of the proclamations and orders issued by the president for the earlier period, which are most readily found in the *Federal Register* after 1936. House and Senate *Documents* and *Reports* on investigations contain a wealth of material on lynching, mobbing, riots, and murder. These sources were particularly useful for the section on the Seminole War as a black freedom movement.

The opinions of the Supreme Court, published in *United States Reports*, of the courts of appeal, published in the *Federal Reporter*, and the federal district courts, published in the *Federal Supplement*, were used to ascertain when and how the judicial process was brought to bear on the perpetrators of racial violence. In a few cases, court opinions shed some light on the extent of the president's powers in cases of domestic disorder.

In the executive field, the *Messages and Papers of the Presidents* made important materials accessible through the administration of Woodrow Wilson. There is a gap in the series from Wilson to the administration of Franklin D. Roosevelt when commercial publishers began publication of *Public Papers and Addresses* of succeeding presidents. For the period after 1936, most official executive materials on the topic under consideration were found in the *Federal Register*, or after 1957 in the "Report of the Assistant Attorney General for Civil Rights" in each *Annual Report of the Attorney General of the United States*. After 1964, the annual reports of the Community Relations Service of the Department of Justice contain a wealth of information. The agency's reports omit the names of individuals involved in incidents but many were identified by using newspapers, court cases, and other materials.

NEWSPAPERS

Although one can find some information on official practices in the newspapers of particular communities at the time of a racial incident, such as the *Detroit Free Press* during the 1943 and 1967 riots, the issues of governmental practice and power are usually not given much attention. After the *New York Times* began publication in 1851, it increasingly became the best newspaper for the kind of information required for this study. It usually contained summaries of official statements and an analysis of policy, followed by interviews with government spokesmen.

GENERAL STUDIES AND SECONDARY ACCOUNTS

There is no one book or article on this subject. The facts of some disturbances, however, may be found in monographs on the more general subject of civil disturbances. I found Bennett Rich, *The Presidents and Civil Disorder* (Washington, D.C.: Brookings Institution, 1941), a useful constitutional analysis, although it contains only a note on the subject of racial domestic disorder. Frederick T. Wilson, "Federal Aid in Domestic Disturbances," *Senate Document* 209 (1903), contains significant information for the period before its publication. Staughton Lynd, *Slavery Class Consciousness and the Constitution* (Indianapolis: Bobbs-Merrill, 1967), sheds light on the white supremacist goals of politicians in the early national period. Robert K. Carr, in *Federal Protection: The Quest for a Sword* (Ithaca: Cornell University Press, 1947), succinctly describes the unsuccessful attempt to use the federal criminal code to punish the perpetrators of racial violence after the Civil Rights Section was set up in the Justice Department in 1939. Burke Marshall, *Federalism and Civil Rights* (New York: Columbia University Press, 1964), explains Justice Department policy during his tenure in the 1960s. John Elliff, "Aspects of Federal Civil Rights Enforcement: The Justice Department and the FBI, 1939–1964," *Perspectives in American History* V, 1971, gives insight into the civil rights agency's efforts in the early years. Harvard Sitkoff, "Racial Militancy and Interracial Violence in the Second World War," *Journal of American History*, December, 1971, pp. 661–81, contains illuminating detail and interpretation.

Individual riot studies, such as James L. Crouthamel, "The Springfield Race Riot of 1908," *The Journal of Negro History* 44 (1960), pp. 164–81; Edgar Schouler, "The Houston Race Riot, 1917," *The Journal of Negro History* 29 (1944); Elliot M. Rudwick, *Race Riot at East St. Louis, July 2, 1917* (Carbondale: Southern Illinois University Press, 1964); Alfred McClung Lee and Norman D. Humphrey, *Race Riot* (New York: Dryden Press, 1943); Robert Shogan and Tom Craig, *The Detroit Race Riot: A Study in Violence* (Philadelphia: Chilton Books, 1964); Ben W. Gilbert, *Ten Blocks from the White House* (New York: F. A. Praeger, 1968); John D. Weaver, *The Brownsville Raid* (New York: W. W. Norton, 1970); and William M. Tuttle, Jr., *Race Riot: Chicago in the Red Summer of 1919* (New York: Atheneum, 1970), were relied upon heavily for chronology in the first edition of this book.

Studies published since the publication of the first edition in 1971 support the conclusion that federal executive branch response to black complaints of violence and to black resistance activities have reinforced black inequality and subordination. Herbert Shapiro's *White Violence and Black Response from Reconstruction to Montgomery* (Amherst: University of Massachusetts Press, 1988) is a valuable study which covers the incidents of white violence against blacks for the period indicated in more detail. However, Shapiro does not focus on the legal and constitutional issues or black militancy or compare federal action when blacks were the victims and when they were the perpetrators. Leon Higginbotham, *In the Matter of Color: Race and the America Legal Process: The Colonial Period* (New York: Oxford University Press, 1981), discusses some instances of racial violence in the colonial period and legal responses. Eugene Genovese, *From Rebellion to Revolution: Afro-American Slave Revolts in the Making of the Modern World* (Baton Rouge: Louisiana State University Press, 1979), interprets the meaning and impact of black rebellion. Richard E. Ellis, *The Union at Risk: Jacksonian Democracy, States' Rights, and the Nullification Crisis* (New York: Oxford University Press, 1987), reinforces the view that a key ingredient in the Nullification Crisis in South Carolina was Jackson's disinterest in weakening the slave system in that state. Robert Kaczorowski, *The Politics of Federal Judicial Interpretation: The Federal Courts, the Department of Justice and Civil Rights, 1866–1876* (New York: Oceana, 1985), discusses the limited way in which the Justice Department interpreted the civil rights statutes during Reconstruction. Allen Trelease, *White Terror: The Ku Klux Klan Conspiracy and Southern Reconstruction* (New York: Harper and Row, 1971), treats the white violence of the Reconstruction period and the federal government's attitude.

There are numerous studies of individual riots or other incidents of extra-legal execution which provide greater detail about particular incidents. Ann J. Lane, *The Brownsville Affair: National Crisis and Black Reaction* (Port Washington, N.Y.: Kennikat Press, 1971), and Jack D. Foner, *Blacks and the Military in American History* (New York: F. A. Praeger, 1974), includes a discussion of the Brownsville incident. Mary Frances Berry and John W. Blassingame, *Long Memory: The Black Experience in America* (New York: Oxford University Press, 1982), explain that on September 28, 1972, the U.S. Army voided the dishonorable discharges for the men involved in the incident, ruling out back pay for survivors, however, or allowances for their descendants. In 1973, Congress passed a bill granting the only living survivor, eighty-six-year-old Dorsey Willis of Minneapolis, $25,000 in compensation and medical care in a veteran's hospital. Pete Daniel, *The Shadow of Slavery: Peonage in the South, 1901–1969* (Urbana: University of Illinois Press, 1972, 1990), remains useful for treating one form of violence against blacks. Robert Haynes, *A Night of Violence: The Houston Riot of 1917* (Baton Rouge: Louisiana State University Press, 1976), adds detail to earlier accounts of this disturbance. Richard C. Cortner, *A Mob Intent on Death: The NAACP and the Arkansas Riot Cases* (Baton Rouge: Louisiana State University Press, 1988), discusses the defense effort in the case of the Elaine, Arkansas, rioters. James McGovern, *Anatomy of a Lynching: The Killing of Claude*

Neal (Baton Rouge: Louisiana State University Press, 1982), sheds more light on this 1934 Florida incident. Jacquelyn Dowd Hall, *Revolt Against Chivalry* (New York: Columbia University Press, 1979), and Robert Zangrando, *The NAACP Crusade Against Lynching 1909–50* (Philadelphia: Temple University Press, 1980), provide information on lynching and the struggle to gain an effective antilynching law.

There have also been studies of specific incidents that were not included in the 1971 study. William Ivy Hair, *Carnival of Fury: Robert Charles and the New Orleans Race Riot of 1900* (Baton Rouge: Louisiana State University Press, 1976), details the conflict between Charles, other blacks, and the New Orleans police in 1900 after an incident of police brutality. Domenic Capeci, "The Lynching of Cleo Wright: Federal Protection of Constitutional Rights during World War II," *Journal of American History*, March 1986, pp. 859–87, discusses the lynching of Wright, a Sikeston, Missouri, cotton-mill worker who allegedly assaulted a white woman.

Tony Freyer, *The Little Rock Crisis: A Constitutional Interpretation* (Westport, Conn.: Greenwood Press, 1984), and Michael Belknap, *Federal Law and Southern Order: Racial Violence and Constitutional Conflict in the Post-Brown South* (Athens: University of Georgia Press, 1987), discusses the use of white violence to prevent the desegregation of schools in the South in the late 1950s and early 1960s.

Kenneth O'Reilly's *Racial Matters: The FBI Secret File on Black America, 1960–1972* (New York: Free Press, 1989) used papers that the Justice Department would not make available to me during my research earlier, as well as other materials. He confirms the view that the FBI and the Justice Department refused to punish most of the violence against blacks during the civil rights movement and used disinformation and other tactics to destroy the black revolutionary movements of the late 1960s and 1970s. My 1971 conclusion, which some critics found exaggerated, that "Federal law enforcement . . . endorsed and contributed to rigorous campaigns of surveillance of rebellious blacks," was actually understated. Manning Marable, *Race Reform and Rebellion: The Second Reconstruction in America 1945–1982* (Oxford: University Press of Mississippi, 1984, 1991), contains some information about incidents in the 1970s and 1980s from newspaper accounts.

Memoirs of participants, especially the *Eyes on the Prize* documentaries, provide important detail about the participants in the civil rights movement and the rebellions and the federal government responses. The videorecordings, *Eyes on the Prize: America's Civil Rights Years* (1986), and *Eyes on the Prize II: Back to the Movement, 1979 to the mid–1980's* (1990), both from Blackside Productions; the documentary by producer Henry Hampton, *Voices of Freedom: An Oral History of the Civil Rights Movement From the 1950's to the 1980's* (New York: Bantam Books, 1990); and Clayborne Carson et al., *The Eyes on the Prize Reader: Documents, Speeches, Firsthand Accounts from the Black Struggle 1954–90* (New York: Viking, 1991), offer indispensable insight into the period.

A number of useful theses and dissertations on incidents analyzed in this book are also available, including Domenic Capeci, "The Harlem Riot of 1943" (Ph.D. diss., University of California, Irvine, 1970); Hayumi Higuchi, "White Supremacy on the Cape Fear: The Wilmington Affair of 1898" (M.A. thesis, University of North Carolina, 1980); Gregory Mixon, "The Atlanta Race Riot of 1906" (University of Cincinnati, 1989); Clark Miller, "Let Us Die to Make Men Free: Political Terrorism in Post-Reconstruction Mississippi, 1877–1896" vols. 1 & 2 (Ph.D. diss., University of Minnesota, 1983); Walter Thomas Howard, "Vigilante Justice: Extra-Legal Executions in Florida 1930–1940" (Ph.D. diss., Florida State University, 1987); and William Fitzhugh Brundage, "Lynching in the New South: Georgia and Virginia, 1880–1930" (Ph.D. diss., Harvard, 1988).

Every major disorder brought forth official state or national government studies and hearings. The most informative ones were the Chicago Commission on Race Relations Study of the 1919 riot and the Kerner Commission on the riots in the 1960s, and the Hearings Before the U.S. Congress, Select Committee To Study Governmental Operations With Respect to Intelligence Activities of the United States Senate, 94th cong., 1st sess., 7 vols., VI (Hearings in 1975) (Washinton D.C.: U.S. Government Printing Office, 1976), pp. 76–77, 94–95.

Appendix:
Excerpts from the
United States Code

TITLE 10, CHAPTER 15—INSURRECTION

§ 331—Federal Aid for State Governments

Whenever there is an insurrection in any State against its government, the President may, upon the request of its legislature or of its governor if the legislature cannot be convened, call into Federal service such of the militia of the other States, in the number requested by that State, and use such of the armed forces, as he considers necessary to suppress the insurrection.
Aug. 10, 1956, c. 1041, 70A Stat. 15.

§ 332—Use of Militia and Armed Forces to Enforce Federal Authority

Whenever the President considers that unlawful obstructions, combinations, or assemblages, or rebellion against the authority of the United States, make it impracticable to enforce the laws of the United States in any State or Territory by the ordinary course of judicial proceedings, he may call into Federal service such of the militia of any State, and use such of the armed forces, as he considers necessary to enforce those laws or to suppress the rebellion.
Aug. 10, 1956, c. 1041, 70A Stat. 15.

§ 333—Interference with State and Federal Law

The President, by using the militia or the armed forces, or both, or by any other means, shall take such measures as he considers necessary to suppress, in a State, any insurrection, domestic violence, unlawful combination, or conspiracy, if it—

(1) so hinders the execution of the laws of that State, and of the United States within the State, that any part or class of its people is deprived of a right, privilege, immunity, or protection named in the Constitution and secured by law, and the constituted authorities of that State are unable, fail, or refuse to protect that right, privilege, or immunity, or to give that protection; or

(2) opposes or obstructs the execution of the laws of the United States or impedes the course of justice under those laws.

In any situation covered by clause (1), the State shall be considered to have denied the equal protection of the laws secured by the Constitution.

Aug. 10, 1956, c. 1041, 70A Stat. 15.

§ 334—Proclamation to Disperse

Whenever the President considers it necessary to use the militia or the armed forces under this chapter, he shall, by proclamation, immediately order the insurgents to disperse and retire peaceably to their abodes within a limited time.

Aug. 10, 1956, c. 1041, 70A Stat. 16.

TITLE 18, CHAPTER 13—CIVIL RIGHTS

§ 241—Conspiracy against Rights of Citizens.

If two or more persons conspire to injure, oppress, threaten, or intimidate any inhabitant of any State, Territory, or District in the free exercise or enjoyment of any right or privilege secured to him by the Constitution or laws of the United States, or because of his having so exercised the same; or

If two or more persons go in disguise on the highway, or on the premises of another, with intent to prevent or hinder his free exercise or enjoyment of any right or privilege so secured—

They shall be fined not more than $10,000 or imprisoned not more than ten years, or both; and if death results, they shall be subject to imprisonment for any term of years or for life.
June 25, 1948, c. 645, 62 Stat. 696; Apr. 11, 1968, Pub.L. 90-284, Title I, § 103(a), 82 Stat. 75. As amended Nov. 18, 1988, Pub.L. 100-690, Title VII, § 7018(a), (b)(1), 102 Stat. 4396.

TITLE 18, CHAPTER 13—CIVIL RIGHTS

§ 242—Deprivation of Rights Under Color of Law

Whoever, under color of any law, statute, ordinance, regulation, or custom, willfully subjects any inhabitant of any State, Territory, or District to the deprivation of any rights, privileges, or immunities secured or protected by the Constitution or laws of the United States, or to different punishments, pains, or penalties, on account of such inhabitant being an alien, or by reason of his color, or race, than are prescribed for the punishment of citizens, shall be fined not more than $1,000 or imprisoned not more than one year, or both; and if bodily injury results shall be fined under this title or imprisoned not more than ten years, or both; and if death results shall be subject to imprisonment for any term of years or for life.
June 25, 1948, c. 645, 62 Stat. 696; Apr. 11, 1968, Pub.L. 90-284, Title I, § 103(b), 82 Stat. 75. As amended Nov. 18, 1988, Pub.L. 100-690, Title VII, § 7019, 102 Stat. 4396.

§ 245—Federally Protected Activities

(a)(1) Nothing in this section shall be construed as indicating an intent on the part of Congress to prevent any State, any possession or Commonwealth of the United States, or the District of Columbia, from exercising jurisdiction over any offense over which it would have jurisdiction in the absence of this section, nor shall anything in this section be construed as depriving State and local law enforcement authorities of responsibility for prosecuting acts that may be violations of this section and that are violations of State and local law. No prosecution of any offense described in this section shall be undertaken by the United States except upon the certification in writing of the Attorney General, the Deputy Attorney General, the Associate Attorney General, or any Assistant Attorney General specially designated by the Attorney General that in his judgment a prosecution by the United States is in the public interest and necessary to secure substantial justice, which function of certification may not be delegated.

(2) Nothing in this subsection shall be construed to limit the authority of Federal officers, or a Federal grand jury, to investigate possible violations of this section.

(b) Whoever, whether or not acting under color of law, by force or threat of force willfully injures, intimidates or interferes with, or attempts to injure, intimidate or interfere with—

(1) any person because he is or has been, or in order to intimidate such person or any other person or any class of persons from—

(A) voting or qualifying to vote, qualifying or campaigning as a candidate for elective office, or qualifying or acting as a poll watcher, or any legally authorized election official, in any primary, special, or general election;

(B) participating in or enjoying any benefit, service, privilege, program, facility, or activity provided or administered by the United States;

(C) applying for or enjoying employment, or any perquisite thereof, by any agency of the United States;

(D) serving, or attending upon any court in connection with possible service, as a grand or petit juror in any court of the United States;

(E) participating in or enjoying the benefits of any program or activity receiving Federal financial assistance; or

(2) any person because of his race, color, religion or national origin and because he is or has been—

(A) enrolling in or attending any public school or public college;

(B) participating in or enjoying any benefit, service, privilege, program, facility or activity provided or administered by any State or subdivision thereof;

(C) applying for or enjoying employment, or any perquisite thereof, by any private employer or any agency of any State or subdivision thereof, or joining or using the services or advantages of any labor organization, hiring hall, or employment agency;

(D) serving, or attending upon any court of any State in connection with possible service, as a grand or petit juror,

(E) traveling in or using any facility of interstate commerce, or using any vehicle, terminal, or facility of any common carrier by motor, rail, water, or air;

(F) enjoying the goods, services, facilities, privileges, advantages, or accommodations of any inn, hotel, motel, or other establishment which provides lodging to transient guests, or of any restaurant, cafeteria, lunchroom, lunch counter, soda fountain, or other facility which serves the public and which is principally engaged in selling food or beverages for consumption on the premises, or of any gasoline station, or of any motion picture house, theater, concert hall, sports arena, stadium, or any other place of exhibition or entertainment which serves the public, or of any other establishment which serves the public and (i) which is located within the premises of any of the aforesaid establishments or within the premises of which is physically located any of the aforesaid establishments, and (ii) which holds it-

self out as serving patrons of such establishments; or

(3) during or incident to a riot or civil disorder, any person engaged in a business in commerce or affecting
commerce, including, but not limited to, any person
engaged in a business which sells or offers for sale to
interstate travelers a substantial portion of the articles, commodities, or services which it sells or where
a substantial portion of the articles or commodities
which it sells or offers for sale have moved in commerce; or

(4) any person because he is or has been, or in order to
intimidate such person or any other person or any
class of persons from—

(A) participating, without discrimination on account
of race, color, religion or national origin, in any
of the benefits or activities described in subparagraphs (1)(A) through (1)(E) or subparagraphs
(2)(A) through (2)(F); or

(B) affording another person or class of persons opportunity or protection to so participate; or

(5) any citizen because he is or has been, or in order to
intimidate such citizen or any other citizen from lawfully aiding or encouraging other persons to participate, without discrimination on account of race,
color, religion or national origin, in any of the benefits or activities described in subparagraphs (1)(A)
through (1)(E) or subparagraphs (2)(A) through
(2)(F), or participating lawfully in speech or peaceful
assembly opposing any denial of the opportunity to so
participate—

shall be fined not more than $1,000, or imprisoned
not more than one year, or both; and if bodily injury
results shall be fined not more than $10,000, or im-
prisoned not more than ten years, or both; and if
death results shall be subject to imprisonment for any
term of years or for life. As used in this section, the
term "participating lawfully in speech or peaceful as-

sembly" shall not mean the aiding, abetting, or inciting of other persons to riot or to commit any act of physical violence upon any individual or against any real or personal property in furtherance of a riot. Nothing in subparagraph (2)(F) or (4)(A) of this subsection shall apply to the proprietor of any establishment which provides lodging to transient guests, or to any employee acting on behalf of such proprietor, with respect to the enjoyment of the goods, services, facilities, privileges, advantages, or accommodations of such establishment if such establishment is located within a building which contains not more than five rooms for rent or hire and which is actually occupied by the proprietor as his residence.

(c) Nothing in this section shall be construed so as to deter any law enforcement officer from lawfully carrying out the duties of his office; and no law enforcement officer shall be considered to be in violation of this section for lawfully carrying out the duties of his office or lawfully enforcing ordinances and laws of the United States, the District of Columbia, any of the several States, or any political subdivision of a State. For purposes of the preceding sentence, the term "law enforcement officer" means any officer of the United States, the District of Columbia, a State, or political subdivision of a State, who is empowered by law to conduct investigations of, or make arrests because of, offenses against the United States, the District of Columbia, a State, or a political subdivision of a State.

(d) For purposes of this section, the term "State" includes a State of the United States, the District of Columbia, and any commonwealth, territory, or possession of the United States.

Pub.L. 90-284, Title I, § 101(a), Apr. 11, 1968, 82 Stat. 73. As amended Pub.L. 100-690, Title VII, § 7020(a), Nov. 18, 1988, 102 Stat. 4396; Pub.L. 101-647, Title XII, § 1205(b), Nov. 29, 1990, 104 Stat. 4830.

TITLE 18, CHAPTER 102—RIOTS

§ 2101—Riots

(a)(1) Whoever travels in interstate or foreign commerce or uses any facility of interstate or foreign commerce, including, but not limited to, the mail, telegraph, telephone, radio, or television, with intent—

(A) to incite a riot; or

(B) to organize, promote, encourage, participate in, or carry on a riot; or

(C) to commit any act of violence in furtherance of a riot; or

(D) to aid or abet any person in inciting or participating in or carrying on a riot or committing any act of violence in furtherance of a riot;

and who either during the course of any such travel or use or thereafter performs or attempts to perform any other overt act for any purpose specified in subparagraph (A), (B), (C), or (D) of this paragraph—

Shall be fined not more than $10,000, or imprisoned not more than five years, or both.

(b) In any prosecution under this section, proof that a defendant engaged or attempted to engage in one or more of the overt acts described in subparagraph (A), (B), (C), or (D) of paragraph (1) of subsection (a) and (1) has traveled in interstate or foreign commerce, or (2) has use of or used any facility of interstate or foreign commerce, including but not limited to, mail, telegraph, telephone, radio, or television, to communicate with or broadcast to any person or group of persons prior to such overt acts, such travel or use shall be admissible proof to establish that such defendant traveled in or used such facility of interstate or foreign commerce.

(c) A judgment of conviction or acquittal on the merits under the laws of any State shall be a bar to any prosecution hereunder for the same act or acts.

(d) Whenever, in the opinion of the Attorney General or

of the appropriate officer of the Department of Justice charged by law or under the instructions of the Attorney General with authority to act, any person shall have violated this chapter, the Department shall proceed as speedily as possible with a prosecution of such person hereunder and with any appeal which may lie from any decision adverse to the Government resulting from such prosecution.

(e) Nothing contained in this section shall be construed to make it unlawful for any person to travel in, or use any facility of, interstate or foreign commerce for the purpose of pursuing the legitimate objectives of organized labor, through orderly and lawful means.

(f) Nothing in this section shall be construed as indicating an intent on the part of Congress to prevent any State, any possession or Commonwealth of the United States, or the District of Columbia, from exercising jurisdiction over any offense over which it would have jurisdiction in the absence of this section; nor shall anything in this section be construed as depriving State and local law enforcement authorities of responsibility for prosecuting acts that may be violations of this section and that are violations of State and local law.

Pub.L. 90-284, Title I, § 104(a), Apr. 11, 1968, 82 Stat. 75. As amended Pub.L. 99-386, Title I, § 106, Aug. 22, 1986, 100 Stat. 822. Subsection (a) was enacted without a paragraph (2).

§ 2102—Definitions

(a) As used in this chapter, the term "riot" means a public disturbance involving (1) an act or acts of violence by one or more persons part of an assemblage of three or more persons, which act or acts shall constitute a clear and present danger of, or shall result in, damage or injury to the property of any other person or to the person of any other individual or (2) a threat or threats of the commission of an act or acts of violence by one or more persons part of an assemblage of three or more persons having, individually or collectively, the ability of immediate execution of such threat or threats, where the performance of the threatened act or acts of violence would constitute a clear and present danger of, or would result in, damage or injury to the property of any other person or to the person of any other individual.

(b) As used in this chapter, the term "to incite a riot," or "to organize, promote, encourage, participate in, or carry on a riot," includes, but is not limited to, urging or instigating other persons to riot, but shall not be deemed to mean the mere oral or written (1) advocacy of ideas or (2) expression of belief, not involving advocacy of any act or acts of violence or assertion of the rightness of, or the right to commit, any such act or acts.

Pub.L. 90-284, Title I, § 104(a), Apr. 11, 1968, 82 Stat. 76.

Index

A & T College, 146
Abernathy, Ralph, 156, 181
Abernethy, Thomas G., 156, 171,
    176–77
Abolition movement, 46, 48, 53–60,
    253n., 254n.
  denial of civil liberties and, 55
  Quaker petitions and, 8–9, 10–13,
    42, 59
  suppression of, 17, 54–55
  suppression of literature during, 17,
    54
  See also Civil liberties; Jay, William;
    Quakers; Slavery
Abrams, Creighton, 152
Adams, John Quincy, 12, 20, 37
Adams, Kent, 210–11
Adams-Onis Treaty, 35
Adjunct patrols, 3
  See also Militia, patrol and
Afro-American Council, 95
Agnew, Spiro, 186
Ahmed, Fred, 180
Alabama, 17, 65, 271n.
Albert, Carl, 176
Algiers Motel, 177, 183
Allen, Alex, Jr., 235
Allison, C. B., 124
Ambrister, Robert, 34, 35, 47
Amelia Island, 32
American Colonization Society, 17
American Nazi Party, 148–49
American Railway Union, 91

American Revolution, 3, 4, 29
Americans for Democratic Action
    (ADA), 57
Andrews, George W., 158–59
Andry Revolt, 16
Anniston, Alabama, 147
Appalachicola Fort Affair, 33, 35,
    251n.
Appalachicola River, 33
Arbuthnot, Alexander, 34, 35, 47
Arkansas, 79
Armed Settler Bill, 48, 253n.-54n.
Army, see U.S. Army
Arthur, Chester, 85–86
Articles of Confederation, 4, 5, 8, 30
Aryan Nations, 221, 225, 226
Atkinson, William (Frankie), 206
Atlanta, Georgia, 103–4, 172
August, Ronald, 177
Aurand, Henry, 130, 131

Baird, Absalom, 75
Baird, Lourdes, 234
Baker, Frazier B., 93
Baker, Newton D., 93, 119, 121, 132
Bakke v. California, 196
Baltimore, Maryland, 179
Banks, Corinne, 126
Banks, Nathaniel, 63
Barbour, James, 20–21
Bard, David, 11
Barnett, Ross, 149, 151, 152, 154, 156
Barr, William, 217, 226

Barron v. Baltimore, 53
Batson, Ruth, 190
Battle of New Orleans, 33
Beattie, Taylor, 88
Bell, Griffin, 196, 199
Bennett, Thomas, 19
Benson, David, 205
Benton, Thomas Hart, 41, 42, 46–47, 48, 59, 253*n*.–54*n*.
Bermudez, Anthony, 208
Biddle, Francis, 133–34
Bill of Attainder, 182
Bill of Rights, 53
  See also Constitution, U.S.
Birmingham, Alabama, 157–59, 175, 201
Black, Hugo L., 136, 161
Blackburn, Thorton, 255*n*.
Black Codes, 71–72
  See also Reconstruction
Black liberation movement, 166–87
  nonviolent phase of, 169, 181
  violent phase of, 180–81, 184–86, 187–88
  See also Black radicalism; Civil rights movement
Black militancy, 180, 181, 185
Black Muslims, 167–68, 217
Black nationalism, 166, 167
Black Panther Party, 180, 182, 185, 186, 187, 188–89
Black power, 166, 171
Black protest, 88, 123
  through bus boycott, 139–40
  through civil rights organizations, 87, 95–96, 97, 109, 111, 114, 120–21, 123, 125, 126–27, 136–39
  through letter of protest to government agencies, 93, 103, 111–12, 124–25
  marches and mass meetings and, 88, 95, 128, 168
  migration and, 85, 95
  petitioning and, 88
  through public statements, 88, 104, 168
  strikes and, 88, 181
  See also Black liberation movement; Civil rights movement; CORE; NAACP; SCLC; UNIA
Black radicalism, 119–20, 123

"Black Republicans," 60, 62, 83
Black Scholar, The, 212
Black Seaman's Act, 20
Black Seaman's Controversy, 22, 23
Black Student Unions, 189
Blaine, James, 83
Blair, Henry, 89
Blair bill, 89
Blankenship, Kenneth Ray, 218
Blewett, Jeffrey, 236
Boggs, Hale, 176
Bohndorff, William, 208
Bolshevism, 112, 118, 120
Boston, Massachusetts, 56, 57–58
Bourbons, 83
Boutwell, Albert, 158
Bova, Gino, 208
Bratton, U. S., 117
Brawley, Tawana, 221
Brennan, William, 161–62
Brewer, David J., 100–101
Brewster, Benjamin, 85–86, 87
Brimmer, Andrew, 216
Briseno, Theodore J., 231, 238
Brooke, Edward, 245
Brooke, George, 38
Brotherhood of Sleeping Car Porters and Maids, 125
Brown, H. Rap, 178, 181, 182, 184
Brown, John, 59, 60, 63
Brown, William, 116
Brownell, Herbert, 140, 141
Brownsville, Texas, 101–2
Brown v. Board of Education, 139, 142, 146
  See also Civil rights; Education
Buchanan, James, 60
Budzyn, Walter, 235–36
Bumpurs, Eleanor, 221
Bureau of Indian Affairs, 37
Burges, Tristam, 24–25
Burgreen, Bob, 222
Burns, Anthony, 57
Busbee, George, 202
Bus boycott, 139–40
Bush, George, 216–17, 223, 224, 229, 231, 232–34, 243
Butler, Benjamin, 51, 63–64
Butler, John M., 156
Byrd, Robert C., 169, 171
Byrd, William, 171

Caffrey, George, 208
Calhoun, John C., 19, 23, 36, 59
Camp Chickamauga, 104
Camp Moultrie Treaty, 37, 38, 39
Camp Pike, 117
Camp Zachary Taylor, 120
Caraway, Thaddeus, 118–19
Carey, James, 138
Carmichael, Stokely, 181, 182, 184
Carolina colony, 3
Carter, Jimmy, 195, 196–97, 200, 203, 204, 214, 243
Cass, Lewis, 23
Cato, Gavin, 227
Cato, Will, 99
Cavanaugh, Jerome, 172, 173
Cease-and-desist proclamation, 153
Celler, Emanuel, 138–39
Chaney, James, 160–63, 175, 183
Charleston, South Carolina, 18–19, 88, 112–13
Charleston Employees' Strike, 181
Cherokee Indians, 38, 45, 46, 252*n.*
Chicago, Illinois, 92, 93, 95, 115, 179, 187
Chicago Commission on Race Relations, 115
Chicago Defender, 113
Chiles, Nick, 111–12
Chin, Vincent, 207
Choctaw Indians, 51
Christopher, Warren, 173
Cincinnati, Ohio, 54, 172, 197
CIO, 138
Citadel, The, 219
Citizens Committee to Investigate the FBI, 189
Civil liberties, 55
    freedom of assembly, 75–77, 95
    freedom of the press, 17, 54, 55
    freedom of speech, 53
    See also Abolition movement; Civil rights
Civil rights, 69–70, 81, 143, 183, 243
    equal accommodations, 85, 87, 137, 139, 148, 183, 184
    equal employment, 129
    franchise, 79, 81, 140
    legislation, 170–71, 183
    petition, right to, 59, 88

Supreme Court decisions, 100–1, 118, 126, 127, 142, 161–62, 164, 175
    violations, 125, 136
    See also specific subjects and organizations associated with civil rights
Civil Rights Act:
    of 1866, 69–70, 72, 73, 74, 100, 101, 109, 162, 183
    of 1875, 87
    of 1957, 140, 155
    of 1964, 159, 168, 190, 269*n.*
    of 1966, 170
Civil rights cases, 101, 262*n.*
Civil Rights Commission, 136, 140, 149, 197, 200, 214
Civil Rights Congress, 87
Civil rights movement, 146–50, 156–62, 242
    fair employment campaign, 156–57
    freedom ride of, 147–50
    Freedom Summer of, 160, 162–64
    marches and, 156–59, 164
    sit-ins and, 146, 147–48, 168
    See also specific subjects and organizations associated with the civil rights movement
Civil War, 61–68, 72, 241
Clark, Elmore, 126
Clark, Mark, 187
Clark, Ramsey, 173, 175–76, 179, 188, 274*n.*, 275*n.*–76*n.*
Clark, Tom C., 137–39, 161
Clay, Henry, 42
Clayton Antitrust Act, 108
Cleveland, Grover, 87–88, 91, 107
Clifford, Nathan, 50
Clinton, Bill, 234, 238–39
Coffin, William Sloane, 149
Cokley, Peggy, 210–12
Cokley, Warren, 210–12
Coleman, William T., 195
Collins, Cardiss, 245
Colmer, William, 163
Colonial period, 1–3
Colonization, 89
Commerce Clause, 183, 187
Commission on Civil Rights, U.S., 136, 140, 149, 197, 200, 214
Communism, 169, 185, 186

Communist Party, 139
Compromise of 1850, 59
Compromise of 1877, 80, 81, 98, 181
Confederacy, 62, 65–68
  See also Civil War
Confederate Congress, 66, 68
Confederate Hammerskins, 225
Confederation Congress, 247*n*.
Confiscation Act of July 1862, 64
Congress, U.S.:
  debates of, 8–9, 29, 41–42, 44–45,
    56–57, 83–84, 89
  First, 8, 9
  Fourth, 9
  Gag Resolution, 42, 58–59
  legislation of, 32, 62, 64, 69–70, 71,
    72, 77, 79, 91, 111, 152, 167
  powers of, 6, 7, 10, 35, 53, 64, 95,
    136
  Second, 8
  See also House of Representatives;
    Senate, U.S.
Congressional Record, 143, 154, 155,
  162, 176, 182
Congress of Industrial Organizations
  (CIO), 138
Congress of Racial Equality (CORE),
  147, 168
Connor, Eugene "Bull," 156, 158
Conrad, Charles M., 56
Constitution, U.S., 6–7, 17–18, 99,
  100, 157, 191, 240, 242
  apportionment of representation in,
    6
  Article I, 182
  Article II, 152
  Article IV, 51, 62, 78, 82–83, 175
  Article VI, 141
  Bill of Rights, 5
  Commerce Clause, 183, 187
  Domestic Violence Clause, 65, 80
  enforcement of, 7
  Fifteenth Amendment, 70, 97, 98
  Fifth Amendment, 85
  First Amendment, 158, 182
  Fourteenth Amendment, 70, 72, 79,
    80, 100, 121, 127, 139, 142, 147,
    161, 184, 262*n*.
  Fourth Amendment, 188
  Fugitive Slave Clause, 7, 30, 57, 64
  Military Clauses of, 5–8, 30, 121

proslavery compromises, 6, 7, 9, 10,
    22, 25, 30, 36, 43, 52, 62–65, 70
  provisions for military aid requests
    in, 19, 22, 25, 82–83, 121, 175,
    179
  ratification of, 7, 30
  relegation of war-making power in,
    35
  Tenth Amendment, 11, 20
  Thirteenth Amendment, 65, 69, 74,
    80, 100, 101
  See also United States Code
Constitutional Convention, 5–7
Constructualism, 23
Continental Congress, 3, 29
Convention of 1864, 75–77
Conyers, John, 174, 182
Coolidge, Calvin, 125
Cooper Union, 95
Cooper v. Aaron, 142
CORE, 147, 168
Corman, James, 171
Court of King's Bench, 2
Cox, George, 88
Cox, Henry, 88
Cramer, William C., 171, 181
Cramer anti-riot bill, 181
Crawford, William, 33
Creek Indians, 28, 30–39, 44, 254*n*.
  removal westward, 38–52
  treaties with, 28, 31–32, 36, 50
Cuba, 156
Cuomo, Mario, 221
Cushing, Caleb, 51

Daniels, Josephus, 114
Darrow, Clarence, 129
Daugherty, Harry M., 123
Davies, John, 238
Davies, Ronald, 141
Davis, Angela, 188
Davis, Jefferson, 56, 61
Davis, Kenneth E., 209–11
Day, William, 101
Days, Drew, 196–200
Debs, Eugene, 91, 92
Decatur, Alabama, 201
Declaration of Independence, 4
Deering, William L., 209–11
Dees, Morris, 220, 226
Democratic Convention of 1968, 182

Democratic Party, 202, 232
  black voters in Indiana and, 84–85
  Cleveland's election and, 87
  Harpers Ferry Affair and, 60
  Reconstruction acts and, 84
  in the South, 89, 90, 103, 124–25
  See also Readjusters; Redeemers;
    Jacksonian Democrats
Denny, Reginald, 234, 235, 237
Department of Justice, *see* Justice
  Department, U.S.
Department of War, *see* War
  Department, U.S.
Depression, 128
Dershowitz, Alan, 234
Desegregation, 139–43, 150–56, 158,
  162, 184, 187, 190–91
  See also Civil rights; Education;
    Integration; Segregation
Detroit, Michigan, 128–29, 172–74,
  177, 180–81, 206–7, 274n.
Devens, Charles, 83
Devlin, Francis X., 206
Dewey Report, 178
Dick Act of 1903, 108
Dies Committee, 131
Diggs, Charles, 174
Dillon, C. Douglas, 157
Dirksen, Everett, 184
Dismukes, Melvin, 177
District of Columbia, 58, 59
District of Columbia Bar Association,
  134
Dixon, Richard, 98
Doar, John, 173
Domestic Violence Clause, 65, 80
Dorn, Roosevelt, 235
"Doughface administrations," 54,
  59
Douglas, Freddie, 235
Douglas, Paul H., 155
Douglas, William O., 136, 161–62
Douglass, Frederick, 87, 104
Douglass, Lewis, 104, 262n.
Downing, Charles, 46
Dred Scott v. Sanford, 59
Duke, David, 224
Dulles, Allen, 160
Dunne, John, 224
Dyer, Leonidus, 109, 121
Dyer, Bill, 123

Eastland, James O., 143, 154, 155, 156,
  162, 184, 187
Ebens, Ronald, 207
Edmunds, George, 83–84
Education:
  desegregation of, 139–43, 150–56,
    158, 162, 184, 187, 190–91
  federal aid to, 85, 89
  integration of, 139–43
  segregation in, 139, 159
  See also Brown v. Board of Education;
    Civil rights; NAACP
Edwards, Don, 171, 182
Eisenhower, Dwight D., 135, 139, 142,
  144, 145, 155, 177, 191
Election riots, 77, 85–88, 94, 124,
  258n.
Elkison v. Deliesilline, 20
Ellender, Allen J., 155
Elliott, J. D., 22
Ellis, W. H., 107
Emancipation Proclamation, 65, 67,
  241
Emergency Plan White, 119, 130, 131,
  132
Eppes, Richard, 21
Erie v. Tompkins, 155
Ervin, Sam, 139, 155–56, 184
Everglades, Florida, 45
Evers, Medgar, 159
Ex Parte Milligan, 72, 74
Export tax, 6

Fair Employment Practices
  Commission (FEPC), 136–37
Fair Housing Act, 183, 184
Farmer, James, 147, 149, 169
Farrakhan, Louis, 217
Faubus, Orval, 140–41
FBI, 138, 144, 145, 147, 148, 150, 160,
  162, 166, 168, 178–79, 182,
  188–89, 200, 210, 222, 226–27,
  230, 231
Federalists, 7
Federal Party, *see* Whigs
Fillmore, Millard, 56
First Battalion of the District of
  Columbia, 113
Fisk University, 159
Fitts, William, 111
503rd Military Police Battalion, 153

Florida, 27–52, 253*n.*-54*n.*
  Adams-Onis Treaty, 35
  Armed Settler Bill, 48, 253*n.*-54*n.*
Foraker, Joseph, 102
Force Act of May 31, 1870, 83
Force Bill, 24
Ford, Gerald R., 176, 191, 195
Forrester, Elijah, 143
Fortas, Abe, 161
Fortress Monroe, Virginia, 21, 22, 60, 63, 73
Foster, William Z., 112
Franchise, 70, 79, 81, 91, 97, 98, 140, 163, 183, 195
  black attempts to exercise, 81
  black elected officials, 195
  black illiteracy and, 71
  election riots, 77, 85–88, 94, 124, 258*n.*
  Fifteenth Amendment and, 70, 97, 98
  Force Act, 83
  Freedom Summer, 160, 163–64
  intimidation of blacks in exercise of, 79, 85, 98, 103, 120–21, 124
  Lodge Bill, 89–91
  See also United States Code, Section 245; Voting Rights Acts
Frankfurter, Felix, 136
Franklin, Joseph Paul, 202–3
Freedom ride, 147–50
Freedom Riders Coordinating Committee, 149
Frelinghuysen, Theodore, 24
Fremont, John C., 65
French, Peggy Jo, 209–10, 211, 212
French and Indian War, 7, 29
Fries Rebellion, 12, 22, 247*n.*–48*n.*
Fugitive Slave Act:
  of 1793, 9–10, 27, 36, 37, 38, 51, 56, 255*n.*
  of 1850, 55–58, 63, 64, 140
Fugitive Slave Clause, 7, 30, 57, 64
Fugitive slaves, *see* Slavery

Gag Resolution, 42, 58–59
Gaines, Edmund, 33, 34, 252*n.*
Garfield, James, 85
Garner, Loyal, Jr., 222–23
Garvey, Marcus, 123
Gaston, A. D., 157

Geary, David E., 236
Georgia, 3, 28–34, 36–37, 43–44, 49, 50, 65
Giddings, Joshua, 253*n.*
Glover, Joshua, 58
Goetz, Bernard, 220
Goodman, Andrew, 160–62, 163, 175, 184
Gorsuch, Edward, 57
Grady, William, 206
Grant, Ulysses S., 74, 79
Great Britain, 1, 2, 20, 28, 29, 32–33
Great Strike, 82–83, 108–9
Green, Malice, 235
Greenback Party, 85
Greenberg, Jack, 152
Greensboro, North Carolina, 146
Gregory, Thomas, 109
Griffin, Robert P., 177
Griffith, Michael, 220
Guevara, Che, 185
Guihard, Paul, 153
Guinier, Lani, 239
Gulf, Mobile, and Ohio Railroad, 104
Guthner, William, 130

Haiti, 11, 15, 16
Hale, Gene, 208
Haley, Harold, 188
Hall, Robert, 136
Halleck, Charles, 64
Hamer, Fannie Lou, 166
Hampton, 21
Hampton, Fred, 187
Hampton, Wade, 16
Hansen, George, 170
Hanway, Castner, 57
Hardin, A. T., 126
Harding, Warren G., 123
Harlan, John Marshall, 101, 162
Harlem, New York City, 168
Harper, Robert Goodloe, 11, 247*n.*
Harpers Ferry, West Virginia, 59
Harrington, Oliver, 138
Harrison, Benjamin, 88–90
Hart, Phillip A., 177
Hate Crimes Statistics Act, 226–27, 228
Hawkins, Yusef, 225
Hayes, Rutherford, 82–84

Hays, Brooks, 141
Haywood, Big Bill, 119
Hebert, F. Edward, 176
Heflin, Thomas, 118
Hell's Angels, 205
Henderson, Jerry Albert, 218
Hicks, Louise Day, 190, 191
Hill, Robert L., 117, 118
Hodges v. United States, 100, 107, 112,
    124, 136, 139, 157, 161
Hoffman, Clare, 132
Holiday, George, 231
Holland, Paul, 124
Hollifield, Chet, 176
Hood, James, 159
Hooks, Benjamin, 232
Hoover, Herbert, 171–72, 178, 189,
    200, 204–5
Hoover, J. Edgar, 119, 120, 163
House, James, 22
House of Representatives:
  bills in, 89–90, 91, 109, 121, 127,
      171, 182
  committee of, 7
  debates in, 8–12, 17–18, 24–25, 35,
      45–46, 114–15, 118–19, 132, 143,
      156, 158–59, 163, 170, 171,
      176–77
  reports to, 35, 77
  resolutions of, 109
House Un-American Activities
    Committee (HUAC), 131, 185–86
Houston, Charles H., 134
Houston, Texas, 110
Hruska, Roman, 184
HUAC, 131, 185–86
Humphrey, Hubert H., 155
Hunter, David, 65
Hurst, Cornelius, 90

Ichord, Richard H., 170
Illinois, 82
Import tax, 71–72
Indian removal, 38–52
Indian Removal Act of May 1830, 38
Indians:
  colonial defense and, 2
  removal westward, 38–52
  treaties with, 28, 30, 31–32, 36,
      38–39, 50
  See also individual tribes

Industrial Workers of the World
    (IWW), 103, 112, 118, 119
Integration, 139–43, 150–52, 155, 156,
    179–80
  See also Education; Desegregation;
    Segregation; Supreme Court; U.S.
    Army
International Labor Defense (ILD),
    126, 266n.
Interposition, 143
Interstate commerce, 125, 148, 181,
    183–84
  transportation and, 147
  travel and, 161–62
Interstate Commerce Act of 1887, 147
Interstate Commerce Commission,
    147, 149
IWW, 103, 112, 118, 119

Jackson, Andrew, 23, 25, 33–36, 38, 43,
    45, 47, 252n.
Jackson, Chan, 119
Jackson, Charlie, 119
Jackson, James, 8
Jackson, Jesse, 181, 196, 217
Jackson, Jonathan, 188
Jackson, Lynn, 207
Jackson, Mississippi, 149, 151, 152, 159
Jackson, Robert, 136, 268n.
Jacksonian Democrats, 41–42, 48
Jacob, John, 232
Jacobs, Donovan, 222
James, Joe, 105
Javits, Jacob, 143, 154, 155, 158, 162,
    169, 171
Jay, William, 27, 52
Jefferson, Thomas, 15–16
Jeffries, Edward, 130
Jeffries, Leonard, 217
Jencks, Isaac, 117–18
Jesup, Thomas, 42–46, 48, 49, 50
Jim Crowism, 110, 133, 170
Johnson, Andrew, 70–71, 75–77
Johnson, Frank, 164
Johnson, James W., 120, 125
Johnson, Lyndon B., 159, 160, 162,
    164, 168, 169, 173–78, 191
Johnson, Nelson, 201
Johnson, Paul, 151
Johnson, William, 20
Jones, James, 196

Jones v. Alfred Mayer Co., 101
Jordan, Vernon, 202–3
Joyce, William, 206
Justice Department, U.S., 149, 150,
   172, 189, 196, 232, 233, 243
   Civil Rights Division (CRD),
      190–91, 197–207, 209, 212–15,
      217–20, 223–26, 229
   civil rights opinions and, 87, 124,
      126–27, 134, 144–45, 158, 264*n.*,
      268*n.*
   Civil Rights Section of Criminal
      Division of, 128, 136, 140
   Community Relations Service
      (CRS), 189–90, 197, 200, 201,
      204, 205, 206, 212, 213, 214, 217,
      218–19, 222, 223, 224, 227, 229,
      230
   correspondence of, 118, 125–27
   Dyer Bill and, 123
   federal intervention and, 109, 152,
      157, 174
   General Investigating Division of,
      119
   integration and, 151, 155, 156
   interstate travel and, 149
   peonage and, 264*n.*
   racial violence cases and, 143–44
   states rights and, 99, 107, 124

Kansas, 85
Kansas City, Kansas, 179
Katzenbach, Nicholas, 158
Katzenbach v. South Carolina, 155, 158
Keating, Kenneth B., 155, 158
Kelley, William, 77
Kelly, Harry, 130–31
Kennedy, John F., 146, 147, 149–50,
   153–56, 158, 159, 177, 191
Kennedy, Robert F., 148–52, 155, 159
Kern, Scott, 220
Kerner Commission, 178
King, Martin Luther, Jr., 139–40, 147,
   148, 156–58, 166, 168, 170, 178,
   179, 181, 183, 189
King, Mel, 190
King, Rodney, 223, 231–39
King, Rufus, 6
Kirchner, Robert, 236
Knights of Labor, 88
Knox, Henry, 31

Knoxville, Tennessee, 116
Koch, Edward, 207–8
Kohut, Mark, 237
Kokomo, Indiana, 181
Koon, Stacey, 231, 238
Krech, August M., 129–30
Kuchel, Thomas H., 143
Ku Klux Klan (KKK), 79, 123, 129,
   140, 147, 148, 161, 200–3, 205,
   208–11, 214, 217, 218–21, 224,
   225, 228, 237, 243

Labor movement, 92, 113
Ladner, Thomas, 223
Ladone, Jean, 220
La Guardia, Fiorello, 132–33
Lambertson, William, 132
Layton, John B., 179
Leaken, W. R., 99–100
Lee, Robert E., 59–60
Lester, Jon, 220
Levenson, Laurie, 237
Lewis, Elijah, 57
Lewis, John, 169
Lexington, Kentucky, 120
Lincoln, Abraham, 61–65, 105
Little Rock, Arkansas, 124, 140–43,
   145, 155
Liuzzo, Viola, 183
Locke, Hubert, 274*n.*
Lodge, Henry, 89
Lodge Bill of 1890, 89–91
Lord, Jeremy, 228
Lord Lyttleton, 3
Los Angeles, California, 128, 230–39
Louisiana, 65, 66, 79
Louisiana Purchase, 17, 51
Louisville, Kentucky, 87
Lovejoy, Elijah, 55
Lovett, Robert, 132
Lozano, William, 233, 238
Lucy, Autherine, 140, 142
Luther v. Borden, 175*n.*
Lynching, 95, 144, 220
   demands for antilynching legislation
      and, 92, 111, 121, 127–28, 137,
      138
   Dyer Bill and, 121
   instances of, 89, 91, 98, 116–17, 120,
      125, 127–28, 138–39
Lyon, Cecil, 107

McCarthyism, 135
McClellan, John L., 143, 186
McCormack, John, 176
McDowell, Joseph, 10
McDuffie, Arthur, 199, 200
McEnery, Samuel D., 88
McGrath, J. Howard, 139
McGregor, Paul, 206
Mack, John, 238
McKinley, William, 93, 95, 97
McKinley Tariff of 1890, 90
McLaughlin, Melvin, 114
McNamara, Robert, 157, 173
Macon, Nathaniel, 10
Madison, James, 7, 10, 32
Mahone, William, 86
Malcolm X, 167–68, 217
Mallory, Patrick, 126
Malone, Vivian, 159
Mansfield, Michael, 169
Manumission, 9, 16, 37
    See also Slavery, and fugitive slaves
Marshall, Burke, 150, 157, 166, 189
Marshall, Thurgood, 131, 137
Marshals, U.S., 56–58, 83, 151–53,
    164, 242
Martin, James D., 170
Maryland, 3, 82
Mason, John, 50
Mason, Vernon, 220
Massachusetts, 16
Mays, Maurice, 116
Meese, Edwin, 214, 217
Memphis, Tennessee, 73–74, 90–91,
    152, 154, 190
Meredith, James, 150–56
Metzger, John, 226
Metzger, Thomas, 202, 226
Mexican-Americans, 128
Mexican War, 59
Mexico, 51
Miami, Florida, 139, 199–200, 213,
    224, 233
Miccio, Anthony, 208
Militarism, 180
Military Police, 110, 153
Military Reconstruction Act, 77
Militia:
    division of authority over, 7–8
    establishment of, 2
    in Fries Rebellion, 12

local responsibility for, 2, 14
Negro organization of, 16
patrol and, 14, 15, 66–67
racial disturbances, 54, 56, 57, 82,
    86, 87, 89, 95, 98, 99, 103, 104,
    106, 126
during Reconstruction, 70, 78, 79
during Seminole War, 44, 48, 50
slave control and, 1, 3, 16, 19, 21
state control of, 7
strengthening of, 2, 15
in strikebreaking, 82, 88
weaknesses of, 5, 15, 20–21
in Whiskey Rebellion, 12
Militia Act:
    of 1792, 8, 14
    of 1795, 8
Miller, Antoine, 235
Miller, Glenn, 218
Miller, Reginald D., 236
Milwaukee, Wisconsin, 58
Mississippi, 62, 65, 67, 149
Mississippi Freedom Democratic
    Party, 166
Mississippi River, 38, 44, 84
Missouri, 17
Missouri Compromise, 18, 51
Mitchell, Clarence, 191
Mitchell, William, 125
Mobile, Alabama, 77
Mohammed, Elijah, 167
Mondale, Walter F., 169
*Mondou v. New York, New Haven, and
    Hartford R.R. Co.*, 126
Monroe, James, 15, 20, 32, 34, 37
Monroe, John T., 74–77
Montgomery, Alabama, 139–40, 148
Moody, William H., 99
Moore, Harry T., 139
Moore, Patricia, 237
Moore v. Dempsey, 118
Morgan State College, 118
Mormando, Paul, 208
Morris, Gouverneur, 6
Morse, Wayne, 155, 156, 158
Moss, Theodore, 90, 91
Motley, Constance Baker, 152
Murder, *see* Police murders; Racial
    murders
Murphy, Frank, 128, 129, 132, 136
Murphy, Patrick V., 179

NAACP, 97, 105, 109, 111, 114, 118, 119–21, 123–27, 129, 131, 135–37, 144, 150, 152, 155, 159, 167, 191, 201, 203, 218, 219, 230, 232, 239, 266*n.*
Nashville, Tennessee, 158
Natchez, 21
National Association for the Advancement of Colored People, *see* NAACP
National Association of Colored Women (NACW), 138
National Bar Association, 134
National Convention of Colored Men (NCCM), 87
National Council of the Churches of Christ, 139
National Guard, 231, 233, 238
of Alabama, 148, 164
civil rights enforcement, role in, 127, 148, 157, 163, 164
establishment of, 108
federalization of, 121
of Illinois, 110
integration, role in enforcing, 140–42, 153, 159
of Michigan, 130
militarism and, 180
of Mississippi, 153, 163
Negro units of, 113
riot control, role in, 101, 110, 113, 116, 127, 130, 137, 169, 173–77
riot training of, 179
of Texas, 101, 110–11
National Urban League, 232
Navigation Acts, 2
Navy, U.S., 22, 35, 114
Nazis, 134
Neal, Claude, 127
Nelson, Lemrick, 228
Nesmith, Kevin, 219
Neuberger, Richard L., 143
Nevers, Larry, 235–36
New Abolitionists, 147
Newark, New Jersey, 172
New Bethel Church, 180, 181
New Deal, 134, 135, 267*n.*
New Orleans, Louisiana, 16, 74–77
Newport, Rhode Island, 141
New York, New York, 54, 132–33, 207–8, 220–21, 224–25, 227–28

New York *Age*, 104
New York *Herald Tribune*, 138
New York *Times, The*, 119, 232, 234
Nicholas, George, 7
Nitz, Michael, 207
Nix, Robert, 156, 182
Nixon, Richard M., 181, 185, 191
Norfolk, Virginia, 73
North Carolina, 3, 7, 9–10, 95
Northern Pacific Railroad, 84
Northwest Territory, 16, 31
Nowack, Michael, 206
Nullification Acts, 24
Nullification Crisis, 23–25, 42, 45, 250*n.*

Oakland, California, 180, 197
O'Bryant, John, 191
Oklahoma Skinhead Alliance, 225
Oklahoma State University, 219
Olney, Richard, 91–92
Olney, Warren, III, 143
Omaha, Nebraska, 116–17, 181
O'Mahoney, Joseph C., 143
Osceola, 41
Otis, Harrison Gray, 11, 18, 247*n.*
Ouderkirk, John, 237
Oxford, Mississippi, 150–54

Page, Horace, 83–84
Paille, Robert, 177
Palmer, A. Mitchell, 119
Parker, Mack C., 144, 161
Patronage, 103, 106
Patterson, John, 148, 149
Pearl River, 144
Pellet, Jeff Ray, 237
Penn, Lemuel, 161, 169
Penn, Sagon, 222
Pennsylvania, 3, 12, 82
Pennsylvania State University at State College, 219
Pensacola, Florida, 33
Peonage, 117, 264*n.*, 266*n.*
Perkins, Frances, 132
Petition, right of, 59, 88
Philadelphia, Mississippi, 160
Philadelphia, Pennsylvania, 5, 54
Phillips, Kevin, 232
Pickins, William, 118
Pierce, Franklin, 51

Pippen, Dan, 126
Pirone, Michael, 220
Plessey v. Ferguson, 101, 262*n*.
Plumer, William, 17–18
Poinsett, Joel, 44–45, 47, 48
Police brutality, 115, 133, 144–45,
     168–73, 180–81, 190, 194, 196,
     197, 199–200, 205, 212–18, 221,
     222, 229–39, 243
Police murders, 180, 181, 186–87
Polk, James, 50
Posse comitatus act of 1878, 152, 259*n*.
Potomac River, 4
Powell, Adam Clayton, 170
Powell, James, 168
Powell, Joseph, 208
Powell, Larry, 186
Powell, Laurence M., 231, 234, 238
President's Committee on Civil
     Rights, 136–37
Preston, William, 47
Price, Cecil, 161, 162, 188
Progressives, 97, 107
Progressivism, 107
Proslavery compromises, 6, 7, 9, 10,
     22, 25, 30, 36, 43, 52, 62–65, 70
Prosser, Gabriel, 14, 15
Prosser plot, 15, 19
Providence, Rhode Island, 197
Pullman Strike, 91–92, 109

Quaker Pennsylvania Society for
     Promoting the Abolition of
     Slavery, 8
Quakers, 8–12, 57

Racial murders, 93–94, 107, 111, 124,
     126, 136–39, 144, 159–64,
     179–80, 220
  Equal Protection Clause and, 79,
     127
  murder as a state crime, 107, 108,
     124, 136, 183–84
  United States Code Section 245 and,
     183
Racine, Wisconsin, 58
Rainbow Coalition, 217
Rainey, Lawrence, 160
Rakestrau, Keith, 208
Randolph, A. Philip, 125–26, 128, 168
Rankin, John E., 132

Readjusters, 86
Reagan, Ronald, 203–5, 214–16, 224,
     232, 243
Reconstruction:
  amendments and statutes, 69–72,
     77–79, 83–84, 91, 241
  legislation, 91, 100
  Military, 77–80
  Presidential, 70–77
Redeemers, 81
Reed, Isaiah, 92
Reed, Paul, 99
Reed, Stanley F., 136
Reiner, Ira, 234, 235
Removal Act of 1830, 45
Reno, Janet, 238
Republican Party, 178, 232
  black disfranchisement and, 77,
     81–87, 90
  black militancy and, 185
  civil rights legislation and, 69–70
  colonization and, 89
  under Garfield, 85
  under Harding, 123
  under Harrison, 88–89
  under Hayes, 82
  1900, 1904, 1908 platforms of, 97
  1920 platform of, 123
  patronage and, 93, 106
  Reconstruction and, 77, 78, 83–84
  riots during the ascendancy of, 98
  secession and, 61–62
  under Taft, 106–107
Republic of New Africa, 180
Resnick, Joseph, 182
Restore Our Alienated Rights (ROAR),
     190
Resurrection City, 181
Reverse discrimination, 196
Revolution, American, 3, 4, 29
Revolutionary Action Movement
     (RAM), 185
Reynolds, William Bradford, 204, 205,
     224
Rich, Charles, 18
Richardson, George, 105
Richmond, Virginia, 15
Riggs, Thomas, 222
Riot Control Act, 182
Riots, 54–58, 73, 75–78, 87, 90–91,
     94–95, 102–5, 108–10, 113–19,

Riots (*cont.*)
128–32, 146, 156–59, 169–81, 196, 199, 201, 217–18, 231–34, 242, 274*n.*
abolition, 53–60
armed services, 73–74, 101–2, 109–11, 129, 133
civil rights, 148, 163
election, 77, 85–88, 94, 124, 258*n.*
jailhouse, 89, 99, 105–6, 115–17, 120, 137, 181
police brutality, 132–33, 168, 173, 181
prevention, 181–82
zoot suit, 128
See also Cramer anti-riot bill
Rivers, L. Mendel, 176
Roberts, Owen J., 136
Robinson, Joseph, 124
Robinson, Robert E., 226
Robinson, Skip, 200
Rochon, Donald, 230
Rockwell, George Lincoln, 148–49
Rogers, William P., 144
Romney, George, 173–77, 275*n.*
Roosevelt, Franklin D., 126, 127–28, 131, 132, 146
Roosevelt, James, 170
Roosevelt, Theodore, 97, 99, 102, 103, 107, 109
Roper, Lori, 209–10
Roper, Michael, 209–10
Rosenbaum, Yankel, 228
Rourk, Charles, 237
Rowe, Gary Thomas, 147
Russell, Richard, 169
Rutledge, John, 6, 11, 247*n.*
Rutledge, Wiley, 136
Ryan, Leo J., 196
Ryan, William F., 156

St. Augustine, Florida, 19
St. Clair, Arthur, 31
St. Louis, Missouri, 108–9
St. Marks, Florida, 34–35
Sandiford, Cedric, 220
Schwerner, Michael, 160–64, 175, 184
SCLC, 147, 156, 181
Scott, Winfield, 23, 42, 43, 45, 58
Scottsboro, Georgia, 127
Screws v. United States, 136, 139, 161

SDS, 185, 186
Seale, Bobby, 182, 186
Secession, 56, 58, 61–62
Segregation, 81, 123, 132, 139, 142–43, 146–47, 157, 170, 275*n.*–76*n.*
See also Desegregation; Education; Integration
Selden, Armistead, 158, 170
Selfridge Air Force Base, 173–74
Selma, Alabama, 163, 175
Seminole Indians, 27–28, 31–34, 36–49, 59, 253*n.*–54*n.*
removal westward, 38–52
treaties with, 37, 38–39, 50
See also Treaty of Payne's Landing
Seminole War:
First, 27–40
Second, 41–52
Senak, David, 177
Senate, U.S.:
bills in, 89–90, 121, 127
debates in, 42, 47–48, 143, 154–56, 158, 162, 169, 171, 177
Finance Committee, 44
Internal Security Committee, 187
Judiciary Committee, 104
reports to, 35
resolutions in, 109
Seraw, Mulugeta, 226
716th Military Police Battalion, 153
Seven Years' War, 3, 29
Shadrach, 56, 58
Sharpton, Al, 217, 220
Shays's Rebellion, 5, 12
Sheridan, Philip, 75–76, 77
Sherman, Lawrence, 109
Shillady, John, 124
Siddon, John, 10
Sit-ins, 146–47, 168
Slavery:
under Articles of Confederation, 4
under the British government, 2
during the Civil War, 62–65
colonization and, 15–17
congressional opposition to antislavery discussion, 9–12, 15, 42, 58, 62
under the Constitution, 7
in the District of Columbia, 58
establishment of, 17–18, 47–48

Slavery (*cont.*)
fear of slave revolts and, 3, 10–11,
15, 22, 59, 61, 63–64, 66–68
federal responsibility for slave
control, 6–8, 22, 23, 25, 36, 43–44
fugitive slaves, 6–10, 28–31, 36–38,
42–43, 51, 55–58
legislation during, 4, 59
rendition of fugitive slaves, 29–30,
37–38, 57
slavecatchers, 9–10, 57
slave revolts and, 3, 10, 11, 14,
15–19, 21–22
slave trade, 2, 6, 9, 11, 15
See also Abolition movement;
Confiscation Acts; Emancipation
Proclamation; Fugitive Slave Act
Slidell, John, 61
Smathers, George, 184
Smilie, John, 11–12
Smith, Carlton, 222
Smith, John, 172
Smith, William, 9, 10
Smith, William French, 204
SNCC, 146, 160, 169, 172, 182
Sojourner Truth Federal Housing
Project, 129
Southard, Samuel, 46
South Boston, Massachusetts, 190–91
South Carolina, 3–4, 11–12, 19–20, 23,
27–28, 29, 45, 62, 79, 92, 95
Southern Christian Leadership
Conference (SCLC), 201, 202
"Southern Manifesto," 139
Southern Poverty Law Center, 218,
220
Spanish-American War, 82, 93
Speed, James, 74
Speer, Emory, 99–100
Spencer, John, 50
Spencer, W. Thomas, 233, 238
Springfield, Illinois, 5, 247*n.*
Springfield, Ohio, 98–99
State sovereignty, 20, 23
States' rights, 7, 9, 11, 53, 83, 144,
196–97
Stennis, John, 155, 158, 162–63
Stewart, Allen, 91
Stewart, Potter, 101, 106
Stewart, Robert P., 120
Stimson, Henry, 131, 132

Stoli, Daniel, 208
Stone, Harlan F., 124, 136
Stoneham, George, 74
Strange, Robert, 47–48
Strikes, 90, 91, 112, 129, 132
Student Non-violent Coordinating
Committee (SNCC), 146, 160,
169, 172, 182
Suits, Jerry Douglas, 218
Suits, Mary Vestal, 218
Supreme Court:
Cherokee Indians and, 38
civil rights decisions of, 69, 87, 100,
101, 118, 139, 142, 147, 161, 183
economy and, 134
federal intervention and, 175
integration decisions, 139, 140, 142,
155, 271*n.*
interposition and, 143
interstate commerce and, 126
military courts and, 72, 74
slavery and, 53, 59
state sovereignty and, 53, 136, 156
Swanick, John, 9
Sweet, Ossian, 129

Taft, William, 97–98, 106–7
Tallmadge, James, 17
Talmadge, Herman C., 155–56
Tampa, Florida, 171
Tariff, lowering of, 23–24, 249*n.*
Taylor, Zachary, 42, 48, 49
Terrell, Lyndon, 209–12
Texas, 59, 65, 67, 72
Texas Rangers, 128
Thacher, George, 11
Third Regiment of United States
Colored Artillery, 73
Thomas, Neval, 119–20
Thompson, Charlie, 125
Thompson, Wiley, 41
Thornburgh, Richard, 223–24, 226
Three-fifths Compromise, 6, 17
Thurmond, Strom, 169, 184
Tilden-Hayes election, 80, 81
Till, Emmett, 139
Tillman, Ben, 94, 98
Tolbert, T. P., 94
Topeka Plaindealer, 111
Toucey, Isaac, 50
Treason, 57

Treaty of Fort Jackson, 28
Treaty of Indian Springs, 36
Treaty of Payne's Landing, 38–39, 43,
    44, 45, 47, 51
Truman, Harry S., 135–38, 145, 146
Tucker, St. George, 91
Tuffo, Edward J., 206
Tulsa, Oklahoma, 124
Turks, Willie, 207
Turner, Nat, 21–22
Turner Revolt, 21–22
Turney, Hopkins, 46
Tuscaloosa, Alabama, 126
Twenty Negro Law, 66–67
Tyler, John, 50

UNIA, 123
Uniform Crime Report System, 227
U.S. Army, 25, 82, 98, 110, 231, 241
    need for, 6
    racial riots in, 73–74, 101–2, 109–11,
        129, 133, 242
    riot control instructions of, 179
    role in Civil War, 62–66
    role in enforcement of integration,
        141, 142, 152, 153
    role in Reconstruction, 70–80
    role in riot control, 12, 16–18, 21,
        56, 60, 73–78, 104, 105–6, 112,
        173
    role in slave control, 20, 43, 60
    role in strikebreaking, 83, 92
    in Seminole War, 34–35, 38, 41–50
    See also Emergency Plan White;
        Riots, armed services
U.S. Civil Rights Commission, 136,
    140, 149, 197, 200, 214
U.S. Marine Corps, 57, 112, 113, 125,
    231
U.S. Navy, 22, 35, 114
United States Code:
    Article IV, Section 4, 176
    Chapter 15, 175
    Section 231, 182
    Section 241, 158, 161–62, 183, 188,
        275n.–76n.
    Section 242, 161, 183, 188, 198, 202,
        207, 234, 238, 275n.–76n.
    Section 243, 183
    Section 244, 183
    Section 245, 184–85

Section 331, 174–76, 179
Section 332, 140, 143, 159, 162, 164,
    175, 179
Section 333, 132, 157–59, 162–64,
    175, 179
United States v. Guest, 161–62, 177,
    183, 188
United States v. Louisiana, 143
United States v. Price, 161, 162, 177,
    183, 188
Universal Negro Improvement
    Association (UNIA), 123
University of Alabama, 140, 159
University of Michigan, 219
University of Mississippi, 150–53, 155,
    156
University of Missouri at Columbia, 219
University of Wisconsin, 219
Urban League, 97, 119

Van Buren, Martin, 48
Vance, Cyrus, 153, 173–74, 175
Vance, Robert S., 226
Vardaman, James, 105
Venable, Abraham, 10
Vesey's Plot, 18–20, 23
Virginia, 2, 3, 7, 15–16, 250n.
Voting rights, *see* Franchise
Voting Rights Act:
    of 1957, 162
    of 1960, 162
    of 1965, 90, 163, 242

Waggoner, Joe D., 159, 176
Wallace, George, 157–58, 159, 164,
    272n.
Waln, Robert, 10–11
War Department, U.S.:
    Civil War and, 63
    correspondence of, 23, 251n., 252n.,
        254n.
    Emergency Plan White and, 119
    Reconstruction and, 63, 72, 78
    reports to, 22, 34, 35
    response to riots, 75, 117, 124
    Seminole War and, 39–40, 45, 49,
        253n.–54n.
    on size of army, 82
    slave revolts and, 21
War of 1812, 32
War on Poverty, 169

Warren, 21
Warren, Earl, 161–62
Warrington, Lewis, 22
Washington, Booker T., 97
Washington, George, 12, 31
Washington, Walter, 179
Washington, D.C., 113–15, 179
Washington Post, 113–14
Watson, Henry, 235
Wayne, Anthony, 31
Weaver, Robert C., 195
Webster, Daniel, 42
Wells-Barnett, Ida, 93
Western Federation of Miners, 103
West Virginia, 59, 82
Whigs, 42, 46, 47
Whiskey Rebellion, 12, 22, 247*n.*–48*n.*
White, Byron, 148
White, Walter, 137, 139
White Citizen's Council, 140
White Knights of Liberty, 218, 219
White Patriot Party, 218
Whitten, Jamie L., 156
Wickersham, George W., 106, 107
Wilkins, Frederic, 56, 58
Wilkins, J. H., 125
Wilkins, Roger, 173
Wilkins, Roy, 144, 168, 187, 188
Wilkinson, Bill, 208
Williams, Harrison A., Jr., 158
Williams, Hosea, 220, 228

Williams, John, 266*n.*
Williams, John Bell, 143, 163
Williams, Damian, 235
Williams, Robert F., 167, 273*n.*
Williams, Willie, 236
Williams v. Wallace, 164
Wilmington, Delaware, 180
Wilmington, North Carolina, 94
Wilson, Christopher, 237
Wilson, James, 7, 31
Wilson, Woodrow, 108, 109, 114, 119,
    120, 123
Wind, Timothy E., 231, 238
Windom, William, 84
Wise, Henry, 45, 46
Witherspoon, John, 130
Wood, Leonard, 116–17, 120
Wood, Mailon Paul, 209–11
World War I, 111
World War II, 135, 138
Worth, William, 49–50
Wright, Jasper, 85
Wright, Silas, 4, 59
Wrightsville, Georgia, 202

Yamassee Indians, 3
Young, Andrew, 195
Young, Whitney, 168

Zoot suit riots, 128
Zoot suits, 128